Strategic Management

Strategic Management

Process, Content, and Implementation

Hugh Macmillan

Independent Management Consultant, formerly Professor of Business Policy, University of Edinburgh

Mahen Tampoe

Independent Management Consultant and Visiting Fellow, Henley Management College

OXFORD
UNIVERSITY PRESS
Great Clarendon Street, Oxford OX2 6DP
Oxford University Press is a department of the University of Oxford.
It furthers the University's objective of excellence in research, scholarship,
and education by publishing worldwide in
Oxford New York
Auckland Bangkok Buenos Aires Cape Town Chennai
Dar es Salaam Delhi Hong Kong Istanbul Karachi Kolkata
Kuala Lumpur Madrid Melbourne Mexico City Mumbai Nairobi
São Paulo Shanghai Taipei Tokyo Toronto
Oxford is a registered trade mark of Oxford University Press
in the UK and in certain other countries
Published in the United States
by Oxford University Press Inc., New York

British Library Cataloguing in Publication Data
[Data available]
Library of Congress Cataloging in Publication Data
[Data available]
ISBN 0-19-878229-2
5 6 4
Typeset in OUP Swift
by RefineCatch Limited, Bungay, Suffolk
Printed in Great Britain by
Antony Rowe Ltd
Chippenham, Wiltshire

Preface

STRATEGIC management must form a core element of any business course as it provides the glue that holds the other business subjects together. The body of literature on strategic management has grown rapidly and this increase means that many textbooks on the subject have become very large. There has not, however, been a corresponding increase in the time available for teaching strategic management so that few students read the thick textbooks. This suggests the need for a textbook shorter than the full texts but more comprehensive than the 'Basics' or 'Essentials' books on the subject.

Secondly, most students are hoping to derive some usable knowledge from the time that they spend on strategic management as well as the academic knowledge to pass their examinations. This requires an approach to strategic management that takes practice into account as well as the academic literature and gives full weight to the problems of implementing strategy.

Our aim in writing this book has been to provide a text which has enough academic content to meet the requirements of degree courses but which is also practical enough to be useful to business practitioners. It is, in short, the book we would like to have to support the teaching we do and have done. We hope to provide a summary of those elements of strategic management that will be useful to students who want to put what they have learnt into practice.

The study of strategy in action endeavours to understand and explain why some enterprises have been more successful than others in the past. This is useful knowledge to the future strategist but it is not enough. Winners in today's or tomorrow's world will need to break outside the box of existing thinking. An effective strategist must be able to understand the current rules of the game but must also be able to invent new rules for the future. In addition, strategic management is not just about ideas, it also requires the ability to implement those ideas in practice. We hope that this book will help its readers to do this.

Targeted readership

The book is intended for students who wish to acquire a broad understanding of strategic management quickly. It will be easier for those who have had a few years of work experience to understand and interpret its contents. It should, therefore, be particularly suitable for both core MBA courses and for shorter professional management courses in strategic management. It will also be of help as a strategy primer for those studying for other professional examinations such as personnel management, accountancy, company secretarial practice, or law.

We hope that the style is accessible so that the book will also be of value to general managers already in leadership positions in enterprises who wish to gain an overview of the subject of strategic management from their own reading.

It is likely that both lecturers and readers will want to supplement the book with reading in areas where greater depth of discussion is relevant to their specific needs. Many suitable books and articles are referenced in the text and in the bibliography.

Structure of the book

The book is divided into six parts. Part I defines the meaning of strategy and describes the structure and content of the book as a whole. Part II examines the importance of context in determining the agenda for strategic management and describes some distinctive classes of context. Part III describes the process by which strategies are formulated. Part IV looks at the content of strategy and suggests the questions to which business and corporate strategies should provide the answers. Part V examines how the practical problems of implementing strategy can best be approached. Part VI consists of case examples referenced in the text as examples of the principles described. Chapter 1 describes the overall structure in more detail.

Learning aids

The book aims to help readers to understand how the principles of strategic management apply in the real world. To assist in this aim we have incorporated a number of learning aids:

- Clear division into parts to give focus to particular aspects of the subject as needed;
- Diagrams to illustrate the overall logic of the subject;
- Summaries of each part in the first chapter of that part;
- Summaries at the end of each chapter;
- Case examples to demonstrate the principles described in the text in practice;
- A brief commentary and questions for discussion on each case example;
- A glossary for easy reference to the definitions of special terms.

Acknowledgements

We should like to thank the various people who have helped to bring this book to completion. First of all, we should like to thank Roger Lovell and Gary Saunders for contributing case examples, each of which is from an enterprise with which they have been associated over several years. Secondly, we must acknowledge the helpful comments of the two anonymous reviewers, who reviewed as it was written; we hope that they will recognize the effects of their comments in the final result. Thirdly, we should like to thank Brendan George, Ruth Marshall, Miranda Vernon, and Virginia Williams of Oxford University Press who have helped the writing of the book from inception to publication. Fourthly, and perhaps most importantly, we should like to thank Sheina and Judith for their support during the writing of this book.

Summary of Contents

Part VI **Case Examples**

Contents

Part VI **Case Examples**

Introduction

STRATEGIC management is the most exciting of the management disciplines. Strategic management is about success and failure, about the ability to plan wars and win them. Big mergers—perhaps the most visible sign of strategic management in action—catch the headlines. Effective strategic management can transform the performance of an organization, make fortunes for shareholders, or change the structure of an industry. Ineffective strategic management can bankrupt companies and ruin the careers of chief executives.

Strategic management is both a skill and an art. It is a skill because there is a body of knowledge that can be learnt and techniques that can be used with greater or lesser competence. It is an art because it deals with the future that is unknowable and with the hearts and minds of people that transcend reason. Good strategic management requires both clear thought and sound judgement.

Strategic management is the formal and structured process by which an organization establishes a position of strategic leadership. Strategic leadership is about the achievement of sustained comparative advantage over the competition. Strategic leadership is the outcome of the strategic management process. It is a state of being rather than a management mechanism. So strategic leadership does not replace strategic management; it results from it.

Strategic management skills are not only critical for those who have made it to the top. Executives and managers at earlier stages of their careers need to have an understanding of strategic management to increase the value of their contribution in their present assignments. It can help them to master the corporate jungle and to achieve individual career aims. It instils the habit of reaching an identified goal by developing the necessary competence and seizing available opportunities. In short, an understanding of strategy enhances performance and improves career prospects.

Aims of this book

OVERALL our aim is to provide a summary of strategic management that will be useful to readers who not only want to pass exams but also to put what they have learnt into practice. In support of this aim we have applied four principles throughout the book.

First, we hope that this book is easy to understand. It is intended to give easy access to strategic management to readers who have not studied the subject before. Strategic management is not a simple subject but its difficulty should derive from applying effective ideas to the complexities of a unique context rather than from the application of complex theories. Managers fail when they do not apply relatively simple principles properly, not because they had not read the latest research article.

Secondly, we believe that it is necessary to combine the best of the accepted theory in the subject with a pragmatic viewpoint. We are concerned not just with the theory itself but also with how best to apply it in practice. To do this we have drawn on our own experience as managers and management consultants. We have tried to balance academic and pragmatic perspectives and to take the best from each.

Thirdly, we believe that good strategic management requires a particular way of thinking and a mental discipline rather than a specific body of knowledge. This book aims to provide an intellectual framework for the study and application of strategic management. We hope that this framework is clear enough to be quickly understood by all readers and yet robust and flexible enough to form a sound base for a lifetime of learning from further reading and experience. We have not tried to include everything that may be valuable to the body of knowledge of a strategist. As a result this book is significantly shorter than many of the textbooks in the field.

Fourthly, we have not attempted to chase too many of the current hares. Over the years, managers have been offered mantras and quick fixes that purport to avoid fundamental and hard thinking about the appropriate strategy for their particular enterprise. The quality movement and the concept of excellence both had their day. Most recently, E-commerce and knowledge management have been offered as strategic panaceas. We do not deny the importance of either E-commerce or knowledge management but they are not a substitute for a proper process of strategic management to address all the relevant issues in a full perspective of the context. Our view is that a robust strategy making process effectively applied will take into account the constant stream of new ideas and new technological opportunities and position the enterprise to take advantage of them.

Fifthly, we hope that this book will help readers not only to think strategically but also to act to achieve strategic change in real organizations. Good strategic thinking is necessary and a good start to successful strategic management but it is not enough. Strategic thinking that does not lead to action that meets customer needs better is a waste of time and resources. We hope that this book will enable readers to understand the nature of the action that will be needed to make strategy happen. For this reason, this book gives as much weight to the implementation of strategy as to its formulation.

Distinctive contributions to thinking on strategic management

PRACTITIONERS, academics, and management consultants have all contributed to the current understanding of strategic management. Each group has strengths and weaknesses so that the fullest understanding depends on combining their different perspectives.

The personal experience of practitioners can demonstrate an intensity of involvement that often lends strength and credibility to their perceptions. There are undoubtedly both specific lessons and more general principles to be deduced from studying exactly how the movers and shakers of successful companies achieved what they did and in their perspectives on what was important in achieving their success. The strength of these contributions is in their depth and coherence. They are also likely to be particularly credible to practising managers because they appreciate the manager's perspective and the constraints within which managers have to operate. One limitation is that they may be describing particular circumstances of limited general relevance. Sometimes, too, their views may reflect individual eccentricity as much as universal truth.

Good academic work contributes rigour and scholarship to the subject. There are few universal truths about business but good analysis can clarify the balance of probability by objective observation. Every strategist should have some of this cool objectivity to temper his or her enthusiasm. Another valuable contribution from the academic world is diversity of thinking about strategy. Academics have come to strategy from a wide variety of previous disciplines. Each discipline brings its own perspective to the subject. Originality is more likely to emerge from this diversity of thought than from any single view of the way the world works. One limitation of the academic contribution is that it sometimes seems a little weak in its appreciation of how managers work in practice to achieve results in real enterprises.

Management consultants have also made a notable contribution to thinking in strategic management. It may even be that more genuinely new ideas have come from consultants than from academics. Management consultants are paid to solve problems. Nothing focuses the mind as much as the need to come up with a solution to a problem in a limited time. Management consultants have to make ideas work in real enterprises and among real people. Good strategic management does not usually depend on the most complex or sophisticated ideas but rather from working with ideas that are relevant, understandable, and workable. Management consultants usually understand how to do this.

We hope that this book will help readers to understand strategic management and to apply this critical management discipline.

Part I

Introduction to Strategy and Strategic Management

Chapter 1
The Structure of this Book

THIS book is divided into six parts. Readers who want a quick overview of the scope and content as a whole should read the first chapters of Parts I to V—that is Chapters 1, 4, 6, 13, and 16.

Part I is concerned with the basics of strategic management. Chapter 1 describes the structure of the book with more explanation than in the Table of Contents. Chapter 2 considers the nature of strategy and how ideas about strategy have originated from military, academic, and practical origins. Chapter 3 attempts to structure the currently accepted body of literature on strategic management.

Parts II, III, IV, and V address each of the four elements of strategic management—context, the strategy formulation process, strategy content, and the strategy implementation process. Figure 1.1 illustrates how these four elements form a conceptual framework for strategic management. This figure is the basis of the structure of this book.

Part II is devoted to examining the first element—**Context**—which forms the background to the model in Figure 1.1. Strategy and strategic management can only exist in a particular context. The context is unique for each enterprise and has numerous characteristics—both of the enterprise itself and of its external environment. The context determines the issues which strategic management must address and hence the agenda and scope of strategic management for that enterprise. The context may present a range of strategic issues or a single strategic dilemma which strategic management has to resolve. All effective strategic management must start from a deep understanding of the context. Chapter 4 is concerned with context in general. Chapter 5 discusses some of the diverse contexts that exist in an attempt to alert the reader to the impact that different industry and organizational factors may have on strategy formulation and implementation.

Part III addresses the second element of strategic management—the **Strategy Formulation Process**. This is the process by which strategies are thought about, conceived, compared, and chosen within a particular enterprise over time. It is the process of strategic thinking in that enterprise. There is no universally correct process that will generate successful strategies nor are there any proven means by which

Figure 1.1 The four elements of strategic management

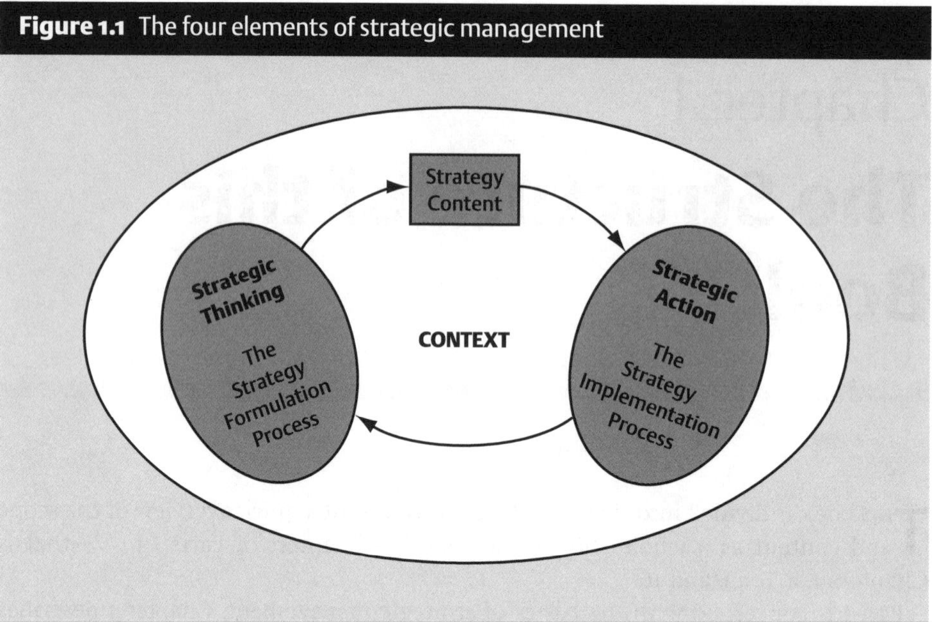

infallible strategic thinking can be caused to occur. Some processes may be formal and involve a large number of people; other processes may be completely informal and involve only a handful; a sudden flash of insight may sometimes be worth more than years of analysis. The purpose of the strategy formulation process is to arrive at an agreed view of how the enterprise will succeed in the future.

The strategy formulation process has three logical elements, as illustrated in Figure 1.2 and described further in Chapter 6.

Strategic Intent is the highest level purpose of the enterprise. It is therefore a driver of the strategy process since all meaningful action must originate in purpose.

Figure 1.2 The strategy formulation process

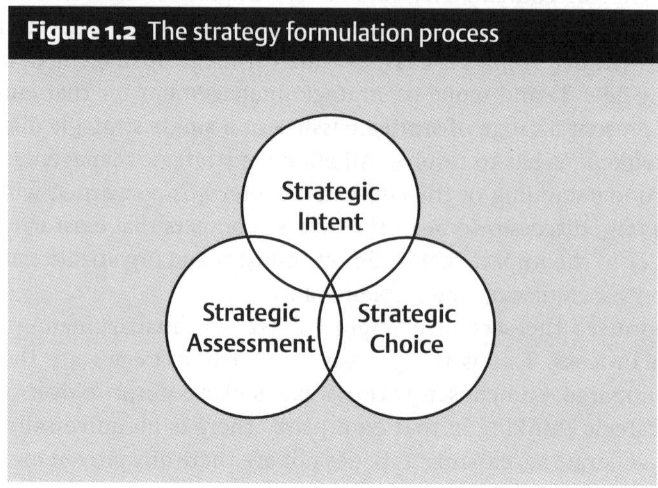

Strategic intent may also change or develop as a result of the strategy formulation process. Strategic intent is described at more length in Chapter 7.

Strategic Assessment is an overall assessment of the context at a particular time and the effects of possible future actions. Strategic assessment involves standing back from the everyday activities of the business. It requires consideration in broad terms of the capabilities of the enterprise and the characteristics of the business environment in which the enterprise operates. Strategic assessment considers how likely the enterprise is to realize its strategic intent as the business environment changes. Strategic assessment takes into account current performance, expected future trends, the aims of the enterprise, and the success of past strategies. Strategic assessment involves both analysis and judgement. The principles of strategic assessment are described in Chapter 8. Some of the tools and techniques that may be useful in practical strategic assessment are described in more length in Chapters 9 and 10.

Strategic Choice involves deciding what action to take and how to take it for the future health and direction of the enterprise. It requires faith that actions taken now will improve future outcomes. The degree of uncertainty in strategic choice is often very high. But if there are no choices to be made, there is no value in the strategy formulation process. Strategic choices should address strategic issues or resolve the strategic dilemma posed by the context in a way that fits with the strategic intent. Strategic choice is described in more detail in Chapter 11.

Formulating strategy usually involves analysis and the manipulation of data and ideas. Chapter 12 describes how analytical tools (usually programs running on personal computers) can support the strategy formulation process in practice.

The strategy formulation process delivers the **Content of Strategy**. This is the third element of strategic management and is addressed in Part IV. Chapter 13 examines the content of strategy in general and discusses what results can reasonably be expected from a strategy process. Chapter 14 focuses on **Business Strategies** and on what is likely to make the business strategy of an enterprise more effective. Chapter 15 is devoted to the subject of **Corporate Strategy**—the additional component of strategy required if an enterprise has more than one business.

Strategic management is incomplete and of little value without effective implementation. The final element of strategic management is the **Strategy Implementation Process** described in Part V. Implementation is too often seen as separate from strategic management. Our view is that implementation is an integral part of strategic management so that the process and content of strategy should take the needs and capabilities for implementation into account. Many strategic change initiatives fail to achieve their stated objectives. Often this failure is due as much to underestimation of the difficulties of implementing the changes as to poor execution.

Figure 1.3 shows the parts of the strategy implementation process.

Chapter 16 summarizes the key themes of the strategy implementation process. Chapters 17 and 18 distinguish between the leadership of strategic change and the management of a change programme. Leadership and management are both essential for successful implementation and form the vertical dimension of Figure

Figure 1.3 The strategy implementation process

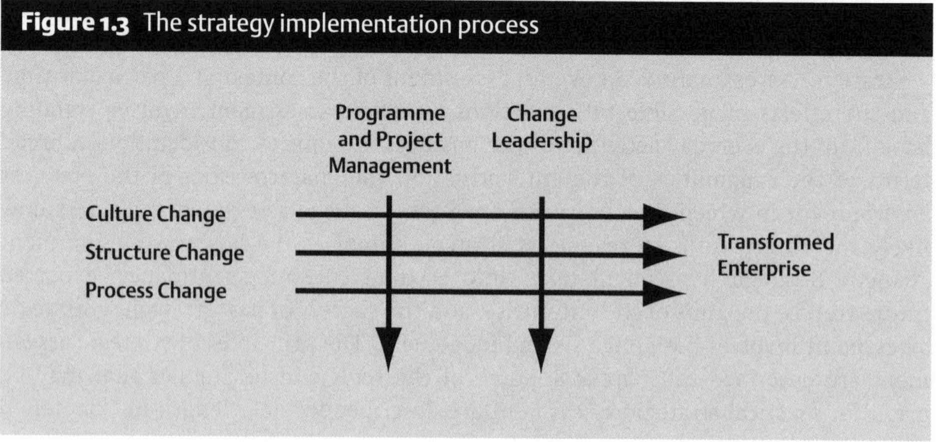

1.3. To implement a new strategy it is likely that change will be needed in the business processes, the culture, and the structure of the enterprise. Practical approaches for causing change in each of these three are described in Chapters 19 to 21.

Chapter 22 addresses the question of **Adaptability**—an organizational competence which adds to the chances of future success in an unpredictable world.

The four elements of strategic management relate closely to each other. The context sets the scene, poses the issues to be resolved, and constrains the style of the strategic management process. The quality of the strategy formulation process and its suitability to the context will tend to determine the quality of the strategy content that results. The strategy content is of little value unless it has taken implementation issues into account and leads to an effective process of implementation that turns ideas into realities. The results of the strategic implementation (and other unrelated changes) will in due course affect the context so that the elements of strategic management interact in a cycle. Figure 1.4 combines the content of Figures 1.1 to 1.3 into a single diagram.

Figures 1.1 to 1.4 are original to this book. They are derived from classical models of strategic management. The main extensions to other models are that context is specifically represented and implementation is given more emphasis.

Part V ends with a brief Epilogue to conclude the book.

Part VI contains six case examples. A case example differs from a case study in that it is structured to be useful as an example of principles described in the text. Specific references to these case examples occur throughout the book. It is hoped that the case examples give a fuller understanding of the context than is possible in brief vignette examples on their own. Readers may find it useful to read the case examples through in parallel with the main text to get a wider feel for each of the six contexts.

We hope that we have avoided unnecessary jargon. Terms that are defined in the text are also listed in the Glossary for easy reference.

The structure of the book was designed to focus on key elements of strategic management. Each element stands on its own and will offer a grounding in the themes

Figure 1.4 Our complete model

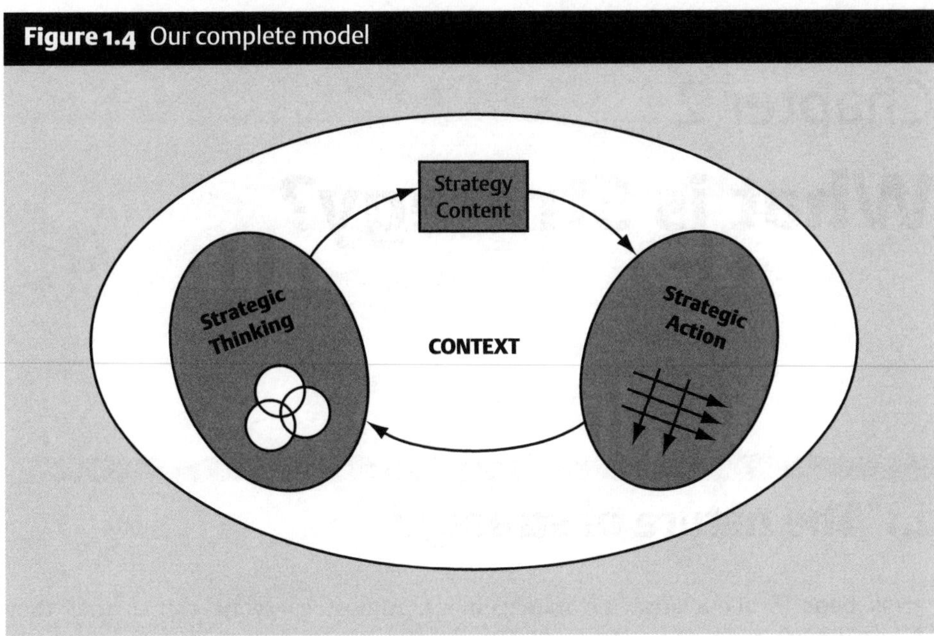

covered. Taken as a whole the book offers, in a comprehensive and digestible format, a manual of strategic management from which either students or practitioners can benefit quickly.

Chapter 2
What is Strategy?

2.1 The nature of strategy

THIS book is about strategic management. Almost everyone thinks that they know what strategy is. However, if you ask what the word strategy means to them, the range of replies is surprisingly varied. To some the term 'strategic' is no more than a synonym for 'important'; to others it may be a plan of action and for a third group it might be a blueprint for success. More considered replies are likely to reveal different shades of meaning within this broad range. To us, strategic management is about envisioning and realizing the future. Note that this definition requires that strategy should both provide an idea of the future and generate the action necessary to realize that idea. Implementation is part of strategy and not a separate activity.

2.2 Strategy from the manager's point of view

MANAGERS are responsible for the health of their enterprises both in the present and in the future. Strategic management is the part of their job that relates to the future. Strategic management is about taking action today to achieve benefits in the future. The future is always uncertain so that strategic management decisions must be made with information that is always incomplete and often wrong. This is not a new issue. Peter Drucker (1955: 85) put this very clearly:

> Management has no choice but to anticipate the future, to attempt to mould it and to balance short-range and long-range goals. It is not given to mortals to do either of these things well. But

lacking divine guidance, business management must make sure that these difficult responsibilities are not overlooked or neglected, but taken care of as well as is humanly possible.

It is not easy for managers to manage strategically. Henry Mintzberg (1989) has observed and most managers will be personally aware that: 'Managers work at an unrelenting pace and their activities are characterised by brevity, variety and discontinuity'. Managers have to manage strategically within this pattern of work. The objective of strategic management is to prepare an enterprise for future success—to conceive and secure the future of that enterprise. The objective of this book is to help managers to achieve this.

Strategic management requires both thinking and action. Strategic management only takes place when action follows thought. Thought on its own may be intellectually stimulating but it is not strategic management. There are limits to the ability of managers to foresee the future, to understand the significance of changes, to conceive strategies, and to implement strategies successfully. Managers need to be aware of these limits but cannot avoid their responsibility for taking action.

In summary, the manager's perspective of strategy has three characteristics. First of all, the concern of managers is with a particular enterprise at a particular time. Secondly, they need to have a concept of what the future will be like. Thirdly, they have to take action. This is the essence of strategic management.

2.3 Definitions of strategy

MANY writers have attempted to define strategy. Such definitions emphasize one or more of the aspects described above. A definition that included all the aspects would have to be very long.

One of the earliest definitions of strategy comes from the ancient Greek writer Xenophon (Cummings 1993: 134): 'Strategy is knowing the business you propose to carry out'. This definition stresses that strategy requires a knowledge of the business, an intention for the future, and an orientation towards action. This definition also emphasizes the link between leadership and strategy formulation. Xenophon saw strategy as a direct responsibility of those in charge, not as a spectator sport.

Kenneth Andrews (1971) defined strategy as: 'The pattern of major objectives, purposes or goals and essential policies or plans for achieving those goals, stated in such a way as to define what business the company is in or is to be in and the kind of company it is or is to be'.

Note that in this definition strategy is concerned with both purpose and the means by which purpose will be achieved. It implies that strategy must address the fundamental nature of the business in the future. This suggests that strategy will be sensitive to values and culture as well as to business opportunity. It also implies that managers are able and responsible for making deliberate choices about the future nature and scope of their business.

Igor Ansoff (1987: 1965) offers a brief definition: 'Strategy is a rule for making decisions'. Ansoff also distinguishes between policy and strategy. A policy is a general decision that is always made in the same way whenever the same circumstances arise. A strategy applies similar principles but allows different decisions as the circumstances differ.

Kenichi Ohmae (1983: 92) defines strategy as: 'The way in which a corporation endeavours to differentiate itself positively from its competitors, using its relative strengths to better satisfy customer needs'. This definition addresses both the competitive aspect of strategy and the need to build capabilities. It also explicitly mentions customers and the satisfaction of their needs as a driver of strategy.

More recently and reflecting his perspective as a practising management consultant, Michael de Kare-Silver (1997) suggests that strategy should have just two elements—future intent and 'sources of advantage'. He is therefore restating the view that intent and strategy are inseparable. The word 'source of advantage' has a similar meaning to capability but emphasizes that capabilities only have value when they meet the real needs of customers.

Our own definition of strategy is: 'Ideas and actions to conceive and secure the future'. This definition highlights the fact that strategy requires thought about the future but also effective action to realize the conception. This definition, though brief, does not imply that strategy cannot have the many aspects discussed above.

It is apparent that definitions of strategy vary. To understand the reasons for this variation, it may help to have some understanding of where the ideas come from. Military thinkers, political thinkers, academics, and practitioners have all considered the issue of strategy.

2.4 The military origins of strategy

THE concept of strategy is an ancient one and originated in the study of success in war. The word strategy comes from the Greek '*stratos*' (army) and '*agein*' (to lead). The '*strategos*' in Athens was an elected general, a post created when Athens was at war with Persia in 506 BC. The Greeks saw strategy setting as one of the responsibilities of a leader, a connection that continues in modern thinking. The Greeks also gave serious thought to what kind of person would be suitable to the role and how they should be trained. Interestingly, they concluded that intellectual skills, while essential for a good strategist, were not sufficient unless supported by practical learning gained from experience.

At about the same time, and quite independently, the Chinese general, Sun Tzu (tr. 1997) wrote about strategy, also relating it closely to the duties of a leader: 'Only a brilliant ruler and an excellent leader, who is able to conduct their intelligence with superiority and cleverness, is certain to achieve great results. The entire force relies on this for every move. This is the essence of strategy'.

Sun Tzu saw the aim of strategy as defeating the enemy by fighting as few battles as possible. He defines priorities for gaining advantage over an adversary. The highest priority is to foil the enemy's plots, second to ruin his alliances, third to attack his armies, and lowest of all to besiege his castles. In his view, strategy is as much about avoiding battles as it is about fighting them. Sun Tsu's book *The Art of War* has sometimes been used as a management text because of the relevance of its insights to business strategy.

Perhaps the best-known military strategist of more recent history is Carl Von Clausewitz (1832). One often-quoted sentence highlights an important paradox about strategy in that good strategies are inherently simple but hard to conceive: 'Thus, then, in Strategy everything is very simple, but not on that account very easy'.

Von Clausewitz saw good strategies as difficult to conceive and even more difficult to implement so that only very few people ever succeed as strategists:

> A Prince or General who knows exactly how to organize his war according to his object and means, who does neither too little nor too much, gives by that the greatest proof of his genius.
>
> But to follow that way straightforward, to carry out the plan without being obliged to deviate from it a thousand times by a thousand varying influences, requires besides great strength of character, great clearness and steadiness of mind, and out of a thousand men who are remarkable, some of mind, others for penetration, others again for boldness or strength of will, perhaps not one will combine in himself all those qualities which are required to raise a man above mediocrity in the career of a general.

Military thinking certainly has some relevance to business strategy. Its emphasis on winning, on the importance of leadership, and on taking action to achieve desired results are all themes which resonate. On the other hand, war campaigns are a limited analogy to the realities which modern enterprises face. The military analogy lacks any equivalent to the customer. Modern enterprises rarely have the simple hierarchical structures nor obedience to orders which military models assume. Military writers and particularly Clausewitz saw war as a zero-sum game. Business competition often allows opportunities to avoid the destructive results of a zero-sum game by creating diversity.

If we accept the analogy that business is a war then the military model of strategy can be an important starting point for an exploration of business strategy. Strategy also has a political role.

2.5 The political role of strategy

NICCOLO Machiavelli (tr. 1961) added a political dimension to the study of strategy. *The Prince* published in the early sixteenth century was notable for its detached observation of events. Francis Bacon said of Machiavelli (Jay 1987) 'He set forth openly and sincerely what men are wont to do and not what they ought to do'.

Machiavelli is also the earliest writer to concern himself with the realities of implementing strategies. One particular example of this quoted by Jay is how to handle take-overs. Machiavelli was, of course, writing about a prince taking control of a country. His advice was that it was necessary either to treat the powerful citizens well or to crush them so completely so that they could not retaliate. Jay points out that there is a parallel in how to manage companies which have been recently taken over and that advice on such matters is rarely available in conventional management books. Machiavelli moved beyond the ancient writers in his concern for effectiveness as much as describing ideals.

2.6 The academic contribution to strategy

ANOTHER major source of knowledge about strategy is provided by academics. Modern thinking on business strategy first evolved into a recognizable form in the 1960s in the USA. Writers such as Drucker (1955), Chandler (1962), Ansoff (1987, 1965), and Andrews (1971) studied the development of large successful American corporations before and during the Second World War. Their work set the scene for what is now usually referred to as the 'Classical School' of business strategy. The classical school saw direction setting (strategy formulation) as an important responsibility of top managers and believed that it could be separated from strategy implementation. Corporate thinkers in headquarters headed by the chief executive formulated the strategy; divisional management teams implemented it. The analogy with the general and his headquarters staff and field officers is clear so that the classical school seems to have its roots in the military model of strategy. One major addition to thinking was the introduction of ecomomic goals—particularly return on capital—as the driving objective of business.

The thinking of the classical school has never been replaced by a better total view of what business strategy is all about but it has come in for significant criticism from at least three directions. First, the companies that based their strategies on the classical theories have not necessarily been more successful than others who did not. Over-rigid application of classical approaches led to strategic planning becoming a staff role separated from, and often not well regarded by, line management. As a result, the concepts themselves were rejected even though the failures may have resulted from poor application of the concepts as much as from the limitations of the concepts themselves.

Secondly, it was suggested that the techniques and concepts of the classical school could well have been appropriate to large companies based in the USA at a time when America had a dominant share of world economic activity. The same techniques and ideas might be less relevant in other business contexts. For example, it might be possible for DuPont in 1960 in a growing chemical market to set world-wide strategies centrally and to expect them to be implemented successfully. It might not be possible for a small company struggling in a depressed economy to go about strategy making in the same way.

Thirdly, the classical school thinking was too closely tied to its military and economic models. Other fields of thought—particularly psychology, sociology, and biology—offered new and relevant ways of thinking about strategy.

The volume of academic writing in the field of strategic management is both very large and diverse. The value to the business strategist is in providing multiple different ways of thinking about strategy. It is, however, important to realize that academics are looking for general patterns that they can prove by analysis. This may not be directly helpful to the strategist who is seeking a unique solution to a unique strategic dilemma for a particular enterprise. The academics are seeking to understand the rules; the manager is seeking to get round the rules for the advantage of his or her own enterprise. In addition, academics can sometimes seem unaware of the realities of the constraints and pressures within which managers have to work. Political pressures and imperfect knowledge can make cold logic less relevant to the needs of the practising manager. Business success may often come from carrying people along with an imperfect strategy.

2.7 The contribution of practitioners

MANAGERS have to face strategic issues and take action to resolve them. Some have written convincingly about their experiences. Alfred P. Sloan (1963) was president and then chairman of General Motors between 1923 and 1946. The strategic issues facing Sloan were how to handle the vast enterprise that General Motors had become and how to catch Ford who had taken a lead in mass production techniques. Sloan (who writes of 'policy' rather than 'strategy') pioneered the Divisionalized Corporation that became a model for many large companies. The divisionalised form allowed policy making by the centre to be separated from execution by the divisions. It thereby allowed General Motors to become more diverse than Ford without giving up any economies of scale. The central strategy makers were able to gather detailed knowledge of what execution involves and so set strategies for the separate divisions that were both different from each other and achievable. Sloan faced a particular dilemma and describes his solutions.

John Harvey-Jones (1988) wrote his book *Making it Happen* just after he retired as chairman of ICI. One of his principal dilemmas was how to make the board of ICI work better. As a result, his particular contributions to the concept of strategy include his insights into how boards should operate and on the mix of people necessary to devise strategy for a large organization at the highest level. He also emphasizes the responsibility for communicating the strategy to all concerned and stresses the importance of people in making any strategy happen. To him success lies in getting a larger part of a strategy implemented rather than conceiving a more brilliant strategy. Again Harvey-Jones's solutions were effective for the particular issues faced by ICI at the time.

Andrew Grove (1996) wrote as president and CEO (chief executive officer) of Intel Corporation. Intel faced particular issues in the micro-electronic industry. This industry may be atypical of business in general because of its rapid speed of technological advance. Such a rapidly changing environment provides an opportunity to study strategic change at higher speed—just as geneticists study fruit flies because their reproduction cycle is so short. Grove describes strategic inflexion points in which radical changes in business parameters require radical strategic change in response. His ideas are relevant to other industries as they face moments of radical change but may be less useful in slower-moving strategic contexts.

The advantage of studying strategy as seen by practitioners is that they approach the issues of strategy from the perspective of practising managers—the need to take action to solve a problem. The disadvantage is that the dilemma is different for each case and so the lessons may not be relevant to other situations.

Case studies have had an important role in the teaching of strategic management. The purpose of a case discussion is to cause the participants to address the two generic questions: 'What are the strategic issues in this case' and 'What would you do?' While the particular dilemma described in a case will never reoccur, each will build a useful body of knowledge for tackling other dilemmas. Case studies therefore illuminate strategic management from the same perspective as reading the accounts of practitioners. We have included six case examples in Part VI of this book. Each case example describes a different context and therefore different issues and dilemmas to be resolved.

2.8 A theoretical general solution to strategic dilemmas?

One interesting question is whether it will ever be possible to have some general theory for strategic management. John Kay considered this question and concludes that strategy is still at a level of development equivalent to early medicine when doctors based their conclusions on unscientific categorization such as humours and elements. He observes (Kay 1993) that: 'The prestige of a doctor rested more on the status of his patients and the confidence of his assertions than on the evidence of his cures'. It is evident that an equivalent state of affairs exists in the field of strategy at the present time but Kay seems to be optimistic that greater knowledge will in time make the subject more scientific.

Gary Hamel has also addressed this question by referring to the 'dirty little secret of the strategy industry' (Hamel 1997). The dirty little secret to which he referred is the fact that all methods of devising strategies always leave a gap. Only genuinely creative thought can bridge the gap and no standardized method can provide this.

Our own view is that Kay's optimism about the future of thinking about strategy may not be justified. Strategies are successful partly because they are different. This means that if there were ever to be a method for devising strategies that came to be generally accepted, success would come to those who ignored it or rewrote the rules. Therefore it may be possible to analyse in retrospect why a particular company has been successful but it will always be impossible to devise rules of how to devise such a strategy. While scholars are studying what has made business successful in the past, creative entrepreneurs are finding new ways to make companies successful in the future. It follows that, as soon as all the players in an 'industry' begin to see their strategies in the same way, there is likely to be an opportunity for an outsider to rewrite the rules.

2.9 Summary

THE concept of strategy is more complex than it might at first appear and has a number of aspects. Definitions of strategy tend to emphasize one or two of these aspects but cannot succinctly include all of them. Soldiers, academics, and practitioners have all studied strategy and written about strategy. The perspective of each of these groups is of relevance to the practising manager but each also has its limitations.

While an understanding of the origin of the ideas may be intellectually stimulating, the practical problem for a manager is to understand the nature of the particular strategic dilemma that he or she must address. The manager must select ways of thinking which are helpful in deciding what actions to take now to resolve the dilemma and ensure success in the future. A broad knowledge of the relevant thought should help to achieve this but the ability to select and pursue useful ways of thinking may be as valuable as breadth of knowledge.

The simple view of strategy as a grand plan worked out by some mastermind at the centre of the enterprise is too simplistic. A degree of suspicion is necessary and the nature of cause and effect is often more complex than may appear at first glance.

Our view is that the classical concepts of strategy still usefully form a start point for strategic thinking but are no longer sufficient. Any competent strategist has both to be able to understand other ways of thinking about strategy and have the skill to be able to judge which perspective is most valuable in particular situations.

The greatest generals understood the current state of the art of war for their time but also knew when to break the rules. They entered their battles with a strategy but were still able to act spontaneously on the battlefield. These should perhaps be the ideals for the modern day business strategist.

References

Andrews, K. R. (1971) *The Concept of Corporate Strategy* (Homewood, Ill.: Irwin).

Ansoff, H. I. (1987/1965) *Corporate Strategy*, rev. edn. (London: Penguin; 1st pub. McGraw-Hill, 1965).

Chandler, A. D. (1962) *Strategy and Structure* (Cambridge, Mass.: MIT Press).

Clausewitz, C. Von (1832) *On War*, tr. Graham, J. J. (London: Penguin Classics, 1982).

Cummings, S. (1993) 'The First Strategists', *Long Range Planning*, 26/3: 133–5.

de Kare-Silver, M. (1997) *Strategy in Crisis* (London: Macmillan).

Drucker, P. (1955) *The Practice of Management*, paperback edn. (Oxford: Butterworth Heinemann).

Grove, A. S. (1996) *Only the Paranoid Survive: How to Exploit the Crisis Points that Challenge every Company and Career* (London: Harper Collins Business).

Hamel, G. (1997) Talk to the Strategic Planning Society Conference, Nov.

Harvey-Jones, J. (1988) *Making it Happen* (London: Fontana).

Jay, A. (1987) *Management and Machiavelli* (London: Business Books).

Kay, J. (1993) *Foundations of Corporate Success* (Oxford: Oxford University Press).

Machiavelli, N. (1961) *The Prince*, tr. George Bull (London: Penguin Classics).

Mintzberg, H. (1989) *Mintzberg on Management* (New York: Free Press).

Ohmae, K. (1983) *The Mind of the Strategist* (New York: Penguin; 1st pub. McGraw-Hill, 1982).

Sloan, A. P. (1963) *My Years with General Motors* (New York: Macfadden Books).

Sun Tzu (1997) *The Art of Strategy*, tr. R. L. Wing (London: Thorsons).

Chapter 3

Schools of Thought on Strategy and Strategic Management

3.1 Introduction

CHAPTER 2 introduced strategy and strategic management and looked at the origins of ideas about strategy. The purpose of this chapter is to outline the structure of strategic management as it is now accepted as an academic subject. Readers whose interests are more practical than academic may choose to omit this chapter at a first reading. It will be of more value to those wishing to bridge the gap between practice and the academic literature—a gap which sometimes seems to be wider than it should be.

3.2 Aspects of strategy

STRATEGY has multiple aspects. Some of the more important aspects are listed below.

Strategy as a statement of ends, purpose, and intent

Purpose or intent must act as the driver of the future. No useful activity can occur without some underlying purpose. The role of strategy is to determine, clarify, or refine purpose. This may require creating new visions of the future to inspire the organization to greater efforts or wider scope. It may entail reconciling conflicting purposes or stating purposes in more concrete terms.

Strategy as a high level plan

Strategy is also concerned with the means by which intent or purpose will be achieved. The strategy will define such means in broad and general terms. As detail is added and answers the questions: who, when, where, how, and with what, the strategy develops into a plan or perhaps a set of plans with varying scope and focus. It is impossible to draw a hard distinction between a strategy and a plan. In general, strategies tend to be at a higher level and to take an overall view; plans tend to be more detailed, more quantified, and more specific about times and responsibilities. However, some details may be so essential to the strategy that they become 'strategic'.

Strategy as the means of beating the competition

Many ideas about strategy derive from analogies of war and games. One aim of strategy is to win and this means beating the enemy or the competition in a game which may be won or lost. Strategies are therefore required to keep ahead of the competitors as a bunch. Companies may also have strategies (or stratagems) for out-manœuvring particular competitors at particular times for particular kinds of business.

Strategy as an element of leadership

Strategy has close association with leadership and setting strategy is one of the responsibilities of leaders. Nobody can lead an enterprise if he or she does not agree with its strategy. Conversely, organizations that are leaderless or inadequately led have difficulty defining clear strategies even if they continue to function in their day-to-day activities. When leaders change, strategies tend to change. Conversely, if the strategy needs to change, it may be necessary to appoint a new leader. A change of leader may be both a symbol that a change in strategy has occurred and an opportunity to appoint an individual with a leadership style appropriate to the new strategy. For example, some chief executives specialize in being 'company doctors' and develop the leadership style necessary to achieve clear results in adverse conditions. Other leaders may possess characteristics more appropriate for the long slow building of an enterprise over many years.

Strategy as positioning for the future

Strategy may be seen as preparation for the uncertainty of the future. Some trends may be apparent but other changes may occur which may contradict the general direction of the trend. All trends eventually end but it is often difficult to predict turning points. One purpose of strategy is therefore to position the enterprise for the future so as to be prepared for this uncertainty. One way to achieve this is to make the enterprise more adaptable.

Strategy as building capability

Certain capabilities may be seen as improving the chances of future success so that strategy may relate to building these capabilities. The capabilities of an enterprise may be exceptional or even unique. The essence of any firm is partly defined by the unique set of skills and knowledge of its people and teams. Strategic building of capabilities can exploit this uniqueness. For example, this may involve maintaining a lead in specific technical skills or investing to sustain a general ability to react fast to unexpected circumstances.

Strategy as fit between capabilities and opportunities

One aim of strategy is to achieve survival and future success. Success results from a good match between the capabilities of the enterprise and the opportunities to serve the needs of customers better than competitors. One aspect of strategy is to improve the fit between capabilities and the opportunities available and thereby to make the business more successful.

Strategy as the result of deep involvement with the business

This aspect contrasts with the idea of strategy as detached thinking about the business. Mintzberg (1987) coined the term 'crafting strategy' and uses the analogy of a potter throwing a pot on a wheel. While the potter will have had an original intention for the design of the pot, the final shape of the pot depends also on the interaction of the potter's hands with the clay as it rotates on the wheel. It has been suggested that Japanese firms are particularly good at allowing their strategies to emerge from deep involvement of managers with the business rather than doing abstract exercises in strategy formulation.

Strategy as a pattern of behaviour resulting from embedded culture

Every enterprise has its own culture. This culture is easy to observe but hard to change. The strategies that an enterprise is able to adopt are partly determined by this culture. Those within the enterprise see the outside world through their own conditioned perspective and this influences everything they do and permeates their strategy even though they may be unaware of this. In addition, since cultures are hard to imitate, culture may sometimes be a source of competitive advantage.

Strategy as an emerging pattern of successful behaviour

Few strategies are implemented in their entirety in the form in which they were formulated. Similarly, the reasons for success when analysed retrospectively may be different from what was expected in advance. Part of strategy may therefore be in recognizing the patterns that seem to have led to success even if these patterns arose by chance rather than as a result of planned actions.

These multiple aspects of strategy are separable but not usually contradictory.

Several attempts have been made to classify the literature on strategic management. Two of the best are due to Whittington (1993) and Mintzberg, Ahlstrand, and Lampel (1998).

3.3 Whittington's four generic approaches to strategy

WHITTINGTON (1993) defines four distinct schools: Classical, Evolutionary, Systemic, and Processual, differentiated by their stance on two axes. The first axis separates those who believe that leaders and managers are able to determine what their strategies should be by a deliberate process of thinking. The opposite view is that managers have very limited ability to determine outcomes and that strategy emerges as events unfold. This axis distinguishes between a deterministic view and an emergent view of strategy.

Table 3.1 Whittington's four schools of strategy compared

Characteristics	Classical	Processual	Evolutionary	Systemic
Deterministic/emergent	Deterministic	Deterministic	Emergent	Emergent
Single goal/pluralistic	Single	Plural	Single	Plural
Strategy style	Formal	Crafted	Efficient	Embedded
Influences	Economics/ military	Psychology	Economics/ biology	Sociology
Decade of influence	1960s	1970s	1980s	1990s

Source: Adapted from R. Whittington, *What is Strategy—And Does it Matter?* (Routledge 1993).

The second axis differentiates between those who see strategy seeking as a single goal (usually a financial goal in business) from those who see enterprises as having multiple purposes that may conflict. This axis therefore distinguishes between those who take a single dimensional view of purpose (usually profit or shareholder value) and those who place greater emphasis on complexity and politics in the reality of business.

The two directions of each of the two axes lead to the four schools. Whittington postulated that each of the four schools tended to derive from different contributions to thinking on strategic management from different subjects and that each had tended to be dominant, at least among academic writers, in a particular decade. The subject origins and decades are shown in Table 3.1.

Writing in 1993, Whittington saw sociology as having an increasingly important role in thinking about strategic management. It might be possible to defend this point of view in a debate but it is certainly not true that economic pressures (particularly the search for shareholder value) nor the importance of people and their psychology have in any way reduced in importance during the 1990s. The four schools therefore may be more usefully seen as complementary perspectives rather than evolving truth.

3.4 A safari through the strategic management literature

MORE recently, Mintzberg, Ahlstrand, and Lampel (1998) have outlined three prescriptive and seven descriptive schools of strategic thought, which differ according to their premises and the nature of the strategy process. The characteristics of the schools are summarized in Tables 3.2. and 3.3.

Table 3.2 Three prescriptive schools

School	Nature of Process	Principal Relevance
Design	Conception	Emphasis on chief executive's responsibility and overall simplicity of successful strategies
Planning	Formal planning	Currently blamed for the failure of formal strategic planning departments
Positioning	Analysis	Particularly strong in large companies and where management consultants have an analytical role

Source: Adapted from H. Mintzberg *et al.*, *Strategy Safari* (Prentice Hall, 1998).

The Design School sees strategy formulation as a deliberate process of conscious thought with responsibility resting with the chief executive. Strategies should be unique to the enterprise and to the moment. The process for formulating strategy should be kept simple and informal. The resulting strategies should be explicit and must therefore also be simple.

The Planning School sees strategy as a formal process and provides a clear model of how to do strategic planning using clear and logical methods. The model defines clear steps to be performed in sequence: objective setting, external assessment, internal assessment, strategic choice, and strategy implementation. Strategies result from analysis with little need for intuition or synthesis. Mintzberg (1994) has pointed out that strategic planning of this kind can often prevent strategic thinking.

The Positioning School sees the formation of strategy as depending on an analytical process. This school owes much to the work of Michael Porter and thrives on the use of analytical techniques and frameworks. It is particularly strong in larger companies and where management consultants are active in defining the process of strategy formation.

These three prescriptive schools may all be seen as variations of what we and Whittington called the Classical School. The Design School is the Classical School in its original form; the Planning School is recognisable as the Classical School distorted by excess bureaucracy; the Positioning School is a development of the Classical School, structured and extended by later work. These prescriptive models are the most obviously relevant to the needs of practising managers to help them form strategies and to take action.

The seven descriptive schools add insights into the nature of strategy. They are summarized in Table 3.3.

The Entrepreneurial School emphasizes the importance of a clear vision of the future, probably promoted by a single-minded or even obsessional leader. The premises of this school are that the process of strategy formation is semi-conscious at best and that strategy exists in the mind of the leader. Strategy is therefore deliberate in long-term direction but emergent in detail. This school may be particularly relevant to start-ups, turnarounds, and owner-managed businesses.

The Cognitive School studies strategy formation as a cognitive process which takes place in the mind of the strategist. Flashes of insight are often a significant element of strategy formation. There is value in understanding and perhaps changing the mental maps inside the heads of key managers. This school certainly has relevance to the successful implementation of strategy in large organizations where obsolete mental models can often block progress.

The Learning School takes the view that the complex and unpredictable nature of the environment precludes deliberate control so that strategy must take the form of learning, which only occurs as a result of action. The Learning School thus recognizes the importance of emerging as opposed to deliberate strategy. Strategy formation cannot therefore be neatly separated from strategy implementation. The end result of an effective strategy may be an adaptive organization as much as it is a plan of action.

The Power School, which resembles Whittington's Processual School, sees strategy formation as a process of negotiation among the relevant possessors of power within the enterprise. It also sees power as important in determining the interaction between the enterprise and its external environment. This school certainly is relevant to practice as power structures may be as important as logic in determining strategies.

The Cultural School, which is like Whittington's Systemic School, sees strategy formation as a collective process. The culture can both be a constraint to be overcome

Table 3.3 The seven descriptive schools

School	Nature of Process	Principal Relevance
Entrepreneurial	Vision	Emphasis on vision for the future. Relevance for business start-ups, turnarounds, or where there is a charismatic leader
Cognitive	Mental process	Examines the mental processes and maps of leaders. Examines the flashes of insight from which strategy may originate
Learning	Emergent	Sees planning as leading to learning. An enterprise which can learn and adapt may succeed in uncertain world
Power	Negotiation	Examines the processes of power and negotiation by which strategies are formed in enterprises
Cultural	Collective process	Strategies derive from a collective process and the culture of the enterprise which may be unique and hence a source of advantage
Environmental	Reactive process	Organizations cluster in distinct ecological niches until resources become scarce or conditions hostile. Then they die
Configuration	Transformational process	Organizations exist in stable configurations for considerable periods but then have to transform themselves

Source: Adapted from H. Mintzberg *et al.*, *Strategy Safari* (Prentice Hall, 1998).

for implementing change but also a potential source of competitive advantage because cultures may be unique.

The Environmental School sees strategy formation as a reactive process and hence has much in common with Whittington's Evolutionary School. Organizations cluster together in distinct ecological-type niches where they remain until resources become scarce or conditions too hostile. Then they die.

Finally, the Configuration School sees strategy as a process of transformation from one stable configuration to another. This view sees enterprises as being in stable configurations for long periods. These stable periods are interrupted from time to time by radical transformations involving major change with multiple dimensions.

3.5 Summary

STRATEGY has many aspects. Different writers tend to emphasize particular aspects, possibly under the influence of their own original academic discipline.

Two comprehensive attempts to provide an overview and structure for the academic literature on strategy have been summarized. These may be valuable as frameworks within which to place further reading and to understand differences between differing academic perspectives.

References

Mintzberg, H. (1987) 'Crafting Strategy', *Harvard Business Review*, 65/4: 66–75.

—— (1994) *The Rise and Fall of Strategic Planning* (London: Prentice Hall).

—— Ahlstrand, B. and Lampel, J. (1998) *Strategy Safari* (London: Prentice Hall).

Whittington, R. (1993) *What is Strategy—And Does it Matter?* (London: Routledge).

Part II

Context

Chapter 4
Why Context Matters

4.1 Introduction

Sound strategic management depends on understanding the context. The overall objective of Part II is to consider the significance of context in more depth. This chapter will discuss what context is and why it is important. Chapter 4 explores some of the diversity that exists in contexts at a general level. Detailed techniques for assessing contexts are described in Part III (Chs. 8 to 10).

Figure 4.1 shows again the basic model of strategic management on which this book is based. Context is the environment within which an enterprise operates.

Figure 4.1 Context: the background to strategic management

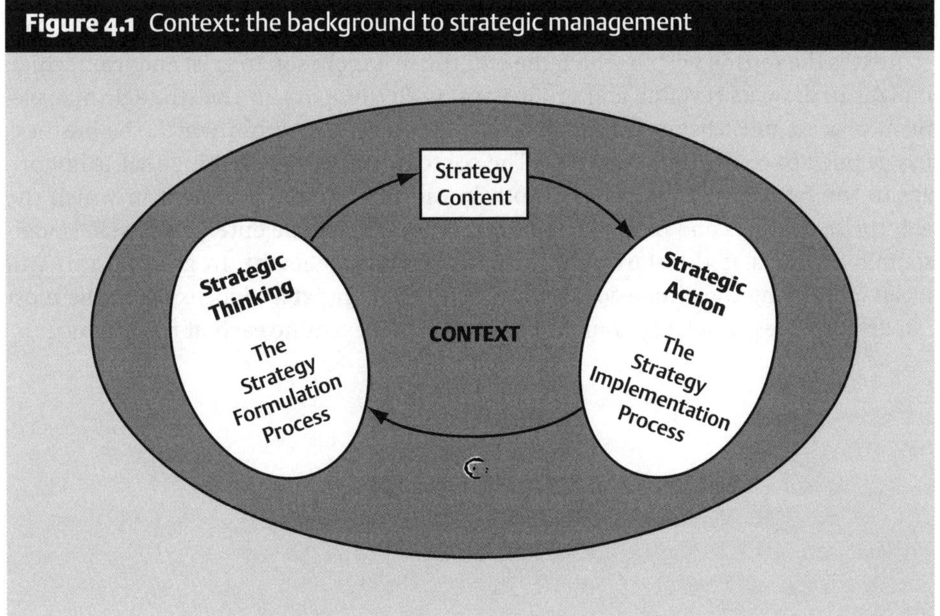

Context sets the scene for strategic management and therefore forms the background to the model. All the other elements of strategic management have to be appropriate to the context. Poor strategies often result from a failure to take into account some important aspect of the context.

4.2 What do we mean by context?

CONTEXT is an elusive reality of strategic management because contexts consist of both fact and perspective. Every context involves some hard facts. For instance, the enterprise will currently be offering particular services to particular groups of customers and in competition with known competitors. Such facts are important to the context but the context is also influenced by how you interpret the facts. Context is both objective and subjective. As Theodore Levitt (1960) pointed out in his famous article 'Marketing Myopia', how you see your context influences the strategies which you will pursue at least as much as the facts. For instance, railway companies can see themselves as in the train business or the transport business or indeed in the entertainment (leisure travel) business. If you are running a railway what you see as your context depends on which of these views you choose. You could, of course, choose to be in all three. If you did, your context would be different from if you chose to be in passenger transport and different again if you choose to be in freight transport. Thus the perspective of context is fundamental to the whole of strategy. It has to be clear even before deciding your strategic intent. In this chapter we try to peel the onion of context.

Any enterprise exists in a context that is unique to that enterprise at that time. The context is the setting within which the enterprise has chosen to exist and from which it plans to draw its revenue and profit streams. Because of this the strategic management process must begin by understanding the context within which the business has decided to compete and survive. The context includes everything that is important to the future of the enterprise both in the external environment in which the enterprise operates and in the internal characteristics of the enterprise itself. Understanding context is the start point for strategic management. In general, this will mean identifying the dimensions and scope of the context and focusing on the most important issues which the context poses. We shall examine each of these in turn.

4.3 The dimensions of context

THE context is likely to have several dimensions which may include:

- an industry context (i.e. is our mythical railway company competing in the people transport industry or the leisure industry?);
- a national or international context (i.e. is our mythical railway company in a single country or is it multi-national and if so in which part of the globe?);
- an organizational context (i.e. the particular characteristics and capabilities of our railway company and its people);
- a self-perception context (i.e. is our railway catering only to a special group, (e.g. commuters in limited comfort or luxury coaches for a small exclusive group such as the Orient Express?);
- an intention context (i.e. is it aimed at displacing the road transport of its passengers or just filling up its available rolling stock to make a profit?).

4.4 Focus in context

AS our definition of context is all-embracing, it is impossible to say what may be important in practice, but what we can say is that not defining the context within which the company plans to compete would make strategic management invalid.

While the dimensions above may be useful, a more important classification is between the more important and the less important aspects of the context so that the organization can prioritize its investments and sharpen its focus. For example, the privatized railway companies in the UK need to decide whether they wish to please:

- shareholders;
- passengers;
- the regulator;
- the government;
- or all of them at the same time.

Similarly, they need to decide whether the service is aimed at:

- protecting the existing base;
- attracting road users to abandon their cars and 'let the train take the strain';
- attracting inter-city airline passengers to abandon the shuttles and take the train.

Failure to answer these questions will result in weak strategic direction and a tendency to react to each media-driven crisis without addressing more fundamental issues such as infrastructure and rolling stock. In an industry where it is almost impossible to increase capacity overnight, a lack of strategy and vision may prove disastrous.

It is apparent that the focus within any particular context derives from identifying what the right questions are to address. This is why the first step in many case study discussions is: 'What are the issues in this case?' Similarly an early question for strategic management is: 'What are the important issues for us now?' The context presents the questions, issues, and dilemmas which strategic management needs to resolve and so sets the agenda for strategic management.

4.5 The significance of the uniqueness of context

It is apparent that enterprises face very different issues as they contemplate their futures. It is, therefore, important to understand that there are limits to the relevance of studying other contexts. There may, of course, be similarities between one context and others but there will also always be dissimilarities. The exact combination of characteristics in any context will never have occurred before nor will it ever occur again. There can, therefore, be no alternative to studying the context as it is and devising and implementing a unique strategy in response.

This uniqueness means that, while general models of strategic management are of value, it is necessary always to consider the relevance of a particular model to a particular context and to choose the most relevant models. General models may help to understand a particular context but will rarely provide the whole truth.

No organization can survive unless it is able to read its context well both for the present and the future and understand the issues presented by its context. If a context does not present any questions or issues, there is no need for strategic management as everything can run on quite happily as it is. Some enterprises enjoy this happy state at times but far more often the context presents management either with a single major dilemma or with multiple issues which require action if the enterprise is to survive and prosper. A single major dilemma may require a single major and obviously strategic choice. For example, a failing business may demand a turnaround strategy of a slash and burn type to ensure survival as a first step before taking action to bring itself back into profitability. Multiple issues may require changes which are both more subtle and more inter-related so that there is a need for a coherent strategy which responds to the issues and to the relationships between them. In either case, the context sets the agenda and the response must be appropriate.

Because contexts are unique, each context presents a unique dilemma or set of issues to a single enterprise. A strategy is the unique response. It is therefore meaningless to transfer a strategy from one enterprise to another. This is one reason why imitation strategies are almost always ineffective. The imitator necessarily faces different issues from the imitated. Even in the case of direct competitors in the same industry, the actions of the first mover will have altered the context. The context is also different for the imitator because the imitator has different organizational capabilities and inclinations.

It is because contexts are unique that case studies are so commonly used to teach strategic management. A case study attempts to describe a particular context and the dilemmas that it imposes on a particular enterprise at a particular time. The effective discussion of a case depends on understanding the context and identifying the dilemma or the issues that have to be resolved. This is the closest it is possible to get in the classroom to posing the strategic dilemmas faced by managers in real contexts. Needless to say, the nature of the issues in a case may be arguable. The strategic issues facing a real enterprise may be just as arguable. Arguments about the nature of the issues are an important step on the way to devising good strategies; effective strategic management depends on resolving these arguments.

Strategic management is about resolving the issues and dilemmas that the strategic context presents using whatever frameworks and approaches help. The strategic context and the issues are the start point; the frameworks and analytical models are secondary. Many of the best strategies result from an intuitive response to the issues presented by the context, but flashes of insight are only effective if they result from a correct understanding of the context.

4.6 Typical issues and dilemmas posed

It is impossible to provide a comprehensive checklist of all the issues and dilemmas which contexts may pose for strategic management to address. The following quite often play a significant part:

- the action of a dominant competitor may require a response;
- resources are scarce so that priorities have to be set;
- technological change affects products, processes, or both;
- key people are dissatisfied with the current situation or are in conflict with others;
- new owners set different kinds of objectives or expect a different level of result;
- political change requires new patterns of behaviour;
- customers and suppliers are affected by economic change;
- environmental concerns and pressure groups require changes in practice.

Each enterprise has to understand the separate dimensions of its context, to identify its own issues and dilemmas, and to formulate and implement its own strategies in response. Effective strategic management starts with a good understanding of context.

4.7 Theoretical models of the relevance of context

One way of thinking about strategic context is to draw a parallel between an enterprise and its context and an animal and its habitat. An animal species becomes adapted to its environment by natural selection. Similarly, an enterprise makes management decisions and takes action to survive and thrive in its context. Animal species are able to get it right by evolution over many generations; enterprises cannot do this, so they have to make the needed adjustments by competent strategic management. The enterprise has to define a 'viable system' which will allow it to live within its context and exploit that context to maximum advantage. To do this it is necessary to understand both the external environment and the organizational capabilities that lend themselves to exploiting the context in which it lives. Beer (1984) describes a viable system as one that can: 'Survive under considerable perturbations because it can take avoiding action, because it can acclimatize, because it accommodates, because it is adaptive'.

This means that the enterprise is able to adjust its structure, systems, culture, and the attitudes of its people at the same rate of change as the environment in which it is and hopefully do so faster than its competitors. Espejo (1989) points out that:

Viable systems are those that:

1. Are able to maintain a separate existence.
2. Have their own problem-solving capacity.
3. Have the capacity to respond to familiar disturbances.
4. Have the potential to respond to unknown disturbances.

Strategic management is about giving an enterprise the advantages that Beer and Espejo claim for viable systems and the first step must be to understand the context in depth.

Recently there has been a general view that business contexts are becoming more complex and turbulent. This has led to attempts to apply complexity theory to business. Complexity theory has created the concept of Complex Adaptive Systems (CAS) which by the interactions between components following relatively simple rules can achieve spontaneous self-organization. A commonly used example of a CAS is a group of birds or fish forming themselves into orderly flocks or shoals. Each fish or bird applies a few simple rules that define, for instance, how close and in what position to swim or fly in relation to its nearest neighbours. Complexity theory suggests that CASs that are too chaotic can improve their performance by imposing tighter rules whereas CASs which are too rigid can improve their performance by allowing more flexibility. A successful CAS will therefore move towards a state of equilibrium between the forces of organization and disorganization. This stable state has been called the 'edge of chaos'. Applying this idea to strategic business contexts suggests that the essence of strategy is to hunt for the right rules to allow the enterprise to live on the edge of chaos in relationship to its strategic context (Waldrop 1992).

There are some dangers to the application of complexity theory to business. The theory has its roots in biology where evolution takes many generations of trial and error to achieve its results; managers only have one, or at most a few, chances to get it right. One attempt to demonstrate how complexity theory is relevant to business (Lissack and Roos 1999) differentiates complex contexts from complicated contexts. They point out that the word 'Complicated' is derived from the Latin word to fold whereas the word 'Complex' is derived from the Latin word to weave. Complex contexts have far more inter-relationships than merely complicated contexts. They suggest that coherence is the essential ingredient for success in complex contexts. This sounds like good general advice but coherence may not be the only ingredient needed for success; some contexts also require the right decisions and actions.

4.8 Examples of differing contexts and dilemmas

SOME important features of the context and the strategic issues or dilemmas of each of the six case examples in Part VI have been tabulated in summary form in Table 4.1.

The features of the contexts and the nature of the issues or dilemmas faced are necessarily very briefly stated in Table 4.1. There is certainly much more to each context than can be shown. Clearly someone who knows an enterprise, an industry and its environment well can describe the context and the issues in far more detail. Conversely an independent observer may have the detachment or a comparative perspective to see the issues more clearly. An effective understanding of a context depends on the ability to focus on the right issues—not on the length of the list of issues.

There are two important points to make about Table 4.1. First, it should be apparent that each of the contexts is completely different from the others. Six examples are not many but if there were six thousand or six million they would each still be different. This is why strategic management has to start with the unique context not with some theoretical model offering a universal solution.

Secondly, there are patterns of similarity between different contexts and similar kinds of dilemma present themselves to different enterprises. The theories of strategic management are derived from study of these similarities and help to transfer experience from one context to another. However, it is essential to start by thinking about the particular context and then to use theories that seem genuinely relevant and helpful. It is usually disastrous to impose a theoretical framework without having thought very carefully about the particular context. One of the weaknesses of the 'strategy industry' is that it has sometimes failed to recognize this point.

Table 4.1 also illustrates that it may be difficult to agree what the strategic issues which the context poses really are. This may happen in practice because no two people have exactly the same knowledge or perspective of the context. Typically

Table 4.1 Case examples—contexts and issues

Example	Some Important Features of the Context	Some Strategic Issues and Dilemma(s)
Nolan, Norton 1986	■ Small knowledge-intensive company ■ Increasing impact of computers on business ■ Owned by two individuals with personal ambitions ■ Growing healthily in short term but vulnerable in economic downturns	■ Resource limits at present scale ■ Continue internal growth or sell out? ■ Choice of partner ■ Product/service direction in post-mainframe world
ICL 1981	■ Emergent new technologies such as microprocessors and desktop computing ■ Long-standing strategy of being a universal supplier of mainframe computers ■ Financial crisis ■ Preferential procurement strategies of government and public bodies challenged and eroded ■ Distribution channels unsuited to selling new products ■ Introduction of solution selling in the market by minicomputer suppliers ■ Reluctance of financial institutions to back a failing organization	■ Survival in the short term ■ Return to profit and growth in longer term ■ Need for new strategy in changed computer business ■ Choice of partners to enhance resources ■ Managing expectations of several stakeholder groups
BMW 1994–9	■ Car market maturing and becoming global ■ Erosion of margins in principal markets of Europe and USA ■ Brands weakening as cars tend to become commodities ■ BMW much smaller than principal direct competitors but with a strong brand ■ R&D spend to maintain diverse product range growing exponentially	■ Several strategic directions possible: 1. Grow by evolution risking margins and brand image 2. Become niche provider 3. Grow by acquisition but most attractive acquisitions already gone 4. Seek 'White Knight' to avoid risk of hostile take-over 5. Do nothing for the present ■ Implementation difficult in technical and people terms

Marks & Spencer 1999	■ UK base threatened by changing tastes of once loyal customers—demand for designer labels etc. ■ Reluctant consumers forcing all UK retailers to reduce margins ■ Traditional UK supply strategies failing after long period of success ■ Overseas investments not paying off	■ How to stem the downward spiral? ■ How to meet new customer expectations without eroding values and trading principles of the company ■ How to recover past glory? ■ Difficulties in succession to Chairman/CEO
Intervention Board for Agricultural Produce 1990–3	■ Public Sector ■ New managerialism ■ External pressure to produce more for less ■ General policy directives applied to whole public sector	■ Mismatch between general directives and needs of the enterprise itself. ■ Need to change culture, systems, and organization at the same time ■ Lack of experience of change or culture for change
EuroPharm UK 1993–8	■ National subsidiary of European parent ■ Increasing purchasing power of customers ■ Increasing costs of R&D ■ Pharmaceutical industry consolidating ■ Strong values of staff	■ Choice of future Vision ■ Retaining independence ■ Vision-driven change ■ Achieving change in multi-functional company ■ Internal development of needed capabilities ■ Sustained implementation process

there may be a divide between outsiders who can more easily see the big picture but lack knowledge of the detail and insiders who know the details but may be unable to see the wood for the trees. There may also be differences in perception between people in different functions or at different management levels. This can often lead to arguments about what the really strategic issues to be resolved are. These arguments may be among the most important in the whole strategic management process.

An interesting example of this argument occurred in the motor industry in the late 1990s. The conventional wisdom at the time was that the car industry was consolidating. Alex Trotman the former Chairman of Ford stated publicly that there would soon only be five global car producers in the industry. The many take-overs and mergers in the industry between 1995 and 1999 suggest that Trotman was expressing a view widely held among senior managers in the industry. BMW bought Rover in 1994 ostensibly to increase its scale of operations. Daimler Benz and Chrysler merged in 1998 with the apparent aim of achieving a place as one of the surviving giants of the industry. Ford acquired Volvo in early 1999. Renault and Nissan formed a strategic alliance in 1999. John Kay (1999), however, argued that the facts did not support the view that the car industry was actually consolidating. He compared the figures for the car industry in 1996 with 1969 and concluded that the degree of consolidation had decreased over that period. The combined market share of the largest three producers had declined over this period from 51% to 36%. The number of manufacturers producing over a million cars a year had increased from 9 to 14 and the number of companies with more than 1% of the global market had increased from 15 to 17. Kay's view was that the economies of scale (which might be expected to drive the industry towards consolidation) did not apply in modern manufacturing and that consumer preference would drive the industry towards continuing and increasing diversity.

It may be that these apparently conflicting views were both correct. The number of car market niches may continue to increase as had already occurred in the 1990s with the emergence of Sports Utility Vehicles, the rebirth of the soft-top sports car, the arrival of the mini-people carriers such as the Renault Scenic and the Mercedes A Class, as well as the resurgence of the hyper-performers such as the Jaguar 220. At the same time, the number of manufacturers or assemblers may diminish as car conglomerates such as Ford, Fiat, and Volkswagen successfully prove that it is possible to sustain different brands within the same home without harming customer perceptions. The strategic 'battle' may be about which form of organization—the conglomerate or the diversified—will prove the best able to manage the uniqueness of the brands it manages into discrete market niches.

There is another aspect to this. Increasingly, the big and small manufacturers are sourcing whole units from third party suppliers such as Bosch in Germany, TRW in the USA, and Magna in Canada. *Time* magazine (1 March 1999) reported that:

> These system-manufacturing firms provide large chunks of car across the entire range of established auto companies and are taking on their own global role alongside the global auto assemblers. The advantage to the major carmakers includes faster delivery times, more flexibility and more manageable inventories, as well as redefined labor arrangements.

If this trend escalates, being able to put price and performance pressure on these system suppliers will be a significant factor in the showroom price of cars. To achieve such buying power the auto-assemblers have to be big. The role that procurement policies have on car makers' profits is illustrated by the significant impact Volkswagen derived by employing Lopez and asking him to take charge of their supplier management.

Our point is that it is crucial for any strategist in the car industry to consider the arguments in this debate that is essentially about the nature of the context of this industry. The perception of which dilemmas their strategies will have to resolve will depend on what they come to believe about the nature of their context. If the leaders of the car industry believe that they have to merge to survive then there are likely to be plenty of mergers even if Kay's analysis was correct. Perception may be as important as truth; dispassionate analysis will have to wait for business historians who will, of course, write history from the point of view of the victors. Dispassionate strategy may be an oxymoron. As we said at the start of this chapter, context is subjective as well as objective.

The BMW case example illustrates these general points on the context of the car industry with the particular story of BMW's acquisition of Rover. It may be that BMW read the context wrongly and addressed the wrong issues.

4.9 Summary

EACH context is unique, many faceted and continuously changing. Contexts consist of both facts and perspectives. The context poses the issues and dilemmas to which strategic management has to respond. The nature of the strategic issues and dilemmas may be arguable and it is essential to resolve this argument. The aim of strategic management is to enable the enterprise to respond to its context in a way that improves its chances of remaining viable.

Strategic management should start from a good understanding of the unique context.

References

Beer, S. (1984) 'The Viable System Model: Its Provenance, Development, Methodology and Pathology', *Journal of Operational Research Society*, 35. Reprinted in Espejo and Harnden (1989).

Espejo, R. (1989) 'The VSM Revisited', in Espejo and Harnden (1989).

—— and Harnden, R. (eds.) (1989) *The Viable System Model* (Chichester: Wiley).

Kay, J. (1999) 'Sometimes Size is Not Everything', *Financial Times*, 3 Mar.

Levitt, T. (1960) 'Marketing Myopia', *Harvard Business Review*, July–Aug.

Lissack, M., and Roos, J. (1999) *The Next Common Sense: Mastering Corporate Complexity through Coherence* (London: Nicholas Brealey).

Waldrop, M. M. (1992) *Complexity: The Emerging Science at the Edge of Order and Chaos* (New York: Simon & Schuster, 1992; Penguin, 1994).

Chapter 5
The Diversity of Context

5.1 Introduction

IN Chapter 4, we emphasized the importance and uniqueness of the context within which an enterprise operates. Our point was that an effective strategy for an organization must be built to exploit the opportunities afforded by the environment in which it operates. However, the organization needs to put its aspirations within the context of the bigger grouping of which it is a part. In the private sector this wider group is often called an industry. In the public sector it tends to be collections of similar service providers such as Local Government or Public Utilities. Each of these collective groupings has its own context with its own peculiarities, similarities, and general principles. Specific research results and relevant literature exist for some of these collective entities. The purpose of this chapter is briefly to review some of the more important of these. We hope that this chapter will achieve two objectives. First, it will assist readers with interests in particular classes of context to find relevant work in that field. Secondly, we hope that by describing some differences in context, it will help readers to become more sensitive to differences in context and become more able to understand the particular contexts with which they happen to be involved.

5.2 'Normal' businesses

MOST strategic management writing is concerned, either explicitly or tacitly, with businesses which:

- are privately owned;
- are moderately large;

- have significant investment in tangible assets;
- are growing or intending to grow.

This class of enterprise has tended to be accepted as 'normal' and it is certainly a very common class. These businesses are run principally for the benefit of their shareholders as the dominant stakeholders. Success is measured mainly, but not entirely, by the ability to deliver value to shareholders.

In practice, success for this class of enterprise may be achieved either by improving operational performance or by financial means. Operational performance can be improved by either increasing revenues or increasing efficiency or a combination of both. Financial methods may increase the value as perceived by the market without any necessary change in operational performance. Common financial methods include leveraging equity with debt and restructuring. Sophisticated financial means may be referred to collectively as financial engineering and may be undesirable if taken to extremes and without improvements in operational performance.

Most of the companies that catch the newspaper headlines fall into this 'normal' class which therefore is seen as the dominant model and the 'normal' context. It is, however, important to remember that the assumptions and habits of thought which defined the normal class do not necessarily apply to other types of business, to non-profit-making enterprises, and to the public sector.

It is possible to build a model of strategic management in which the maximization of shareholder value is built into the model itself. Mathur and Kenyon (1997), for instance, base their analytical framework for strategic management on the assumption that the only objective of a business is to create value for its shareholders. This assumption has the advantage that it allows rigorous analysis for those cases where it applies but the disadvantage that it limits the scope of the model. Our model of strategic management is intended to be relevant to all forms of enterprise so that the nature of the context and the aims which that context imposes have to be considered from first principles and not assumed.

In practice, there are few enterprises that can focus on the creation of shareholder value to the exclusion of all other aims. Some may be constrained by the needs of other stakeholder groups, some distracted by the personal whims of key individuals. For example, none of the case examples in Part VI fits perfectly within the 'normal' context. IBAP (Intervention Board for Agricultural Produce) is in the public sector; personal characteristics and aims clearly carried some weight in Marks & Spencer and BMW; professional stakeholder groups had other aims than just profit making in Nolan, Norton; ICL was fighting for survival, EuroPharm was gearing up to ensure an independent future among giants.

In this chapter we are interested in the contexts of enterprises that do not fit the tacitly accepted 'normal' model of context.

5.3 Knowledge-intensive enterprises

OVER the last several years there has been an increasing awareness of the importance of knowledge as a wealth creator in its own right. Large organizations have sprung up that package and sell know-how. In these knowledge-intensive enterprises the intellectual assets embodied in the systems, databases, products, people, and processes are more important than fixed assets and financial capital. For a general description of this type of enterprise see, for instance, Stewart (1998). In many such enterprises, the intellectual capital that knowledge generates becomes the wellspring for long-term profitable growth. Into this category fall software producers, media companies, and some distance-learning organizations. The issues to do with how these types of business should be managed have attracted thought and research. (See e.g. Quinn 1992; Leonard-Barton 1995; Fruin 1997; Kennedy 1989; Rosenbloom and Spencer 1996; Sakaiya 1991.) Clearly the knowledge-intensive enterprise is a modified form of the normal business context in which the value of knowledge has to be given more weight.

Professional service firms (including accountants, lawyers, investment banks, advertising agencies, and management consultants) are knowledge-intensive enterprises who sell knowledge directly. They have few physical assets and their success depends on how well they develop the knowledge of their staff and transmit it as benefits to their customers. This sector has attracted a literature of its own (see, for instance, Maister 1993 and Scott 1998; Kelly 1985; Katz 1988; Shapero 1985; Sveiby and Lloyd 1987; and much earlier Langrish *et al.* 1972 and Carr-Saunders and Wilson 1933). Professional service firms are likely to provide some useful models of best practice relevant to all knowledge-intensive enterprises and which have yet to be fully explored.

Creating strategies for these types of organizations is different in many ways from developing strategies for asset-based businesses. Protecting the rights to exploiting knowledge is a critical competence and tends to be taken seriously. For instance, software vendors, such as Microsoft, have established an organization to monitor infringement of copyright and with a remit to identify and prosecute those who reproduce products for commercial exploitation without the originator's approval. Copyrights, patents, and similar legal means can protect some forms of knowledge to some degree.

On the other hand, knowledge tends to migrate. The competitive advantage that the knowledge bestows can often be fleeting. Ideas are often easy to imitate and the cost of entry may be lower for the followers. For example, offering a net-based service costs very little and the expertise is often found among young computer buffs.

Obviously one would expect many of the strategic issues and dilemmas in knowledge-intensive enterprises to relate to knowledge, its management and deployment. Successful strategic management will depend on understanding the knowledge dimension of the context and the issues to be resolved. It will be important to know what knowledge is valuable, how it is generated, and how it is transmitted to customers. Among the most important strategies are likely to be those relating to managing the people and computers in whose heads and databases so much of the knowledge resides. Managing knowledge within the organization is another critical competence and in some ways the most daunting. It is necessary to capture the knowledge of the firm in reusable form and to encourage employees to share their knowledge. Unless the means of easy knowledge transfer are in place, a knowledge-intensive firm will find that it does not have the critical mass necessary to offer a credible service or to build on its initial advantage. For these and other similar reasons, keeping a significant competitive edge is the most daunting of strategic challenges for knowledge-intensive businesses.

Knowledge intensity does not change the principles of strategic management but it will affect the content of all the elements of strategic management. The implementation of strategy for these firms is likely to require changes in the culture, processes, reward strategies, and structure to improve the flow of knowledge.

5.4 Mature businesses and declining industries

THE normal model assumed that the enterprise is intending to grow. Some businesses find themselves in circumstances in which an industry is declining. Managers face the task of devising future strategies in a context that seems to offer few new opportunities. It is apparent that many firms in Western Europe and the USA are in relatively mature industries.

Baden-Fuller and Stopford (1992) specifically studied this context and the question of suitable strategies for mature businesses. Their argument starts by dispatching the myth that industry is a significant factor in determining the profitability of a business. They quote research by Rumelt (1991) which showed that only about 8% of a business's profitability could be explained by choice of industry compared with about 46% that could be explained by choice of strategy (44% could not be systematically explained at all). Such research results confirm the everyday observation that some companies are much more profitable than others in the same industry. It also appears that while there is a correlation between market share and profitability, there is little evidence that a large market share *causes* profitability. It may be just as true to say that firms become profitable because of their ability to innovate and that their profitability in turn allows them to price at a level which gives them a large market share. Baden-Fuller and Stopford argue that it is strategic innovation—the ability to rewrite the rules within which the industry operates—which is the real key to success in mature industries. It follows that the issue for the strategist to address in such businesses is to understand the present rules and then devise some imaginative way of changing these rules. Baden-Fuller and Stopford suggest that rejuvenation should be accomplished in four steps:

- galvanize: create a top team dedicated to renewal;
- simplify: cut complexity;
- build: develop new capabilities;
- leverage: maintain momentum and extend advantages.

These findings are of wider significance to many contexts as they emphasize the importance of innovation and creativity for achieving success. It would seem that while the principles of strategic management still apply to declining industries, the ability to innovate and create innovative strategies is even more important for them than in more prosperous conditions.

5.5 Turnaround, recovery, and end-games

ANOTHER type of strategic context occurs often enough for it to have been examined by researchers. This is the enterprise that is suffering relative decline within a generally healthy industry. The issue is to change the trend from decline to renewed growth. This area has generated a vocabulary of its own. Corporate recovery covers all attempts to recover from a decline and also includes the specialized roles of receivers and administrators who have to work within a specific legal framework. Turnaround covers businesses that do manage to change decline into growth. Sharpbenders are those who do this at a late stage and so form the most extreme examples of turnaround.

Bibeault (1982) investigated the causes of decline. His survey concluded that internal deficiencies were about twice as likely to cause the decline as external causes (see summary in Table 5.1).

A major research study of the phenomenon of Turnaround was carried out on 26 UK manufacturing companies between 1982 and 1987 (Grinyer *et al.* 1988). This study differentiated between early-stage, intermediate-stage, and late-stage turnarounds (sharpbenders) and identified differences in the causes, triggers, and actions taken for each of the three stages. The study led to a general model of how enterprises react to unsatisfactory performance. The model is shown in Figure 5.1. This model suggests that the first reaction is cost-cutting. Only if this fails will enterprises make strategic changes within their existing operating patterns, beliefs, and rules (OBR). Only if this fails again will they change the OBR itself.

This research finding tends to support the field observation that organizations change only when they have to and that fundamental change rarely occurs except in dire circumstances.

Slatter (1984), updated and reissued as Slatter and Lovett (1999), provides more general guidance on the issues likely to occur in enterprises which are facing adverse circumstances and need to recover.

Table 5.1 Common causes of decline

Internal (67%)
- Management defects
- Management errors of omission
- Management errors of commission

External (33%)
- Decline in government demand or change in regulations
- Increased foreign competition
- Economic variables
- Changes in demographic/social variable
- Changes in product technology

Source: Adapted from D. B. Bibeault, *Corporate Turnaround: How Managers Turn Losers into Winners* (McGraw-Hill, 1982).

Figure 5.1 Progressive reaction to unsatisfactory performance

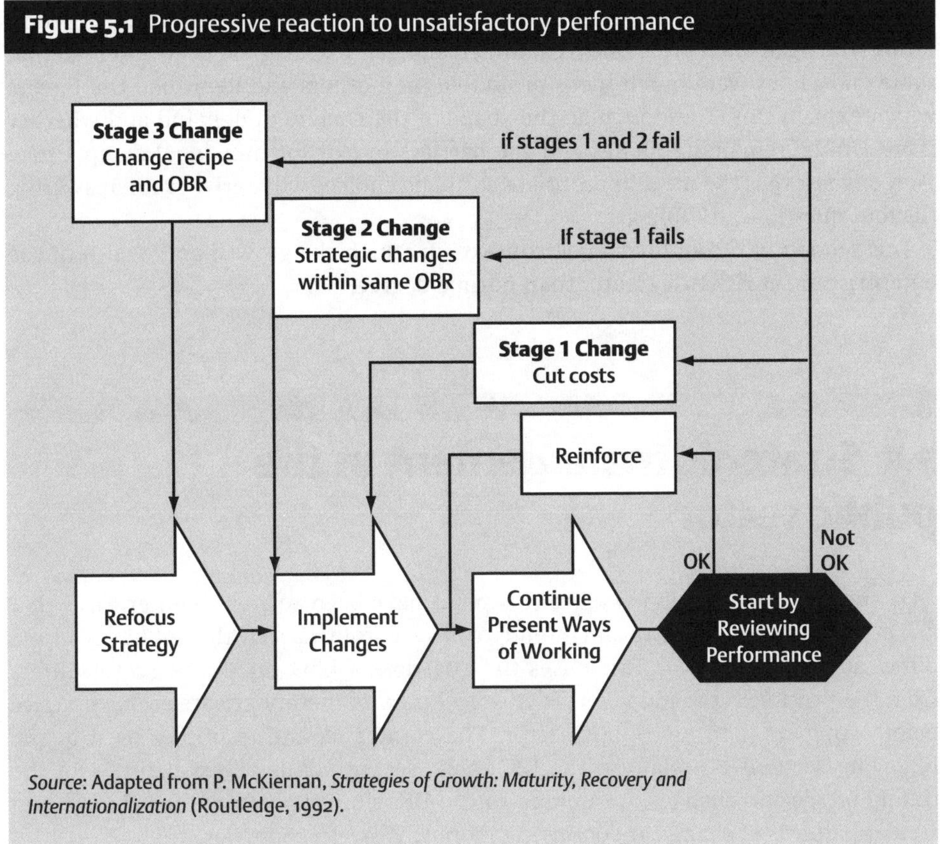

Source: Adapted from P. McKiernan, *Strategies of Growth: Maturity, Recovery and Internationalization* (Routledge, 1992).

Table 5.2 Choosing an end-game strategy

Can the structure of the industry support a profitable decline phase?
Indicators of profitable decline include slow and predictable decline with well-defined remaining niches.

What are the exit barriers for each significant competitor? Who will exit quickly and who will remain?
Exit barriers are lower if assets are fully depreciated or easily converted, reinvestment needs low and plants shared.

Do your company's strengths match remaining pockets of demand?
This is easier to achieve if there are a few large well-defined residual markets rather than general decline in all segments.

What are your competitors' strengths in these pockets? How can their exit barriers be overcome?
Possible suggested gambits include offering to take over customer support or acquire unwanted assets.

Source: Adapted from K. R. Harrigan and M. E. Porter, 'End-Game Strategies for Declining Industries', *Harvard Business Review*, July–Aug. (1983).

Industries eventually move towards terminal decline. This raises the need for 'end-game' strategies to provide the best returns from a business that has no long-term future. Harrigan and Porter (1983) examined end-game strategies. They observed that some end-games were much more profitable than others and identified the factors which explain this. These include the shape of the decline in demand and whether there will be remaining niches and the barriers to exit for individual competitors. They suggest that the most appropriate strategic choices will derive from answering the four questions in Table 5.2.

This section has examined some contexts in which the growth and health of the enterprise are at risk to a greater than normal degree.

5.6 Strategic management in the public sector

ALL the contexts mentioned up to this point have been related to enterprises that are in private ownership and intend to make a profit. Clearly the public sector is a different class of context. This raises the question of how the public sector differs from the private sector and whether it is necessary to modify private sector practice before applying it to the public sector. The comments and examples used in the following sections all relate to the UK public sector. While the structure and the timing of specific changes are unique to the UK, similar pressures for change and similar patterns of change are occurring in most Western countries.

It has generally been assumed during the 1980s and 1990s that public sector management can be improved by importing management ideas and practices from the private sector. This trend has been called (Pollitt 1991) the 'new managerialism'. Examples of the specific actions taken to implement new managerial ideas include:

- transfer of approaches to strategy and planning from the private sector;
- appointment of more 'professional' managers into public services;
- setting explicit standards for performance;
- measuring the quantity and quality of outputs;
- reorganization into smaller units with clearly defined objectives;
- introduction of real or synthetic competition.

It is questionable whether this new 'managerialism' has been of benefit to the public sector but there is no doubt that it has occurred. Serious doubts have been expressed (see e.g Willcocks and Harrow 1992; Farnham and Horton 1993). The questions raised include the following.

- Will management practices that have become widely accepted in the private sector necessarily be appropriate to the differing needs of the public sector?
- Have all the transplanted practices truly reflected the current best practice in the private sector?
- Have the new practices been well implemented?

Whatever the objections, many managers in the public sector have to do their best to make these initiatives work. Many of them read books and articles or attend courses on strategic management in the private sector and then have to modify what they learn to their own contexts.

5.7 Traditional public sector management

Any examination of the public sector strategic context must take into account the ways in which management in the public sector in general tends to differ from the private sector. One important difference is that managers in the public sector have different aims from those in the commercial sector. This colours the way strategy is devised and implemented in these two contexts. Managers in the commercial or private sector generally aim to optimize shareholder value and to serve customers' needs. Managers in the public sector generally aim to provide 'public service' meaning the expenditure of public money to meet public needs as expressed by the policies of the government of the day. The commercial drivers within the public service generally aim to ensure that budgets are not exceeded and that money is legitimately spent to deliver the promised services. Public sector strategies attempt to be fair, even-handed, and consistent when judged by all those who are entitled to the benefits of the service. The Cabinet Office published a pamphlet entitled *A force for improvement in the UK Public Service* in 1991. This listed the duties for public servants. An extract from this list published in Tampoe (1994) is given below.

- Give undivided allegiance to the Crown
- Put official duty before private interests and not use their official position to further their private interests
- Be honest and avoid bringing discredit to the public service
- Serve Ministers with integrity and ability
- Keep the confidence to which they are party
- Carry out decisions with energy and goodwill, whether or not they personally agree
- Assist in the communication of government policy and decisions
- Deal sympathetically, efficiently and promptly with the public

Notice how much emphasis this charter puts on service to the Crown and Ministers rather than voters and taxpayers. The concept of the customer can also vary from that in the commercial sector. In the public services the recipient of the service is not necessarily seen as the customer. For example, a patient in a hospital is not seen as a customer of the hospital. Neither is a person claiming unemployment benefit seen as a customer by the department that administers social security payments. The patient and the unemployed person are better described as beneficiaries of the service. Customers of the public services are more likely to be the Ministers than the general public to whom the specific Secretary of State and the departmental heads have to account for their stewardship. Neither party pays for the services provided. This honour goes to the taxpayer who funds the public services through various forms of direct and indirect taxes.

Public servants can broadly be categorized as either advisers or providers. The advisers tend to be close to Ministers and convert policies into strategies, green papers and white papers which enable the framework of government to be built. The providers are those civil servants who are closer to the beneficiaries. In recent years more and more of these service providers have found themselves working in Executive Agencies and have been floated free from the operational net of the civil service. It is the Executive Agencies in which the pressure to introduce private sector management approaches has been the strongest (see the IBAP case example).

5.8 Comparison of private and public sector management

A GENERAL distinction has been made between 'management' in the private sector and 'administration' in the public sector (Keeling 1972). Keeling wrote before the new managerialist drive but it seems fair to assume that the traditional attitudes of the public sector persist in spite of the new initiatives. Some of the traditional characteristics of administration in contrast with management as practised in the private sector are listed in Table 5.3 below.

While Keeling was describing a difference in the attitude to the role of management among ex-administrators, there are also identifiable differences in the situations in which managers find themselves in the public sector. Some of these differences are summarized in Table 5.4 below.

From the point of view of strategic management, it would seem that public sector enterprises generally have less opportunity to develop their strategic intent as this is defined by a political process outside the control of management. Strategic choices are consequently focused more on how policy directives may best be achieved rather than on what those policies should be. Figure 5.2 taken from Tampoe (1994) summarises the links between policy, strategy, and strategy delivery.

Table 5.3 Characteristics of administrative systems compared with management systems

- Administrative systems express objectives in general terms and these are rarely reviewed or changed
- Administrative systems tend to give weight to avoiding mistakes
- Administrative systems place efficient use of resources as of secondary importance to meeting service goals
- Administrative systems have tightly defined responsibilities and hierarchies with limited delegation
- Administrators tend to refer problems upwards in contrast to managers who are expected to take decisions
- The role of administrator is one of arbitration and rule interpretation, whereas the manager is a protagonist

Source: Adapted from D. Keeling, *Management in Government* (Allen & Unwin, 1972).

Table 5.4 Differences in management between public and private sectors

Public Services	Private Sector
Statutory regulation	Boards of directors
National needs	Market-place signals
Relatively open	Relatively secret
Attention of general public	Mostly attention of shareholders only
Multiple goals—primarily social	Simple goals — primarily shareholder value
Funded by taxes	Funded by operational returns, loans, and financial markets
Responsible to political masters	Responsible to shareholders
Complex and debated measures of performance	Mainly quantifiable measures of financial performance
Ill-defined policy directives	Policies less ambiguous

Source: Adapted from L. Willcocks and J. Harrow, *Rediscovering Public Services Management* (McGraw-Hill, 1992, p. xxi).

Figure 5.2 Government policy and its implementation

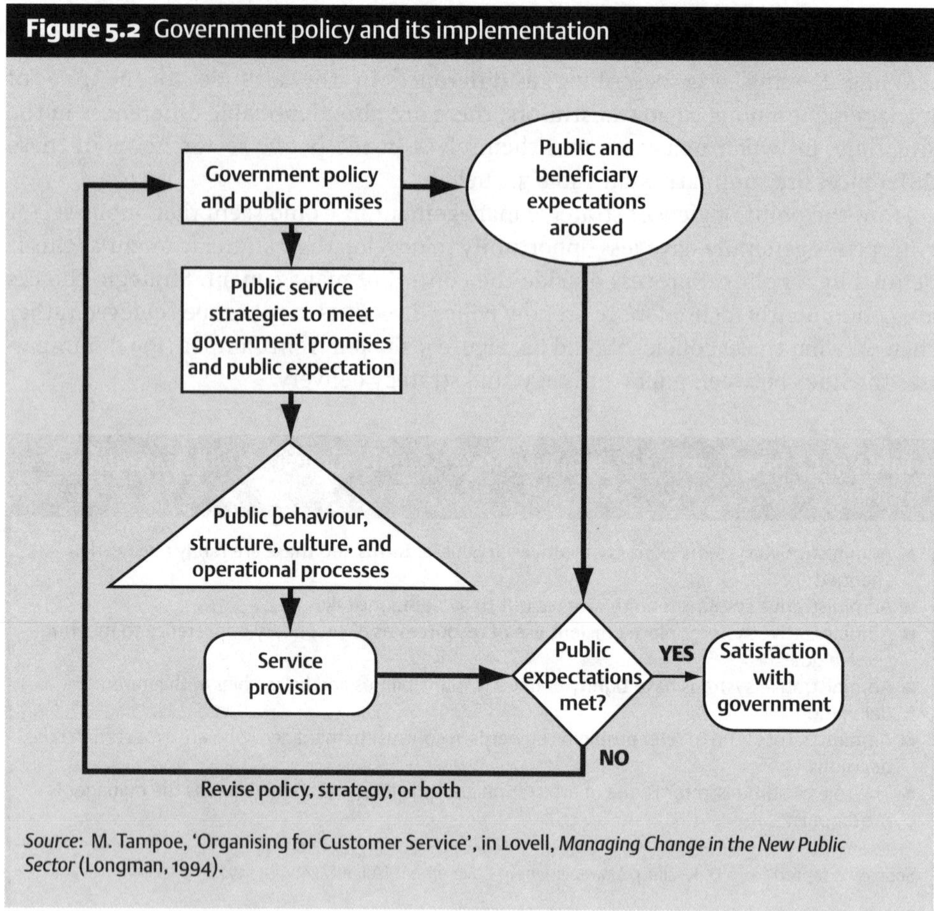

Source: M. Tampoe, 'Organising for Customer Service', in Lovell, *Managing Change in the New Public Sector* (Longman, 1994).

5.9 Differences among public sector entities

GENERALIZATIONS about the public sector are of limited value as there is a large range of strategic context within the public sector. Tomkins (1987) has suggested that a spectrum (see Table 5.5) is a better model than a simple division between public and private sectors.

This spectrum would suggest that the approaches to strategic management developed for the private sector can be most directly applied at the upper end of this spectrum and be least helpful at the lower end. Executive agencies, such as the IBAP case example, are perhaps in about the middle of the spectrum.

Specific contexts in the public sector also have their own peculiar characteristics unrelated to the public/private spectrum.

Table 5.5 Diversity in the public sector: a spectrum of organizational types

Fully private
Private with part state ownership
Joint private and public ventures
Private regulated
Public infrastructure—operating privately
Contracted out
Public with managed competition
Public without competition

Source: Adapted from C. R. Tomkins, *Achieving Economy, Efficiency and Effectiveness in the Public Sector* (Keegan Paul, 1987).

Local government

Local governments provide a set of services (e.g. schools, policing, rubbish collection, libraries) which have very little in common except that they are paid for out of the same pool of taxes and provided for the same population. The strategy for the local authority as a whole is likely to determine the total level of spending and how the total resource available should be allocated among the different services. This strategy may also encourage certain values such as the extent to which services should be contracted out or public sector jobs protected. This overall strategy is determined more by a political process than by the strategic management approaches typical of the private sector.

Each separate service will have its own 'strategy'. This is likely to focus on using the defined level of resources to achieve goals such as levels of service. The strategic choices to be made will be on the relative priority of different goals and on how to achieve the best overall achievement of goals within the resource constraints.

It is apparent that the local authority context tends to resemble a set of independent enterprises linked by a political entity.

The National Health Service (NHS)

The NHS has been more affected by new managerial initiatives than most parts of the public sector. There have been so many new initiatives that one major initiative has rarely had a chance to be implemented before a new one has started. In general, it would seem that 'strategy' in the NHS is determined by central government. Individual Trusts are expected to develop plans as to how they will implement the latest directive.

The service is run by a very efficient and proficient group of medical practitioners from nursing auxiliaries, nurses, and doctors. The service they provide is in increasing demand as the population ages and lives longer. The cost of the service increases in geometric progression as new high-technology solutions to illness are discovered and used, but unlike a commercial organization the cost-effectiveness of these increasingly expensive and skilled services are not questioned—just demanded in ever-increasing quantity and speed by the population at large.

Hidden away in all of this is the constant battle between the healers and the administrators. The healers take the view that life cannot be measured out on a cost-benefit basis; besides unless new techniques are tried new cures cannot be discovered. The administrators on the other hand use management and decision paradigms from the commercial and quasi-commercial world to manage a highly sensitive and invaluable service. This supposes that the demands made on it and its response to this demand can be predetermined and managed. Unfortunately, this is not the case. To all intents and purposes it is a crisis-management organization. Its workload cannot be predicted, neither can it be managed as an even flow as, for example, in a factory making widgets. This issue of crisis management lies at the heart of the problems that government, consultants, and academics have tried to solve. The problem is made worse by the news media highlighting resource shortages during periods of epidemics. Another very important consideration for the planner is the evaluation of the cost of a life. The NHS offers a benefit to anyone who comes for help. Some of these benefits cost significant sums of money to provide. How is a doctor to decide who is worth curing by spending the money and who should be allowed to die as his or her life is not worth saving? These sorts of questions lie deep in the strategy and decision-making processes in the Health Service. As far as we are aware the politicians who finance the service have never provided clear answers to these questions. Because of this the NHS presents particular difficulties to strategists.

Universities

Most of the genuine strategic choices about higher education are made by central government, influenced of course by major strategy reviews such as the Dearing Committee (Dearing 1997). Government would appear to be applying a simple strategic model in which input (funding) is expected to produce outputs (graduates and research results). Quality assessment mechanisms have been introduced to prevent quality eroding too rapidly under the pressure to produce more at decreasing cost. The Dearing Report on higher education provided numerous detailed recommendations but was less clear in providing answers to strategic questions on the purpose and future of higher education. It therefore seemed to accept the principle that strategies for universities are set politically and that the role of strategy within individual institutions is merely to implement this design.

In practice, each university has limited strategic freedom within a funding framework determined by central government. The main strategic choices which it can make are on the relative priority of subject areas, the relative emphasis to place on teaching as against research, and the degree of effort to supplement government funding by other sources of income—such as fees from foreign students or commercial research. In practice, the management energies of universities are largely devoted to playing the funding rules to increase their revenues. Real strategic change, such as major restructuring and increasing diversity between institutions, seldom occurs and appears to be almost impossible to initiate within the present arrangements for funding and decision making.

Executive agencies

In principle, each executive agency provides a service and the government department to which it reports makes the policy. This separation of policy and service provision, it was thought, would enable the executive agencies to adopt methods analogous to the private sector to improve service quality and to reduce costs. The structure of executive agencies looks much like those of commercial enterprises with a Chief Executive and a management board. Each agency was set up to be self-funding and encouraged, where possible, to find ways of generating new revenue streams. For example, the Vehicle Licensing Agency has taken to selling personalized number-plates as a means of revenue generation. Many government research establishments now undertake research for the private sector as well as for the government department of which it was once a member. Among the many critical issues facing these agencies is that of changing cost-based cultures into customer-focused and revenue-generating ones. Some of the agencies developed service charters in accordance with the ideas put forward by the Prime Minister of the time, John Major. By March 1994 it is reported in Lovell (1994) that: 'Of 51 agencies serving the public directly, 40 had charters in place'. Some went even further and published core values (Bichard 1994) covering such areas as service to customers, value for money, caring for staff, and a bias for action. Salt (1994) writing about pay and grading in HMSO points out that the HMSO had been operating as a Trading Fund since 1 April 1980. This meant that HMSO had to:

> Introduce commercial approaches with clear financial targets, rigorous management disciplines and a much sharper approach to all activities, particularly after April 1982 when government departments which previously had no choice were free to choose whether or not to use HMSO's services. The Trading Fund environment and the growing competition guaranteed that HMSO's efficiency and effectiveness were under constant scrutiny as a result of the pressure of market forces.

The strategic challenge to these organizations is that of marrying policy and provision. Policy makers tend to become distanced from the customers of the agency and this begins to impose on the ability of the agency. This also means that the policy makers can make promises to the customers of the agency that the management of the agency has to satisfy. But policy makers are not called to account for the policies they make at the operational level neither are they required to take heed of what the management of the agency say about the viability of the policies they are asked to enact. The politicians and policy advisers have in one stroke passed the buck to the agency management for any shortfalls between policy and execution while being able to take all the credit for what does go right.

Formulating strategy in this environment is extremely difficult. However, there is a case for developing a strategy for operational excellence even if it is difficult to formulate a strategy to conceive and secure the future of the enterprise.

5.10 Summary

THIS chapter has examined some contexts that differ from the business context which much strategic management literature assumes as normal. Our aim in very limited space is to draw attention to the enormous diversity of context that exists and to emphasize yet again that strategic management must start with an understanding of the context and the strategic issues which it poses.

The principles of strategic management laid out in the rest of this book broadly apply to all these separate contexts but will need to be supplemented by additional ideas relevant to each specific context.

References

Baden-Fuller, C., and Stopford, J. M. (1992) *Rejuvenating the Mature Business: The Competitive Challenge* (London: Routledge).

Bibeault, D. B. (1982) *Corporate Turnaround: How Managers turn Losers into Winners* (New York: McGraw-Hill).

Bichard, M. (1994) 'Change and Managing it in the Benefits Agency', in Lovell (1994).

Carr-Saunders, A. M., and Wilson, P. A. (1933) *The Professions* (Oxford: Oxford University Press).

Dearing, R. (1997) 'Higher Education on the Learning Society: Report of the National Committee' (London: HMSO).

Farnham, D., and Horton, S. (1993) *Managing the New Public Services* (London: Macmillan).

Fruin, W. Mark (1997) *Knowledge Works, Managing Intellectual Capital at Toshiba*. (Oxford: Oxford University Press).

Grinyer, P. H., and McKiernan, P. (1990) 'Generating Major Change in Stagnating Companies', *Strategic Management Journal*, 11: 131–46.

—— Mayes, D., and McKiernan, P. (1988) *Sharpbenders: The Secrets of Unleashing Corporate Potential* (Oxford: Basil Blackwell).

Harrigan, K. R., and Porter, M. E. (1983) 'End-Game Strategies for Declining Industries', *Harvard Business Review*, July/Aug.

Katz, R. (ed.) (1988) *Managing Professionals in Innovative Organizations* (Cambridge, Mass.: Ballinger Publishing Company).

Keeling, D. (1972) *Management in Government* (London: Allen & Unwin).

Kelley, R. E. (1985) *The Gold Collar Worker*. (Reading, Mass.: Addison Wesley).

Kennedy, N. (1989) *The Industrialization of Knowledge* (London: Unwin).

Langrish, J., Gibbons, M., Evans, W. G., and Jevons, F. R. (1972) *Wealth from Knowledge* (London: Macmillan).

Leonard-Barton, D. (1995) *Wellsprings of Knowledge* (Cambridge, Mass.: Harvard Business School Press).

Lovell, R. (1994) *Managing Change in the New Public Sector* (London: Longman).

McKiernan, P. (1992) *Strategies of Growth: Maturity, Recovery and Internationalization* (London: Routledge).

Maister, D. H. (1993) *Managing the Professional Service Firm* (New York: Free Press)

Mathur, S. S., and Kenyon, A. (1997) *Creating Value: Shaping Tomorrow's Business* (Oxford: Butterworth Heinemann).

Pollitt, C. (1991) *Managerialism and the Public Services: The Anglo-American Experience* (Oxford: Blackwell).

Quinn, J. B. (1992) *Intelligent Enterprise* (New York: Free Press).

Rosenbloom, R. S., and Spencer, W. J. (eds.) (1996) *Engines of Innovation*. (Cambridge, Mass.: Harvard Business School Press).

Rumelt, R. (1991) 'How Much does Industry Matter?' *Strategic Management Journal*, 12 Mar. 167–86.

Sakaiya, T. (1991) *The Knowledge Value Revolution* (Tokyo: Kodansha International).

Salt, M. (1994) 'HMSO: Restructuring Pay and Grading in an Executive Agency', in Lovell (1994).

Scott, M. C. (1998) *Profiting and Learning from Professional Service Firms* (Chichester: Wiley).

Shapero, A. (1985) *Managing Professional People* (New York: Free Press).

Slatter, S. (1984) *Corporate Recovery: A Guide to Turnaround Management* (London: Penguin).

—— and Lovett, D. (1999) *Corporate Turnaround: Managing Companies in Distress* (London: Penguin).

Stewart, T. A. (1998) *Intellectual Capital* (London: Nicholas Brealey).

Sveiby, K. E., and Lloyd, T. (1987) *Managing Know-How* (London: Bloomsbury).

Tampoe, M. (1994) 'Organising for Customer Service', in Lovell (1994).

Tomkins, C. R. (1987) *Achieving Economy, Efficiency and Effectiveness in the Public Sector* (London: Kegan Paul).

Willcocks, L., and Harrow, J. (eds.) (1992) *Rediscovering Public Services Management* (London: McGraw-Hill).

Part III

The Strategy Formulation Process

Chapter 6

The Strategy Formulation Process: Overview

6.1 The importance of the strategy formulation process

IN Part I we defined strategy as ideas and action to conceive and secure the future of the enterprise. In Part II we emphasized the importance of the context within which all strategic management takes place. Part III focuses on the process for formulating strategies within enterprises. The strategy formulation process leads to a chosen strategy, the content of which is described in more detail in Part IV. These relationships are illustrated in Figure 6.1.

The purpose of the strategy formulation process is to cause strategic thinking that conceives the future of the enterprise and how that future may be secured. The strategy formulation process should provide a mechanism to ease the communication of ideas and to co-ordinate efforts. It should inject structure but not rigidity into the thinking.

Every enterprise has a strategy at any time. It may be that nobody has ever used the word strategy and that no deliberate or disciplined process has ever taken place. The strategy may be to continue to do tomorrow what was done today. This is a somewhat neutral strategy but it may sometimes be appropriate and effective. It certainly has the advantage that it is easy to implement and it may be more likely to secure the future than ill-conceived radical departures into new activities. More often in practice, however, it is apparent that the future of the enterprise is less secure than it might be so there is a need to consider and formulate suitable new strategies which will increase the chance of success. Such new strategies do not just happen; they result from a formulation process. The strategy formulation process is important

Figure 6.1 Strategic thinking: the second element of strategic management

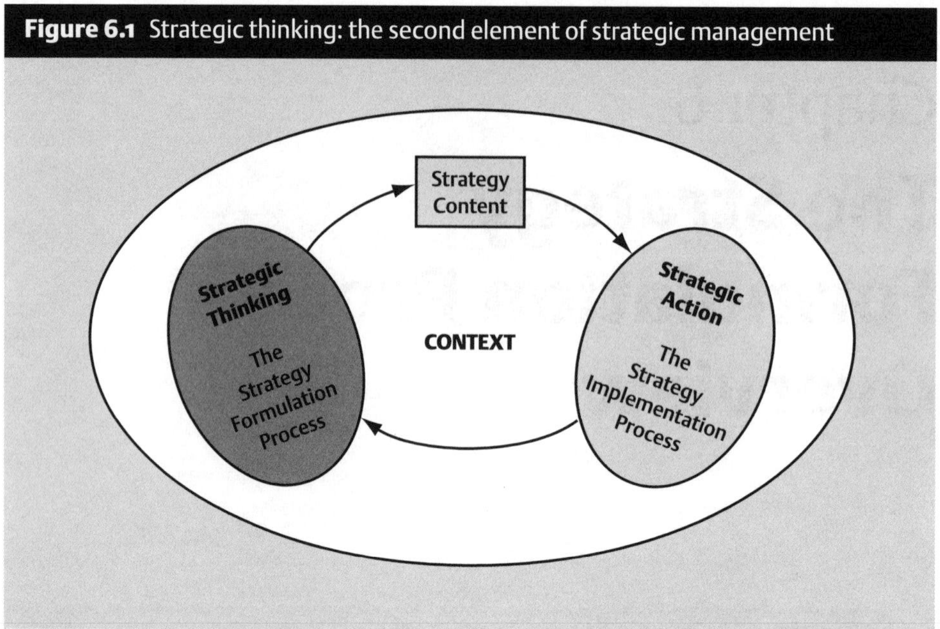

because a 'better' process should produce better strategies. It is, of course, arguable what 'better' means.

Good strategies are judged by the results achieved not by the quality of the process that generated them. In Chapter 3 we outlined ten schools of strategic management thinking, each of which postulated a different view on the nature of the strategy formulation process. It is apparent that there is considerable divergence of view among academic thinkers on what the 'best' strategy process would look like. Successful enterprises adopt a formulation process that matches their business, their culture, and the specific issues of the context. They certainly do not all go about formulating strategy in the same way. Management consultants specializing in strategy may offer their clients a proprietary method for formulating strategy and may claim that this approach offers advantages over alternative approaches. Such claims are hard to substantiate and the same process is likely to work better in some contexts than others. Certainly no standardized approach can ever guarantee success. Gary Hamel (1997) has referred to this as the 'dirty little secret of the strategy industry'. He meant that, when management consultants guide their clients through a process, it is originality, creativity, and effective implementation that lead to future business success and not the process itself. It is impossible to be prescriptive about what process will generate the best strategies. In spite of this awkward fact, most enterprises do find it useful to think about the process by which they formulate their future strategies and to try to improve the process so as to increase the chances of creative thinking happening.

In practice, strategy processes may be formal or informal, complex or simple. They may be exactly analytical or based on a broad understanding of important trends. The process may involve many people or just a few. In one very successful life insurance company the process is almost entirely informal. The senior six or seven executive directors meet regularly and discuss strategy among other more immediate matters. Strategic ideas may be discussed at committees chaired by the same directors so that any difficulties or objections become apparent. After a period of gradual agreement, the strategies will be reported to a meeting of the full board. The expectation is that the board will nod them through. There are no strategic plans written down and very little documentation of any kind. All the executive directors maintain, however, that the strategy is very clear. The company has been highly successful over a long period of time.

At the other end of the scale, many large multi-divisional companies still operate formal processes in which individual companies or divisions present their strategies to the board for review. Such formality may have the important advantage that it causes busy managers to think about the future. On the other hand, formality may also have the disadvantage that thinking that is undertaken only to meet the requirements of a bureaucratic process may be stiff and unimaginative.

The case examples give some indication of the broad range of formality, style, and time-scale that occurs within planning processes. In ICL, under the pressure of a crisis, one or two people conceived a radically new strategy in a period of a few weeks. Marks & Spencer, also experiencing a crisis, found it appropriate to have an off-site meeting for the entire board and to study a strategy document several hundred pages long.

The strategy formulation process has to be tailored to the current needs of the organization. The task for the manager is to understand the process that has generated strategies in the past in that enterprise and to consider how to develop that process in the future. This may require minor adjustments, such as changes of emphasis, involvement of new groups of people, or new analyses of data. There is some evidence (Brews and Hunt 1999) that planning processes need several years to bed down and begin to produce results. This argues for gradual development of the existing process. Sometimes, however, it may be appropriate to introduce an entirely new process for formulating strategy so as to generate new insights about the future of the business and to break out of accepted patterns of thought. The value of the process is that it can trigger new ideas, capture ideas for discussion, and clarify ideas for implementation. The process must lead to ideas about how the future can be secured and must lay the ground for effective action. The strategy formulation process should, in short, lead to good strategic thinking.

Effective strategic thinking usually has certain characteristics. It considers the enterprise as a whole and is more about the longer term than the immediate. Strategic thinking must address both the relationship of the enterprise with its external environment and its own capabilities and resources. Good strategic thinking is based on fact and reality and is supported by rigorous analysis. On the other hand, analysis is not enough; good strategic thinking also requires imagination. An effective strategic thinker has a good understanding of the present, is able to imagine the future, and is also able to think beyond the current constraints in an original way.

The design of the strategy process must cause strategic thinking to happen. It is important that all parts of the strategy process are appropriate to the context. The process must be coherent. Good strategic thinking requires the right combination of analysis and imagination. Kenichi Ohmae (1983:5) puts this point well:

> In my opinion, these two are complementary. For the strategic mind to work creatively, it needs the stimulus of a good, insightful analysis. In order to conduct a good analysis, it takes a strategic and inquisitive mind to come up with the right questions and phrase them as solution-oriented issues. Analyses done for the sake of vindicating one's own preconceived notions do not lead to creative solutions. Intuition or gut-feel alone does not ensure secure business plans. It takes a good balance to come up with a successful strategy.

Sometimes a strategy formulation process may fail to achieve this balance. This may be because it is too analytical. The highly formalized approach to strategic planning which became very common in the 1960s and 1970s often involved large planning departments. These did extensive analysis but often failed to generate or communicate strategic thinking. This may have been because of a lack of imagination or because they failed to relate well to the line managers with the detailed knowledge of the business. Mintzberg (1994) suggests that highly formalized strategic planning of this kind may actually prevent strategic thinking.

Processes that are totally informal or not supported by sound analysis can also fail. They may result in unrealistic lists of desired future outcomes for which the resources are not available and for which there is no drive to find the resources or to build the capabilities.

6.2 The three logical elements of the strategy formulation process

THE three essential elements of the strategy process are illustrated in Figure 6.2.

Strategic Intent is the driver of the strategy process. Without an underlying intent, strategy lacks an overall sense of direction and there is no reason to choose one direction rather than another. Strategic intent provides the answer to the question 'Where do we want to go?' Strategic intent is addressed in Chapter 8.

The fundamental role of **Strategic Assessment** is to provide relevant knowledge about the strategic context. It has to assess both the outside world and the relative capabilities of our own enterprise. The role of strategic assessment is to anchor future strategies in reality. Strategic assessment must address the question 'Where are we now?' Potential future strategies also have to be assessed. Strategic assessment is described in Chapters 8 to 10.

Strategic Choice is fundamental to the strategy process because it is the link to action. It must address the question 'Which options will we choose for getting where we want to be from where we are?' If strategy is to be anything more than an intellectual relaxation then actions must result from the strategy process. Strategic choice is examined in more depth in Chapter 11.

The model in Figure 6.2 is useful as a start point but needs to be refined to differentiate between the process and the results which the process achieves. This distinction in made is Figure 6.3.

The strategy formulation process has three interlocking activities: intending, assessing, and choosing. Each of these activities relates to the other two. In a good strategy process, the activities fit together into a coherent whole and are in balance. These interlocking activities produce related results: strategic intent, strategic assessment, and available options. Note that the eventual strategy which is chosen

Figure 6.2 The strategy formulation process: three inter-locking aspects

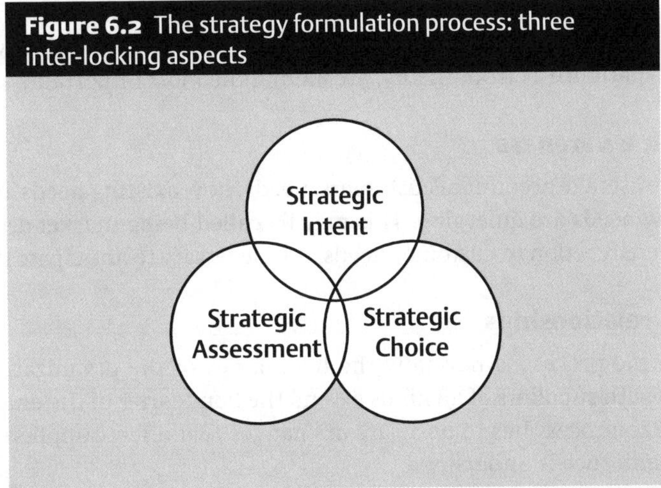

Figure 6.3 Process and results both inter-relate

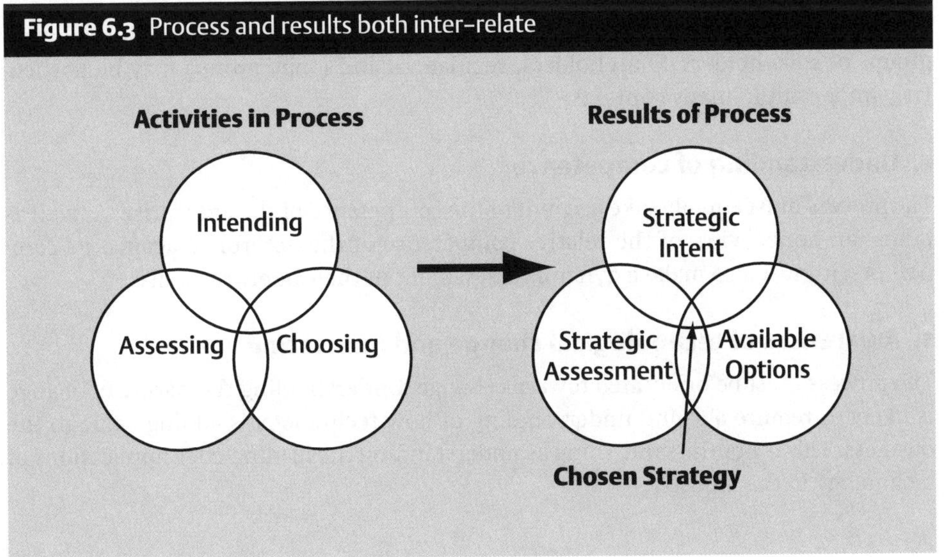

depends on all three elements as shown in Figure 6.3. The methods described in Chapters 7 to 11 are built on the structure of Figure 6.3.

6.3 Effective strategy formulation processes in practice

While it is impossible to define a universal strategy formulation process that will work for any enterprise in all circumstances, it is possible to observe the characteristics that seem to lead to success in practice. The eleven points below, derived as much from experience as from theory, are among the most important.

1. Customer awareness

The process must take account of customers' needs, how existing needs are changing, and what new needs are emerging. This may be called being market-driven but it is more than mere reaction to customer needs; it is necessary to anticipate future needs.

2. Supplier relationships

The scope of the process is normally the boundaries of the organization. External relationships with suppliers of all kinds extend the boundaries of the enterprise in an untidy way. The process has to be aware of changes that affect suppliers and ensure that their significance is understood.

3. Stakeholder influences

The process must take into account the expectations and influences of all important groups of stakeholders. Shareholders, regulators, and lobby groups may be particularly important in many contexts.

4. Understanding of competence

The process must equally take account of the competence of the enterprise. As well as taking an honest view of the relative competence of the enterprise against its competitors, it must also make a dynamic assessment of their likely response.

5. Awareness of technological change and innovation

The process must be orientated towards change. Understanding the nature of change is likely to require a sound understanding of how technology is adding value to the business. This is not the same thing as understanding the leading-edge applications of technology in the industry.

6. Mix of people involved in the process

Businesses are usually complex so different people have different perspectives and different fields of knowledge. Marketing people see the world differently and know different things from development engineers; long-serving employees differently from newcomers, board members differently from middle managers, central staff differently from field staff. No one group has a monopoly on useful perspectives so an effective mix of views is important. An effective moderator may be essential to ensure that views are heard.

7. Encouragement and understanding of top management

Ultimately the power to take action resides with senior managers and particularly the chief executive. If the process does not have top management actively behind it then it will usually fail.

8. Communication of results and reaction to feedback

Good strategies do not appear suddenly. A good raw idea needs to find support from those who have to make it work. The raw edges of the idea have to be rubbed off. This is achieved by good two-way communication. Ideas are improved by valid criticism. Secret strategies are rarely implemented if they affect a large number of people.

9. A sound logic and balance to the process

Figure 6.3 illustrated the nature of the balance that is necessary. If the process has been unbalanced in the past, one of the three elements may need more emphasis than the other two at a particular time to redress the imbalance. Conversely, one element may already be in place and so can be given less attention.

10. Process design but not over-design

The design of the process requires some thought. It is useful to consider the strengths and weaknesses of the existing strategy process. The process should be tailored to address current strategic issues and hence ensure relevance. Some outline of time-scale and method is necessary. However, the methods must be flexible enough to allow time to react to findings and to delve into critical detail. The balance between analysis and synthesis is important. The process needs to develop from year to year to avoid the process becoming a boring and bureaucratic routine.

11. Considered role of external support

Management consultants can make a valuable contribution provided that their role has been thought through. Consultants can help with process design, provide analytical support, offer a comparative perspective, and contribute to strategic thinking. They can also catch attention, contribute objectively in political discussions, and cut across organizational boundaries. Consultants cannot, however, take responsibility for implementation nor are they likely to understand their client's business in as much depth as insiders do.

It is essential that the strategy formulation process is designed to meet the needs of the enterprise and its business needs. There are dangers in imitating processes that seem to have worked well in prominent and successful companies. This point is made very clearly by Campbell (1999) who comments that there is still widespread dissatisfaction among managers with the strategic planning processes as they are practised in their companies even after many years of refinement. He attributes much of the problem to imitating the processes of leading companies rather than designing a process appropriate to the specific needs. In particular it is critical that the process should be clear about how the enterprise is trying to create value. Campbell illustrates his article with examples of three different processes in use. The value-creation focus is different for each of the three cases. In one the focus is to make dramatic increases in profit; in the second it is on cost reduction; for the third it is to find incremental performance gains. In each case the process is successful because it is focused on a particular kind of value and because it fits the style of the chief executive. The planning techniques, the form of the process, role of different functions in the process, length and tone of meetings and follow-up are all tailored to be coherent with the required focus and style in each case.

6.4 Results from the strategy formulation process

THE strategy formulation process results in strategic choice and supporting strategies whose content is discussed in Part IV. Robert Grant (1995: 8) suggests four critical elements to the results that have to be achieved from a strategy formulation process:

1. Goals that are simple, consistent and long term
2. Profound understanding of the competitive environment
3. Objective appraisal of resources
4. Effective implementation

Grant's list echoes the framework of Figure 6.3. Clear strategic intent may be expressed as goals. The results of strategic assessment are an objective and profound understanding of resources and an objective appraisal of the competitive environment. A good strategic choice is one ingredient of effective implementation. Other relevant ingredients are discussed in Part V.

On the other hand Grant's list does not guarantee success. There may also be other necessary useful results that are not on his list. The four items on the list beg further questions. 'Clearly stated goals' may sound good but may be extremely woolly in their practical meaning. 'Profound understanding of the competitive environment' is a worthy aim but how can one know what degree of profundity is adequate? What if the present competitors are all equally blind to the nature of future change like a group of dodos? 'Objective appraisal of resources' may not be enough as it may be possible to find new resources to stretch the organization to meet future challenges. Certainly the strategy formulation process must generate strategies which are capable of implementation but actions will have to be modified in the light of events so that what is implemented is not the same as what seemed capable of implementation.

More generally, the strategy formulation process will produce both 'hard' and 'soft' results. The hard results of the strategy process form the content of strategy described in Part IV. Softer results include the increased awareness of opportunities, increased commitment of staff, a clearer understanding of the future direction of the industry, and appreciation of the extent of change required. These may often be as important as the hard results, as illustrated in the EuroPharm case example.

The interaction between any two of the three elements of the process produces intermediate results, which may be of value in providing supporting arguments and justification for the strategic choice. These issues are discussed further in Chapter 11.

6.5 Summary

THE overall aim of the strategy formulation process is to ensure that strategies are conceived which will secure the future of the enterprise. The process has to be designed within the unique context of a particular enterprise at a particular time. The strategy process has three logical elements (strategic intent, strategic assessment, and strategic choice). These three elements are closely related and need to be balanced in a good process. There is no perfect process for formulating strategies but there are some characteristics that are more likely to lead to a process being successful. Strategy formulation processes produce hard and soft results. Both are important.

References

Brews, P. J,. and Hunt, M. R. (1999) 'Learning to Plan and Planning to Learn: Resolving the Planning School/Learning School Debate', *Strategic Management Journal*, 20/10.

Campbell, A. (1999) 'Tailored, not Benchmarked: A Fresh Look at Corporate Planning', *Harvard Business Review*, Mar.–Apr.

Grant, R. M. (1995) *Contemporary Strategy Analysis* (London: Blackwell).

Hamel, G. (1997) Talk at the Strategic Planning Society Annual Conference, London, Nov.

Mintzberg, H. (1994) *The Rise and Fall of Strategic Planning* (Hemel Hempstead: Prentice-Hall).

Ohmae, K. (1983) *The Mind of the Strategist* (New York: Penguin; 1st pub. McGraw-Hill, 1982)

Chapter 7
Strategic Intent

7.1 The concept of strategic intent

STRATEGIC intent is the first of the three logical elements of the strategy process outlined in Chapter 6. Strategy is concerned with both ends and means. Strategic intent is concerned with the ends and purposes of the enterprise and combines a vision of the future with the intent to make that vision a reality.

A vision is a picture in the mind. Sight is the most vivid of the senses and the word vision suggests an image of the future that is both three-dimensional and in colour. The vision must go beyond defining the future products or services which the enterprise will offer to conceiving also how the enterprise will operate as an entity, what its values will be, and what it will be like to work in. To say that the enterprise will double in size in a given period fails to meet our criteria for a vision statement. In our view a vision statement provides a visual image which is exciting and emotionally energizing. Vision is a necessary part of strategic intent but a vision on its own may be imaginary or lacking in substance. Strategic intent must therefore combine vision with the will and the means to make the vision become reality.

Nearly all writers on strategy have agreed that clarifying and extending the fundamental purpose of the enterprise is a necessary part of strategy. Andrews (1971) saw the creation of clear purposes and objectives as central to strategy and a clear responsibility of senior management. More recently, Hamel and Prahalad (1989 and 1994) (who first used the phrase strategic intent) see it as the heart of strategy and as providing an animating dream for the future. They see it as providing a sense of direction, discovery, and destiny for every person in the company. Clearly it is a prime responsibility of top management to generate such strategic intent and to ensure that it is compelling. Hamel and Prahalad take the view that strategic intent should stretch the aspirations and should not be constrained by existing resources. Rather strategic intent should focus the search for the necessary resources and so drive the enterprise beyond the constraints of its present resources.

Strategic intent may be seen as the apex of a pyramid of purpose as shown in Figure

Figure 7.1 The pyramid of purpose

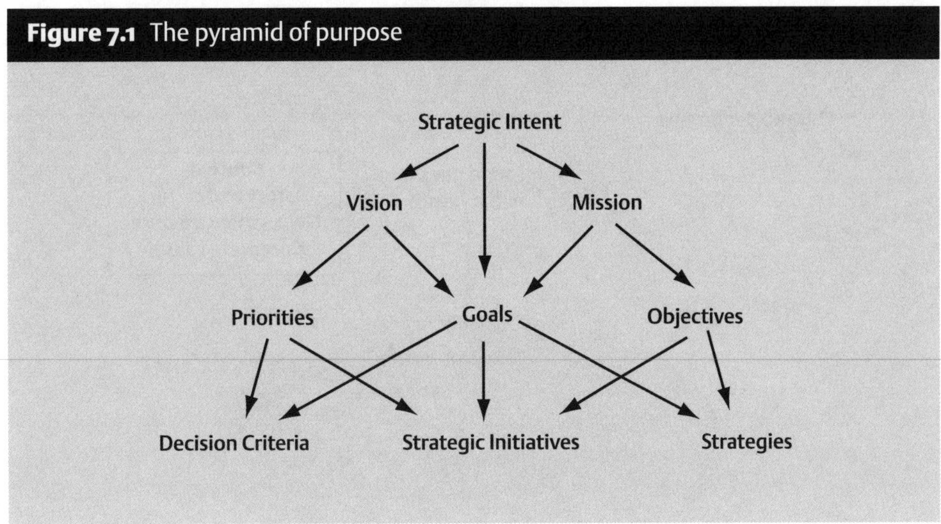

7.1. The figure shows some of the words typically used. Such a pyramid of terms tends to be formed when purpose and strategic intent are discussed. Because different groups of people will interpret the terms differently and because some of the terms will tend to overlap in their meanings, there is some value in defining such terms to improve communication.

7.2 Strategic intent in practice

FIGURE 7.2 illustrates the main factors likely to influence strategic intent in practice. The strategy formulation process should result in the strategic intent becoming clearer, more developed, and more widely understood. This occurs in practice by a process of continuing discussion informed by the results of strategic assessment and strategic options. There are no magic methods to achieve quick results.

The strategic intent has to be acceptable to the various individuals or groups who are stakeholders in the enterprise. The shareholders are normally the dominant stakeholder group in a publicly owned business but they are not the only stakeholders to have a degree of influence on the strategic intent. The strategic intent will owe something to the history and culture of the enterprise. For many enterprises, success will gradually slip away unless the strategic intent stretches the enterprise to strive beyond its present aspirations and practices. One of the key responsibilities of leaders is to cause this stretching of intent to occur. Finally, the strategic intent may be in part based on an inspired guess of what the future will be like—a combination of evolving trends and deliberate effort to affect the future.

Figure 7.2 also illustrates the fact that strategic intent is likely to include both goals

Figure 7.2 Influences on strategic intent

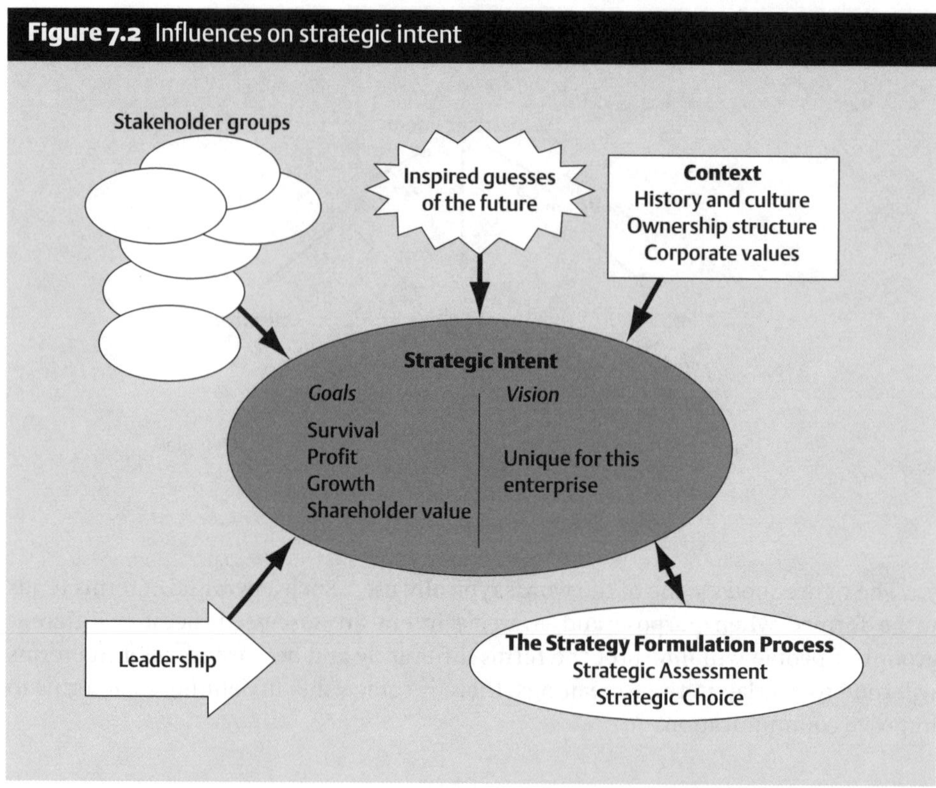

and vision. Goals are tangible and quantifiable. When times are hard, the goal will be survival. Once survival seems assured, the goal for business enterprises is likely to be to increase revenues, profits, or both. The relative importance of these goals will vary according to the context. In most publicly quoted companies, the dominant goal is to increase shareholder value. Goals are necessary but not sufficient for a strategic intent. Goals on their own do not inspire people. The strategic intent must also outline something unique and inspirational. Great enterprises seem always to have aspirations beyond producing a profit, something that makes them unique.

The strategic intent should inspire everyone who works for the enterprise and perhaps also have an effect on customers and suppliers. It follows that there may be benefits if the strategic intent can be expressed in a memorable form or as a slogan. This form of strategic intent may act as a rallying cry. On the other hand slogans can in time degenerate into meaninglessness. The British Airways slogan 'The World's Favourite Airline' may be an example of both the value and limitations of slogans. British Airways, if challenged, would have been hard pressed to prove this claim. During the early 1990s British Airways was certainly successful at improving its customer service and image. By the middle 1990s British Airways was receiving high ratings in opinion surveys suggesting that it was at least one of the world's favourite airlines. The slogan may have been instrumental in achieving this position and in inspiring staff to improve their service to customers. Certainly both the slogan and

Box 7.1 What is the strategic intent of the Virgin Group?

Richard Branson made the following three points in a public television broadcast:

1. The Virgin Group operates in widely different businesses, including music shops, an airline, rail services, cola soft drinks, cinemas, and financial services. In each of these businesses the Virgin brand is important to success.

2. The Virgin Group will enter businesses that have most of these characteristics:
   - previous competitors who tended to monopolize the business;
   - opportunities to improve customer service and value;
   - an opportunity for the Virgin brand to add a perception of value;
   - an opportunity to introduce a sense of fun.

3. The relative priority of stakeholders is employees first, customers second, and shareholders third. The rationale for this is that happy employees provide good service that keeps customers happy which in turn will lead to profits.

Comment. It would seem from the above that the strategic intent of the Virgin Group is centred on exploiting its brand. The clear criteria for entering new markets support this intent and focus the use of the brand. The stakeholder priorities support the brand image. It may be that the objectives and priorities also reveal a deeper motivation such as 'Kill sleeping giants' or 'Rock complacent boats' that makes the strategic intent particularly suitable to Branson's personal inclinations and style.

Source: Notes on talk by Richard Branson, BBC Money Programme, 5 July 1998.

the attempt to be passenger friendly were very visible for a time. Later in the 1990s, however, the slogan seems to have passed its sell-by date. British Airways seemed to become more concerned with painting the tail fins of its aircraft. The connection between colourful tail fins and passenger favour is obscure. British Airways' customer service no longer stood out from among its competitors. The business results of the company declined. The slogan had lost its value as a statement of strategic intent.

An effective strategic intent can usually be expressed in relatively few words—a slogan may be more effective than a long document. A **Mission Statement** may be used as a means of publicizing the strategic intent of an enterprise. Good mission statements are pithy and credible. When genuine strategic intent exists, everyone is aware of it; the mission statement is therefore only a record of what is already known and understood. Few mission statements achieve this. Too many mission statements consist of motherhood statements or are the subject of mild scepticism or even mirth among staff. Lucy Kellaway (1999) has suggested that the only way for a company to stand out is by not having a mission statement at all as they all seem to be the same.

7.3 The role of leadership in forming strategic intent

THE strategic intent may reflect the views of a single inspirational leader. Such leaders tend to be highly visible and to surround themselves with people who agree with their vision of the future. As a result the strategic intent becomes closely related to the leader but also widely shared and understood. There are obvious examples of this in Jack Welch and Bill Gates who are often personally associated with the strategic intents of GE (US General Electric) and Microsoft respectively.

Unfortunately, strong leaders sometimes fail to recognize that their personal objectives may not be of value when the organization has reached a watershed in its development. At such times they need to move on and allow a new leader to take control of the helm but this rarely happens. For example, Geneen at ITT held sway for so long that the company reflected his persona. It would seem in hindsight that he built a conglomerate that only he could manage. It took his successors many floundering moves to right the ship once he left and to steer it to calmer but equally lucrative waters.

The case examples illustrate the importance of leadership in determining strategic intent. In the ICL case example, it was Robb Wilmot's leadership that caused ICL to adopt a new and clearly stated strategic intent that drove the company forward. Conversely, the problems of Marks & Spencer might have been addressed sooner if Sir Richard Greenbury had been less totally dominant at a time when strategic change became necessary.

It would seem that leadership has a critical role in forming strategic intent and that it may be a force for weakness as well as for strength.

7.4 Stakeholders and their ability to influence strategic intent

STAKEHOLDERS are any group with an interest in the activities and results of the enterprise. The most obvious stakeholder groups are shareholders, managers, employees, and customers. Suppliers, bankers, the government, society at large may also be significant stakeholders. Shareholders are generally the dominant stakeholder group.

Different groups of stakeholders tend to differ in their values and hence will tend to have different views about what the strategic intent of the enterprise should be.

Some stakeholder groups are more powerful than others and some are more inclined to exercise their power than others. It may be useful to classify stakeholder groups on this basis as shown in Figure 7.3.

Analysis of stakeholder power cannot be precise but it is usually useful to identify the main stakeholder groups and to consider how their values and expectations for the enterprise may differ. Some groups of stakeholders may be less coherent than expected. For instance, among employees, the long serving may have different views from recent recruits. The analysis has therefore to consider these as separate stakeholder groups. The role of management is to achieve a strategic intent that satisfies most of the stakeholders or at least ensures that no powerful stakeholders are left too unhappy. Unexpected stakeholder groups may suddenly form and have greater power than expected.

A group of stakeholders who rarely get a mention are the middle managers of companies. While directors tend to make the decisions that often take organizations into new directions, many of the strategic decisions that make evolutionary change possible depend on the goodwill of middle managers to carry them through. In attempting to pursue their personal ambitions these managers can derail or divert a company from its chosen strategic direction. Because this happens by stealth it is often not detected or corrected. For example, two managers in charge of different business units who are competing for recognition will set out to sell the virtues of their respective organizations and seek support and patronage for their business unit strategies. If, however, resources are scarce, this lobbying can take a sinister turn. The individual with the cash cow may divert resources to it at the expense of the individual with the emergent star, thus starving the future business for short-term gains.

The Nolan, Norton case example gives some insight into stakeholder power in practice. The owners, principals, and staff of Nolan, Norton all had different perspectives and interests about the future of the firm. The success of the merger with KPMG

Figure 7.3 Model for analysing stakeholder power

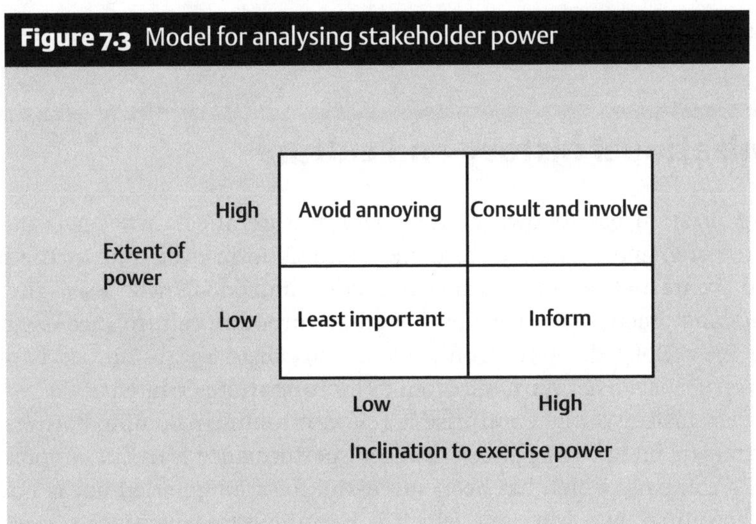

Box 7.2 Example of power of an unexpected stakeholder group

Sometimes relatively unlikely groups of stakeholders can influence the outcome in very surprising ways. For example, in 1995 Shell decided after consideration of environmental issues to sink its Brent Spar oil platform in deep water in the Atlantic. German drivers boycotted Shell filling stations and these eventually forced Shell to reconsider this decision. Brent Spar was towed to a Norwegian fiord instead.

Nobody in advance of this event would have predicted that fuel consumers were powerful stakeholders in Shell. This story does, however, illustrate a trend away from an orderly model of stakeholder power. A more appropriate view for the twenty-first century may have to include the power of the media as both significant and unpredictable.

Source: Extensive newspaper coverage.

depended on, among other things, balancing these different perspectives. In the BMW case the interests and attitudes of the Quandt family dominated the decisions taken, suggesting that a dominant shareholder can significantly affect the direction and future of an organization.

7.5 Impact of context on strategic intent

IN Part II, we discussed the importance of the context as defining the background to strategic management. Context is also a factor in determining strategic intent. Some of the most common ways in which context matters are as follows.

Organizational history and culture

Every organization has its own culture. This culture affects what gets done, why things are done, and how they are done. Cultures form over time as the result of historical events and the influence of particular individuals who leave their mark. Academics and practitioners have both studied corporate culture. (See e.g. Deal and Kennedy 1982; Hofstede 1991; Trompenaars 1993; Bate 1994). Culture is of fundamental importance in defining and often in limiting strategic intent.

The recent history of the enterprise is relevant to understanding both its culture and its strategic intent. The pattern of recent performance is usually important. For instance, a company which has been successful for a long period but is now under threat reacts differently from one which is beginning to experience success after a long period of struggle. Recent traumatic events may have left specific scars in the culture and be crucial in defining the attitudes of key individuals.

Mergers cause two different cultures to come together. The two separate cultures often remain discernible for many years after the merger. In take-overs the acquiring company's culture will tend to dominate and may eventually eradicate the acquired company's culture. Even when the two merger partners are supposedly equal, in practice one culture usually seems to dominate.

In some organizations the strategic intent has become so much a part of tradition that they do not need slogans to transmit them. For instance, Daimler Benz has a long-standing tradition of excellence in engineering. It is clearly a part of the strategic intent of Daimler Benz to maintain this excellence whatever its business goals at a particular time.

Just as culture can influence strategic intent, so a change in strategic intent is likely to require a change in culture. There is clearly a balance in practice between the view of the Cultural School and the prescriptive view of strategies. The Cultural School would hold that strategic intent is little more than the expression of the culture of the enterprise and that it is culture which determines its future. The prescriptive schools would expect a change in culture to be a requirement of a radically new strategic intent and so require deliberate action to cause a change in culture. Most contexts involve an element of both of these perspectives as described in Chapter 20.

Ownership and power structure

The ownership of larger businesses is usually divided between a mixture of individual and institutional shareholders. With this form of ownership the drive of the strategic intent is likely to be towards increasing shareholder value. The major institutional shareholders cannot easily dispose of their holdings without lowering the share price. This may lead them to place specific demands on the management or to seek to replace managers. Individual shareholders may vary in the relative value they place on dividends as against increases in share price. Managers have to understand the mix of ownership and the specific forces at work.

Other common ownership structures include family firms, entrepreneurial enterprises, mutuals, and co-operatives. For each of these cases, the owners may have distinctive purposes that will influence the strategic intent of the enterprise. Family firms are often concerned to maintain continuity of control within the family. They may be unwilling to raise capital for attractive investments since this would dilute family shareholdings. Family firms may not concentrate on maximizing profits since an adequate flow of profits to meet their own needs may be perfectly acceptable and less risky. Handover of authority from one generation to another can be a particularly delicate issue and may cause a distortion in strategic intent and strategy in general over several years.

If the founder (or founders) of the firm is still an active participant in its management, there is likely to be a close connection between the strategic intent of the firm

Box 7.3 Examples of impact of personal goals on strategic intent

Virgin is an example of the relationship between corporate and personal goals. The Virgin Group is engaged in an airline, retailing, entertainment, financial services, cola, and trains. Large parts of the group are unprofitable and the profitability of the entire group is less than would be acceptable in a publicly owned company. At the same time the Group as a whole certainly provides adequate income for Richard Branson to pursue his interest in ballooning and a platform on which he can remain a national figure.

The strategic intent of the Virgin Group is acceptable to its present owner but might have to change if, for instance, Virgin was to become a public company.

Source: Based on 'Behind Branson', *The Economist* (2–7 Feb. 1998: 81).

and the personal objectives of the entrepreneur for his or her own life aims and style. This may result in decisions that appear irrational from the point of view of the business as an entity.

Customers, policyholders, or members own mutuals, co-operatives, and associations. The owners may therefore be a large group of people with no natural way of forming a consensus or of applying clear pressure on managers. The managers may be free to act in broad accordance with the principles on which the institution was founded. This sometimes results in great clarity and simplicity of intent; at other times it seems to lead to stagnation or sleepiness.

While power may in theory emanate from ownership, this is not necessarily the case in practice. It is useful to study the real power structure of the context.

7.6 Contrasting views on the nature of strategic intent

IN sharp contrast to this view that strategic intent is at the very heart of strategy, other writers have supported the views of Simon (1964) and Cyert and March (1963) and have denied that it is possible for organizations to have either purpose or intent. Their view is that only individuals can have intents and purposes. They see organizations as consisting of a number of individuals who negotiate with each other and form temporary alliances through contracts with other individuals. The outcomes of these behavioural processes determine the direction that the enterprise takes. This view of the world has a ring of truth to anyone who has observed the workings of a company board at close quarters; individual agendas are often as important as any shared intent; committees make decisions which owe more to compromise than to principle.

A third view is that the intent of an organization is deeply embedded in its culture. Under this view, managers have very little scope to make the intent any different from the embedded purpose. Real change in intent can only occur after a change in culture and this will necessarily take time. There is evidence to support this point of view from observing how hard it is for any organization to make dramatic changes in its way of doing things. For example, IBM was outstandingly successful as a provider of mainframe computers and this culture had become deeply embedded. IBM has, therefore, found it much more difficult to succeed in a world where it is selling personal computers and services. Both these businesses involve selling different products to different customers through different channels.

These divergent views on the nature and possibility of strategic intent may be more or less useful depending on the context, so it is necessary to judge how relevant and valid each point of view might be in any specific context. Most managers will probably find themselves more in sympathy with the Andrews–Hamel–Prahalad perspective as a starting point. They will be wiser, however, if they are also aware that this model may not be the whole truth.

7.7 Summary

STRATEGIC intent is one of the three essential elements of the strategy formulation process. Strategic intent interacts with strategic assessment and strategic choice in the thinking process from which strategies emerge. Strategic intent is particularly concerned with the purpose of the enterprise and hence the ends of strategies. Strategic intent may be seen as the apex of a pyramid of purpose.

Strategic intent describes what the enterprise means to become in the future. Strategic intent will outline the unique vision of the enterprise in the future and set goals to be achieved. The strategy formulation process, leaders, stakeholders, and context all influence strategic intent.

Strategic intent depends on the differing aspirations of stakeholder groups, particularly the most powerful. Strategic intent may also be influenced by the history of the enterprise and its ownership structure.

The strategy formulation process must concern itself with the fundamental purposes for which the enterprise exists. The purposes nearly always include the need for survival and to make a profit. Most businesses also aim for growth and to provide their shareholders with value. Great enterprises need a greater strategic intent than just making money.

References

Andrews, K. R. (1971) *The Concept of Corporate Strategy* (Homewood, Ill.: Irwin).

Bate, P. (1994) *Strategies for Cultural Change* (Oxford: Butterworth Heinemann).

Cyert, R. and March, L. (1963) *A Behavioural Theory of the Firm* (New York: Prentice Hall).

Deal, T. and Kennedy, A. (1982) *Corporate Cultures* (New York: McGraw-Hill and Penguin, 1988).

Economist (1998) 'Behind Branson', 21–27 Feb.: (81–3).

Hamel, G. and Prahalad, C. K. (1989) 'Strategic Intent', *Harvard Business Review*, 67/3, May/June.

—— (1994) *Competing for the Future* (Boston: Harvard Business School Press), 63–76.

Hofstede, G. (1991) *Culture and Organizations: Software of the Mind* (Maidenhead: McGraw-Hill).

Kellaway, L. (1999) 'Full of Sound and Theory, but Signifying Nothing' *Financial Times*, 10 May.

Simon, H. (1964) 'On the Subject of the Organisational Goal', *American Science Quarterly*, 9 June: 1–22.

Trompenaars, F. (1993) *Riding the Waves of Culture* (London: Nicholas Brealey).

Chapter 8
Strategic Assessment: General Principles

8.1 The purpose of strategic assessment

STRATEGIC assessment is the second logical element of the strategy formulation process. The role of strategic assessment is to anchor future strategies in reality. Thus strategic intent drives towards the future but strategic assessment relates strategies to the present.

The scope of strategic assessment must address both the internal and external aspects of the context. External assessment is concerned with changes in the business environment that will affect the business, with changes in the industry, and with the activities of competitors. Internal assessment is concerned with the internal resources, capabilities, and competencies of the enterprise and the potential for these to meet future customer needs.

Strategic assessment combines analysis with judgement. Analysis without judgement is sterile while good judgement depends on sound analysis. Assessment is more than analysis alone. Doing more and more analysis does not necessarily lead to better assessment. Rather it is important to relate the focus of the analysis to testing potential judgement. Analysis on its own tends to give undue weight to what can be readily measured and this can distort judgement. As Albert Einstein is supposed to have said: 'Not everything that can be counted counts and not everything that counts can be counted'. Einstein was, of course, talking about science rather than about management and his view has to be balanced against another well-known saying: 'If you can't measure it, you can't manage it'. When it comes to strategic assessment and analysis, these two apparently contradictory statements are both relevant and have to be weighed against each other. Good assessment leads to the conviction that one has achieved a balanced understanding of the context and the issues to be resolved. This conviction comes partly from emotional commitment and partly from the support of sound analysis.

This chapter examines the general principles of strategic assessment. Chapters 9 and 10 describe some of the more useful analytical tools and frameworks for external and internal assessment respectively. The principles of strategic assessment are easily lost in a rush to apply the tools. It is important, therefore, that Chapters 9 and 10 are read in the light of this chapter.

8.2 Strategic assessment as part of the strategy formulation process

THE processes that form strategy vary widely as we have discussed in Chapter 6. Strategies may result from formal processes but probably just as often they result from informal conversations, chance meetings, or sudden insights at unexpected moments. Strategy making may happen continuously or in fits and starts so there are dangers in thinking of a beginning or an end to the process of formulating strategy. However, if strategy is formulated using a purposeful process at a particular time, it is likely that it will prove useful to carry out a strategic assessment early in the process.

The purpose of strategic assessment is to come to a view on the current position of the enterprise as a whole in its relationship to the outside world. Strategic assessment relates to a specific enterprise at a specific time. The strategic assessment attempts to answer the question 'Where are we now?' The answer to this question is partly absolute but partly dependent on strategic intent, strategic choice, and implementation. The answer to 'Where are we now?' depends partly on the answers to the questions: 'Where do we want to go?', 'How are we intending to get there?' and 'Do we have the ability to implement the necessary changes?'. Ultimately, the answers to all these questions must be coherent so strategic assessment cannot be complete in isolation.

Figure 8.1 illustrates the factors that are usually important in strategic assessment. The strategic assessment is set against the background of the context. The aim of strategic assessment is to understand the context better in relationship to the strategic intent and potential strategic choices.

Strategic intent defines the underlying purpose for the enterprise and so sets the foundation for strategic assessment. Strategic assessment cannot have any clear basis unless there is strategic intent. The assessment of how well we stand today depends on where we want to be in the future. Equally, strategic assessment may constrain or expand strategic intent. This is why the arrow between strategic intent and strategic assessment is double-headed in Figure 8.1. Similarly there is a close two-way link between strategic assessment and strategic choice. Some options may seem more attractive as a result of strategic assessment; some may seem less attractive or even impossible.

Recent operational results are usually relevant in making a strategic assessment. It may well be that one of the reasons for considering a change in strategy is that recent performance has not been acceptable. In addition, the process of formulating strategy

Figure 8.1 Factors likely to influence strategic assessment

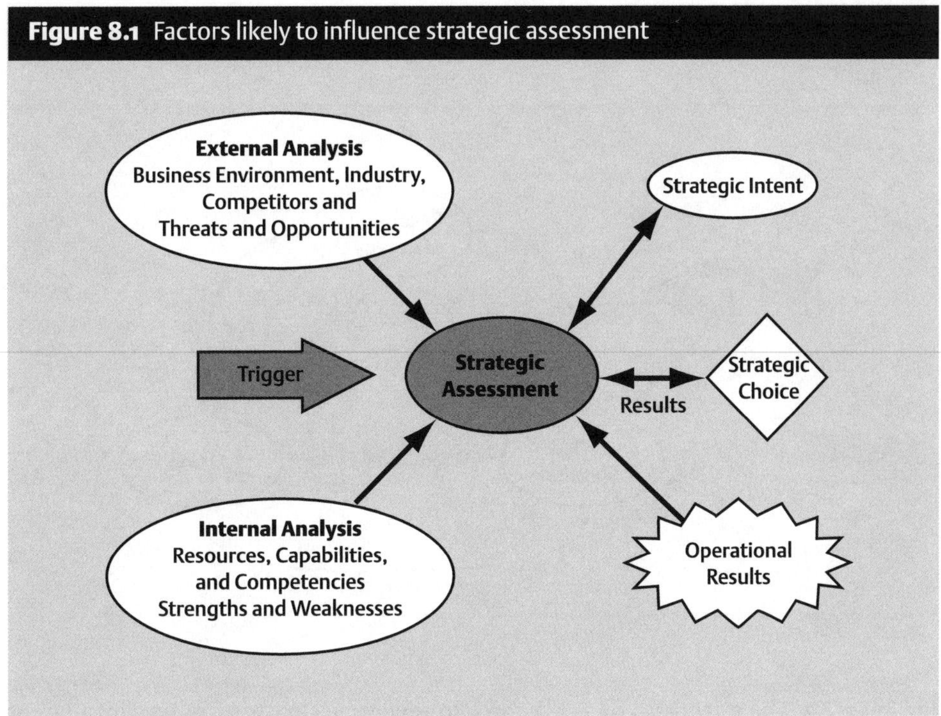

is often cyclical so that the assessment in this iteration will take into account the thinking of previous iterations and the results of attempts to implement earlier strategies. Strategy formulation will be more credible if earlier strategic thinking and action has led to visible operational results. Even if earlier strategies have failed, the causes of failure will inform the present discussion and enrich the strategic assessment.

There are normally particular reasons that trigger the need for strategic assessment at a particular time. For much of the time, enterprises operate within existing strategies. Results will not exactly meet targets but the discrepancies can be handled by doing better tomorrow what was done yesterday. Occasionally it becomes clear that the gap between expectations and achievement requires more fundamental change. The awareness of this gap may act as a trigger for new thinking and new strategies. Other common triggers include the arrival of a new chief executive or a merger. A trigger may occur in recognition of the need to respond to strategic issues imposed by the strategic context. The nature of the trigger is likely to influence the agenda and scope for the strategic assessment.

A fundamental type of trigger occurs when the business is undergoing a change in the rules that apply in its industry. Andrew Grove (1996) refers to these as strategic inflection points and suggests that such inflection points occur when there is a '10× [*sic*]' (ten times) change in any basic business parameter such as cost per unit or time to develop a new product.

Whatever the root cause of the trigger, the effect of such a trigger is to cause a shift from an operational cycle (that is 'business as usual') to a strategic cycle as illustrated

Figure 8.2 When do enterprises reconsider their strategies?

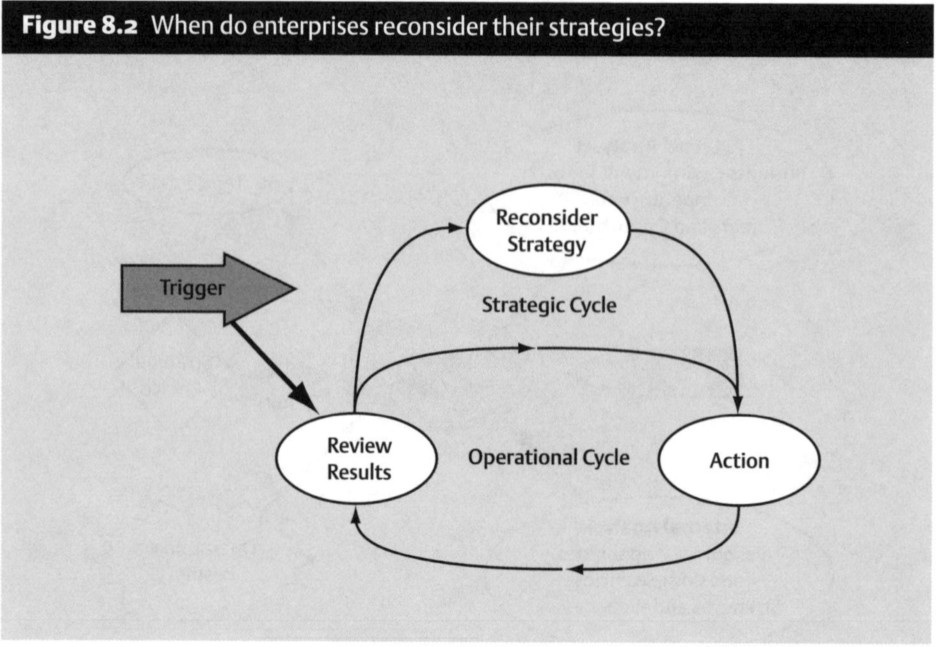

in Figure 8.2. The setting up of a task force to review strategy or the appointment of external consultants to assist with a strategic review are common symptoms that an enterprise has embarked on a strategic cycle.

Figure 8.2 is a simplified version for strategic reviews of reasonably healthy enterprises which may be seen as an early stage of Figure 5.1 which applied to sharp-bending and turnaround enterprises.

8.3 The questions that strategic assessment should address

A STRATEGIC assessment requires conclusions and judgements that never directly follow from analysis alone. These judgements follow from a process of setting and answering questions. A good strategic assessment will pose and answer relevant strategic questions. Examples of the kinds of questions that may be relevant are:

What are our chances of survival if we continue as we are?
Where are the best opportunities for growth given our existing capabilities?
Where are our competitive advantages and disadvantages?
Where can we invest to improve our capabilities most efficiently?
What changes can we realistically implement?

It is very important that strategic assessment should identify and address the particular questions that are relevant to the context. In Chapter 4, we discussed how a context poses issues or a single strategic dilemma. The strategic assessment starts the process of identifying the response to these issues. Time and effort need to be spent in formulating the questions before attempting too much detailed analysis. A key question to ask is 'Which questions are the right questions in the current circumstances?'

There is a tendency for students on strategic management courses to rush into applying the many analytical frameworks available without considering what the important questions are. This is likely to make the analysis less useful than it might be. Analysis for its own sake may be a complete waste of time.

Naturally, the answers to early questions tend to raise other questions. Strategic assessment is a process not a single analytical framework. It is an art as much as a science.

8.4 Selecting analytical frameworks and tools to support strategic assessment

THE range of analytical tools, techniques, approaches, and frameworks available to support strategic assessment is very large. Some of the most commonly used tools and techniques are described in Chapters 9 and 10. Particular contexts are likely to require analyses peculiar to that context as well as some of the general frameworks. Each of the ten schools of thought about strategy described in Chapter 3 tends to suggest a different set of questions for strategic assessment to answer. Particular frameworks tend to be effective at answering particular types of questions and to relate to particular ways of thinking about strategy.

It is usual to employ more than one framework for analysis. A survey by Wilson (1994) produced the data in Figure 8.3 from a survey of fifty companies in various industries and countries.

The survey demonstrates clearly that most companies in the survey were using more than one technique. The popularity of core competencies may reflect the date of the survey which was just after the publication of Hamel and Prahalad's *Competing for the Future* (1994). It is also intriguing that Business Process Redesign should be included as a technique of strategic analysis. The survey suggests that the variety of techniques in use was broad. Hopefully this would mean that all the companies concerned had carefully considered what the questions for their strategic assessment should be and had selected the techniques appropriate to their particular needs. Wilson's survey did not examine whether this was the case. It is also apparent from this survey that some possible ways of thinking about strategy—such as the Cultural School or the Environmental School—were not being applied in the field at that time.

As well as being relevant to the questions asked, the selection of techniques will in

Figure 8.3 Techniques in use in strategic planning processes

Technique	% Using
Core competencies analysis	72
Scenario planning	69
Benchmarking	56
Total quality management	44
Shareholder value analysis	44
Value chain analysis	44
Business process redesign	33
Time-based competition	25

Source: Adapted from I. Wilson, 'Strategic Planning Isn't Dead—It Changed', *Long Range Planning*, Aug, 1994.

practice depend on what information is available or obtainable within limits of time and effort.

Many of the frameworks provide ways of thinking which help to link strategic intent, assessment, and choice. Thus, in practice, the tools that prove effective for assessment will be coherent with the strategic intent and capable of providing a rationale for strategic choice. The tools and techniques are grouped in Chapters 9 and 10 for the convenience of the reader but logically they should be spread across Parts II, III and IV of the book.

8.5 Assessing competitive advantage

ONE of the most important aims of strategic assessment is to discover whether the proposed options and eventual choices deliver **competitive advantage**. Successful business strategies are those that use the capabilities of the firm to address customer needs in a way that leads to sustainable competitive advantage. Competitive advantage has characteristics similar to the Holy Grail: it is highly desirable, hard to define or measure, and may even be imaginary. Because of its central role in ensuring success there has been more written about competitive advantage than about almost any other single aspect of strategic management.

Observations of most industries would suggest that clear-cut competitive advantage is the exception rather than the rule and strategic choices can rarely guarantee to deliver it. More often, within a group of competitors, there are one or two clear leaders and one or two clear stragglers. Each of the rest of the group often has strengths and weaknesses in particular segments of a market that is not completely homogeneous. The decision-makers have to make their choices based on an accurate assessment of the current positioning and a realistic view of what is possible for the future in terms of competitive leadership. A clearly expressed strategic intent is often helpful in this decision-making process.

Competitive advantage may more often be relative rather than absolute. The story of the bear hunters may provide a relevant allegory (see Box 8.1).

While admitting that competitive advantage may be a little hard to nail down, no one denies its importance and its central role in determining business success. This role has been well summarized by John Kay (1993:4):

> Corporate success derives from a competitive advantage which is based on distinctive capabilities, which is most often derived from the unique character of a firm's relationships with its suppliers, customers, or employees, and which is precisely identified and applied to relevant markets.

This neatly balances the need to identify capabilities and to choose appropriate markets. Competitive advantage comes from matching internal capabilities to external opportunities. Assessing competitive advantage is therefore likely to require combinations of the frameworks and techniques described in Chapters 9 and 10.

In assessing whether the options and eventually the choices will deliver sustainable competitive advantage it is necessary to test the proposals against the different ways in which competitive advantage can be achieved for a time. These are:

1. Cost-based advantage

This is the most obvious way of achieving competitive advantage. Customers are always aware of the price and will choose the lowest price if all else is equal. Low prices are only sustainable if costs are low.

2. Advantage from a differentiated product or service

If the offering is different in a way that customers value then it may offer a competitive advantage.

3. First mover advantage

The first player to adopt some new product or approach may derive competitive advantage just because it was first. Such advantage may occur if the first mover is able to grab a large share of the available market while its offering is still unique. By the time that competitors have imitated the offering, the first mover may have achieved economies of scale or brand recognition which sustain its advantage. Obviously if

Box 8.1 The bear hunters

Two young men were preparing for a bear-hunting expedition. One suggested that he wanted to buy new trainers to be able to run fast. His friend pointed out that he could not run faster than a bear whatever trainers he wore. The first replied: 'That's not the point; I only have to be able to run faster than you'.

there are high costs for customers to switch suppliers, this will contribute to the first mover's advantage.

Unfortunately while it is easy to find examples of companies who have done well by being first into a new market, there are also many examples of fast followers who have been able to grab the lead even after a late start. Later starters can avoid the mistakes of the leaders and so save both time and money in their launch. Table 8.1 gives some examples.

Table 8.1 also shows the risks of offering such examples. Many of the 'winners' may be winners only for a limited time. The successful first mover may yet be overtaken by a fast follower yet to appear or a first mover into a new direction. Successful fast followers may be overtaken by even more successful followers of followers.

Table 8.1 Examples of success of first movers and fast followers

Industry/Product	First Mover	Fast followers
Passenger Jet Aircraft	De Havilland Comet	**Boeing 707**
Direct Motor Insurance	**First Direct**	Churchill, many others
Pocket calculators	Bowmar	**TI, Casio**
Personal Computers	Apple	**Compaq**

Note: Winners in bold type.

4. Time-based advantage

There are other occasions in which time can be a source of competitive advantage. Time can often be as important as price in modern business. For instance, the time to bring new products to market can be critical in high technology and fashion markets where product lives are short. The earlier offering has longer to earn its development cost in the market place. Much play has been made of the ability of Japanese manufacturers to design and produce new models more quickly and to manufacture them more cheaply than Western competitors. These examples were cited more often before Japanese industry encountered the difficulties of the 1990s but these difficulties are certainly not because the Japanese are fast developers of new products!

In other circumstances the ability to deliver quickly or within very tight time limits may be as important as price. Many customers will pay more for fast or reliable delivery. For instance, some specialized components may be essential for work to proceed in a large building project. Since delays in the delivery of the component will stop the whole project, the ability to deliver faster than the competition provides a competitive advantage. The value of this advantage may be very high as it relates to the cost of delay.

It is clear that time can be a factor in competitive strategy. For further discussion of this issue see Stalk (1988).

5. Technology-based advantage

Rapid advances in technology can have important effects on the basis of competition. The most obvious examples of this result from the rapid advances in computer and communications technology. One relevant current example is the Internet (and E-commerce)—a technology which generates new business opportunities for providers of services and new ways for existing business to communicate with their customers. The shares in many companies providing services on the Internet have achieved very high prices in stock markets even though many of them are only serving very limited needs of their customers. The biggest winners in Internet service provision will be those who harness the power of the Internet to serve day-to-day needs. For example, Charles Schwab, a stockbroker, has stolen a lead in selling securities on the Internet. As a result, Schwab has moved from being a small brokerage company to being a very significant one.

The Internet will affect most enterprises as users rather than as providers. There are already pressures on companies to participate in E-commerce and the implied threat that those who do not will be left behind. In fact, inappropriate participation may be worse than non-participation. Those who succeed will have made sure that they deliver real benefits to their customers and have developed the right internal capabilities to deliver quality results. Past experience of other technologies suggests that those who get it wrong may experience the 'bleeding edge' of technology for themselves.

The overall lessons on technology-based advantage are that innovation may be a source of business advantage and that innovation may be based on technology. The trick of achieving competitive advantage from technology is to harness the technology to create business innovation rather than exploit technology for its own sake.

Any of the above means of achieving competitive advantage may be relevant in a particular context. The practitioner, however, cannot rely on general prescriptions but must rather understand the true basis of competition of their particular business. This basis of competition is likely to be changing and the winners will be those who understand the present rules of competition and how those rules will change in the future. It is also essential to remember that success in the future will depend on finding new patterns of competitive advantage since the old patterns are known to all and therefore commonly available. Thinking outside the 'box' seems to be the prime means of achieving competitive advantage.

8.6 Assessing corporate advantage

COMPETITIVE ADVANTAGE is the means by which one business can win in competition with another. **Corporate advantage** is the means by which a multi-business corporation can add value to its businesses beyond what they would be worth on their own. Strategic assessment of multi-business companies will need to assess how much and by what means the corporate headquarters adds value. It may be that the value added by corporate headquarters is small, or even negative, in many enterprises. This issue is of interest both in practice and for research.

In practice, the cost of a headquarters is relatively easy to measure. If the headquarters is adding little value, the costs of floating and operating the constituent businesses as separate businesses might be less than the cost of the headquarters. Shareholders could then hold shares in the separate companies and choose to buy or sell these as they pleased. The argument is, in short, that stock markets are better at sorting out investment portfolios than corporations. Many managers of subsidiary companies and divisions will support the general view that 'group' is a waste of their time and money!

Collis and Montgomery (1998) conducted a research study among a group of fifty companies who were struggling to create corporate strategies by which corporate headquarters could add value to the separate businesses. They found that some of the companies were working on core competence, some were restructuring their portfolios, while others were concentrating on building learning organizations. They concluded that it was necessary to pull these dimensions into a coherent whole to optimize corporate advantage. This thinking resulted in their Triangle of Corporate Strategy (see Fig. 8.4). This provides a possible framework for the strategic assessment of corporate advantage.

The centre of the triangle is vision, goals, and objectives which is what we have referred to as strategic intent. The three sides of the triangle are resources, businesses, and the organization, systems, and processes. Competitive advantage is shown at the corner of the triangle where resources and businesses meet. Corporate advantage is the result of a good match between a business and its resources—being well fitted to its opportunities. The other two corners are marked co-ordination and control. Appropriate co-ordination and control occur when the organization, systems, and processes are appropriate to resources and businesses respectively.

Figure 8.4 The triangle of corporate strategy

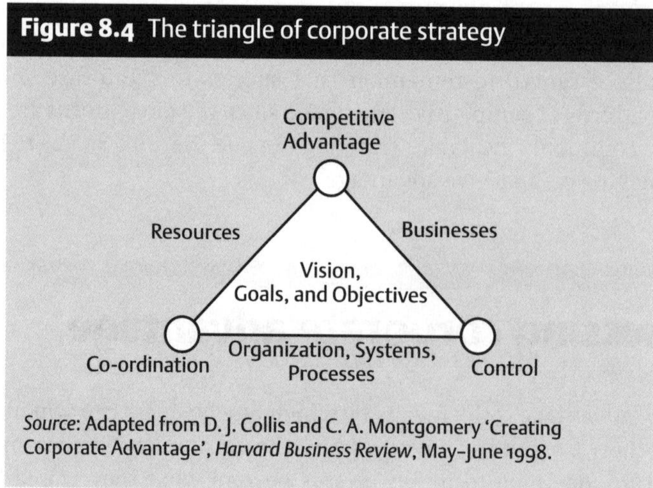

Source: Adapted from D. J. Collis and C. A. Montgomery 'Creating Corporate Advantage', *Harvard Business Review*, May–June 1998.

Figure 8.5 Successful enterprises tend to make coherent choices

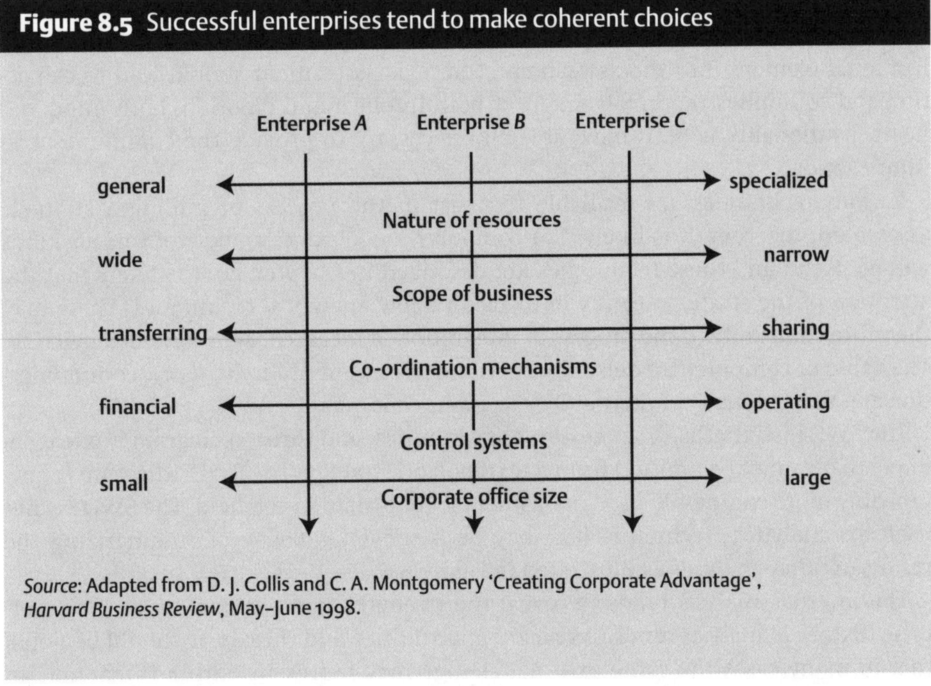

Source: Adapted from D. J. Collis and C. A. Montgomery 'Creating Corporate Advantage', *Harvard Business Review*, May–June 1998.

Collis and Montgomery claim that their research demonstrated that better corporate advantage resulted when there was a balance between the various elements of their Triangle of Corporate Strategy. Because of the inter-relationships implied, there is no single solution that will lead to the best pattern of strategy. Rather strategies will vary along a number of dimensions and the most successful strategies were aligned in these dimensions as indicated in Figure 8.5.

This framework is not highly quantified but it does suggest a way of considering corporate advantage in the strategic assessment of multi-business companies. Other possible techniques are described in Chapter 10.

8.7 Pulling the strategic assessment together

STRATEGIC assessment involves asking questions, using analysis to answer questions, reformulating better questions, refocusing analysis, and so on. The end result is a rich picture of the strategic context and the potential choices to be made in the light of a strategic intent which may itself be evolving and becoming clearer.

It is important that the results of strategic assessment are shared among a group of people—the strategy team. However rational the question/analysis mechanism may have been, the values and inclinations of the people involved will introduce an irrational element into the assessment. Strategic assessment should lead to conviction and so implies the involvement of both intellect and emotion, both mind and heart. Irrationality is both inevitable and necessary to provide the commitment to future action.

Various techniques are available to assist in the process of pulling a strategic assessment together. It is likely that computer models and support of various kinds will be useful and these techniques are described in Chapter 12. It is likely that the attention of the strategy team will focus on a few analytical techniques. These may therefore contribute to the process of integration of ideas, consensus, and conviction. The value of computer models may be as much in their ability to assist communication and agreement as in their ability to extend analysis.

The SWOT (strengths, weaknesses, opportunities, and threats) diagram is one technique that cannot be omitted from a textbook on strategy. The SWOT diagram is now probably more commonly used in business schools than in the field. The SWOT is not itself an analytical technique but may be a convenient way of summarizing the results of other analyses as illustrated in Figure 8.6.

The internal analysis tends to reveal the strengths and weaknesses of the enterprise. External analysis tends to reveal opportunities and threats. It should be noted that in many cases the same external change may represent both a threat and an opportunity. An appropriate response can change a threat into an opportunity.

One particular contribution of the SWOT diagram is that it may highlight the relationships of strategic intent and strategic choice to strategic assessment. Strengths and weaknesses are not only related to competitors but also to where we want to go and how we intend to get there.

The SWOT diagram is usually most effective when only the most important half dozen or so points are listed in each quadrant. Reducing much longer lists of

Figure 8.6 The SWOT diagram may summarize the results of analyses

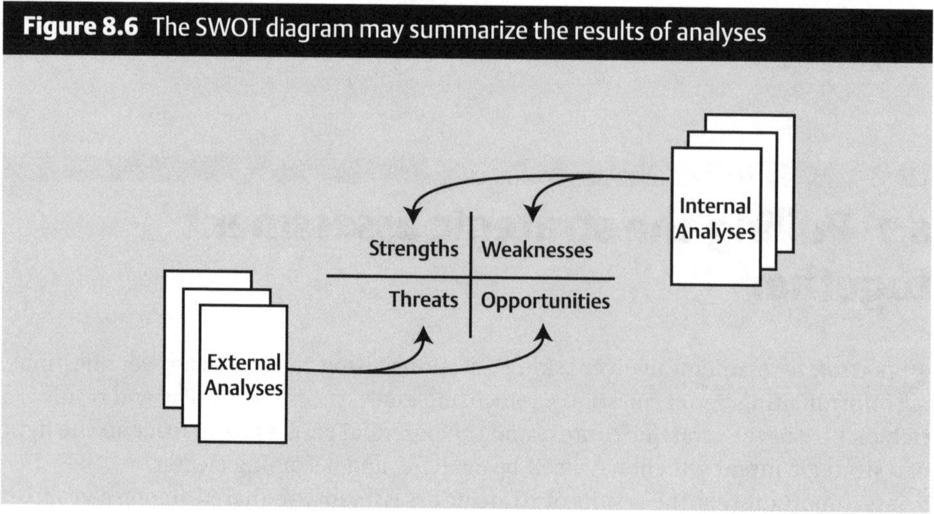

strengths, weaknesses, opportunities, and threats can be a valuable source of discipline and insight. This reduction process involves making judgements about relative importance between variables that cannot be related analytically—for instance, the cost of providing improved service versus the value to the customer of that service.

An ideal strategy would use the strengths to exploit the opportunities while at the same time defending against the threats and hiding the weaknesses. In practice, it is rarely so simple!

8.8 Strategic assessment of a business as a whole

ONE of the dangers of many analytical techniques is that the mass of detail can obscure the big picture so that the integrity and essence of the business is lost. A powerful technique for broader assessment is to ask more general questions. Examples of good questions (originally suggested by Levitt 1960 as antidotes to marketing myopia) include:

- What business are we really in?
- What real customer needs do we satisfy?
- What problem do we solve for our customers?

These kinds of questions tend to relate the strategic assessment to the strategic intent. Questions such as these can lift the process of formulating strategy away from a routine perspective of the nature of the enterprise. This may help to generate thinking outside the constraints of everyday work and bring creativity to the formulation of strategy. See Box 8.2 for an example.

Box 8.2 Examples of broadening thinking on the nature of a business

Electric Drills. The need of the customer is for a hole or for support to hang something on a wall. The drill is a means. There are many other ways of meeting these needs.

Cosmetics. The customer need is for personal recognition or some psychological benefit. A cosmetic manufacturer who sees the purpose of its business as improving the customer's self-image will define their business more broadly than one that sees itself in the market for face paints.

Source: Adapted from T. Levitt, 'Marketing Myopia', *Harvard Business Review*, July–Aug. 1960.

8.9 Summary

STRATEGIC assessment is an essential element of the strategy formulation process. The aim of strategic assessment is to take stock of the current business situation with a view to realizing the strategic intent. Strategic assessments tend to be carried out formally in response to some clear trigger which may be poor performance or the arrival of a new chief executive.

Strategic assessments will include analysis of the external business environment and how it is changing. Internal resources and capabilities are also analysed. There is a wide selection of techniques to support this analysis. The purpose of the strategic assessment is to provide a rich and shared understanding of the context and the issues which it imposes.

One critical requirement of strategic assessment is to build an understanding of the nature of current and future competitive advantage. This can be one means of taking a broader view of the business as a whole. This can have the effect of integrating the analyses and should also lead to conviction among the members of the strategy team.

Chapters 9 and 10 describe some general tools and techniques that are often used to assist in strategic assessment. These tools will be most effective when they are deployed within a clear idea of what the strategic assessment is aiming to achieve as described in this chapter.

References

Collis, D. J. and Montgomery, C. A. (1995) 'Competing on Resources', *Harvard Business Review*, Jul–Aug.

—— —— (1998) 'Creating Corporate Advantage', *Harvard Business Review*, May–June.

Grove, A. (1996) *Only the Paranoid Survive* (London: HarperCollins Business; paperback edn., 1998).

Hamel, G. and Prahalad, C. K. (1994) *Competing for the Future* (Cambridge, Mass.: Harvard Business School Press).

Kay, J. (1993) *The Foundations of Corporate Success* (Oxford: Oxford University Press).

Levitt, T. (1960) 'Marketing Myopia', *Harvard Business Review*, Jul–Aug.

Stalk, G. (1988) 'Time—the Next Source of Competitive Advantage', *Harvard Business Review*, Jul–Aug.

Wilson, I. (1994) 'Strategic Planning Isn't Dead—It Changed', *Long Range Planning*, 27/4 Aug.

Chapter 9

Strategic Assessment: Analysis of the External Environment

9.1 The purpose of external analysis

STRATEGIC assessment requires an understanding of both the external business environment and of internal resources, capabilities, and culture. This chapter examines some of the more commonly used frameworks for analysing the external business environment. It is important that this chapter should be read in conjunction with Chapter 8 which described the general principles of strategic assessment. In general, the tools described in this chapter are only of value when they are appropriate to the particular context and are applied with understanding of the wider principles.

The purpose of the external analysis is to understand what may affect the future of the enterprise as a whole from outside itself. The external analysis may often be usefully considered at three levels:

- general changes in the business environment;
- change within the industry;
- known activities of immediate competitors and other specific events.

9.2 Analysis of the overall business environment: PEST analysis

THE PEST analysis is the most common approach for considering the external business environment in general. PEST (standing for political, economic, social, and technological change) roughly defines the scope of what is required but the word PEST is no more than a convenient mnemonic. Each of the four broad areas subdivides into a longer list of areas that are likely to be worth considering. This longer list will tend to vary according to the context. PEST is not a rigorous analytical technique but rather a broad framework for reviewing changes in the outside world that may affect a particular enterprise.

The underlying thinking of the PEST analysis is that the enterprise has to react to changes in its external environment. This reflects the idea that strategy requires a fit between capabilities and the external environment and so it is necessary for an enterprise to react to changes.

Political change might be expected to include, for instance, general changes in the domestic political climate, the effects of European integration, the after-effects of the break-up of the Soviet Union, government change, world power shifts, as well as specific legislation and regulation. Changes in legislation tend to occur in a cycle extending over several years. The initial ideas may first become apparent as a political concern, followed by discussion and policy documents before the changes become law. It may therefore be possible to discern and possibly influence the likely shape of future legislation in advance.

Regulation, and particularly change in regulation, is critical to many businesses including, for instance, brewing, financial services, and waste disposal. Most regulation is announced some years before it becomes effective and future trends may become apparent even before legislation is formulated. Regulation also tends to have effects that are both wider and different from what the regulators intended.

Economic change is likely to include the effects of economic cycles, patterns of world trade, currency conversion rate changes, commodity prices, changes in capital markets, labour markets and rates, and economic effects on suppliers and particular groups of customers.

Economic cycles affect nearly all businesses but some may be hit early in recessions, while others tend to recover late in the cycle. Some businesses are counter-cyclical. Examples include insolvency practitioners (for obvious reasons) and perhaps book selling (because reading is cheaper than some other forms of entertainment). Economic cycles also occur in different geographic markets at different times and each recession tends to have slightly different characteristics. This means that simple extrapolation from the last recession is not enough. Capital market cycles relate to economic cycles but not in a simple way. Timing in the capital markets can be very critical for raising capital or for mergers and acquisitions. Mass labour markets are becoming less important for businesses that depend more on brainpower than elbow power. However, the shortage and hence high price of particular skills can often be significant enough to merit the attention of a strategic assessment.

Social change includes the effects of demographic patterns, tastes and habits, and concerns about the environment and sustainable development.

Many products and services, for instance, pensions or popular CDs, tend to cater to the needs of particular age groups so that demographic trends will affect the total number of available customers. Demographic trends are more predictable than most long-term social trends. Changes in tastes and habits, on the other hand, can occur very fast and may be totally unpredictable. For this reason, businesses that are highly exposed to fashion tend not to attempt to predict the future but rather to gear themselves to be able to react fast to change as it occurs.

Environmental concerns have increased over the last couple of decades and are now a major issue for many businesses. Legislation normally sets the lower limit of what is required but many businesses will want to exceed the legal minimum or to plan their long-term investments so that returns are not at risk from future legislation. The effects of environmental concern reaches far further than merely the control of emissions. For instance, property loans can be affected by the long-tail liabilities of landowners.

Technological change covers the effects of technological change on products, processes, and distribution channels.

Obviously, particular technologies have direct relevance to the industries that depend on them. For instance, the future of a pharmaceutical company depends to an important extent on the flow of new patents and the expiry of old ones. Changes in fields such as telecommunications and information technology have a wider impact and are likely to affect almost all enterprises. The impact of the Internet and E-commerce is the latest (but unlikely to be the last) wave of change derived from technological advance in this field. Biotechnology may be as important as a driver of technological change in the twenty-first century as information technology has been for the later part of the twentieth.

Product innovation tends to be particularly important for young and high technology businesses. Many start-up businesses are founded to exploit a particular innovation so their initial growth and success depends on being at the leading edge of technology. Interestingly it seems that the second phase of growth depends on developing the ability to 'cross the chasm' and sell high-technology products to mainstream customers (Moore 1991)—a technological change of a different kind but which would still be highly relevant in a PEST review.

Process innovation may be more important in more mature businesses where the rate of change in the product has decreased. Developments in transport and communications are particularly likely to affect distribution businesses while lean production techniques particularly affect the manufacturers of mass consumer products such as cars. Changes in technology may often lead to the entry of new competitors whose skill is in the technology rather than in the business as it was. Such competitors can initiate rapid change in industry practices and structure.

It is important that any part of the PEST analysis should focus on those changes in

Box 9.1 Example of change of critical importance to a particular business

The increasing use of mini and personal computers in large companies was of great signifiance to Nolan, Norton by the middle of the 1980s. These new types of computer were often outside the control of the central information technology (IT) department that might therefore lose its monopoly control of IT budgets.

This change was a threat to Nolan, Norton whose principal customers were the IT director and the board member to whom he or she reported. The focus of the board on information technology became more diffused. Nolan, Norton's services became less directly relevant as they could no longer offer the board a total view of IT across the organization. The central IT budget from which Nolan, Norton's fees were paid was also often cut back.

Nolan, Norton's strategic response was to seek to win assignments related to the transformation of business enabled by information technology. This new strategy required changes in marketing, new individuals as principal contact, a larger scale of assignments, and new skills among consultants.

A few computers outside the control of the central IT department probably rarely seemed 'strategic' to the companies concerned but it was to Nolan, Norton.

the external environment that are of importance to the business, not just change in general. Many major changes for society at large may have little or no significance to a particular enterprise. On the other hand, particular changes which may seem insignificant in general may be crucial to a particular enterprise (see Box 9.1).

Clearly a PEST analysis will require many and diverse sources of information depending on the business in question. In larger enterprises, much of this information may already be collected for other purposes. The task is to ensure that relevant information becomes visible to the strategy process to interpret its strategic significance.

A PEST analysis should address the drivers of change as well as the change itself. One of the dangers of PEST and of many analytical techniques is that they tend to be unduly sensitive to historical data and past trends. All trends eventually end but turning points are hard to predict. Anecdotal evidence may be critically important in detecting new trends early, as anecdotes may highlight the exceptions which give early indications of new trends before they have shown up in formal reports. Useful anecdotes often come from people who are in direct contact with customers. They may notice changes in customer attitudes that occur before changes in customer behaviour. When a change in trend is suspected, it is necessary to track the effect of the previous trend on the business historically to isolate the probable future effect of a change in the trend.

The PEST analysis is very general in nature and this makes it difficult to give clear rules on how best to apply it in varying circumstances. Global or geographically dispersed enterprises will have to conduct separate PEST analyses for different regions as trends occur at different rates in different places. Some choices may have to be made across these regions so that the PEST analysis will give results that are of doubtful value even if correct.

The value of the PEST is likely to relate directly to the quality of the effort put into it. This time spent thinking about how external change will affect the enterprise and its industry is likely to be well spent.

9.3 Stakeholders, corporate governance, and responsibility

THE PEST analysis is concerned with general change in the business environment. This section is concerned with changes in how the enterprise views the external environment. Changes in perspective of the external world may be as significant as changes in the external world itself.

The concept of stakeholders and their influence on strategic intent was discussed in Chapter 8. Strategic assessment is likely to be most concerned with shifts in the pattern of stakeholder power. This may be seen as particularly relevant to the Power School of thought about strategy (Chapter 3). Such shifts can occur gradually as a result of social or technological change. For instance, a craft group may gradually lose power as a result of their skills being automated. Shifts in stakeholder power may also occur rapidly, particularly if there is a change of ownership. For instance, a private firm may have to increase its focus on profitability when it floats on the stock market.

Corporate governance is concerned with the balance of power between the owners (shareholders), managers, the employees, the government, and the public at large. It can therefore be seen as a force that regulates the power of groups of stakeholders. Conflicts of interest tend to occur between shareholders and managers and between managers and employees. The managers and shareholders may have different views about the relative contribution made by capital as against managerial skill. The non-executive directors on the board have a particular duty to represent the interests of the shareholders so that differences of opinion between the executive and non-executive members of the board may be superficial indicators of underlying issues of corporate governance.

The balance of power between managers and employees has its roots in the relative value of capital and labour in contributing to success. Skills and knowledge are now often as or more important than capital which tends to increase the power of employees and requires managers to lead and co-ordinate rather than command.

Corporate governance has come to the public attention in the UK over the last several years as a result of the Cadbury (1992), Greenbury (1995), and Hampel (1998) reports. The Cadbury committee addressed issues relating to the structures of boards and laid down a code of best practice relating to board structure. In particular, it advocated the separation of the roles of chairman and managing director, the appointment of non-executive directors, and clear responsibilities for audit and remuneration committees. The Greenbury committee dealt with directors' pay. It laid down a code of best practice for how remuneration should be determined and reported in annual reports.

The patterns of corporate governance differ between countries. The USA and the UK have systems that are broadly similar to each other. In this model the shareholders own the company and elect the directors as their representatives. All directors, including the chairman, have equal legal responsibilities. There is not usually any formal structure for representing employees at board level. In practice, this form of corporate governance tends to result in most day-to-day authority being held by a small group of directors. The non-executive directors may become critical at particular times—for instance, if there is a need to replace the chief executive. Financial analysts are an important stakeholder group as they have considerable power in forming the opinion of shareholders.

In continental Europe, employees more often have rights of formal representation at board level. There may be two levels of board. The overall result is for a larger group of people to be involved in major decisions. This may curb abuses of individual power but may slow the decision-making process. The power of the financial markets has traditionally been less although this is beginning to change.

The Japanese model of corporate governance is different again as a result of the interlocking shareholdings of the Kairetsu system. Michel Albert (1994) has summarized the characteristics of the three models as shown in Figure 9.1. It is important to remember that there are many exceptions to these broad generalizations. Any analysis of the impact of corporate governance has to examine what governance mechanisms are important in that particular context and not assume that the general rules always apply.

The pattern of corporate governance may affect the way in which strategies are approved and the nature of the strategic intent. General patterns of corporate

Figure 9.1 Different models of governance

	Anglo Saxon	Rhine	Japanese
Ownership	Public	Institutions	Institutions
Board	Shareholder Reps.	Shareholders and Unions	Kairetsu Reps.
Management	Chairman and CEO	Collective (five to seven people)	Collective

Source: Adapted from talk by Michel Albert at the Strategic Management Society, Fourteenth Annual International Conference, HEC Paris, Sept. 1994.

governance are evolving and practices in Europe may tend to coalesce. Much of corporate governance is advisory rather than statutory so that enterprises have choices about their stance on compliance.

Large corporations in particular have to consider their responsibility for the power that they wield. This raises issues of corporate responsibility that are wider than the issues directly affected by corporate governance practices and guidelines. Common issues of corporate responsibility include the preservation of the environment, the proper use of charitable donations, the relationship with disadvantaged social groups, and the reaction to major world events such as the break-up of the communist bloc in Central and Eastern Europe. Legal frameworks may exist and may exert some influence in some of these fields but there remain, and always will remain, grey areas where conscience and the profit motive may be in conflict.

There are no general rules about how corporate responsibility can influence strategic intent but there are few contexts in which corporate responsibility can be wisely ignored. Cannon (1994) attempts to structure the subject of corporate responsibility and describes some of the historical background. Issues of corporate responsibility tend to present themselves in untidy forms at inconvenient moments leaving the practising manager to rely very much on his or her own inner resources.

Shifts in stakeholder power, the influence of corporate governance, and attitudes to corporate responsibility do not lend themselves to neat analysis but certainly any strategic assessment would be incomplete if both the current status and the direction of change are not understood.

9.4 Industry analysis: a word of warning

THE second level of external analysis is likely to focus on the 'industry'. The changes in the overall business environment will affect all the players in the industry but will often tend to benefit some players more than others. The word industry has been put in inverted commas, as it is often very difficult to define what an industry is. For instance, do brewers compete in a beer industry, in a beverages industry, or in the leisure industry? At the most obvious level, a beer drinker merely chooses between one make of beer and another. However, drinkers may also choose between beer and tea to quench their thirst so two beer brands have a common interest in emphasizing the benefits of beer against tea. Similarly, the quenching of thirst is only one possible use of time so that both tea blenders and beer brewers have a common interest in encouraging liquid refreshment breaks rather than TV watching. This simple example illustrates a point that tends to be just as important in more complex 'industries'.

Conversely, some so-called 'industries' are not industries at all from a strategic perspective. For instance, the steel industry covers a wide range of products from steel beams for building to nuts and bolts for domestic use. Steel beams may be more usefully considered as part of the construction industry while nuts and bolts may be more usefully seen as part of a fixtures and fittings industry.

These simple examples illustrate the very real difficulties that commonly occur in trying to define what an 'industry' is and who the real competitors are. It is important to define the industry wisely and be sensitive to the fact that much real strategic change originates at the boundaries of what had been seen as stable industries. The question 'What industry are we in?' is closely related to the question 'What business are we in?' which was discussed in Chapter 8 as a fundamental issue for strategic assessment to address.

9.5 Industry analysis: Porter's five forces model and its extension

MICHAEL Porter made one of the most thorough attempts to analyse the economic forces within an industry. Porter's work has an important place in the Positioning School (Chapter 3) which sees the fundamental role of strategy as positioning the enterprise for the future.

Porter's Five Forces Framework is shown in Figure 9.2. The five forces are the threat of entry of new competitors, the threat of substitutes, the bargaining power of buyers, the bargaining power of suppliers, and the degree of rivalry between existing competitors. Porter's premise is that some industries are intrinsically more attractive than others and the attractiveness is determined by these five forces.

The *threat of entry* is high when the industry appears attractive and when there are low barriers to entry. Industries are attractive when the existing players are making good profits. Examples of barriers to entry can include high requirements for capital, scarce skills, importance of reputation, or difficulties in access to distribution. If barriers to entry are relatively low, the threat of entry places a limit on prices in the industry and may determine the shape and extent of investment required to deter new entrants.

The *threat of substitution* is high when the customer's needs can be met by buying something other than the product of the industry. The magnitude of this is reduced if there are high costs of switching or if the price performance of available substitutes is poor. There is an important theoretical distinction in Porter's model between what constitutes substitution and merely buying from a competitor. This distinction is sometimes more difficult to make in practice than in theory and also depends on how the 'industry' being analysed is defined.

The *bargaining power of buyers* is high when buyers are able to switch between suppliers easily so that they can seek discounts or additional services in return for continuing their custom. Buyers may be powerful if there are relatively few buyers and a large number of suppliers. Buyers may be powerful if they have strong brands.

Figure 9.2 Porter's five forces model

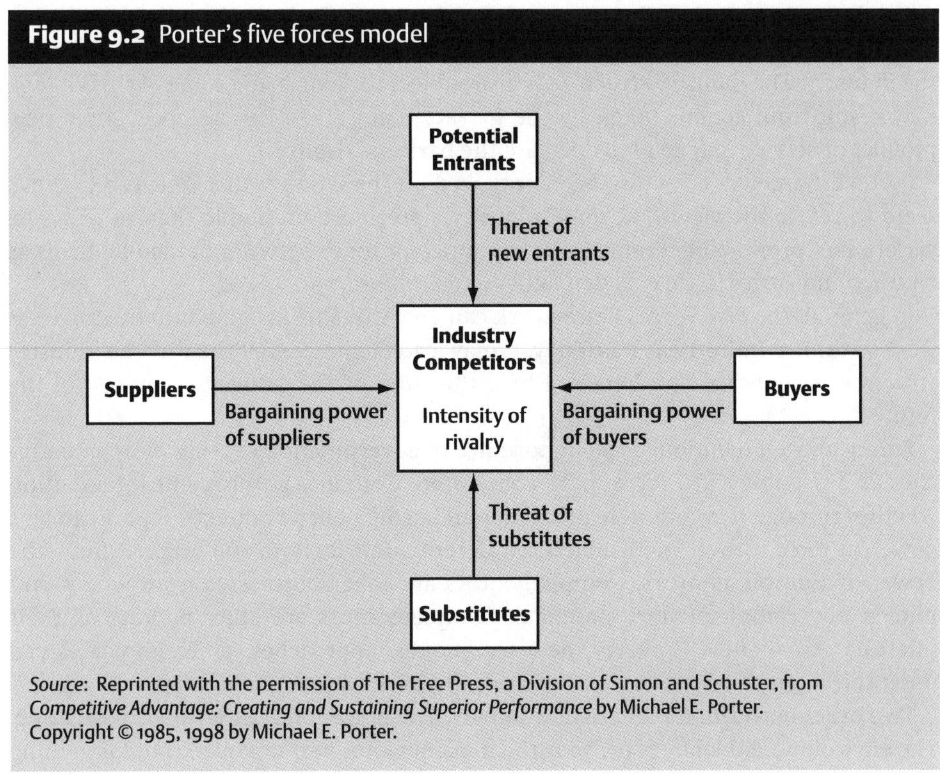

Source: Reprinted with the permission of The Free Press, a Division of Simon and Schuster, from *Competitive Advantage: Creating and Sustaining Superior Performance* by Michael E. Porter. Copyright © 1985, 1998 by Michael E. Porter.

An example of this is large supermarket chains whose own brands are strong enough to make them independent of the manufacturers' brand reputations.

The *bargaining power of suppliers* is high if it is hard to switch from one supplier to another or if the total supply to this industry is only a small part of the supplier's total output. An example of this is the glass industry that depends on specialized chemicals. These chemicals are a relatively minor part of the output of the large chemical companies that make them. As a result the products are more important to the glassmakers than to the chemical companies so prices are high.

The *degree of rivalry among competitors* in an industry is determined by factors such as the rate of industry growth, the tendency for over-capacity to occur, and the strength of brand identities. There are industries in which although competition is apparently intense it is actually limited to very specific fields. For instance, the makers of chocolate confectionery compete heavily in advertising but their prices remain remarkably similar. The three leading competitors in the European market are Mars, Nestlé, and Cadbury who between them have over 70% of the UK market. The barriers to entry are very high and include reputation, brands, and access to distribution. While there appears to be intense rivalry, some of it is perhaps ritualistic.

The Five Forces Framework can provide a powerful analytical tool for understanding the dynamics of an industry. It is, however, difficult to use properly. One major difficulty is in defining the 'industry' (see Sect. 9.4). It is important that industry is defined clearly and that the chosen definition is applied consistently. Interesting findings may result from repeating the analysis with slightly varying definitions of the industry. The industry structure is also subject to change and some of this change may result from actions taken by the players themselves. For instance, some new product or service may tend to decrease the barriers to entry.

Porter's framework has also been criticized on the grounds that research findings seem to refute the view that some industries are more profitable than others. The variation of profitability seems to vary as much or more between individual firms as between industries (see e.g. Baden-Fuller and Stopford 1992:13–34).

In general, the Five Forces Framework can give valuable insights into the forces at work within an industry as it is today. It may lead to glimpses of the way the industry structure is changing and hence of how the rules of the game may change in the future.

Porter himself mentioned the importance of government and regulation on industries as a possible sixth force to be considered. Certainly government intervention whether through legislation, regulation, purchasing policy or direct support can be a powerful force. Grove (1996) added a different sixth force to the original five—the power of **Complementors.** Complementors are other businesses from whom customers buy complementary products. Complementors are allies as long as their interests are aligned. However, new techniques, approaches, or technologies can upset this alignment or change the relative influence of complementors.

Two other powerful forces are now at play. The power of *Lobby groups* is increasing. The environmental lobby is perhaps the most obvious, best organized, and is gaining strength year by year. The demonstrations at the World Trade Organization conference in Seattle in 1999 were just one example of a well-organized lobby group able to thwart an organization from pursuing avenues which are seen to be harmful to the environment or peoples. The activities of lobby groups, whatever their moral justification or lack of it, are able to influence the values of customers and thus change the ground rules within which an enterprise operates.

Finally, changing *fashion* and the *fickleness* of allegiances to brands and lifestyles, particularly among the young and affluent, can seriously damage the health of a business. It seems likely that one of the major effects of the Internet will be to increase fickleness. The Internet makes it easier for consumers to compare a wider range of goods and prices and increase the visibility of choice and so Internet trading has had an effect on the way customers shop. For example, some customers enjoy the 'shopping experience'. They like to browse when buying such items as clothes, books, motor cars, and so on; whereas other customers may be quite happy to order brand-named goods via the Internet. As a result, it is necessary for vendors to rethink the nature of what they are offering their customers and whether they want to be providers of convenience or purveyors of leisure.

The Internet also tends to force a change in the nature of the product itself. For instance, the banks have had to introduce Internet Banking for the benefit of their more computer literate and often more affluent customers. The increased speed and volume of information that can be passed to customers will influence the demands which customers make on banks. Thirdly, the Internet can change the power balance between competitors. For instance, retailers of white goods and non-perishable items are finding that they can reach a much wider customer base by using the Internet as a 'shop-window', thus enabling small enterprises to equal the reach of major players.

It is apparent that the original Five Forces Model needs to be expanded to take into account these additional forces which have become more apparent over the last several years. As the industry to which an organization belongs becomes harder to define, it becomes necessary to understand how these forces threaten the survival of an individual organization. This suggests that the centre of the model should relate to the individual organizations as much as as to the intensity of rivalry among competitors in an industry.

An integrated model of the threats to survival of an organization is shown in Figure 9.3. All the eight forces shown are capable of threatening the survival and growth of the enterprise and therefore need to be considered as part of the process of external assessment.

Figure 9.3 Corporate survival model

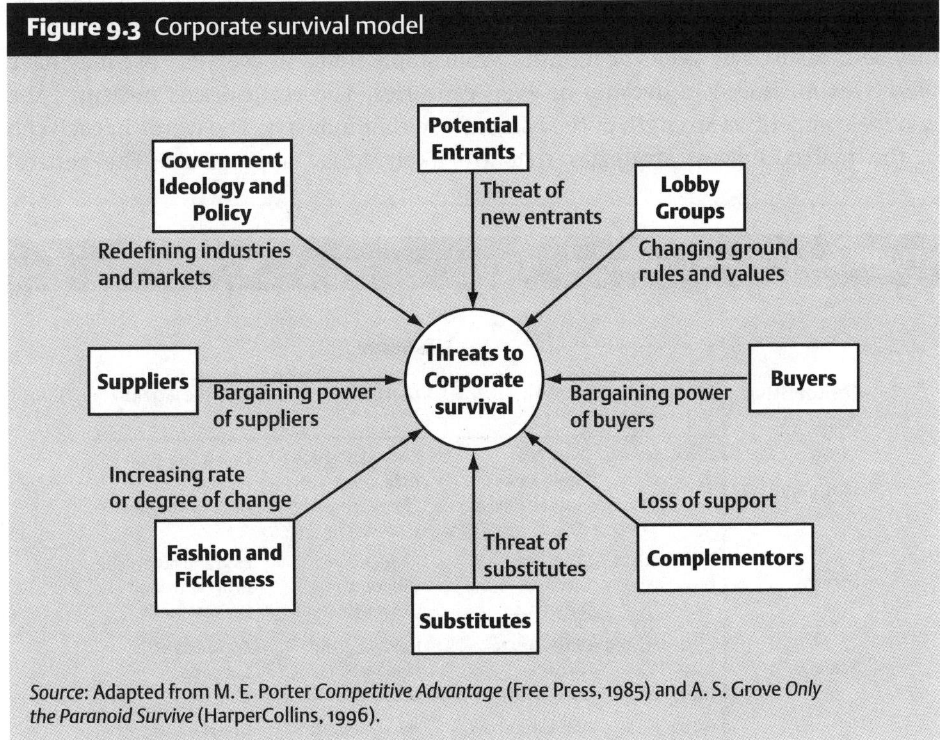

Source: Adapted from M. E. Porter *Competitive Advantage* (Free Press, 1985) and A. S. Grove *Only the Paranoid Survive* (HarperCollins, 1996).

9.6 Life stage analysis of an industry

Most products, services, and the industries supplying them have a life cycle from birth, through growth, then to maturity and eventual decline. Analysis of life stages may give useful insights in those industries where there is a discernible and predictable life cycle pattern. Life cycles may form a useful basis for analysis if, for instance, competition is based on the introduction of new products or if an industry as a whole is moving from maturity towards decline. The life cycle view of the world has its roots in a biological or environmental view of the nature of strategy.

A typical Life Cycle Matrix is shown in Figure 9.4.

Note the two axes. The horizontal axis relates to the life stage of the industry. The terms are self-explanatory. While all industries tend to follow the same overall pattern, the time-scale can vary widely. Life cycles for high technology and high fashion may be measured in weeks or months while staple items in everyday use may have life cycles measured in decades or even centuries. The vertical axis measures the relative competitive strength of the company in that industry. The words in each cell of the matrix suggest strategies that are likely to be appropriate. The general

Figure 9.4 Life cycle matrix

	Life Stage			
Competitive Position	Start -up	Growth	Maturity	Decline/ageing
Dominant	Grow fast	Grow fast Attain cost leadership	Defend position Attain cost leadership Review	Defend position Renew Grow with industry
Strong	Differentiate Grow fast	Grow fast Catch up Differentiate	Reduce costs Differentiate Grow with industry	Find and hold niche Grow with industry Harvest profit
Satisfactory	Differentiate Focus Grow fast	Differentiate Focus Grow with industry	Harvest profit Find niche Grow with industry	Consolidate Cut costs
Weak	Focus Grow with industry	Harvest, catch up Find and hold niche Turnaround	Harvest profit Turnaround Find niche Consolidate	Divest
Very weak	Find niche Grow with industry	Turnaround Consolidate	Withdraw Divest	Withdraw

Source: Adapted from model in common usage believed to have originated in A. D. Little.

principles are those of building on strength, defending against weakness, and recognizing the underlying importance of the life cycle.

The life cycle model can be used for analysing individual product decisions or for the overall positioning in a market area. The general conclusion to be drawn from the model tends to be that in a maturing industry, there is a tendency for the total number of competitors to decline as the stronger players acquire the weaker. This pattern of consolidation may be observed in many maturing businesses.

9.7 Competitor analysis: general

The third level of external analysis is likely to consider competitors both individually and in groups. Although this is often an important piece of analysis, it is difficult to describe in general as the information available, and hence the analysis which is possible, varies markedly from one industry to another. In some industries (such as insurance or many consumer products, for instance), very detailed information is made available by an industry association or independent monitoring agencies. For these industries there is likely to be value in analysing the available data in some detail both for the industry as a whole and for individual competitors. Obviously there are some types of important information that are not recorded in industry databases. In other industries (such as the chemical industry and management consulting, for instance), there is much less systematic and public collection of information. In these cases it may be valuable carefully to aggregate competitive information from the diverse pieces of information collected from multiple sources. In some industries and particularly in emerging markets, all information is scarce. Here competitive intelligence has become a specialized skill with its own professional body of practitioners and with at least some parallels to military espionage.

In some industries, the competitors may divide naturally into strategic groups. These are subsets of the whole that have similar characteristics and tend to compete most closely with each other. Clearly competitors in our own strategic group are worthy of the greatest attention. Some strategic groups may be small enough for the action of one player to cause individual responses from others. In these cases the principles of game theory or military strategy may be useful as the basis for analysis.

If there is enough data it may be possible to analyse competitors using the techniques of internal analysis described in Chapter 10. This may give insights into their likely future strategies, just as analysing our own capabilities informs our own strategies.

9.8 Ohmae's model for analysing competitors

KENICHI Ohmae is Japanese and was head of the managing consulting firm McKinsey in Tokyo for many years, so his ideas tend to be derived as much from practice as theory and have been field-tested. Ohmae is clearly from the Planning School of thought (Chapter 3). Ohmae starts from a straightforward view of a 'Strategic Triangle' of Company, Customers, and Competitors as shown in Figure 9.5.

Note how the company and its competitors are competing on both cost and value in offering a product or service to customers. Notice also how the pool of customers is fragmented so that the total market is divided between the separate competitors. Ohmae's perceptions, particularly of the fragmented nature of customer needs and hence of all real market places, rings true in many situations. It differs from the economic model of perfect competition in a perfect market place.

Ohmae outlined four basic strategies for attaining competitive advantage.

Intensifying functional differentiation

Intensifying functional differentiation is achieved by identifying the Key Success Factors (KSFs) and injecting resources into the most important business functions. The aim is to invest in the parts of the company that matter most.

Figure 9.5 The strategic triangle

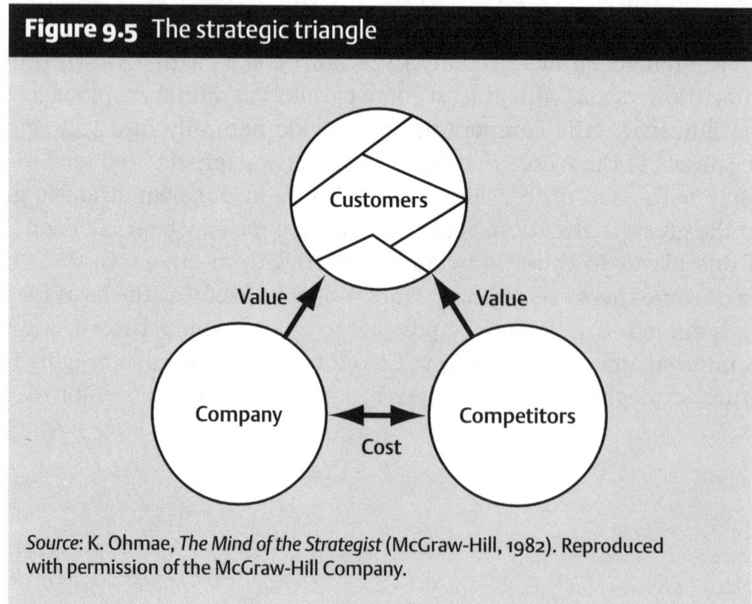

Source: K. Ohmae, *The Mind of the Strategist* (McGraw-Hill, 1982). Reproduced with permission of the McGraw-Hill Company.

Building on relative superiority

Building on relative superiority is achieved by comparing products systematically with competitors and investing selectively either to improve the attractiveness of the product or to reduce the cost. The aim is to invest in improving the product in a way that matters to the customer.

Pursuing aggressive initiatives

Pursuing aggressive initiatives requires challenging prevailing wisdom and practices by asking fundamental questions. Effective aggressive initiatives result from giving new answers to old questions. One example is of Dr Land, the inventor of the Polaroid camera, being asked by his young daughter, 'Daddy, why do we have to wait for photographs to be developed?' This led to the invention of the instant development camera.

Exploiting strategic degrees of freedom

Exploiting strategic degrees of freedom requires defining the strategic degrees of freedom which affect the outcome to the customer and which are within the control of the provider. One example quoted by Ohmae is of a coffee percolator that included water purification and grinding. The taste of coffee is critical to coffee drinkers. The taste of coffee depends principally on the quality of the water and on freshly ground beans. A manufacturer of coffee percolators would be exploiting the strategic degrees of freedom if he built a percolator that integrated these factors into its design. This is an interesting example in that it is clear that coffee drinkers must also have other needs as simpler and cheaper coffee machines still exist!

Ohmae's four basic strategies are constructive in that they tend to focus not on head-to-head competition but in finding particular parts of the overall market which will suit our particular strengths. This point is made even more clearly in a later article (Ohmae 1988).

9.9 Analysis of Competitive Advantage

BEYOND the analysis of the industry, the Positioning School of thought (Chapter 3) also requires consideration of the nature of competitive advantage and the extent to which it can be sustained. Competitive advantage is only useful if it can be sustained long enough to recoup the investment needed to achieve it in the first place. No advantage is sustainable indefinitely since everything can eventually be copied and no customer is loyal for ever. However, some competitive advantages are more difficult to counter than others. It is often possible to estimate the probable degree to which advantage may be sustained in particular contexts.

Sustainability of advantage amounts to finding ways to cheat the principle of economics that suggests that the profits of the competitors in any perfect market will eventually decline to the cost of capital. Managers are concerned to beat this principle by finding ways to make the market imperfect in favour of their own enterprise. Imperfections may occur in practice for a number of reasons including:

- assets that we have acquired in the past for a price lower than the current market value;
- core competencies that are hard to imitate;
- non-tradable assets such as reputation;
- fortuitous geographical position.

Clearly the aim is to do whatever can be done within the particular context to sustain competitive advantage long enough for the investment in the new product or service to pay off. There are no general rules on how to do this. Also, while observing competitive advantage among competitors is a logical part of external analysis, our own competitive advantages are even more interesting as a part of internal assessment (see Chapter 10).

9.10 The Market Commitment Model

The Market Commitment Model suggested by de Kare Silver (1997) attempts to put most of the separate threads of competitive strategy into a single model which is suitable for use in practice. De Kare Silver claims to have tested this in practice with a number of consulting clients in a number of different industries. The model is illustrated in Figure 9.6.

At the centre of the model is long-term commitment to the market place in which the company competes. This is seen as the bedrock for lasting success. Such commitment involves both developing a deep understanding of customers and their needs and taking a long-term horizon in taking decisions.

Surrounding the central commitment are the four 'prime axes' of competitive advantage: price, emotion, service hustle, and performance. Each of these can be provided by a number of more detailed sources of competitive advantage as listed in Figure 9.6. These four prime axes may be seen as analogous at a strategic level with the four P's (Price, Position, Place, and Promotion), well known at the operational marketing level.

The Market Commitment Model provides a general framework for reviewing the probable strategies and chances of success of each of the principal competitors in comparison with our own strategies. It may enable a dynamic strategic assessment of the competitive game being played.

Figure 9.6 The Market Commitment Model

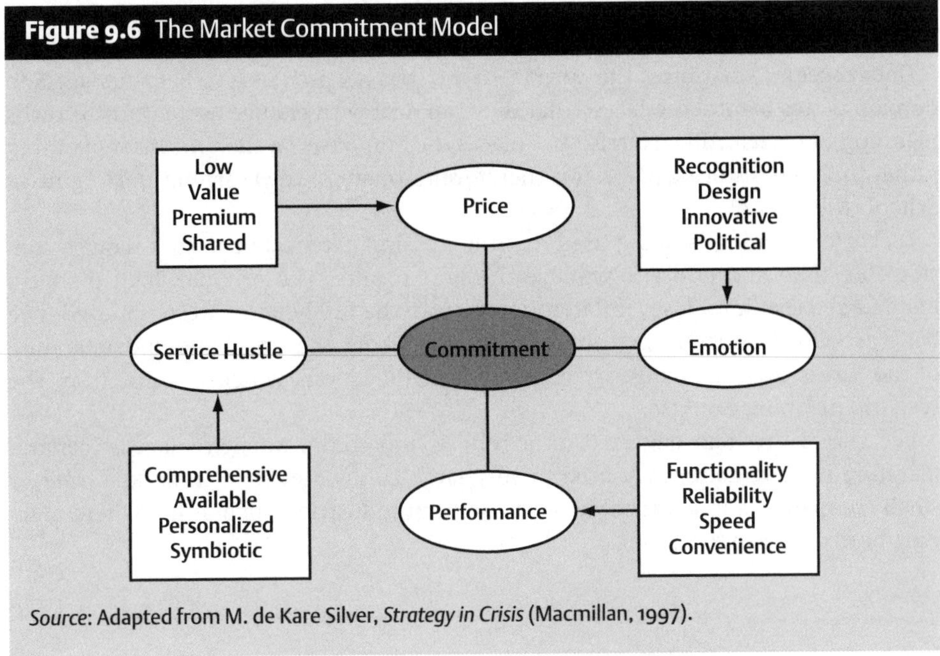

Source: Adapted from M. de Kare Silver, *Strategy in Crisis* (Macmillan, 1997).

9.11 Scenario planning

THE frameworks above all assume that it is possible to analyse the external environment as it currently exists and as it is forecasted to become and that this is a useful thing to do. They are all prescriptive in their approach. It is sometimes argued that it is so difficult to forecast the future that it is better not to attempt forecasting at all. Scenario planning offers a fundamentally different approach that does not depend on forecasting the future. Rather it postulates possible future scenarios without making any assessment of the likelihood that any one scenario will occur. Scenario planning was pioneered in Shell (Wack 1985*a* and 1985*b*; de Geus 1988, Schwartz 1991).

Scenario planning involves the creation of a number (typically two to four) complete scenarios of the future, each of which is self-consistent but significantly different from the others. For instance, one scenario might postulate a serious and long-lasting economic recession coupled with rising trade tariffs—a pattern last experienced in the 1930s. A second scenario might postulate a second Russian revolution resulting in a strongly nationalistic and anti-Western government. A third might postulate some major technological breakthrough transforming the price structure of the industry. The task is then to undertake an assessment of the likely effects of each scenario on the company and to identify the actions necessary to survive and succeed. While the future may evolve like none of the scenarios, the process of planning forces new ways of thinking which may be more valuable than the plans themselves.

Under scenario planning, the purpose of the strategy process is to help managers to develop better mental models so that they can deal with change as it occurs. It turns planning into a learning exercise and places the emphasis on the process of planning rather than the resulting plans. It is therefore resonant of the Learning and Cognitive Schools (Chapter 3).

Scenario planning is being used to an increasing extent, but it does require considerable time and effort to achieve the best results. The original Shell pioneers emphasized that it took several iterations before the full benefits were achieved. The benefits were as much in new ways of thinking about the world and understanding of the forces driving change than in any specific actions which resulted from the scenario planning exercise.

Because of the high degree of time, effort, and commitment required, Scenario planning is more commonly used in very large companies than in middle-sized or small companies and is probably most useful in industries, such as oil, where planning horizons have to be long.

9.12 Summary

THE purpose of external analysis is to understand as much as possible about the external business environment, how it is changing, and the forces driving the change. The analysis is likely to take place at three levels—general changes, industry, and competitors.

The analysis can never be complete because there will inevitably be changes in the future which were not foreseen. Despite this limitation, most enterprises find it useful to attempt an analysis of the external environment using a variety of analytical tools. In practice, some of these tools will prove more powerful in generating insights than others. Often, too, different tools will tend to reveal the same patterns of relevant change through different analytical frameworks.

Scenario planning provides a fundamentally different approach for those who believe that all forecasting is flawed. The main value of scenario planning is in causing managers to think and to learn.

The choice of appropriate tools depends on the requirements of the context and the data available. It may also depend to some extent on preferences for one or other of the schools of strategic thought.

References

Albert, M. (1994) Unpublished talk at the Strategic Management Society's Fourteenth Annual International Conference, Paris, Sept.

Baden-Fuller, C., and Stopford, J. M. (1992) *Rejuvenating the Mature Business* (London: Routledge).

Cadbury (1992) *Final Report of the Committee on the Financial Aspects of Corporate Governance and Code of Best Practice*, 1 Dec. (London: Gee Publishing).

Cannon, T. (1994) *Corporate Responsibility*, (London: Pitman Publishing)

de Geus, A. (1988) 'Planning as Learning', *Harvard Business Review*, Mar.–Apr.

de Kare-Silver, M. (1997) *Strategy in Crisis: Why Business Urgently Needs a Completely New Approach* (London: Macmillan).

Greenbury, R. (1995) *Directors' Remuneration: Report of a Study Group chaired by Sir Richard Greenbury*, 14 Aug. (London: Gee Publishing).

Grove, A. S. (1996) *Only the Paranoid Survive: How to Exploit the Crisis Points that Challenge every Company and Career* (London: HarperCollins; paperback edn., 1998).

Hampel, R. (1998) *Committee on Corporate Governance: Final Report*, 21 May (London: Gee Publishing).

Moore, G. A. (1991) *Crossing the Chasm* (New York: HarperCollins; 1995).

Ohmae, K. (1982) *The Mind of the Strategist* (New York: McGraw Hill and Penguin).

—— (1988) 'Getting Back to Strategy', *Harvard Business Review*, Nov.–Dec.

Porter, M. E. (1980) *Competitive Strategy: Techniques for Analysing Industries and Competitors* (New York: Free Press).

—— (1985) *Competitive Advantage: Creating and Sustaining Superior Performance* (New York: Free Press).

Schwartz, P. (1991) *The Art of the Long View* (New York: Currency Doubleday; 1996).

Wack, P. (1985*a*) 'Scenarios: Uncharted Waters Ahead', *Harvard Business Review*, Sept.–Oct.

—— (1985*b*) 'Scenarios: Shooting the Rapids', *Harvard Business Review*, Nov.–Dec.

Chapter 10
Strategic Assessment: Analysis of Resources, Capabilities, and Competence

10.1 The purpose of internal analysis

THE analysis of the external business environment described in Chapter 9 needs to be matched by a rigorous internal analysis of resources, capabilities, and competence. Traditionally strategy has taken greater notice of the external environment and hence put more emphasis on external analysis. Over the last several years there has been more emphasis on the significance of resources and capabilities as a basis for strategy making. This 'resource-based' view of strategy has become more important for two main reasons. First, the external world is seen as becoming unpredictable and so there are limitations to the value of studying its present state in detail. Secondly, business success may result from exploiting and building upon the unique qualities of the enterprise and these can only be understood by looking inwards. Internal analysis is now seen as at least as important as external analysis and perhaps capable of providing a more stable basis for future strategy. In practice both internal and external analysis are needed and neither can be complete without the other.

The terms used for internal attributes tend to vary between authors so it is important to define the terms as used in this book. **Resources** are tangible, visible, and relatively easy to measure. Resources include plant and machinery, patents, brands, and skilled people. Resources are rarely unique to the enterprise and may usually be acquired. **Capabilities** are less tangible and result from the organization of resources, internal systems, and skills. Capabilities are also seldom unique and many will be widely held by the competitors in the same industry. Distinctive capabilities are those capabilities that are rare enough to be distinctive to customers from among competitors. Distinctive capabilities are visible to the competition and so vulnerable to imitation over time. **Core competence** is the rarest and most valuable internal attribute of all. Core competence is a group of related capabilities that confers competitive advantage. True core competence is rare but worth a great deal when identified.

The overall purpose of internal analysis is to identify those particular characteristics of the enterprise that will either allow it to meet existing or future customer requirements better than present or future competitors. This implies the need for two fundamental tests in assessing capabilities—value to future customers and distinctiveness from competitors. No capability is of any value unless some customer needs it and is willing to pay for it; no competence is of distinctive value if all the competitors have it too and can exercise it with the same or better ability or skill.

One consequence of taking a resource-based view is that strategy making becomes as much concerned with building resources and capabilities as with exploiting business opportunities and gaining market position. Balanced strategies aim to build capability so as to capture future opportunities.

There is a wide range of frameworks and techniques for internal analysis just as there is for external analysis. As for external analysis, the choice of tools will depend on the context and on the data available. The tools fall into two groups. Tools in the first group are concerned with assessing single businesses and therefore particularly relevant to the formulation of competitive strategies (as discussed further in Chapter 14). Tools in the second group relate to the assessment of multiple businesses and so are particularly relevant to the formulation of corporate strategies (see Chapter 15). In each case the assessment tools have an important role in providing the rationale to support the strategy chosen.

The two groups of tools described are listed in Figure 10.1.

10.2 Resource audit

THE resource audit is a straightforward analysis of the quantity and quality of the resources available. It may be useful to consider four general headings, of which the fourth may not meet a rigorous definition of resources:

- physical resources: buildings, equipment, land, and so on;
- human resources: skills, know-how, strong teams, good management, and so on;
- financial resources: ability to raise cash, rich parent, and so on;
- other resources and intangibles: goodwill, brand names, trade relationships, and so on.

The aim of a resource audit is to compare the quality and extent of resources with the resources of present and possible future competitors.

Figure 10.1 Some commonly used techniques for internal analysis

Single businesses
Resource Audit (10.2)
Analysis of Cost and Profit (10.3)
Benchmarking (10.4)
Value Chain Analysis (10.5)
Supply Chain Analysis (10.6)

Both Single and Multiple Businesses
Core Competence (10.7)
Shareholder Value Analysis (10.8)
Distinctive Organizational Capabilities (10.9)

Multiple Businesses
Assessing Parenting Advantage (10.10)
Portfolio Analysis (10.11)

Uniqueness is a particularly important aspect of quality. For instance, any recognized brand name has unique expectations associated with it that can provide opportunities for building credibility for new products or services. Patents, licences, and copyrights may similarly offer unique opportunities during their finite lives.

It may be effective to analyse resources by function. This has the practical advantage that in many businesses the board includes the heads of the various functions. These individuals may therefore report their assessment of the strengths and weaknesses of their function to their assembled board colleagues. This means that responsibility for undertaking the assessment and for subsequently taking action falls to the same person.

Resource audit is a simple and basic technique and may be useful as a first step.

10.3 Analysis of costs and profit

THE overall objectives of the analysis of costs and profit are to understand where the business is making profit currently, the direction of profit trends, and the effects of allocations on reported profit.

It is likely that much information of this kind is already available for analysis. There are usually accountants who can quickly and competently recast figures that have been routinely produced for reporting purposes into new formats so that they give new insights. Many computer systems record multiple codes on their databases and not all these codes may be used for reporting so there are opportunities to provide analyses in new forms. Clearly detailed systems knowledge and skills are needed to do this.

Strategic analysis of financial data requires an interaction between hypothesis and analysis. For instance, it may be that certain groups of customers are suspected of being much more profitable than other groups. This hypothesis may be proved or disproved by recasting the profit and loss to determine the contribution of these groups. Strategic analysis is as much an art as a science. It depends on what data are available but may also require estimates to fill in gaps and realistic allocations to divide cost totals at a more detailed level than the coding system supports.

Analysis of costs and profit is likely to form a part of any strategic assessment but the exact form it takes will vary widely according to what accounting data are available.

It may be useful to analyse whatever data are easily available so as to avoid spending too much effort generating the data that would be ideally required. A pragmatic approach is required to maximize the value of the result within the effort and time available.

10.4 Benchmarking

THE purpose of benchmarking is objectively to compare resources, capabilities, and processes with the highest standards that have been achieved anywhere. This normally requires comparisons with world class—not merely the best in the industry or the best among direct competitors.

In practice, benchmarking clubs of companies that are not in direct competition may carry out the benchmarking. The club members agree the relevant processes or capabilities for comparison and the appropriate measures to apply. Each member collects information on its own enterprise. The pooled information is then tabulated for analysis and comparison.

Benchmarking is simple in theory but it is difficult to achieve convincing results in practice. The main difficulty is in comparing like with like. Generally, the more detailed the comparison becomes, the more uncertainty there is about the basis of comparison. Questions as to whether the differences in observed performance are justified by differences in the parameters are very hard to resolve. Very often the main benefit is in identifying qualitative differences in approach rather than from the detailed performance comparisons themselves.

There is a growing literature giving practical advice on how best to conduct benchmarking. See, for instance, Camp (1989), Karlöf and Östblom (1993), or Watson (1993a, 1993b). Watson in particular differentiates between different forms of benchmarking. He points out that early forms of benchmarking tended to be reverse engineering. According to him, competitive benchmarking followed and led to process benchmarking where the imitator analysed and understood the way things were done by the best in class and followed or bettered the current leader. Watson identifies a fourth stage—strategic benchmarking. He defines this as: 'A systematic process for evaluating alternatives, implementing strategies, and improving performance by understanding and adapting successful strategies from external partners who participate in an ongoing business alliance'. Strategic benchmarking is about imitating the industry leader not at the process or product level but at the strategic level. The results of strategic benchmarking may require radical transformation of the enterprise to achieve the new standards.

10.5 Value chain analysis

MICHAEL Porter (1985) introduced the concept of the value chain. His definition of value is the price that a customer is prepared to pay for an offering. Profit is the difference between this value and the total costs to the enterprise of providing that offering. Value chain analysis divides the enterprise into a chain of activities (See Fig. 10.2 for Porter's generic value chain). Each element, or link, in the value chain delivers a part of the total value to the customer and contributes part of the total profit. The purpose of value chain analysis is to measure the value delivered and the profit contributed by each link of the chain. One concern of strategy is to focus attention and resources onto those parts of the value chain from which the majority of the value comes and reduce or perhaps subcontract those parts that contribute little value.

Value chain analysis is elegant in theory but time-consuming in practice. The costs of the different areas of the value chain model require that all costs be attributed to an activity. Relatively few costing systems contain this amount of detail so the infor-

Figure 10.2 The value chain

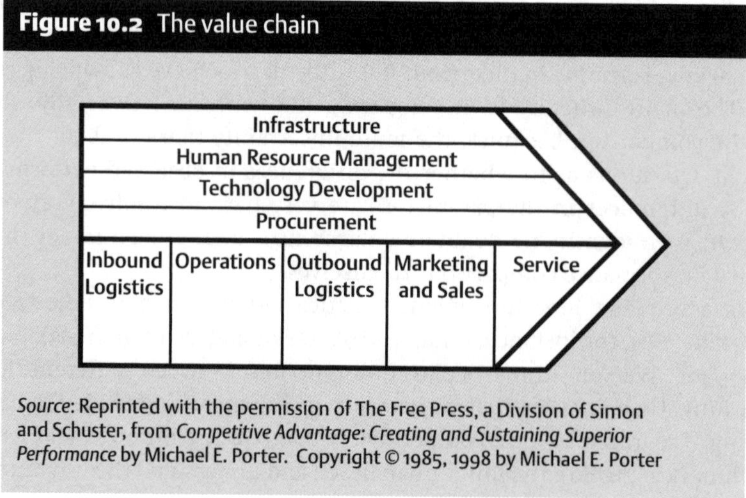

Source: Reprinted with the permission of The Free Press, a Division of Simon and Schuster, from *Competitive Advantage: Creating and Sustaining Superior Performance* by Michael E. Porter. Copyright © 1985, 1998 by Michael E. Porter

mation may be labour-intensive to obtain unless an activity-based costing (ABC) system is already in place. Similarly, the customer may see value in a very general kind of way so that it is difficult to attribute particular parts of the total price paid to specific parts of the product or service. Parts of a service that generate little value may also have the potential to destroy value if done badly so that it may be impossible to act on the results of the value chain analysis. Commercial operations may be more susceptible to value chain analysis than consumer businesses as the customers may be more rational in their purchasing decisions.

Despite these practical constraints on over-detailed reliance on value chain analysis, the concept is useful when the right data is available within time and cost constraints. For a more detailed description of using value chain analysis, see Shepherd (1998).

Like many good ideas, circumstances and time modify the original concept to fit the changing nature of the situation that we first intend to explain. Since first enunciated by Porter the value chains of many companies have seen major changes. For example, Martin (1995) points out that information technology is integral to the value chain. This is exemplified in the way the Internet is transforming trading relationships and redefining the role of those involved in the link between service providers and their customers. Again, there is the growing awareness that information technology can help companies better utilize the knowledge embedded in their processes and people by helping them to better organize, correlate, and retrieve information in a more precise and pertinent form. In businesses more generally and particularly in knowledge-based businesses, people and the whole process of people management and development and knowledge management are also integral to the value chain. Similarly, many businesses depend upon strategic alliances and a more integrated relationship with their suppliers and this too must form an integral part of the value chain model. Finally, it is our view that the value chain should be analysed with the core competence at its heart and Figure 10.3 shows a revision of the original model to reflect both Martin (1995) and our own views as regards people management, information technology, and supplier management.

10.6 Supply chain analysis

Supply chain analysis is an extension of the value chain concept in which the focus is on the value contributed by different players in a supply chain rather than on the different activities of a single enterprise. It is a tool of both internal and external analysis as it reviews the value contributed by each player from raw material supply to final consumer. From the point of view of a single enterprise, the purpose is to review likely profit potential for either backward or forward integration or disintegration.

As an example of supply chain analysis, consider the book supply industry. The

Figure 10.3 Revised value chain

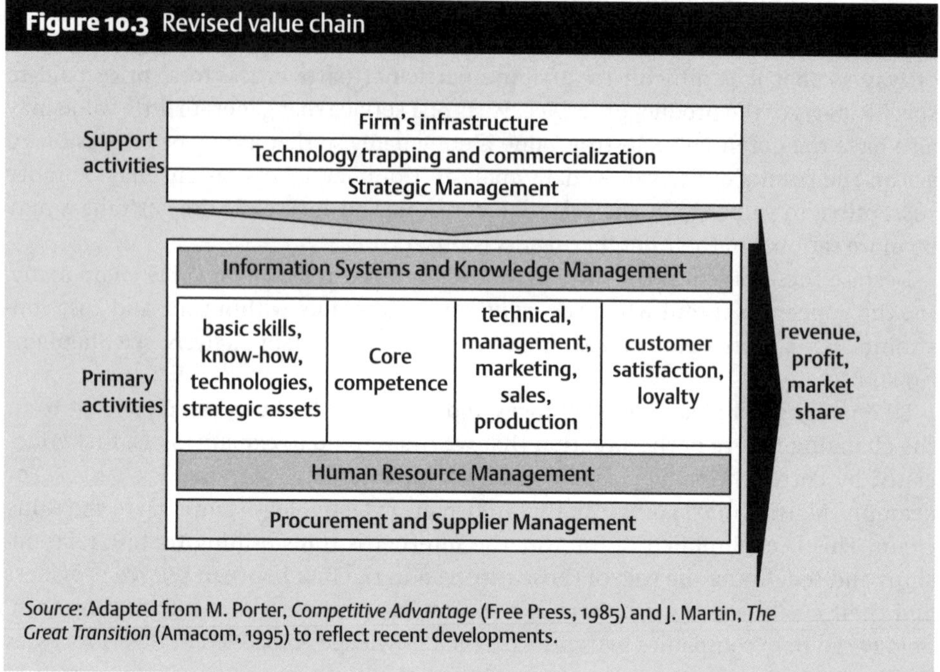

Source: Adapted from M. Porter, *Competitive Advantage* (Free Press, 1985) and J. Martin, *The Great Transition* (Amacom, 1995) to reflect recent developments.

supply chain for books runs from the author, through the publisher, to wholesalers, to retailers, to customers. The author generates the raw material that has some value. The publisher contributes a financial risk by investing in the typesetting, printing, and marketing costs. The wholesalers add value by holding stock and assisting in the distribution process. The retailer holds stock and offers customers the chance to browse before purchase. One publisher discovered that the wholesalers in one European country were returning very high profits whereas their own profit on the same business was small. The publisher also perceived that the value contributed by the wholesalers was modest. The publisher therefore acquired several wholesalers in the country in question so as to capture this profit.

10.7 Identifying core competence

CORE COMPETENCE is defined as 'A technical or management subsystem which integrates diverse technologies, processes, resources and know-how to deliver products and services which confer sustainable and unique competitive advantage and added value to an organisation' (Tampoe 1994).

The core competence of an enterprise is, by definition, hidden and unique. By definition it confers special capability to its owner. An organizational capability often encompasses an organization's core competence and covers a variety of skills, processes, and best practices that convert core competence into products and services. Companies, particularly large companies, may have many capabilities derived from their own extensive resources and their ability to acquire additional resources as needed in the open market. Their core competence, if any, remains unique. The ability to differentiate between general capabilities and true core competence can make the difference between success and failure. The tests for core competence include (Tampoe 1994):

- essential to corporate survival in the short and long term;
- invisible to competitors;
- difficult to imitate;
- unique to the enterprise;
- result from a mix of skills, resources and processes;
- a capability which the organization can sustain over time;
- greater than the competence of an individual;
- essential to the development of core products and eventually to end products;
- essential to the implementation of the strategic intent of the enterprise;
- essential to the strategic choices of the enterprise;
- marketable and commercially viable;
- few in number.

Figure 10.4 illustrates how the concept of core competence differs from and extends previous thinking.

Identifying core competence is much harder than finding the capabilities used by an organization. A starting point for identifying the core competence of an organization is to dissect the different subsystems that make up the total operating entity. Parsons (1960) suggested that an organization might be divided into three main subsystems:

- The Administrative Subsystem which co-ordinates the activities of the organization;
- The Institutional Subsystem which relates the organization to the external world including customers, suppliers, and other stakeholders;

Figure 10.4 The core competence perspective

Traditional Perspective	**Core Competence Perspective**
Market share of present markets	Share of future opportunities
Strategic business unit focus	Corporate competence
Stand-alone	Pattern of alliances
Speed to market	Perseverance towards long-term vision

Source: Adapted from G. Hamel and C. K. Prahalad, *Competing for the Future* (Harvard Business School Press, 1994).

- The Technical Subsystem which, according to Parsons, is: 'The core of what the entity does and which accounts for its distinctive character'.

It therefore makes sense to start the search for the core competence of the organization in its technical subsystem although this may not be where it is eventually found. The reason for this is that the technical subsystem, although unique due to patents and other similar monopoly-providing resources, may not be the eventual source of the organization's competitive strength. In helping organizations identify their core competence, the authors have found that the core competence can reside in any one of these three systems. For example, an asset-based organization found that its core competence was in the technical subsystem and was conceiving, designing, and constructing complex physical networks. Another company with a similar asset profile found its core competence in the administrative subsystem in that its core competence was not in its technical capability but in its ability to manage large volumes of data to gain competitive advantage. A third company in the insurance sector found its core competence in its institutional subsystem in that its core competence was in the way it managed its distribution channels.

Figure 10.5 illustrates how a core competence can be traced for a manufacturing organization. It shows how the different technologies and other skills combine in a core competence that then produces products, sub-components, processes, and knowledge-based person-specific professional services that can be sold directly or incorporated into the process and products. Figure 10.6 shows a core competence

Figure 10.5 The roots of core competence for a typical manufacturing business

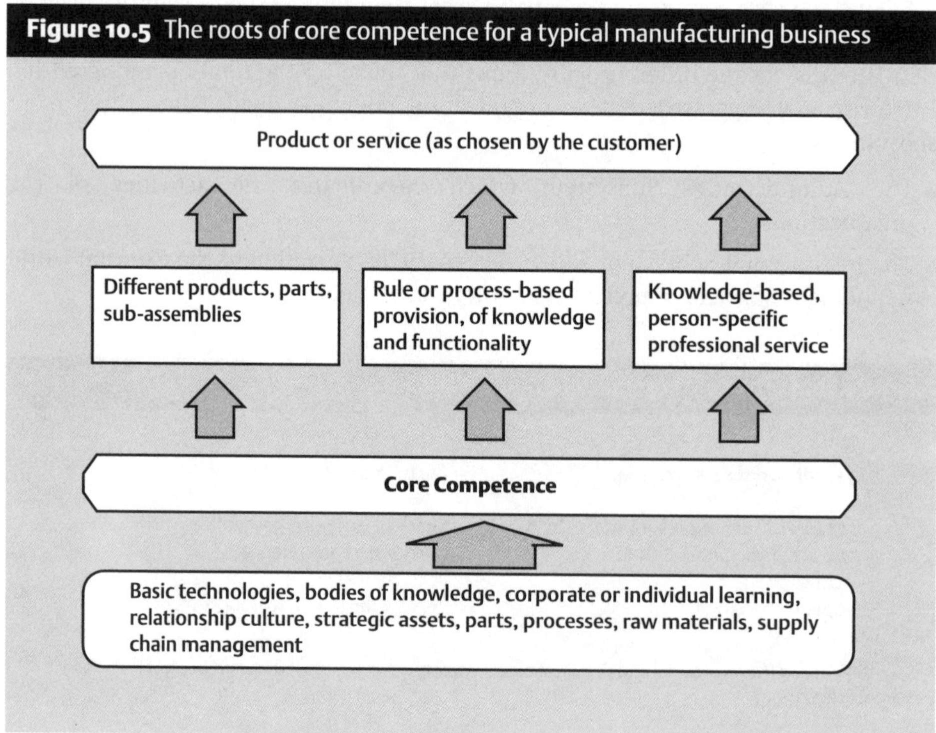

Figure 10.6 The roots of core competence for typical professional services firms

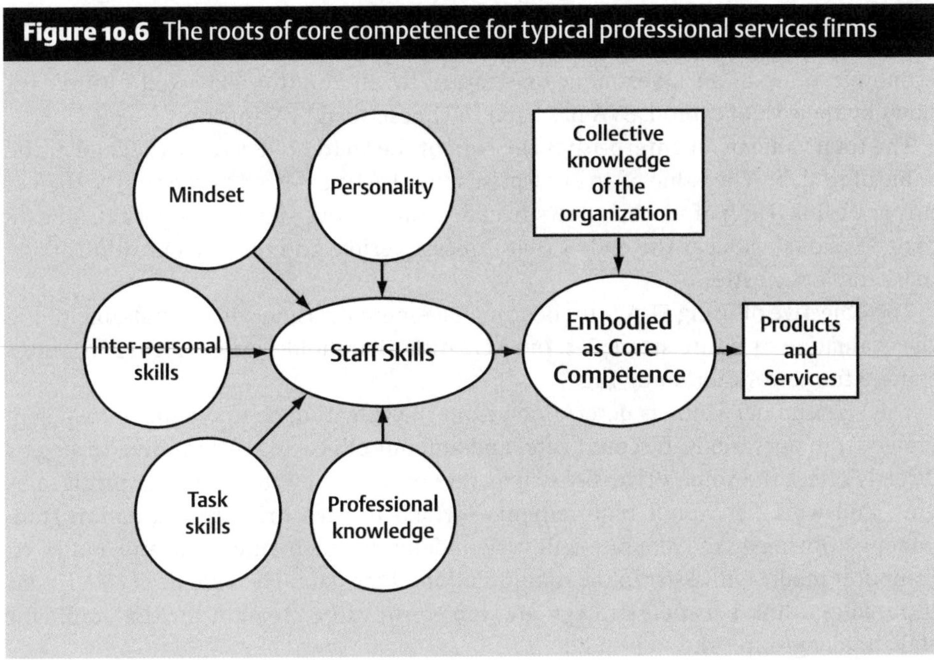

analyser for a professional service organization where the knowledge *is* the business. Here the figure shows that the skills of the staff mingle with the collective knowledge and experience of the organization and its culture to deliver a core competence that is different from that of a similar organization. The culture determines the personality, mindset, and inter-personal skills of the professional staff working for the business and is applied at the time of recruitment and during their working life with the firm.

Core competence has now been used extensively in the field and there is a growing body of literature on how the concept can be used in practice. See, for example, Collis and Montgomery (1995), Tampoe (1994,1998), Campbell and Luchs (1997), Hamel and Heene (1994).

10.8 Shareholder value analysis

STRATEGY is concerned with ensuring the future success of the business and therefore implies a need to define what success means. The traditional measures of business success have included earnings per share (eps), return on investment (ROI), and return on capital employed (ROCE). These measures suffer from shortcomings. All depend on accounting methods that are designed to support reporting requirements rather than long-term value creation. All exclude risk, dividend policy, and the time value of money. Recently many leading businesses have adopted shareholder value analysis (SVA) with a view to avoiding these shortcomings. SVA estimates the economic value of an investment or strategy by discounting expected future cash flows by the cost of capital. SVA has been fully described by Rappaport (1986).

The total value of an enterprise is the sum of the shareholder value (SV) and of the value of its debt. The value of an enterprise may also be assessed as the sum of the net present value (NPV) of its cash flows from operations over a forecast period, an estimated residual value at the end of that forecast period, and the current value of any marketable securities.

The objective of using SVA is to focus management decisions of all kinds, including the evaluation of future strategies, onto creating shareholder value. Figure 10.7 illustrates a framework for doing this.

The Shareholder Value is determined from the valuation components of cash generated from operations, discount rate, and amount of gearing. Alternative strategies directly affect the value drivers—such as rate of sales growth, operating profit margins, and working capital requirements—which in turn drive the valuation components. Obviously the diagram will vary in detail for each enterprise and a tailored computer model will assist in the manipulation of the data. The benefit of SVA is that it provides a link between strategy and long-term value creation for the dominant stakeholder group—the shareholders.

Figure 10.7 Applying shareholder value analysis

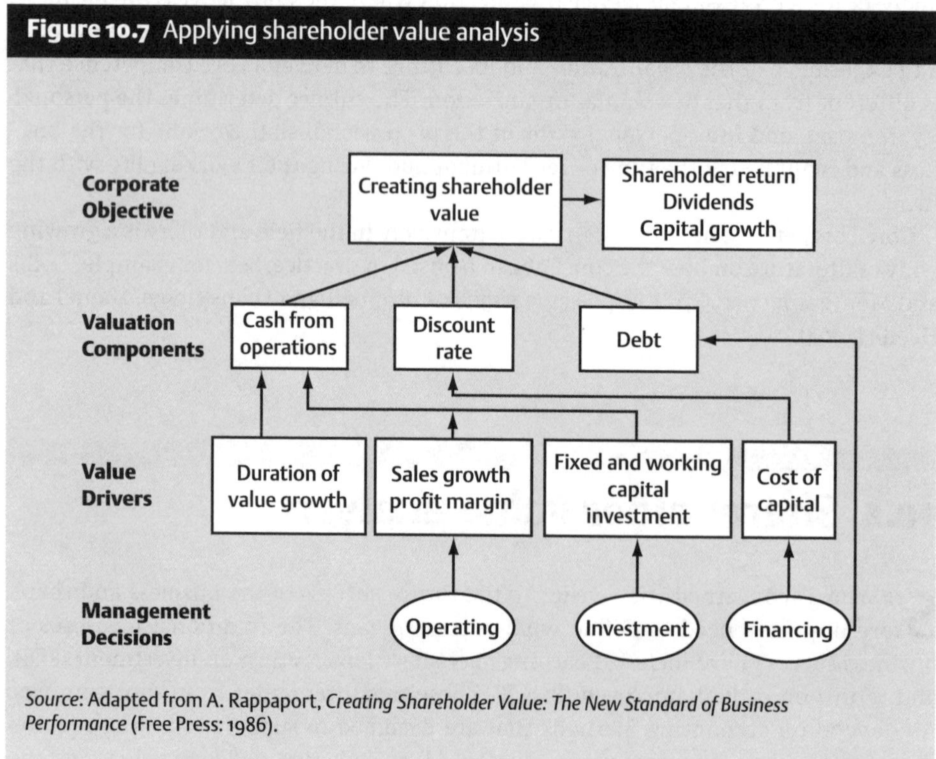

Source: Adapted from A. Rappaport, *Creating Shareholder Value: The New Standard of Business Performance* (Free Press: 1986).

10.9 Distinctive organizational capabilities

As well as analysing the tangible characteristics, there may be value in attempting to focus directly on what makes the particular enterprise distinctive.

Kay (1993) examined distinctive capabilities in his research and claims that such distinctiveness was in practice based on just four sources: architecture, reputation, innovation, and strategic assets. Kay defines architecture as the network of relational contracts, within and around the firm. The value of the architecture rests in the capacity of organizations to create organizational knowledge, to respond flexibly to changing circumstances, and to achieve easy and open exchanges of information. Reputation needs no clarification as a concept. Kay points out that, in many markets, reputation can provide a distinctive capability and suggests ways in which reputations can be enhanced, although this cannot be done in the short term. Kay suggests that innovation is a third source of distinctive capability but points out that the ability to innovate may itself be the result of architecture which allows a continuous process of innovation or enables unusually effective implementation of innovation. He also distinguishes between patent races in which winner takes all and standards battles in which conformity is the key to success. Strategic assets are of three types according to whether they derive from a natural monopoly, the experience curve, or regulation/licensing. Kay's analysis echoes and gives more structure to issues which may well have emerged from the resource audit (Sect. 10.2).

The people, culture, or skills base of an enterprise can be seen as offering a distinctive capability. In their book, Ulrich and Lake (1990) make the point that many organizations have developed the ability to manage people to gain competitive advantage. The issues here are many. First and foremost, the organization must be able to change employee opinions and attitudes and ways of working to meet the competitive environment in which the business operates. This can mean radically changing the organization's values and the values of those working in it. For example, the newly privatized utilities in the UK had to adopt a commercial stance and be accountable to shareholders once they were privatized. However, the ethos of these organizations was one where public service values predominated. Getting staff to evaluate investment programmes and other behaviours and expenditure along cost-effective lines proved very difficult and was only achieved after significant downsizing and in-house training. Getting technical specialists to understand that their knowledge that was once freely available to all suppliers and users in the industry needed to be harnessed and used as a competitive advantage was also hard to accomplish. Historically, they freely shared their knowledge with manufacturers and others in the industry.

Implementation of a new strategy is likely to require that the capabilities of the organization are enhanced or changed. The assessment of capabilities is therefore likely to provide the facts for planning the necessary changes in structure, processes, and culture.

The techniques described up to this point are mainly used to assess single businesses. The two final techniques are specifically for assessing multiple businesses.

10.10 Assessing parenting advantage

ONE of the important questions for internal assessment in multi-business companies is to assess how the parent or headquarters adds value to its subsidiaries. Goold and Campbell (Goold *et al.* 1994) have been particularly associated with tackling this question directly by examining the concept of **Parenting Advantage**. In this view, the headquarters of large multi-business enterprises are competing with each other in their ability to add value to the businesses in their portfolio. It is the duty of the headquarters of an enterprise to understand how it is that it adds value to its subsidiaries. It can then choose to be the parent only to those businesses for which it is a suitable parent. This can provide a rationale for acquisition and divestment.

Figure 10.8 shows how the concept of parenting advantage requires a good fit between a parent and the businesses in its portfolio. The 'fit' between parent and the businesses in its portfolio will tend to decline over time as competitive parents develop appropriate parenting skills. Choices about parenting advantage seek both to make the parent more suitable to its portfolio and to align the portfolio to the existing parenting skills. The overall aim is to maintain parental advantage over time in the light of changes in the external business environment and the activities of other potential parents.

This way of thinking requires consideration of exactly how the parent can add value to its subsidiaries. Goold *et al.* found in their research that successful parents tended to understand their pattern and style of parenting and to be able to describe these coherently. Four possible methods of parental value creation are:

Stand-alone influence:

The headquarters is able to influence the management and operations of the separate businesses directly by reason of superior knowledge of the business or depth of experience;

Linkage influence:

The headquarters influences the relationships between the different businesses to their overall benefit;

Central functions and services:

The headquarters provides common services and functions which are shared by the businesses and offer better value for money than the individual businesses could provide for themselves;

Figure 10.8 Parenting advantage

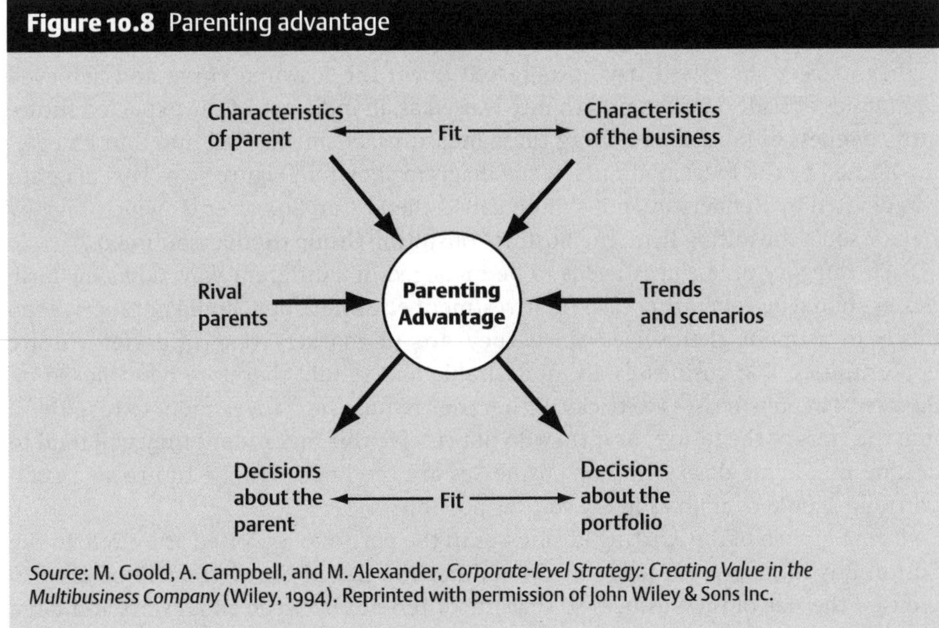

Source: M. Goold, A. Campbell, and M. Alexander, *Corporate-level Strategy: Creating Value in the Multibusiness Company* (Wiley, 1994). Reprinted with permission of John Wiley & Sons Inc.

Corporate development:

The role of headquarters relates specifically to creating or acquiring new businesses for the group and divesting businesses which no longer fit.

It is apparent that the concept of parenting advantage at the very least causes a company to consider its reason for existing in its present form. It does not provide clear prescriptive answers.

For further examples of the use of parenting advantage, see Campbell and Goold (1998).

10.11 Portfolio analysis

PORTFOLIO analysis is a concept that enjoyed great popularity in the 1970s. It has since been criticized on a number of grounds. Portfolio analysis compares the characteristics of the businesses in the portfolio. There is an analogy with an investment portfolio in which investment decisions are made after categorizing the investments according to their characteristics. The overall purpose is to improve the balance of the portfolio so that cash flows from some kinds of business are reinvested in others with greater potential.

Portfolio management is based on an analysis of business by relative market share and market growth rate. Market Share (relative to competitors) is chosen as a surrogate indicator of likely relative cost level on the assumption that those with higher market share will have progressed down the learning curve and achieved economies of scale. Market growth rate is used as an indicator of the expected future attractiveness of the market. Using these measures, businesses fall into four categories defined by the four quadrants of the diagram shown in Figure 10.9. This diagram was devised by Henderson and is often called the Boston Box after its wide usage by Henderson's consulting firm, the Boston Consulting Group (Henderson 1984).

Each category of business needs to be managed in a different way. *Cash Cow* businesses should be generating cash for investment elsewhere but should not receive too much investment themselves since they are in markets that offer few future opportunities. *Dog* businesses are undesirable and should therefore be disposed of. *Question Marks* businesses are tricky. Either they require high investment to turn them into the stars of the future, or if they do not receive this investment they will tend to decline into being dogs. The *Star* businesses are the hopes for the future so a good portfolio should contain as many stars as possible.

Normally each of the existing businesses in the portfolio is plotted as a circle in the Boston Box in its present position. Sometimes the size of the circle may be used to indicate the size of the business so that the difference between small stars and large dogs can be clearly seen. It is also possible to plot future estimated positions under alternative strategies.

Other consulting firms have produced their own variations of this technique but the two axes are always variants on attractiveness of the industry and the relative strength in that industry. For a good description of some of these techniques, see Faulkner (1998).

Figure 10.9 Portfolio analysis

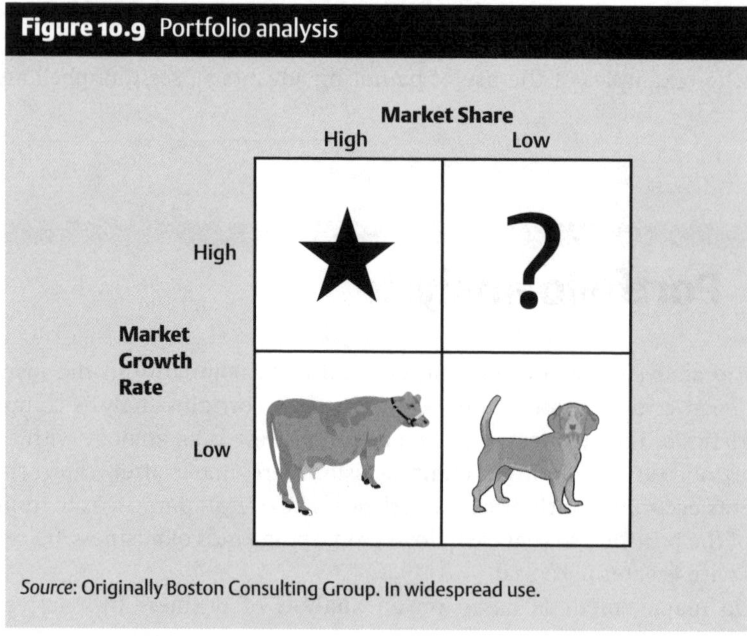

Source: Originally Boston Consulting Group. In widespread use.

Portfolio analysis may sometimes work well but it has been criticized for being naive. Some of the more important snags in practice are:

- 'Markets' are difficult to define with lots of overlaps and complex segmentation.
- Many portfolios in real businesses consist of a high percentage of dog businesses and few, if any star businesses. Portfolio analysis offers little help in these circumstances.
- Contrary to portfolio planning theory, cash cows do seem to need investment. If investment is held back, profits often drop rapidly. Conversely, careful investment in cash cows may often bring better returns at lower risk than investment in stars or question marks.

For a particularly clear and penetrating analysis and criticism of portfolio analysis, see McKiernan (1992).

These criticisms mean that portfolio analysis is unlikely to be adequate if used as the only basis for determining corporate strategy. Matrix analyses of this kind are still quite widely used, however, and have value in comparing and contrasting the various businesses in the portfolio. This must be a useful exercise in the internal analysis of a multiple business enterprise, if only to increase familiarity with the various businesses and to raise discussion of relevant issues.

10.12 Summary: choosing the right frameworks for internal analysis

It is hard to be prescriptive about choosing the right frameworks. However, it is possible to offer some guidelines. It is likely that core competence will form the centre of the analysis so it probably makes sense to:

- start with some simple techniques such as resource audit and cost and profit analysis to gather some basic information, scope the work, and understand the issues;
- consider all the frameworks within the context of the enterprise and identify which are likely to be useful and for which it is likely to be possible to find data;
- define what competitive capabilities the organization needs to achieve its main goals and to list the various elements covering processes, people skills, technologies, resources, and so on that are intimately linked to the competitive capability;
- identify the subsystems that support the competitive capability and the subsystems that are secondary but still essential to achieving competitive capability;
- identify the core competence relative to the competitive capability and dissect the core competence into its constituents.

- determine whether any modifications are needed to enhance or improve the core competence;
- refit the core competence into the other capabilities, fine-tuning them as this is done;
- take a systemic view of the new re-jigged organization and the competitive capability to ensure that it is what was originally needed;
- adjust the methods of analysis in the light of what is found.

References

Ambrosini, V. with Johnson, G., and Scholes, K.(eds.) (1998), *Exploring Techniques of Analysis and Evaluation in Strategic Management* (London: Prentice Hall).

Camp, R.C. (1987) *Benchmarking: The search for industry best practices that lead to superior performance* (Milwaukee: Quality Press).

Campbell. A., and Goold. M. (1998) *Corporate-Level Strategy*, in Ambrosini *et al.* (1998).

—— and Luchs, K. S. (1997) *Core Competency Based Strategy* (London: International Thomson Business Press).

Collis, D. J., and Montgomery, C. A. (1995) 'Competing on Resources: Strategy for the 1990s', *Harvard Business Review*, July–Aug.

Faulkner, D. (1998) 'Portfolio Matrices', in Ambrosini *et al.* (1998).

Goold, M., Campbell, A. and Alexander, M. (1994) *Corporate-Level Strategy: Creating Value in the Multibusiness Company* (New York: Wiley).

Hamel, G., and Heene, A. (eds.) (1994) *Competence-Based Competition* (Chichester: Wiley).

—— and Prahalad, C. K. (1994) *Competing for the Future* (Boston: Harvard Business School Press).

Henderson, B. (1984) *The Logic of Business Strategy* (New York: Ballinger)

Karlöf, B., and Östblom, S. (1993) *Benchmarking—A Signpost to Excellence in Quality and Productivity* (New York: Wiley)

Kay, J. (1993) *The Foundations of Corporate Success* (Oxford: Oxford University Press)

Martin, J. (1995) *The Great Transition* (New York: Amacom).

McKiernan, P. (1992) *Strategies of Growth: Maturity, Recovery and Internationalization* (London: Routledge).

Parsons, T. (1960) *Structure and Process in Modern Societies* (New York: Free Press).

Porter, M. E. (1985) *Competitive Advantage* (New York: Free Press)

Rappaport, A. (1986) *Creating Shareholder Value: The New Standard of Business Performance* (New York: Free Press).

Shepherd, A. (1998) 'Understanding and using value chain analysis', in Ambrosini *et al.* (1998).

Tampoe, M. (1994) 'Exploiting the Core Competences of your Organisation', *Long Range Planning*, 27/4: 66–77.

—— (1998) 'Getting to Know your Organisation's Core Competences', in Ambrosini *et al.* (1998).

Ulrich, D., and Lake D. (1990) *Organizational Capability: Competing from the Inside Out* (New York: Wiley).

Watson, G. H. (1993*a*) *Strategic Benchmarking—How to rate your Company's Performance against the World's Best* (New York: Wiley)

—— (1993*b*) 'How Process Benchmarking Supports Corporate Strategy', *Planning Review (USA)*, Jan.–Feb.: 12–15

Wilson, I. (1994) 'Strategic Planning Isn't Dead—It Changed', *Long Range Planning*, 27/4, Aug.

Chapter 11
Strategic Choice

11.1 Importance of choice in the strategy formulation process

STRATEGIC choice is the third logical element of the strategy formulation process. Choice is at the centre of strategy formulation. If there are no choices to be made, there can be little value in thinking about strategy at all. On the other hand, there will always, in practice, be limits on the range of possible choices. In general, small enterprises tend to be limited by their resources, whereas large enterprises find it difficult to change quickly and so tend to be constrained by their past. In large corporations, managers may find their range of choice limited because some choices are made at a higher level or in another country. In the public sector, the genuine strategic choices may be made by politicians so that the role of the manager is limited to devising how best to implement strategies rather than to ponder fundamental choices of future direction for themselves.

Even when managers are apparently free to make strategic choices, results may eventually depend as much on chance and opportunity as on the deliberate choices of those managers. When considering future strategies, it may seem that there are clear choices to be made. When reflecting on outcomes in retrospect, it is often clear that events, and particularly unexpected events, played a major role in determining results. When considering choice, it is necessary to take a prescriptive view. Descriptive ways of thinking may help to explain the outcomes after the event.

In a tidy logical world, any process of choice could be rationally divided into four steps—identify options, evaluate the options against preference criteria, select the best option, and then take action. This suggests that identifying and choosing options can be done purely analytically. In practice, it may be difficult to identify all possible options with equal clarity or at the same time. Unexpected events can create new opportunities, destroy foreseen opportunities, or alter the balance of advantage between opportunities. Identifying and evaluating options is a useful approach but it has limitations. It is necessary to remember that the future may evolve differently from any of the options.

Good strategic choices have to be challenging enough to keep ahead of competitors but also have to be achievable. Analysis has an important role in making strategic choice but judgement and skill are also critical. For instance, sometimes it may be better to delay making a decision whereas at other times a wrong decision may be better than no decision. Strategic choices that keep options open may be preferable in an uncertain future to defined strategies that depend for their success on uncertain events happening. Such judgements require wisdom as much as analytical skill.

These words of caution lay the ground for this chapter that might otherwise seem to make the process of strategic choice sound too mechanistic.

Since strategic choice tends to be so fuzzy, it is useful to define the words being used. We shall adopt the following definitions.

- *Choice* and *strategic choice* refer to the process of selecting one option for implementation.
- An *option* is a course of action that it appears possible to take. The simplest form of choice is therefore between taking an option and not taking it—doing it or not doing it. Most choices have more shades of possibility than this.
- A *strategic option* is a set of related options (typically combining options for product/markets and resources) that form a potential strategy. For instance, it might be an option to enter a new market in a new country. The entry to that market with a chosen method of distribution and known way of acquiring necessary distribution resources—in fact, a complete business plan of how to enter the new market successfully—would become a strategic option.
- *Chosen Strategy* is the strategic option that has been chosen. The nature of this forms the content of strategy and is addressed in Part IV.

11.2 Structure of strategic choice

FIGURE 11.1 reproduces the right-hand half of Figure 6.3 introduced in Chapter 6. It shows how the three logical elements of the strategy formulation process interlock. The shaded background is a reminder of the importance of context as determining the issues to be resolved by strategic choice.

Figure 11.2 expands the detail to illustrate the significance of the overlaps. The common ground between any two circles is of some interest but it is only where all three circles overlap that logically viable options exist. The chosen strategy emerges as the chosen viable option. It is where the differing requirements of intent and assessment are most fully met—that is, where the three logical elements overlap.

The areas where any two circles overlap are also of interest. The criteria for choice derive from intent and assessment. Feasible options may exist which are not aligned to strategic intent. This, of course, may raise the question of whether the strategic

Figure 11.1 Results of the strategy formulation process

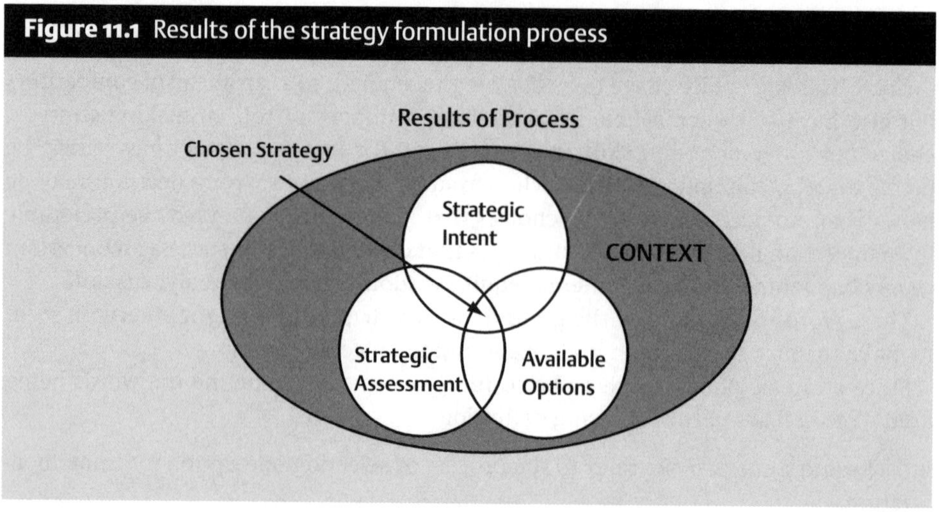

Figure 11.2 Choosing a strategy from among strategic options

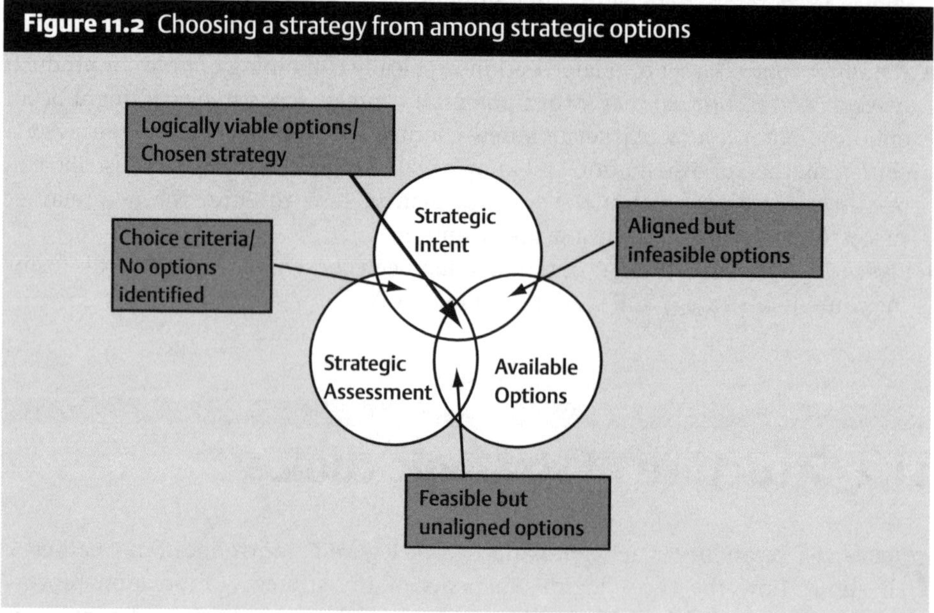

intent should be changed. Infeasible options may seem highly attractive and may have powerful supporters, so the reasons why they are infeasible may need to be carefully argued with clear evidence in support. Choices of what not to do may sometimes be as important as choosing what to do.

In practice, the process for choosing a strategy may be structured something like Figure 11.3, although the reality is likely to be much messier. The structure of this chapter is also based on this figure.

The process of choice starts by identifying available options. The chosen strategy

Figure 11.3 Structure for making strategic choice

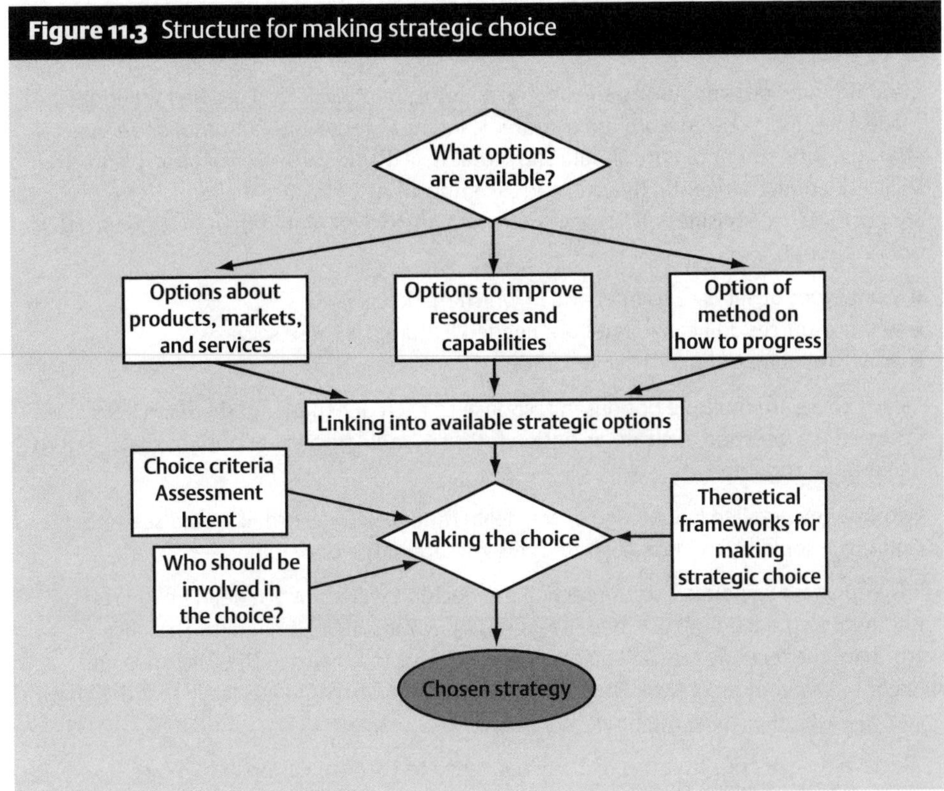

will have to answer the questions 'what', 'how', 'why', 'who', and 'when', so each option will provide provisional answers to each of these questions.

There are likely to be different kinds of options. Figure 11.3 shows three types—products/services/markets, resources/capabilities, and method of progress—that are typical but not necessarily exhaustive.

11.3 Options for markets and products/services

THE most obvious type of option relates to which products or services to offer in which markets. Igor Ansoff was the first to suggest the diagram shown in Figure 11.4 for structuring this decision.

The axes of the diagram are product (including services and any form of offering), market need (which can be any group of potential customers whether defined by their needs, inclinations, or income bracket), and market geography (geographical

Box 11.1 Example of options and a strategic choice

In April 1999, Ford announced the agreed acquisition of Kwik Fit. Ford had therefore made a strategic choice. Ford has a strategic intent to move into automotive services. A strategic assessment of Ford should show that its existing resources of large plants and skills in design, marketing, finance, and assembly of new cars are inadequate to support a service business. The decision to acquire Kwikfit would then be made from options about:

- what types of services to offer and in which markets;
- what resources and capabilities are needed to support these services;
- how to acquire or build these resources.

Clearly there are multiple options in response to each question and there are links between the question. A strategic option for Ford would be a set of options that seem to make sense together.

Without any detailed knowledge of the deliberations within Ford, it would seem that Figure 11.3 could be used to illustrate the structure of the decision.

It is important to notice that in practice the decision will also have been influenced by irrational elements not illustrated in Figure 11.3. For instance, it happens that Alex Trotman, the recently retired Chairman of Ford, and Tom Farmer, the Chairman and majority shareholder of Kwik Fit, are both natives of Edinburgh. It is likely that they have known each other for some time.

We have no evidence that this had any relevance to Ford's decision in this case. The point is that people and events often influence strategic choices. Structured diagrams such as Figures 11.2 and 11.3 only show part of the truth.

location). The model defines four cells for the present market geography. The top-left of these cells represents the present status of the business. The possible future choices about products and markets can be represented as movements within or away from this cell.

One set of choices is possible within the existing product/market set.

- 'Do nothing'—that is, continue present strategies. This strategy is important as it is usual to compare any proposed change with the 'do nothing' option as a baseline. The 'do nothing' option is rarely viable for the long term as it is likely that competitors will gradually take the market by improving their products, their processes, or their relationships.
- 'Withdraw'—leave the market by closing down or selling out. This appears to be a negative option but may be necessary to focus available resources into areas of greater strength. It is common in declining markets to see some of the competitors selling out to others who can operate the combined operation more cheaply.
- 'Consolidate'—attempt to hold market share in existing markets. This is a defen-

sive option which usually involves cutting costs and perhaps prices. It is more common in markets that are mature or beginning to decline.

- 'Market Penetration'—increase market share of the same market. This is a more aggressive option and usually involves investing in product improvement, advertising, or channel development. Acquiring the businesses of competitors who are withdrawing from the market may be a necessary related resource option.

Other possible options (which involve moving out of the front left-hand top cell of Fig. 11.4) are either to develop or acquire new products (product development) or to address new market needs (market development). These two options are easy to understand at the generic level but clearly have to be spelt out in detail before they have any practical meaning for a real discussion in a particular context.

Diversification is entry into new markets with new products. Diversification may be of two kinds—related and unrelated. Related diversification again divides into backward, forward, and horizontal integration. Backward integration is a move towards suppliers and raw materials in the same overall business. An example of this would be a brewer acquiring malting facilities or growing hops. Forward integration is a move towards the market place or customers in the same overall business. An example of this would be a manufacturer acquiring retail outlets or a hop grower beginning to brew his own beer. Horizontal integration is a lateral move into a closely related business such as selling by-products.

Diversification which is not of any of the above types is 'unrelated'. Even unrelated diversification usually has (or is thought to have) some degree of synergy (or fit) with the original business. Examples of synergy are the ability to share facilities—a sales force, for instance—or a balance in the timing of cash flow. Often the fit is less than expected, so less synergy is achieved than was anticipated.

There is a long history of research into how successful diversification has been. Diversification was a particularly popular strategy in the 1960s when there were a

Figure 11.4 Options for markets and products

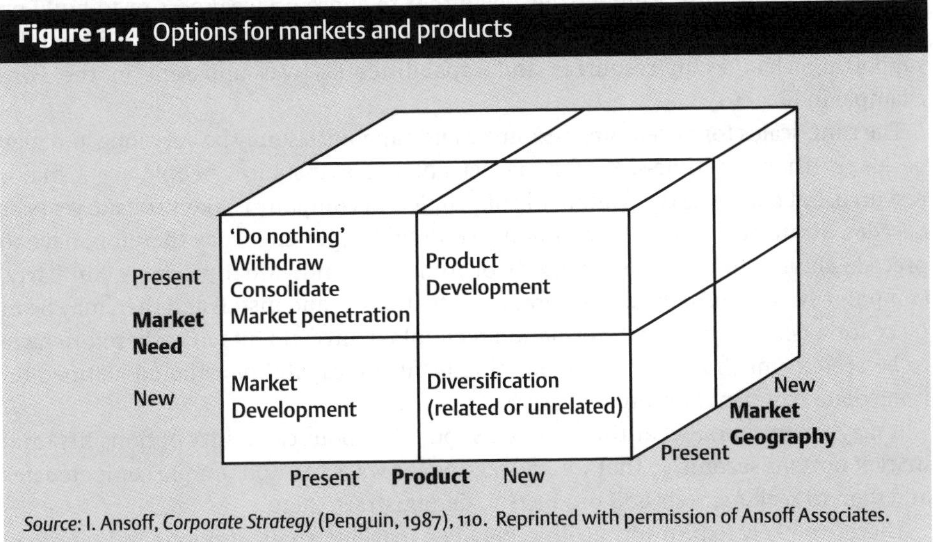

Source: I. Ansoff, *Corporate Strategy* (Penguin, 1987), 110. Reprinted with permission of Ansoff Associates.

number of very well-known and apparently successful conglomerates. Porter, for example, studied the 1950–86 diversification of thirty-three leading US companies and concluded (Porter 1987) that the track record of diversification was poor and that in many cases acquisitions were subsequently divested. More generally, it seems that diversified businesses grow faster and growth tends to be greatest if the diversification is unrelated. However, related diversification tends to be more profitable. In general, there is less fit than anticipated so that the benefits expected are often not fully realized.

While research may measure how successful different forms of market or product development are in general, the management choice has to focus on the relative attractiveness of available options. If the present position is bad enough, even relatively risky alternatives may be preferable to doing nothing.

The third dimension of Figure 11.4 represents choices about geographical markets and represent a third dimension of choice.

11.4 Options for building resources, capabilities, and competence

JUST as strategic assessment was necessarily concerned with both the internal and external perspectives, so strategic choice has to consider options about resources, capabilities, and competencies as well as those for markets and products. It may well be, therefore, that the strategic assessment has identified strengths and weaknesses in existing resources and capabilities in comparison with competitors. This may lead to identifying the improvements needed either to shore up weakness or to build on existing strengths. It is also likely that potential market/product options will require supporting changes in resources and capabilities (as was apparent in the Ford example in Box 11.1).

The time-scales for developing resources and capabilities may be very long and may be longer than the time-scale for market entry. For instance, people are a major resource, but changing the overall mix of people in a company is likely to take years or decades. Strategic options about building skills and experience may therefore have to precede choices to enter new markets or to develop individual products. Similarly, computer systems usually take several years to develop and install and then may be in place for a decade or more. Information technology investments may therefore have to be seen as much as a strategic building of future capability as being justified on immediate cost-benefit grounds.

It may be, of course, that the thinking should be about capability options first and market options second, so that we are looking for ways to build unique competencies and then to seek markets and products to demonstrate them.

There are likely to be multiple links between market/product options and resource/

capability options. Entry into new markets is likely to require acquiring access to new distribution channels and product support. New products may require a fundamental rethink of development resources and field staff skills. While the resource needs are the most obvious, the capabilities needed to succeed may be much more subtle. For instance, the resources may need to be world-class and all the pieces may have to fit into a working whole.

11.5 Options in methods of implementation

THERE are likely to be options in methods of implementation. There are four main methods by which companies can grow their capabilities—internal development, acquisition, contractual arrangements and strategic alliances.

Internal development

Internal development is perhaps the most obvious approach to growth. It involves developing the necessary skills among existing staff and acquiring the necessary production capacity piecemeal. The main disadvantage of internal development is that it takes time during which competitors may move faster or opportunities may be lost. On the other hand, the risks may be lower than for other methods.

Acquisition

Acquisition is a very common implementation option, particularly in countries such as the UK and USA where the structure of financial markets and equity ownership makes take-overs relatively easy to achieve. Take-overs and mergers have sometimes been so dominant as the means of implementing strategies that 'M&A' has sometimes become almost a synonym for 'strategy'. There can be real advantages to acquisition, particularly if there is a good fit with what is acquired. Synergy (by which the whole is greater than the sum of the parts) can occur, although less often than expected. The disadvantages of mergers are that they can cause deep operational and psychological turmoil which can distract the people who have to make them work. Competitors can take advantage of this turmoil, as they are free to concentrate on customers rather than on internal changes. One real problem is that the thinking about mergers and acquisitions is often less than objective. Senior managers and professional advisers tend to benefit from mergers in the short term whatever the long-term outcome. There is also a tendency for the strategic rationale for the merger to be lost in the excitement of the chase. Often, too, pressure from competing acquirers can cause the price to rise to too high a level. Many acquisitions may be beneficial at the right price but may destroy shareholder value at too high a price.

Contractual arrangements

Contractual arrangements come in many different forms. *Consortia* are groups of companies that form a joint entity for a specific purpose—such as building the channel tunnel. When the project is finished, the consortium breaks up and the separate partners may find themselves competing, possibly in different consortia, for the next project. This form is common in the civil engineering and defence industries. *Franchising* is another form of contractual arrangement and is commonest in retailing. Well-known High Street names such as the Body Shop and McDonalds are franchises. The franchisee pays the franchiser a fee for services and royalties, typically for use of the company name, business approaches, and central advertising. The franchisee is half-way between an employee and an independent entrepreneur with his risk limited by the success of the brand name and by the support and advice provided by the franchiser. *Licensing* is a third form of contractual arrangement. A common example is when a small inventive company licenses its product or patent to be manufactured and marketed by others. This can allow quick growth by avoiding the need to build manufacturing or distribution capability. At the same time, the intellectual property rights for the invention are retained. Licensing is probably most frequent in high technology businesses and the creative arts. *Agents* are a long-standing means of doing business, particularly in foreign countries or specialized markets where volumes of business may be too low to justify a permanent presence. The agent is familiar with local requirements and calls for additional support from the principal when opportunities arise. The difficulties with agents include conflicts of interest when the same agent acts for competing principals or is simply inert.

All the above arrangements have in common the need for a written contract which binds the two or more parties into a clear agreement as to who will do what and pay what. Such contracts will normally have a defined duration. The contracts can be very varied to suit the needs of each individual. Disputes can be handled through the courts, by agreed arbitration procedures, or by not renewing the contract at the expiry of the contracted term.

Strategic alliances and partnerships

Strategic alliances and partnerships have come into vogue over the last ten years. While there may be contracts between the parties, there is a wider intention to co-operate at a strategic level, to share information, and to work together in a way that goes beyond a clear contractual arrangement. It is argued that in a rapidly changing world, strategic alliances are the only way in which the necessary speed of response and global spread can be achieved. There are dangers in strategic alliances in that the objectives of the two parties may drift apart over time and the arrangement is hard to terminate neatly because of the lack of firm contracts. The Rover–Honda alliance is an example of an arrangement that seemed to work well for a time but ended messily when Rover was acquired by BMW.

Strategic alliances have been much studied in recent years. See, for instance, Lorange and Roos (1992), Egan (1995), or Faulkner (1992).

11.6 Grouping options into strategic options

Options about product/markets, resources/capabilities, and the method of implementation have to be combined into a much smaller number of strategic options. This may be a bottom-up or top-down process. The bottom-up approach implies linking what might be done in detail into potential strategies that seem to make wider sense. The top-down approach means testing general ideas of future direction against detailed options. In practice, the process is likely to combine top-down and bottom-up thinking.

11.7 General tests of strategic options

Each strategic option has then to pass two tests based on the logic of Figures 11.2 and 11.3. It must be:

- *Aligned* in that it conforms to the strategic intent. This test answers the question 'Does this option take us towards where we want to go?'
- *Feasible* in that the capabilities and resources necessary for success can be made available. This answers the question: 'Will it work?' This test is likely to draw on the analysis of the strategic assessment. The tests of feasibility require serious consideration of what will be required to implement the necessary changes (see Part V).

A third test goes beyond logic to answer the question: 'Will this option be *acceptable?'* Acceptable means that it will win the approval of both those who will have to approve it and those who will have to implement it. This question relates closely to Section 11.8 below.

Any strategic option has to pass all three tests to be viable. If more than one strategic option passes these tests, they may have to be compared with each other to choose the 'best'. The judgement has to take into account both tangible characteristics such as risk and return and less tangible matters such as match to values and culture.

In practice, the number of strategic options is rarely large. The tests, though important, cannot be completely objective.

11.8 Who should be involved with the choice?

STRATEGIC choice is as much a political as a logical process. In a book it is easier to describe the logic than the politics. Each context will have its own pattern of politics which will be important in determining both how and what strategic decisions are made. Questions that may help to reveal the political reality include:

- Who stands to gain or lose from a particular strategic choice?
- What existing coalitions exist and how will these be affected?
- Who may be seen to have originated or supported particular choices or arguments?

Ultimately it is likely that a strategic choice will need approval by the board but this may well be the formal confirmation of a decision that has been made before the actual meeting. For a clear and realistic exposition of how to influence committees, see Parkinson (1960). His advice, in summary, is to focus attention on the members of the committee who are undecided or even perhaps fail to understand the issues.

Formal approval is necessary but no strategy will be effective unless it also has the active support of a far wider range of people who both understand the proposals and are prepared to work to make the necessary changes happen. This issue will be addressed in Part V but one way of achieving this support is to involve these people in the process of making the decision.

Both the logic and politics of the choice may be heavily dependent on the context. In some cases, strategy is driven solely by competitive advantage. In other cases, there may be a strategic intent or vision that determines long-term direction so that the strategic choices are about means rather than direction.

11.9 Theoretical frameworks for assisting strategic choice

SEVERAL attempts have been made to provide theoretical frameworks for making strategic choices. One that was highly influential when first devised was the concept of Generic Strategies (Porter 1985). Porter suggested that the most fundamental choices facing any business are the scope of the markets that it attempts to serve and how it attempts to compete in these chosen markets. The scope can either be broad—tackling the whole market—or narrow—tackling only a particular part of the market. He also suggested that there were only two effective ways of competing in a market.

Companies achieve competitive advantage either by having the lowest product cost (note: this is not the same as having the lowest price) or by having products which are different in ways which are valued by customers. The axes of Figure 11.5 are therefore the scope of the chosen market and the chosen basis of competition.

The four quadrants of Figure 11.5 suggest four possible generic strategies. If the scope is narrow, the distinction between cost and differentiation becomes unimportant so Porter defined just three 'generic' strategies—cost leadership, differentiation, and focus (which combined the two lower squares in the diagram).

Note that differentiation implies a difference in the perception by clients of the product, whereas focus implies a difference in target market. In the Porter view of generic strategy, the worst crime (weakest strategy) is being 'stuck in the middle', that is, being muddled in either of the two dimensions of Figure 11.5.

Practising managers were initially enthusiastic about generic strategies when first published and the ideas were used extensively. Gradually, however, it became clear that reality was less black and white in its distinction between differentiation and cost. There are very few companies that can ignore cost however different their product. Equally, there are very few who will admit that their product is the same as all the others. David Sainsbury, in a public discussion with Michael Porter, pointed out that the Sainsbury's slogan 'Good food costs less at Sainsbury's' was a clear statement of being stuck in the middle but had also proved a successful strategy for Sainsbury's over a long period of time.

Porter's Generic Strategy model has been extended into the Strategy Clock (see Fig. 11.6). This allows for combinations of the original generic strategies.

Figure 11.5 Generic strategies

Competitive Scope		**Basis of Competitive Advantage**: Lower Cost	Differentiation
	Broad Scope	1. Cost leadership	2. Differentiation
	Narrow Scope	3*a*. Cost focus	3*b*. Differentiation focus

Source: Reprinted with the permission of The Free Press, a division of Simon & Schuster, from *Competitive Advantage: Creating and Sustaining Superior Performance* by Michael E. Porter. Copyright © 1985, 1998 by Michael E. Porter.

Box 11.2 Examples of generic strategies

Porter used the car industry as an example of generic strategies in practice.

Toyota is (or was at the time) the low cost producer in the industry. Toyota achieves its cost leadership strategy by adopting lean production, careful choice and control of suppliers, efficient distribution, and low servicing costs from a quality product. Note how the cost leadership must be in all aspects of the business (or value chain).

BMW is an example of a differentiation strategy. BMW still serves a relatively wide range of the total market but its cars are differentiated in the eyes of the customer who is prepared to pay a higher price for a BMW than for a Toyota, for instance, of similar specification.

Morgan is an example of a Focus strategy. It only addresses a very small part of the market—(i.e. those who enjoy getting wet and like the sound of an engine more than conversation!). Each of these three companies has been successful by pushing a particularly generic strategy successfully.

Figure 11.6 The strategy clock

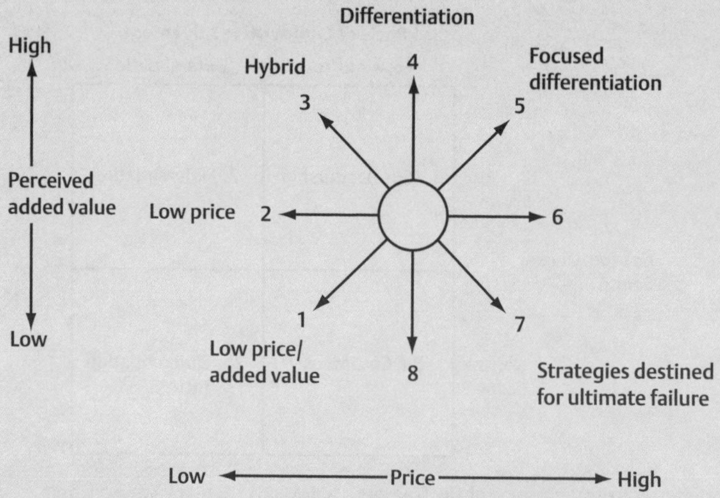

Source: Based on the work of Cliff Bowman. This version from G. Johnson and K. Scholes, *Exploring Corporate Strategy*, 4th edn. (London: Prentice Hall, 1997). Reproduced with permission.

The important addition is the 'hybrid' strategy that is an optimal balance between price and the added value perceived by the customer. This coincides with experience when purchasing household goods. The offerings may often fall into three broad categories. There are 'cheap' offerings which give minimal facilities and appeal to customers to whom price is the most important issue. At the other end of the scale are the 'luxury' offerings that have demonstrably high quality or numerous features and appeal to customers who want the best and the most differentiated. In the middle are the 'good-value' offerings that compromise between the two extremes by offering a good trade-off between price and value. This category often accounts for a sizeable percentage of the total market. The Sainsbury's slogan 'Good food costs less at Sainsbury's' can be seen as an attempt to capture this middle segment. Sainsbury's was the leading food retailer in southern England for many years. If it has lost this position this would seem to be because its original strategy has been successfully imitated rather than because it was a poor strategy.

11.10 Strategic choices in the case examples

THE ICL case example illustrates how a strategic choice was made in a period of a few months. It gives some indications of the strategic options open to ICL at the time and also how the crisis broadened the options that could be considered. The case example also shows how creditors, potential partners, the government, and a new management team were all relevant both to the choice that was made and to how that choice was made.

The relevance of different stakeholder groups to making strategic choice is also clear in the Nolan, Norton case example. In this case, the strategic choice about general future direction was made over a period of years but the eventual choice of a specific partner was necessarily made in a period of just a few weeks.

Marks & Spencer clearly have a large number of options for markets and products on a global basis. This does not necessarily make their strategic choice any easier as, with such a high performance record from the past, options will have to meet rigorous tests of feasibility and acceptability both in terms of financial performance and fit with values.

11.11 Summary

STRATEGIC choice is the third logical element of the strategy process and has a central role. The process of choice can only be described as deciding between different options but this makes the process neater and tidier than it really is.

There are likely to be possible options about product and services and about market segments defined by both customer need and geography. There will also be options on what resources and capabilities are needed and how to build these—implementation options. Indicators of what is possible and what is required may well follow from the results of a strategic assessment.

The various options are likely to be inter-related so it is necessary to identify a small number of strategic options made up of appropriately related options. Strategic choice involves comparing strategic options both logically and politically. Strategic options have to be aligned, acceptable, and feasible. If there is more than one strategic option that meet these tests, they will need to be compared. It is simplistic to treat strategic choice just as the logical comparison of strategic options. The process of decision is also political. It is important that those who will be crucial to implementing the strategy support the choice made.

References

Ansoff, I. (1987) *Corporate Strategy*, rev. edn. (London: Penguin).

Egan, C. (1995) *Creating Organizational Advantage* (Oxford: Butterworth Heinemann), 146–65.

Faulkner, D. (1992) 'Strategic Alliances: Cooperation for Competition', in *The Challenge of Strategic Management*, ed. D. Faulkner, and G. Johnson (London: Kogan Page), 119–46.

Lorange, P., and Roos, J. (1992) *Strategic Alliances: Formation, Implementation and Evolution* (Oxford: Blackwell).

Parkinson, N. (1960) *Parkinson's Law* (London: Penguin).

Porter, M. E. (1985) *Competitive Advantage: Creating and Sustaining Superior Performance* (New York: Free Press).

—— (1987) 'From Competitive Strategy to Corporate Strategy', *Harvard Business Review*, May–June.

Chapter 12
Analytical Tools to Support the Strategy Formulation Process

12.1 Introduction

STRATEGY making is a thinking process. It uses the collective wisdom of a body of theory and practice to help the strategist to collect, analyse, think out, test, and formulate viable alternatives. A variety of intellectual frameworks and structured approaches have been devised to help this thinking process. Many of these were discussed in Chapters 9 and 10. Porter's Five Forces Model, the Boston Box, the Value Chain Analysis, Portfolio Analysis, and similar tested models can be described as *intellectual frameworks.* They have become accepted as generic frameworks for analysing certain specific circumstances when determining strategy. These intellectual frameworks are often supplemented by *structured approaches* that help strategists to think systematically about strategic issues. Into this category fall such techniques as scenario planning, SWOT analysis, PEST analysis, opinion surveys, various competitor analyses, and benchmarking approaches. Thirdly, there are new breeds of thinking tools that are to do with understanding the relationships between people in organizations and between organizations. Among these *relationship mapping* approaches are 360° audits, organization opinion surveys, and impact maps. The 360° audit helps individuals to understand the quality of their relationships with those above, below, and beside them in the organizational hierarchy. Opinion surveys attempt to explain how people feel about the organization judged against a predetermined set of values or behaviours. The impact maps show how people, rewards, and communication systems within the organization influence each other's behaviour.

In the last ten years or so, software developers with an intimate understanding of these thinking frameworks have produced software versions of these intellectual frameworks and structured approaches that make the task of doing a Five Forces or SWOT analysis easier. In addition there is software that enables the layman with an appreciation of advanced statistical and modelling techniques to use them for analysing data. Among this latter group are statistical software, data mining software, expert systems, and neural network software.

The purpose of this chapter is to introduce the subject of strategic modelling and to draw the attention of the strategist to the wide range of software now available and to discuss some of the benefits and pitfalls. Our caution would be that strategists must make deliberate choices about whether to use the available software and to then do so alert to the possibility that they could become slaves to it. Like children and adults who get mesmerized by computer games and net surfing, strategists could also be easily seduced by the software and suspend their thinking and their judgement and produce look-alike strategies which will fail to differentiate one organization from another.

12.2 Models as analytical tools

A MODEL is a representation of reality as understood by the model builder. It attempts to identify the main and secondary influencers associated with an issue and then to hypothesize the causal links between these different influencers so that possible future outcomes can be determined. When the model builder is happy that the model reflects 'reality', he or she begins to use it to test and validate assumptions about the behaviour of the system or the problem being studied. The predictions are tested against past and future scenarios and the model is revised progressively to improve its fit to reality.

Models can help a strategist to review different options and to assess their impact on the results even though they are always imperfect representations of the real situation that they try to imitate. However, models are only as good as the model builder's understanding of the situation. They do not replace the expertise of the model builder, so good models need knowledgeable model builders who take the pains to study the issues associated with the modelling domain or who are very familiar with them. In these cases, the likely outcomes can be predicted with some accuracy. Techniques such as Porter's Five Forces Analysis or the Value Chain, because their logic and validity have been tested, do not require the user to have the same in-depth knowledge as the originator. That is the real value of proven models.

Because model builders have to build their models using known relationships, common data and data sources, and interpretations of current and future actions, models help those building them to gain a greater understanding of the problem they are trying to solve. They can help to structure a problem for management decision making. They may also provide a common language in which people with different mindsets can discuss common issues. Validating the model can highlight logical fallacies and flush out opinions and beliefs in a way that allows better-informed discussion and debate.

Until recently, most models used quantitative data and mathematical relationships. These models, often in the form of business plans, extrapolated the present into the future using growth rates, interest rates, and other incrementing factors. They did not use 'soft' qualitative data and this limited the ability of the model to mimic reality. Now some software packages enable both hard and soft variables to be modelled. Budgets and business plans are examples of hard data. Customer surveys are examples of soft data, for example, views and opinions.

12.3 Using raw data for situation analysis

THERE are situations where the individuals studying them do not understand the relationships that exist between the different entities in the situation domain. In these cases another approach can be taken. The raw data can be made to speak. Using techniques such as neural networks and data envelopment analysis and sometimes factor and cluster analysis it is possible to make sense of large volumes of data by reducing the data into interpretable themes or recognizable and meaningful relationships. Those seeking to use these techniques are referred to Swingler (1996), Goodwin and Wright (1998), Morecroft and Sterman (1994), Rosenhead (1995), Haykin (1994), Checkland and Scholes (1996), and Hair *et al.* (1995). The beauty of using this kind of method to study a situation is that the researcher suspends judgement until the data has spoken. In this way, preconceptions and prejudices are held at bay. The data for such analysis is collected from a wide range of people and circumstances, many of which are unrelated, and then relationships sought. The results need to be interpreted and this is where the knowledge and experience of the researcher begins to pay dividends. These techniques can be classified as inference engines. However, it should be the researcher who does the inferring, not the modelling tools.

12.4 Simulations

SIMULATION is a form of modelling that can help learning and support decision making. Simulations tend to include a deterministic element and a random element. For example, simulations can be used to imitate a specific market situation. As far as the researcher is concerned, he or she would have observed certain variables that impact on the market and noted their behaviours. Using this knowledge, he or she would specify and build a model to represent these variables and their interrelated behaviour. However, how some of the variables will behave will have to be guessed. In order to blind test the behaviour of their variables, the researcher can introduce randomness into the model and study the wide range of outcomes and from that rich picture select one which he or she or a knowledgeable group considers to be the most likely outcome. Armed with this information, the strategist can make assessments, produce options, make choices, and offer a 'best fit' outcome for implementation. Simulations usually attempt to depict a situation or system. The logical relationships built into a simulation represent the model builder's 'best guess' of reality; the randomness allows for the unpredictable. 'Heuristic' simulations are self-learning; they draw on previous runs of the simulation to fine-tune the logical relationships. Expert systems can be algorithmic or heuristic. Users of these models can improve their understanding of the circumstances they are simulating by revising their models using the outcomes of previous runs. Simulations can also speed up analysis. However, to make the outcome useful often requires many hours of data gathering and validation. The 'garbage in, garbage out' motto still applies.

12.5 Strategy software as a tool for strategy formulation

IN recent years, the strategic planners and line managers involved in corporate development have been offered a wide range of inexpensive (£50 to £400) software products, many of them designed and built by strategists for strategists and all claiming to make planning easier. Most emanate from the USA but there are UK-based suppliers too. The products embody generally accepted methods of analysis, offer generic analytical tools, or provide software that acts as a focus for group discussion and decision making, that is, the three categories we mentioned at the beginning. Many of them make no assumptions about the strategic task and do not differentiate between the many different roles of the strategist from visionary to analyst. Users should be wary of software that purports to offer a seamless interface from the vision to the business plan, having, as it progressed through the steps, automatically analysed and validated alternative strategies. Besides these purpose-built modelling tools, models can be built using spreadsheets and database software as the basic building blocks. 'Add-ons' to spreadsheets are now available to help users to carry out specialized analysis using the spreadsheet to structure and input the data. In addition to the software, strategists have available to them a range of computer and telecommunications work tools such as videoconferencing and teleconferencing, software for group working, Email, Fax, and Lotus Notes to enable remote working.

In a survey into the use of software carried out by Tampoe and Taylor (1996) with the help of the Conference Board Europe, the authors found that the strategists who used software gave five main reasons for so doing. These were comfort, time saving, effectiveness, presentation/communication, group working. The details of each main theme are given below.

Comfort

- They were comfortable using computers.
- Approach taken by the software fits the company culture.

Time saving

- Software saves time and effort.
- Package enables them to respond to queries faster.
- Gets people in many parts of the company to develop plans in real time.
- User is able to access data on various electronic media.
- Package captures and maps ideas quickly.

Effectiveness

- Software provides an 'audit trail' and enables the user to check the consistency between different statements.
- Software makes decisions explicit.
- User is able to test more options.
- Package provides a logical structured approach.
- Helps the user to carry out more rigorous analysis.

Communication/presentation

- Package provides more imaginative ways of presenting information.
- Achieves fast and effective communication of information.

Group working

- Imposes a common language and discipline on the planning process.
- User is able to build consensus using the software as a catalyst.
- Software facilitates group learning.

These benefits must be of value to many strategists and can in themselves justify the time and effort needed to develop familiarity and proficiency with specific software products that can enhance the individual's sense of professionalism and expertise.

Despite this, the study found that there were many who chose not to use software primarily for reasons of comfort and time saving. The details for each group are listed below.

Personal comfort or complacency

- 'I have no experience of using strategy software and I am reluctant to start now.'
- 'I don't have time to learn how to use strategy software.'
- 'The organization is hostile to computers except for routine applications.'
- Some had bad experiences with software packages and therefore were reluctant to use them again.
- Software tools operated as 'a black box' and they did not understand how the output was calculated.
- 'I cannot keep up with and evaluate new software and therefore I stick to known methods which are within my own control.'

Not rocking the organizational boat

- 'Strategy is formulated elsewhere in the organization.'
- 'The decision to use strategy software is not taken by us.'
- 'The company depends on financial plans and does not formulate strategic plans.'
- 'The Board is focused on financial control and does little strategic thinking.'

Ignorance of the true use of strategy software

- 'Prefer to discuss strategic options with other managers, building on the manager's experience and judgement rather than depending on computer software.'

Ineffective use of time and effort

- Entering data into the computer and updating the database was too time-consuming.
- Commercial packages did not meet their specific needs and building customized software had proved too expensive.

This study was disappointing. It seemed to suggest that the strategists in some major European organizations were still using either software specifically built for them many years ago or were content to use paper and pencil in this high technology age. Another explanation offered was that board members, rather than junior managers and senior strategists, make many of the major strategic decisions, and that they are likely to depend more on intuition, political manœuvring, and entrepreneurial actions rather than detailed analysis or group thinking. The point being made was that major leaps of strategy such as mergers and acquisitions or divestments are decided on shorter time-frames and by a small, often secretive, group rather than by a strategy function.

12.6 Categories of software

PROPRIETARY software for strategy formulation and strategic thinking falls into six main groups briefly discussed below.

Strategic modelling

These help the strategist to model processes and situations so that they can evaluate the impact of decisions on inter-connected activities. Models can be created to mirror or simulate business processes, financial outcomes of various courses of action leading to ratio analysis, and similar financial indicators of an organization's health. These types of software also enable logic diagrams, decision trees, simulations, and logical relationships such as 'preference diagrams' to be produced to help represent a strategic situation and test its viability. Into this group fall some of the more traditional forecasting methods such as economic and sales forecasting, financial modelling and the assessment of risk and reward, and the application of statistical techniques to test assumptions and to predict future trends and eventualities.

Strategic thinking

These systems include scenario planning, creative thinking, and problem solving. For example, some packages which help the user map the relationship between different aspects of a situation can be used for developing scenarios, simulation of competitive situations, problem analysis and problem solving, thinking creatively, and representing strategic issues in logic diagrams, decision trees, and preference diagrams.

Database analysis

These systems help strategists to acquire, store, retrieve, and manipulate data, for example, marketing databases which can enable users to examine customer behaviour in relation to different types of products. Increasingly, these systems enable access to the vast array of information available on the Internet, thus increasing the volume of information a strategist can access prior to formulating a strategy and testing its viability.

Knowledge transfer

This category covers statistical techniques such as paired comparisons, cluster analysis, conjoint analysis and factor analysis. The researcher understands how to use these techniques and how to interpret the outcomes without necessarily understanding the mathematics associated with each technique.

Expert systems

These may incorporate all four functions discussed above, and they usually provide an elementary form of data storage.

Decision support systems

These software tools help the strategist structure problems into a set of values, a number of options, and various factors which translate the options into results in line with the decision maker's values. The products can help make trade-offs against different outcomes and encourage those involved in the decision process to build a consensus view by a process of debate and discussion. Other benefits claimed for this type of software is its ability to help strategists test many options quickly and to identify factors that do not materially affect the outcomes. The software enables decision makers to carry out sensitivity analyses and risk analysis to discover how changes in different variables will affect the results, often allowing the modeller to include qualitative information as well as numbers. These software products are often designed to evaluate a number of strategic options in the light of certain preferences. The software products offer varying levels and qualities of text and charts. They are either generic in nature giving the user some flexibility in model construction and logic formulation or they are prescriptive and they present an accepted analytical approach.

Strategists would be well advised to use a combination of specialist packages and access to proprietary databases to enrich their own knowledge and expertise.

12.7 Application of these strategy support tools

THE following strategy problems (derived from Tampoe and Taylor 1996) are typical examples of how analytical support tools are used in practice in dealing with strategy formulation:

- the appraisal of new business opportunities and new ventures, for example, new products development and introduction;
- the evaluation of mergers and acquisitions, international expansion, alliances, and joint ventures;
- the assessment of risks and rewards on investment and disinvestment projects, for example, capital projects, disposals, and redundancy programmes;
- the assessment of economic trends and the development of alternative scenarios for the future, for example, in the form of economic models;
- the analysis of trends in an industry, and the relative strengths of competitors. Also analysing the likely results of different competitive strategies;
- debating alternative strategies for a business, examining the logic behind the strategies, and building consensus and commitment in a management team;
- building a detailed budget and plan in the form of a spreadsheet once the assumptions have been agreed;
- ranking competitors;
- building competitor databases;
- modelling the cost structure of organizations.

12.8 How do these tools help the strategist?

STRATEGY software products can help strategists to store, analyse, and interpret large volumes of data. As we have seen, they may provide simple spreadsheets or simulations that model the world the strategist wishes to anticipate. Often the tools can help managers to decide how best to deploy their limited resources to optimize the returns on their investments. The software can also introduce the users to well-established techniques and concepts without requiring them to study these techniques in depth. In addition, strategy software offers speed and flexibility in implementation once the model is built and the data has been loaded.

The speed and flexibility which strategy software offers can also take the user into an unreal world where reality merges into fantasy. When this happens, the user can fall into many traps. Software may constrain management by forcing the user to work within a certain structure. This in-built structure prevents the user from seeing the ambiguity of the 'real' world. Sometimes the software limitations distort the logic applied to a problem and the user can be distracted or seduced by the mechanics of the software. Because software makes the use of complex techniques look easy, it can also cause problems of interpretation because the decision makers do not understand the techniques or the logic that is being used.

The effective use of software requires the user to gain familiarity not only with the software but also with the techniques that it embodies and to acquire a level of computer literacy that enhances rather than inhibits thought processes. In the short term, the vendors will have to work through a transition period in which the management 'generation gap' will limit the use of their tools. It may be another decade before strategists at all levels in the organization are adequately 'computer and model literate' to use the power of strategy software to enhance and support their thinking.

12.9 Points to ponder when choosing software

THERE are no hard and fast rules that strategists can use in choosing software that is right for their specific need. However, many of the rules that apply to the acquisition of any application software apply here also. The points below are useful checks that may help make a suitable choice of software.

Quality of documentation, training, and help

- Ensure that the documentation and help systems provided with the software are such that a user can begin to get results quickly rather than have to spend time relearning the basics. This is vital, as this type of software is not regularly used and most users very quickly forget the nuances and special elements.
- Ensure that there are adequate training aids provided with the software. Look for good quality tutorials and also look for examples in the documentation that reflect the type of work you intend to use the software for. You may also wish to ensure that on-site training is available or failing that, that you can attend a formal course where a tutor will introduce you to the software and help you to familiarize yourself with the essential functionality.
- Ensure that the help line provided by the vendor actually delivers what is promised. It is better to test it while learning how to use the software rather than when a problem occurs in the middle of a live run.

Testing and reliability

- Test the software for reliability. Carry out the routine operations to check that it does not 'hang up' on you or that it fails at critical junctures.
- Test those routines that you are definitely going to use for their ability to handle volumes of data with a high degree of precision (to say, four places of decimals if this is important).
- Ensure that future enhancements can be obtained and that the vendor guarantees upward compatibility. The best way to test this is to ask about previous versions and how customers moved from one version to another. If it is important, ask them for reference sites and speak to the user.
- Check the software to verify if it has fail-safe and recovery procedures. This is particularly important if you have computer runs that take a long time and where a break in the middle will prove expensive in lost time and data.
- Find out how long the product has been in the market and who uses it. It will help you to judge whether you are helping the vendor to test the software and whether the software has had its 'bugs' ironed out.
- Check for audit trails where this is important.
- Ensure that the data handling is secure and will not destroy or over-write existing files.
- Ensure consistency of results. Check that the same routines using the same data produce the same results every time.

Functionality

- Ensure that the models being used and the algorithms used to analyse data and compute results are valid and proven. It does pay to run old data through the model and to check the answers with those already produced to satisfy yourself that the arithmetic and mathematics embedded in the software is correct and meets your standards.
- Check that the software archives data and results so that you can revert to a previous computation rather than start from scratch. This is particularly important when using simulation software.
- Check for language compatibility, particularly in situations where you may have to produce reports in more than one language.
- Check for speed of processing. This can sometimes be a factor of the hardware, but poorly written software can cost both memory and processing time.
- Check the output capabilities of the software. For example, can you produce graphical outputs to the standard expected by those using the results of your work?

Interfaces

- Check whether the software will accept data from other software and transfer data to common formats so that the software can be transported for further processing by another type of software. For example, will the software accept numerical data from an Excel spreadsheet and transfer to it?
- Decide whether it is important to have remote access to the software and if so ensure that this is possible.
- Decide whether the software will be used as a group working support tool and if so whether it is designed and built to support more than one user at the same time.
- Check that you are comfortable with the user interfaces. This is of particular importance when handling graphical inputs such as critical path diagrams, decision trees, and so on, where the model can be input as a diagram or as linkage data.
- Check for compatibility with your hardware and operating system. Look in particular for compatibility with version and releases of the operating system.

Other

- Check the terms and conditions of sale to ensure that your copyright is not infringed in any way.
- Try to talk to people who have worked with the software under operational conditions and with similar needs to your own.

12.10 Summary

It is likely that an increasing number of younger strategists will use some of the strategy tools available to them as a natural part of their way of working. They will benefit from having at their fingertips the distilled knowledge of many academics and practitioners. They will also have access to statistical and other advanced techniques whose use they understand but whose theory and theoretical underpinning may be beyond their grasp.

One concern is that strategy formulation will gradually become single flavoured as all the strategists begin to use the same or similar packages to input data according to the rules of the software designer. This may mean that there would be inadequate differentiation in strategies and lead to copycat strategies rather than innovative industry-leading ones. Another concern is that senior managers who have not participated in the thinking behind the strategies may be mesmerized by the quality of the presentation and narrative set before them and not dig too deeply into the logic and viability of the strategies being offered them.

We need to recognize that many of the major strategic moves carried out by organizations (mergers, acquisitions, demergers) are often done at board level with outside help and often little recourse to the organ grinding of strategists in the organization. This suggests that software tools for strategic management may be of even more benefit in devising department and product strategies rather than corporate or competitive strategies which impact on the long-term future of the business as a whole.

Finally, it is important that whatever use has been made of support tools, the results should be expressed and understood in terms that are independent of the model used. This process of removing the thinking from the 'black box' should ensure that any limitations and possible distortions of the models are also understood.

References

Checkland, P., and Scholes, J. (1996) *Soft Systems Methodology in Action* (Chichester: Wiley).

Goodwin, P., and Wright, G. (1998) *Decision Analysis for Management Judgment* (Chichester: Wiley).

Hair, J. F., Anderson, R. E., Tatham, R. L., and Black, W. C. (1995) *Multivariate Data Analaysis* (Englewood Cliffs, NJ: Prentice Hall).

Haykin, S. (1994) *Neural Networks, A Comprehensive Foundation* (Upper Saddle River, NJ: Prentice Hall).

Morecroft, J. D. W. and Sterman, J. D. (1994) *Modeling for Learning Organizations* (Portland, Ore.: Productivity Press, Systems Dynamic Series)

Rosenhead, Jonathan (ed.) (1995), *Rational Analysis for a Problematic World* (Chichester: Wiley).

Swingler, Kevin (1996) *Applying Neural Networks: A Practical Guide* (London: Academic Press).

Tampoe, M. and Taylor, B. (1996) 'Strategy Software: Exploring Its Potential', *Long Range Planning*, 29/2: 239–45.

Part IV

Strategy Content

Chapter 13
Strategy Content: Overview

13.1 Introduction

IN Part III we described the process that formulates strategies. **Part IV** is concerned with **Strategy Content**, that is, the strategies that emerge from the process and constitute a blueprint of desirable actions that the organization should take to secure its future. Part V will address how these actions are realized. There are, however, some points to be made about the content of strategy. Every chief executive will claim that his or her enterprise has a strategy. What do they mean by this or what should they mean by it? Most enterprises have some form of document describing their intentions for the future. What should usefully be included in such tomes? Part IV aims to answer these kinds of questions. In Part IV, we are concerned at describing in practical terms *how* the transition between thinking and action should take place, even when thinking and action overlap.

The strategies resulting from the strategy formulation process are important but not inviolate. Thinking does not stop because implementation has begun. Strategic thinking is an ongoing process and may require modifications to the implementations in progress. The thinking used to formulate strategy provides the rationale for the strategies that result. It therefore becomes difficult to separate the content of the strategy from the frameworks, such as those described in Chapters 9 and 10, which are used to generate it. It is equally true that the content of strategy can be better expressed when it is described as the actions needed to implement it. The content of strategy is therefore both an output of the formulation process and an input to the implementation process yet needs to be treated separately for purposes of clarity and emphasis. Strategy Content forms a crucial link between formulation and implementation as shown in Figure 13.1.

Figure 13.1 Strategy content: the link between ideas and action

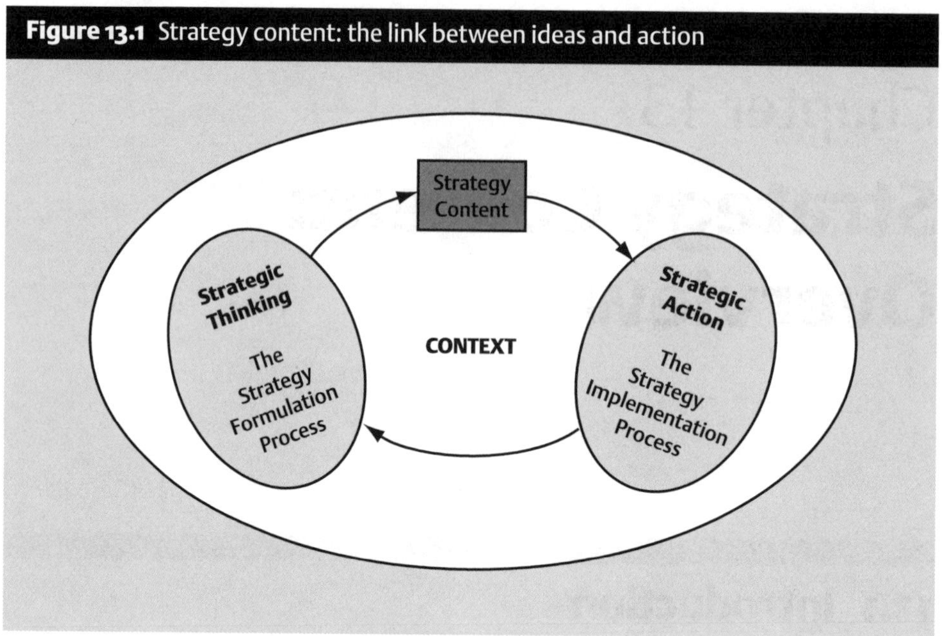

13.2 The form of strategy

THE content of strategy is the set of ideas that will secure the future of a particular enterprise in its particular context at a particular time. The strategy for an enterprise must be explicitly related to its particular needs so there are obvious limitations to the idea of a general-purpose strategy. Mahoney and McCue (1999) have, however, attempted to outline the content of a strategy that may be of value in many business contexts:

- select the right business or businesses to be in and get out of the rest;
- understand what drives success in the business and do these things superbly;
- constantly innovate to renew the business or to redefine it in new, attractive ways;
- maintain financial flexibility to seize on opportunities;
- measure the success of the enterprise by creation of superior shareholder value now and over time. But don't forget the other stakeholders.

Clearly each of the five guidelines would need to be supported with more specific details to be of value in any particular context, but the points have the right kind of shape to outline a strategy. Effective strategies have this kind of look and feel about their content.

The general strategy outlined above contained elements concerned with the choice of business to be in (an issue for the corporation as a whole) and with how to succeed in individual businesses (an issue for each business separately). This introduces the distinction, that we have not made before, between corporate and business strategies.

In practice, it may be helpful to subdivide the overall strategy of an enterprise into corporate, business, and functional strategies. There is just one **corporate strategy.** This will outline the nature and scope of the enterprise as a whole, particularly as it is intended to become in the future. The corporate strategy may outline the general purposes and the core values of the enterprise and express the broadest strategy of the enterprise in a succinct form. The corporate strategy is likely to describe the main activities that the enterprise will undertake or the principles by which such activities will be chosen. Chapter 15 examines corporate strategy in more depth.

If an enterprise has more than one business activity, then each such business should have its own **business strategy.** This should outline how that business intends to compete in its particular market place. It follows that a single enterprise may have as many business strategies as it has separate businesses or activities. The term **competitive strategy** is sometimes used as a synonym for business strategy. (The term business strategy is also sometimes used loosely without clearly differentiating between business and corporate strategy.) Business strategies are examined in more detail in Chapter 14.

If an enterprise has just a single business or activity then there is no distinction between corporate and business strategies. In practice, even in multi-business enterprises the distinction between corporate and business strategies is less clear-cut than the theoretical definitions would suggest. In large enterprises, corporate headquarters are usually responsible for producing the corporate strategy while the management team for each business produces the business strategy. These two groups are likely to differ in how they view the world and so the relationship between the two may be dynamic or even contentious. In particular, the business teams are often competing for corporate resources with other businesses. Corporate headquarters may be concerned to moderate the optimism shown in business unit strategies and projections, particularly when these projections are used as a ploy to gain unfair access to limited corporate resources. Business teams, on the other hand, may see corporate headquarters as remote and incapable of adding much real value to the strategy process. These tensions are healthy if kept within reasonable limits.

Functional strategies may exist for each major function. Marketing strategies, information technology strategies, human resources strategies are all common examples of functional strategies. The purpose of the functional strategy is to focus on improving the performance of that function and aligning it to make the maximum contribution to achieving the goals of the business strategy. In general, functional strategies describe how the resources and energies of that function will be deployed to realize the more fundamental business and corporate strategies. Functional strategies should build a bridge between the overall future direction of the business and the current status of that function. Functional strategies may also set general standards for that function across all businesses.

Recently, it has become common practice to have a knowledge management strategy. It has even been suggested that the knowledge management strategy is the same thing as the business strategy. This trend demonstrates the increase in the perceived importance of knowledge management and that knowledge management is beginning to be recognized as a business function. However, a knowledge management strategy can only be the business strategy for an enterprise whose only business is the generation of knowledge. For most enterprises, the knowledge management strategy is one functional strategy among others.

Functional strategies are not addressed any further in this book as they more naturally form a part of the study of each particular function. In general, functional strategies will be easier to devise and more effective if the corporate and business strategies are well thought through and clearly expressed.

13.3 The documentation of strategy content

IT is usual to record the results of the strategy process and of the strategic thinking that has taken place in a written document or documents. These documents can have a variety of titles of which strategic plan or business plan are probably the most common. The form and style of the documents can affect how useful they are, so it is worth thinking about what form of documentation will be best for a particular context. It is usually helpful to separate strategy documents from plans.

We defined the aim of strategy as defining and securing the future. A strategy is therefore both an idea of how the business will be and a general statement of the means that will be used to realize this idea. Strategy documents should describe general objectives, values, purposes, and means, as well as justifying these with supporting reasons. Strategy documents may outline strategic initiatives in general terms but should not be too specific about time-scales or responsibilities. Strategy documents should not have to be updated unless there is a need for a change in strategy; they should therefore avoid ephemeral detail.

A plan, on the other hand, should be more specific about actions, time-scales, and responsibilities. A plan should describe who will do what and when to implement a strategy or execute a strategic initiative. Plans have to change more often than the underlying strategies because they should reflect progress made and other detailed changes made necessary by the flow of events.

The distinction between strategies, strategic initiatives, and plans may at times be artificial. However, it does seem to be true that documents for communicating strategies are more effective if they are kept short. Too much detail tends to obscure the most important points and usually means that the document is tending too much towards being a plan rather than a strategy. Excess detail may also be politically contentious; readers may focus on individual responsibilities rather than on the central integrating intention of the strategy. Also, of course, the longer the document, the fewer people will read it and the more the opportunity to focus on some parts and ignore others. The most valuable strategy documents are often no more than twenty-five pages long but are widely read, understood, and respected. They emphasize the important themes and directions leaving the detail to be added later in plans of various kinds.

In practice, the various strategies and plans will be documented in a set of loosely connected documents. An example of how such a set might be in practice is shown in Figure 13.2. This is no more than an illustration but it should be possible to draw a diagram of this kind within any real enterprise to show what strategy and high level plan documents exist and the principal relationships between them.

Some companies treat their strategy documents as highly secret. Clearly there may be occasions when a strategy might be in danger if known to competitors. On the other hand, there is a price to be paid for secrecy, as people cannot be expected to support and identify with a strategy if they do not know what it is. This is also an argument for short strategy documents since the secrecy is more likely to be related to specific planned actions than general strategic intentions. Overall, the balance of argument seems to suggest public general strategies and more confidential plans for action.

The case examples offer some interesting contrasts in the form of documentation. The members of the Marks & Spencer board were reported in the press to be meeting over a weekend to discuss a 650-page document. Whatever the nature of Marks & Spencer's difficulties, this does seem a lot. On the other hand, Robb Wilmot at ICL hardly produced any written documents. He depended on numerous presentations to

Figure 13.2 Examples of strategy documentation

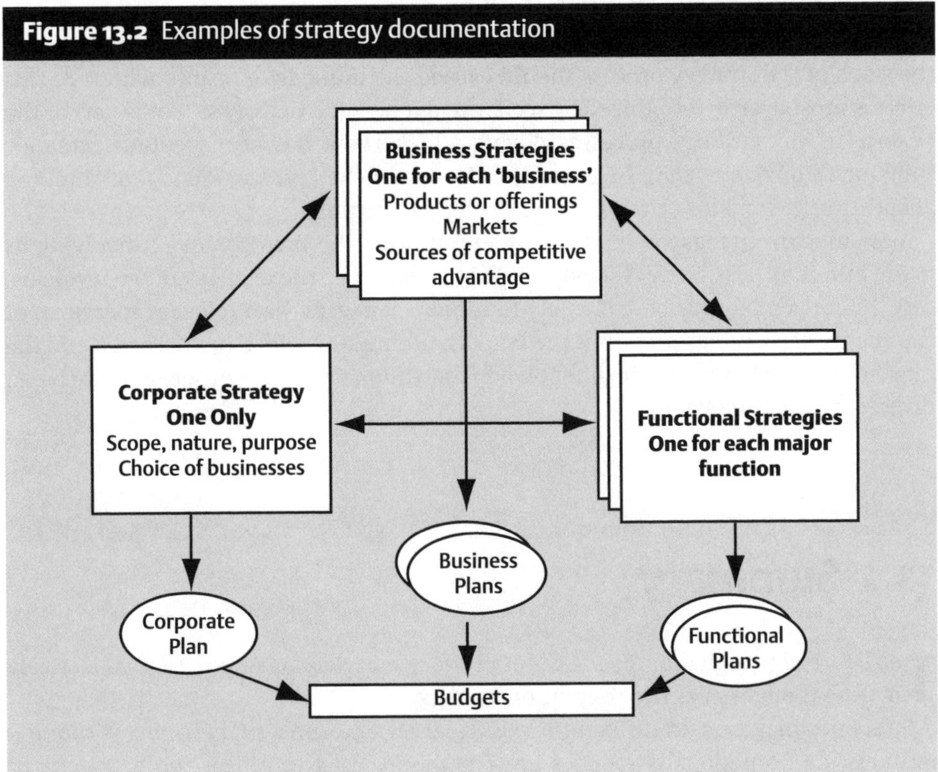

staff in which he put over the key points of the new strategic direction personally and frequently. He had the fervour and intimacy of someone who understood how the strategy was arrived at and had a detailed understanding of all its facets. We suggest that strategies at board level should evolve through the interaction of board members with help from their specialist advisers. Too often it is the other way round, with specialist advisers giving the board an indigestible tome littered with data but little information or knowledge with which to make decisions of significant import to the business. It should be possible to express the essence of a new strategy in relatively few words.

13.4 Other results from the strategy formulation process

WHILE the most tangible contents of strategy are the strategies themselves, there are other less tangible effects of the strategy formulation process that may be just as important. We stressed the importance of involving the right people in the strategy process and of communicating the results widely. The strategy formulation process will therefore cause people at all levels in the enterprise to think about the future of the business. This thinking can lead to new ideas emerging over time so that the value of the strategy process should exceed the immediate results achieved. This effect is most overtly recognized by scenario planners (de Geus 1988) but is part of the essence of any strategy processes during which there has been genuine strategic thinking (Mintzberg 1994). In general, followers of the Learning School of thinking about strategy tend to relate planning closely to learning.

Most modern management thinking emphasizes the importance of involving as many minds as possible with devising ways to improve the chances of business success. No longer can this be left solely to senior managers. Two relevant measures of the quality of a strategy process is the breadth of thinking which has occurred and the range of people who have been involved. The volume of paper produced may be an inverse measure of quality!

13.5 Summary

THE strategy formulation process will produce a variety of results that collectively may be thought of as the content of strategy.

Strategies may exist at different levels in larger enterprises. The terms corporate, business, and functional strategies are commonly used to reflect the hierarchy of strategies that constitute the overall strategy for the company. The relationships between strategies and the related documents should be easy to describe in a particular enterprise.

Strategies are best when recorded in short documents and should be as widely communicated as possible. They should not need updating too frequently. Plans will be more specific, possibly more confidential, and will need to be updated as events occur.

The strategy formulation process, by involving a variety of people, should also lead to some other benefits in terms of new ideas and commitment to the future success of the enterprise.

References

de Geus, A (1988) 'Planning as Learning', *Harvard Business Review*, Mar.–Apr.

Mahoney, R. J. and McCue, J. A. (1999) 'Insights from Business Strategy and Management: "Big Ideas" of the Past Three Decades: Are they Fads or Enablers'. Report published by the Centre for the Study of American Business, Washington University in St Louis. CEO Series Issue No. 29, Jan.

Mintzberg, H. (1994) *The Rise and Fall of Strategic Planning* (Hemel Hempstead: Prentice Hall).

Chapter 14
Business Strategies

14.1 Introduction

A BUSINESS strategy describes how a particular business intends to succeed in its chosen market place against its competitors. It therefore represents the best attempt that the management can make at defining and securing the future of that business. A business strategy should provide clear answers to the questions:

- What is the scope of the business (or offering) to which this strategy applies?
- What are the current and future needs of customers and potential customers of this business?
- What are the distinctive capabilities or unique competence that will give us competitive advantage in meeting these needs now and in the future?
- What in broad terms needs to be done to secure the future of our business?

These questions should have been addressed during the process of strategy formulation. The processes and techniques and processes described in Part III may have contributed to answering them. In this chapter, we are concerned with some of the practical issues that arise when thinking and analysis leads into action and commitment. We are concerned also with what makes the difference between good and indifferent business strategies. We suggest that a good business strategy will meet six tests of quality:

- It will be correctly scoped.
- It will be appropriately documented.
- It will address real customer needs.
- It will exploit genuine competencies.
- It will contribute to competitive advantage.
- It will lay the ground for implementation.

The paragraphs below examine each of these tests in turn.

14.2 The scope of business strategy

EACH separate 'business' should have its own business strategy so that a multiple business enterprise will have a number of separate business strategies. This raises the practical question of how to define the scope for each such business.

Mathur and Kenyon (1997) have examined this question rigorously. They suggest that there should be a separate competitive strategy for each 'offering' defined as the unit of customer choice. The unit of customer choice depends on what the customer is comparing when he or she makes the buying decision. Their many examples of offerings suggest, for instance, that a 100g jar of Nescafé might be a separate offering from a 200g jar of Nescafé if the closest substitute for the customer is the same size jar of another make of instant coffee. They see the two different sizes of jar as being different offerings and therefore requiring different business strategies. This is certainly theoretically elegant but may present a few problems in practice. To divide businesses so finely is likely to be too much work and it is unlikely that it would be possible ever to implement such fine-grained strategies. There is often a conflict between theoretical rigour and practical constraints.

In practice, the problem is more often the reverse of the Nescafé example in that a business is defined too broadly and, consequently, a single strategy is expected to apply to all its facets. One reason for this is that a division or region considers a 'business strategy' for its business that includes several distinct offerings. If the genuinely different needs of the different offerings are not separated, the resulting strategies can only be muddled and less useful than they might have been.

There is a need for a balance in choosing the scope for each 'business'. If the scope of the business is defined at too low a level, the work becomes too much. If the level is too high, the analysis loses its rigour. In practice, the problem is usually that this question of scope is never clearly posed, not that it would be difficult to provide a workable answer.

14.3 Content of a business strategy document

THERE is a tendency for strategy documents to be too long. It should be possible to read the whole document at a sitting and find it easy to understand. However, the document should give clear answers to the questions posed above, concisely and persuasively. Key facts and summarized analysis should support the answers. It may be appropriate to refer to more detailed documents or to include telling details.

It would be wrong to be too prescriptive in terms of the format for a business strategy document but the five headings below are likely to be included:

1. Statement of strategic intent for the business

This should describe in general terms the business as it expects to become in the future. It should outline in practical and tangible terms how this future is different from the present. Clearly, the strategic intent for the business has to relate to the strategic intent for the enterprise as a whole and be coherent with any other corporate strategies.

2. Principal findings of strategic assessment

Typically, the strategic assessment will have involved detailed analyses of both the external business environment and the capabilities of the enterprise. Only the most important or most surprising results need to be recorded. However, this section should provide a reasoned assessment of current status and future prospects of the business if present strategies were to be continued. This then makes the case for change in business terms.

3. Strategic choices which have been made and supporting rationale

This section has to summarize the options that have been identified and the choices made. The reasons for preferring one direction to another have to be spelt out and must be persuasive. The rationale for strategic choice should be based on a rigorous analysis of the basis of competitive advantage and how that will relate to the demonstrable capabilities of the enterprise. It is also desirable to show how the choice matches the strategic intent of the enterprise as a whole.

4. Statement of goals and objectives

The overall goal is to realize the strategic intent of the business. More measurable supporting goals are also very valuable. Objectives should not all be financial. It is important that some objectives set measures that relate to the fundamental nature of the business and to meeting customer and stakeholder needs.

5. Outline of strategic initiatives

This section will outline the principal actions to be undertaken to make the strategy happen.

14.4 Meeting the real needs of customers

THE needs of customers are one major driver of business strategy. It is essential to understand the needs and to identify how to satisfy these needs more fully, more exactly, or more profitably than competitors. Business strategy is therefore about beating competitors in meeting customer needs; beating competitors for other purposes may be fun but it is a distraction.

It follows from this that a deep analysis and understanding of customers' needs is essential to produce a good business strategy. It is necessary to understand the nature and scope of customers' needs, how these needs differ between different groups or individuals, and how these needs are changing. It is normally the responsibility of the marketing function to understand these needs. Business strategy is therefore market driven and likely to have very heavy involvement of marketing people. This does not, however, mean that a business strategy is the same thing as a marketing strategy. Business strategy is also heavily influenced by strategic intent, by financial and human constraints, and in fact by everything that makes the chief executive's job different from the marketing director's.

In the BMW case example, there is no evidence that BMW defined clearly exactly how the BMW/Rover combination was expected to look from the customers' point of view or how it would help BMW to meet customers' needs better. Five years after the take-over, the BMW's brand strategy still looked like two separate companies. In 1999, Rover launched the Rover 75 that appears to compete almost directly with its BMW executive models. At the same time, BMW was developing the MX5, a four-wheel drive vehicle, in apparent competition with Rover's Landrover range. BMW may have had a clear strategy for how the merged entity would meet customer needs but we cannot detect it.

14.5 Exploiting genuine competence in business strategy

THE second major driver of business strategy is the competence of the enterprise. We have described various analytical techniques for measuring resources and identifying capabilities. The ultimate goal is to identify a unique core competence that can provide the basis for differentiating ourselves from our competition. This is not easy to do and probably more business strategies go wrong because they failed to be honest in their assessment of their own capabilities than because they misunderstood customer needs.

In the Nolan, Norton case example, the widening impact of information technologies caused the scope of Nolan, Norton's consulting assignments to broaden and to require larger teams with broader skills in people and change management. This was recognized during the process of formulating strategy and one of the reasons for selling out to Peat, Marwick was to provide this wider skill base.

14.6 Providing sustainable competitive advantage

THE best business strategies are those which use the capabilities of the firm to address customer needs in a way which leads to sustainable competitive advantage. Chapter 8 described how competitive advantage may be assessed, but also suggested that competitive advantage had some of the elusive qualities of the Holy Grail. In practice, business strategies may have to tolerate less lofty achievements than long-term sustainable advantage.

The business strategy has to address the issue of competitive advantage realistically in the context of that business. This may require an admission that former competitive advantages are being eroded so that the strategy is as much defensive as offensive.

As John Kay (1999) has pointed out, businesses, like people, have to go through good times and bad times. It is probably impossible to achieve competitive advantage permanently and the excellent corporation that can achieve a permanent and irreducible lead is a myth.

The business strategy must describe what the basis of competition is, how this basis is changing, and how the strategies take advantage of these changes.

14.7 Laying the ground for implementation

THE business strategy must identify, in broad terms, the principal initiatives that will be necessary to implement the strategies. It must identify the changes in the business processes, culture, and organization that may be needed. It must argue the case for change. It should set tight but achievable targets for the time-scales in which change can be achieved.

14.8 Summary

THE purpose of business strategy is to exploit the capabilities of the enterprise to gain and sustain competitive advantage in serving the needs of customers in a chosen marketplace. An effective business strategy will provide good answers to questions on business scope, customers' needs, how the enterprise will exploit its advantages, and on how competitive advantage will be achieved. It will also describe the main actions necessary to implement the strategy and the reasons why the changes are necessary.

References

Kay, J. (1999) 'The Myth of Excellence', *Financial Times* (London), 26 May.

Mathur, S. S. and Kenyon, A. (1997) *Creating Value: Shaping Tomorrow's Business* (Oxford: Butterworth Heinemann).

Chapter 15
Corporate Strategy

15.1 Introduction

We discussed in Chapter 14 how each business should have its own business strategy to define and secure its future. If an enterprise is involved in several businesses or activities, it will need a corporate strategy as well as a business strategy for each of the separate businesses. Corporate strategy addresses the issues of a multi-business enterprise as a whole. Corporate strategy addresses issues relating to the intent, scope, and nature of the enterprise and in particular has to provide answers to the following questions:

- What should be the nature and values of the enterprise in the broadest sense? What are the aims in terms of creating value for stakeholders?
- What kind of businesses should we be in? What should be the scope of activity in the future so what should we divest and what should we seek to add?
- What structure, systems, and processes will be necessary to link the various businesses to each other and to the corporate centre?
- How can the corporate centre add value to make the whole worth more than the sum of the parts?

Corporate strategy is of particular concern in diverse enterprises to demonstrate, justify, and extend the value of that diversity.

15.2 The historical development of ideas about corporate strategy

IDEAS on what corporate strategy is and how it should be formulated have changed more over time than almost any other part of strategic management. This shows that none of the ideas are completely satisfactory. On the other hand, no new theory completely replaces previous theories in all contexts so none can be rejected as wrong.

The historical development of thinking on corporate strategy has been well summarized by Goold *et al.* (1994). A summary and extension of their summary is shown in Figure 15.1 below:

During the 1950s, many large companies which had previously been organized by function found that this form of organization was overloading headquarters and that they would be more efficient if they divided themselves into divisions. General Motors and other leading US companies had already demonstrated the advantages of divisional organization as was described in books such as Sloan (1963) and Chandler (1962). McKinsey and Co. built its reputation as a firm of management consultants at this time partly through its success in assisting a large number of major companies to make the change from functional to divisional organization.

Figure 15.1 How concepts of corporate strategy have developed

	Issues	Concepts	Corporate Strategies
1950	Overload at centre	Decentralization	Divisionalization
1960	Quest for growth	General management skills	Diversification
1970	Resource allocation	Portfolio planning	'Balanced portfolios'
1980s	Value gaps/raiders Poor performance of diversification	Value based planning 'Stick to the knitting'	Restructuring
1990s	Defining the core business	Dominant logic Core competencies	Manageable portfolio Linked portfolios
	Lasting basis for corporate strategy	Parenting advantage	Managing portfolio to maximize value creation
2000s	Shareholder value	Exceeding cost of capital in all businesses	Focus on value/divest if value being destroyed

Source: Adapted from M.Goold, A. Campbell and M. Alexander, *Corporate-level Strategy* (Wiley 1994).

The 1960s may now be seen as the age of the 'conglomerate'. Conglomerates were companies with a portfolio of unrelated businesses. The conglomerates were created as a result of multiple acquisitions. After acquisition, the conglomerate usually imposed a standard management reporting system. This would typically be more sophisticated than the systems previously in place and had the effect of tightening financial control and making managers very much aware of the importance of 'making their numbers'. On the other hand, these systems could not be tailored to the diverse nature of the businesses acquired. The conglomerates could grow fast partly because the financial markets awarded them high P/E (price/earnings) ratios. The high market valuations were a result of the high visibility of the conglomerates and probably also because analysts admired the tighter control and better financial reporting which the conglomerate parents imposed. There was a belief at the time that a good manager could manage anything and that a good control system could be applied to any type of business. Conglomerates such as ITT under the leadership of Harold Geneen grew from nowhere to being among the largest companies in the world during the decade of the 1960s.

The fashion in corporate strategy changed again in the early 1970s. The Boston Consulting Group (BCG) led by Bruce Henderson grew to prominence at this time. BCG largely built its reputation as a management consulting firm by applying the methods of portfolio analysis (see Chapter 10). This technique offered untidy conglomerates a method of reviewing their portfolio of past acquisitions. Certainly the management control systems of most conglomerates were designed to control each separate business as an entity. Questions about the scope of the enterprise as a whole and the relationships between the different businesses needed a new approach. By the 1970s, investors were becoming more suspicious of conglomerates and portfolio analysis offered a basis for planning some much-needed rationalization.

The trend towards rationalization accelerated in the early 1980s when the best-selling book, *In Search of Excellence* (Peters and Waterman 1982) was published. This book had a major impact on management thinking. The phrase 'Stick to the Knitting' particularly caught the popular imagination and ushered in a period where the fashionable corporate strategy was to restructure around core businesses and to dispose of poorly performing divisions.

During the 1990s, the concern to have a clear core business tended to continue and has deepened into a focus on core competence. There was also a tendency to question the value of scale for its own sake as it became apparent that some large companies were slow moving in a world where the pace of change was increasing. It seemed that there might sometimes be diseconomies of scale. Demergers and management buy-outs increased as larger companies split into separate core businesses or disposed of non-core businesses. This process led naturally to pressure to demonstrate that the headquarters of a multi-business enterprise was adding value as a parent so that the enterprise as a whole was more valuable than the sum of its parts.

While the historical pattern described above is probably a fair sketch of the most important issues with which corporate strategy has been concerned over the last half century, it should be clear that the different frameworks and techniques tended to be suited to addressing particular issues. These issues may still occur and so any of the ideas may still be appropriate in particular contexts. In general, the techniques are now available as a tool kit to answer the questions to be addressed in creating a corporate strategy.

The current emphasis is on achieving value for shareholders over the long term. The techniques for measuring shareholder value were described in Chapter 10. The significance for corporate strategy is to apply these techniques widely to ensure that attention is focused on businesses that create value and to divest those that do not.

15.3 The impact of financial markets on corporate strategy

THE focus on shareholder value relates closely to the fact that most large publicly owned companies, particularly in the USA and UK, are very sensitive to their standing in financial markets. Total shareholder value is determined by the increase in the share price and by the stream of expected future dividends. The former is more important than the latter during bull markets, the latter more important in market downturns. The share price may be heavily influenced by analysts who tend to calculate the price of a share by applying a price/earnings (P/E) multiple to the earnings per share (eps). Both factors in this product are somewhat subjective and sometimes open to manipulation. The expected P/E is determined by somewhat subjective assessments such as whether the share is a 'growth stock' or the nature of the industry. The eps is determined by accounting principles that tend to relate to historic costs more than future value. In general, managers in public companies must be sensitive to the linkages between their strategies and the price of their shares, but also aware that these linkages are somewhat fickle.

One obvious example of this linkage is when a company chooses to demerge one or a group of its businesses. A common motivation for demerging is to increase the value of the set of businesses to shareholders because some parts merit a higher P/E ratio than the whole.

Amram and Kulatilaka (1999) take this argument a step further by suggesting that many strategic choices can be valued directly by markets by assessing them as financial options. To some extent, this allows managers to replace their own judgements about likely future outcomes directly by market valuations. They suggest that this will result in more disciplined decisions and link strategy more directly to building shareholder value. These questions begin to move beyond issues of corporate strategy into the more technical field of financial strategy.

Corporate strategy addresses the question of the extent of the corporation and is therefore necessarily closely related to mergers and acquisitions (M&A). M&A activities involve a wide range of intermediaries such as investment bankers, accountants, and lawyers, all of whom tend to benefit from the number of transactions

Box 15.1 Examples of demergers

ICI demerged Zeneca so that Zeneca's shares could achieve the higher P/E ratio applied to a pharmaceuticals business compared to ICI's chemical businesses. Since the demerger in 1993, the P/E of Zeneca seen as a growth share has moved sharply ahead, while the P/E of the rest of ICI has tended to fall.

British American Tobacco (BAT) diversified into financial services over a number of years by acquisitions including Allied Dunbar, Eagle Star, and Farmers. In 1998, BAT sold off these interests to Zurich Insurance. This sale was at least partly to achieve the higher P/E ratios which insurance businesses will have when separated from the potential claims and litigation over health damage within a tobacco company.

irrespective of the strategic logic of those transactions. Secondly, managers themselves often have personal financial interests and their careers at stake in mergers. There may be attractive stock options or higher compensation on offer from the merged company. There may be a choice between acquiring or being acquired, with power and hence better career prospects tending to move to the acquirer. Top appointments are particularly important. It may be that the crucial reason that the merger proposed between Glaxo-Wellcome and Smith Klein Beecham did not happen in 1998 was because the question of who should get the top job could not be resolved.

It is apparent that financial markets have an extremely potent effect on corporate strategy and have to be taken into account in practice. Market pressures are likely to outweigh the logic laid out in books such as this one—perhaps to the detriment of long-term outcomes.

15.4 Documenting corporate strategy

FORMAL documents on corporate strategy are less common than for business strategies. However, the chairman's statement in the annual report of a public company often gives some indication of the corporate strategy. Chairman's statements rarely answer all the questions suggested in Section 15.1 above. This may be because the enterprise has not addressed all the questions or because the chairman's statement is slanted towards the needs of public relations or to impress financial analysts.

Clearly it is often useful to a corporation to record the answers to the questions of corporate strategy in a short written document. The format of this document is not important but it should describe the following clearly and succinctly.

Strategic intent and values

The corporate strategic intent should describe the general direction and values of the corporation as a whole. If the enterprise consists of several separate businesses, the strategic intents of each separate business should be coherent with the corporate strategic intent.

Business scope

The rationale for overall scope of the business should be explained in terms of core competence, technological focus, shareholder value, parenting skill, geographical scope, or necessary market share to compete. Techniques such as parenting advantage or portfolio management described in Chapter 10 may assist in providing the rationale for the business scope. Visible choices on divestments or acquisitions should be seen to fit with this rationale.

Structure, systems, and processes

It should be apparent what the dominant dimension to organizational structure is. The commonest forms are independent businesses linked by a headquarters umbrella, functional organization, geographical organization, or a matrix combining more than one of these dimensions. There should be a clear rationale as to why this organization is appropriate. The systems and processes should support the organization and there should be an analysis of the principal systems in place, assurances that their quality is adequate, and that their design is appropriate to support the organization.

How the corporate centre is to add value

This should answer the question of the nature of corporate advantage and how it will be enhanced. This is perhaps the least common element to be publicly mentioned in statements of corporate strategy. This may be because it has not been considered or possibly because an honest statement of the facts might lead to embarrassment at high levels in the company.

15.5 Corporate strategy in the case examples

ONLY BMW and Marks and Spencer are large and diverse enough for the distinction between corporate and business strategy to have much significance.

BMW, although a large business, is still predominantly in the motor car market. Its corporate strategy would need to address the issues of the relationship of its dominant business with its other interests in motor cycles and aero-engines. The relationship between Rover and BMW does not seem to have been thought through in strategic terms. This is more an issue of business than corporate strategy because the two companies are in the same business.

M&S has its major businesses in retailing (subdivided into clothes, food, and home furnishings) and financial services. The issues for its corporate strategy certainly include the future geographical scope of each of these businesses. In addition, there is an issue on the extent to which it should focus on a single M&S image and value-set world-wide or seek to exploit its other brand names such as Brooks Brothers. It has issues about how best to organize its logistical processes to support its wide geographical spread and its sharp variations in the degree of market penetration.

15.6 Summary

Corporate strategy must address questions about the direction, values, and scope of the business as a whole and how it intends to operate. Corporate strategy seeks to create value beyond the sum of the individual parts. It is thus concerned with corporate advantage much as business strategies are concerned with competitive advantage.

In practice, corporate strategies are sensitive to the demands of financial markets. These can at times distort the logic of strategic management.

Ideas about how to set corporate strategy effectively have developed over the years but there is no universal theory or analytical framework that will generate an effective strategy. Rather, conviction about the right answers to the questions will evolve within a particular context from a combination of analysis, discussion, and instinct. The answers may be recorded in a brief document.

References

Amran, M., and Kulatilaka, N. (1999) 'Disciplined Decisions: Aligning Strategy with the Financial Markets', *Harvard Business Review*, Jan.–Feb.

Chandler, A. D. (1962) *Strategy and Structure* (Boston: MIT Press).

Goold, M., Campbell, A., and Alexander, M. (1994) *Corporate-Level Strategy: Creating Value in the Multibusiness Company* (New York: Wiley).

Peters, T. J., and Waterman, R. H. (1982) *In Search of Excellence* (New York: Harper and Row).

Sloan, A. P. (1963) *My Years at General Motors* (New York: Doubleday 1963; paperback edn., MacFadden, 1965).

Part V

The Strategy Implementation Process

Chapter 16

Implementing Strategy: Realizing Strategic Intent

16.1 Introduction

IN Part IV we considered business and corporate strategies as ideas. In Part V we are concerned with the implementation of strategy. Strategic ideas have no value unless they are implemented. Strategy implementation is the last element of the strategic management process as shown in Figure 16.1. It is also perhaps the most important.

All the elements of strategic management have to fit together. The strategic thinking in the strategy formulation process has to take into account the need for effective implementation. The content of the strategies has to define the means by which the strategies will be implemented. Strategic thinking, strategy content, and strategy implementation must all be valid within the constraints of the context.

16.2 The importance of strategy implementation

IF implementation is poor, all other elements of strategic management become a waste of time and effort. As Ansoff, Declerk, and Hayes (1976) point out: 'the outcome of strategic planning is only a set of plans and intentions. By itself strategic planning produces no actions, no visible changes in the firm. To effect the changes the firm needs appropriated capabilities; trained and motivated managers, strategic information, fluid and responsive systems and structure.'

Figure 16.1 Strategic implementation: the final element of strategic management

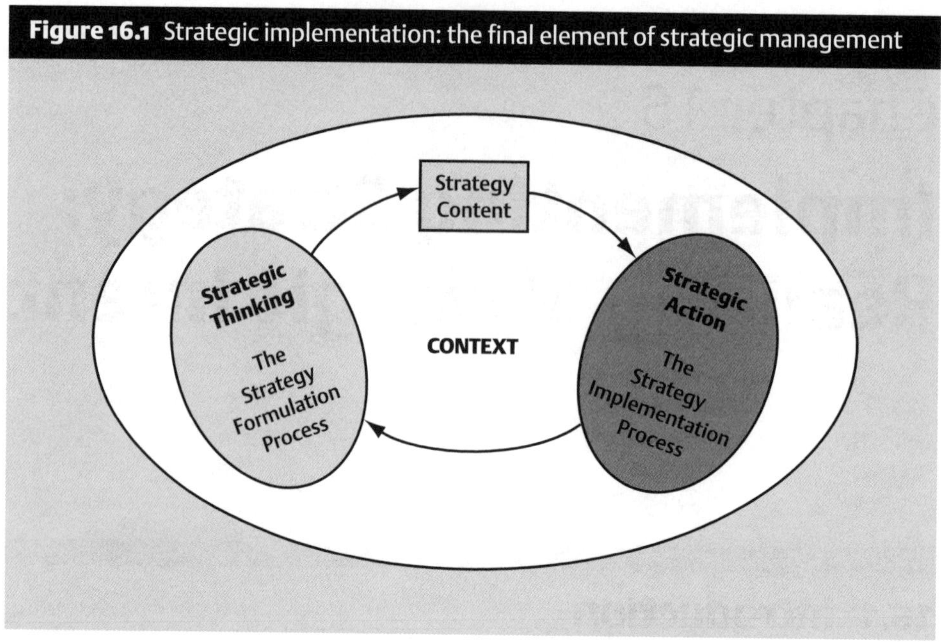

The importance of implementation was shown dramatically in a recent study into why chief executives lose their jobs. Charan and Colvin (1999) found that: 'In the majority of cases—we estimate 70%—the real problem isn't the high-concept boners the boffins love to talk about. It's bad execution. As simple as that: not getting things done, being indecisive, not delivering on commitments'.

Holman (1999) writing on the importance of strategy implementation points out that:

> 80% of Directors believe they have good strategies—but only 14% believe they implement them well, according to a Quest Worldwide survey of 114 international companies. And 'strategy execution' was identified as the most valuable of 39 non-financial performance measures in a recent Ernst and Young survey of 275 US portfolio managers.

The Chief Executive of Lloyds TSB Group made it very clear how important following through on strategy is in the 1998 Annual Report: 'World class performance in shareholder value creation can only be achieved by having clear strategic aims, plans capable of translating strategy into shareholder value, and the determination and ability to implement those plans'.

Several of the case examples demonstrate the importance of implementation. The ICL case does not describe how the new strategies of 1981 were implemented. The sequel to the case is, however, that it was the following decade or so of successful implementation that showed that the strategies put in place in the crisis had been valid. The Nolan, Norton case, on the other hand, demonstrates the dangers of giving too little importance to implementation. KPMG realized less value from the purchase of Nolan, Norton than it might have done, by failing to recognize the desires of many of the staff who valued working for a small and innovative organization. As a result, many staff left because of a sudden and largely unmanaged change of culture. The BMW case seems, in retrospect, to be a failure of implementation rather than an error of strategy. The new board has continued with the strategy pioneered by Mr Pischetrieder and may well reap the benefits of so doing, although the time-scales may be longer than anticipated.

In general, enterprises are successful when they can convert dreams into reality. Effective implementation is crucial to this.

16.3 The scope of strategy implementation

IMPLEMENTING strategy successfully is very difficult. The more radical the degree of change, the more difficult it is. Far-reaching and radical change affects all facets of the business. Above all, change affects people and the success of implementation critically depends on carrying the people in the enterprise along with the new strategy. Strategic change causes significant upheaval to people as they struggle to find their feet with the new arrangements. The changes may be classified under three headings.

Change in systems and processes

Systems and processes determine how work is done. There may be a need to make changes to the processes that underwrite the ability of the enterprise to meet its customer expectations. This may mean devising and implementing new processes, modifying existing ones, and training staff and customers to use these new systems.

Change in culture

Culture determines what it feels like to work in the enterprise. Change can harm the culture of the organization in many ways as the actions that lead to repositioning the organization may contradict the old values of the organization and raise doubts as to the sincerity of the managers who espouse the values. The rules and regulations that sustained the old values may have to be changed to reflect the new behaviours expected from staff. Those administering the new rules and processes may have to shed their old attitudes and approaches, resulting in disorientation to staff, customers, and suppliers.

Change in organizational structure

This determines patterns of communication and responsibility. People are affected when the organization structure is changed or modified. They may have to be moved, either physically and in terms of whom they report to. Structural changes can cause shifts in power bases as old power bases are destroyed and new ones form. In tandem with the redistribution of people and power, the networks that sustain working relationships may be disrupted causing people to feel isolated and vulnerable because they cannot benefit any more from established supportive relationships.

16.4 Strategy implementation: winning combinations?

A GOOD strategy is one that can be successfully implemented. Sometimes, successfully implementing a flawed strategy may be better than devising an elegant strategy that is not or cannot be implemented. If the implemented strategy is out of step with the needs of the business, it is unlikely to be of benefit as it may not exploit the specific window of opportunity it was planned for.

In the main, it is possible to hypothesize seven possible cases where strategic thinking and implementation interact to deliver intended or unintended results. These likely outcomes are summarized in Table 16.1.

Only cases 1, 4, 6, and 7 in Table 16.1 will be acceptable to most people involved in strategic transformation. Case 1 is where both strategic thinking and execution are well done leading to the achievement of strategic intent. Case 4 occurs where, due to the continuously changing nature of the strategic challenge, the only realistic strategy is one which enables the organization to change the way it thinks and acts to meet the circumstances presented to it—a strategy of muddling through and tactical adaptability. Cases 6 and 7 represent rewards to be reaped by building the organizational capability to imitate a successful innovator and exploit the larger and as yet latent market for cheaper yet functionally rich products.

Cases 2, 3, and 5 represent different ways of failing in implementation. Case 2 occurs more often than one might expect. Poor results are attributed to ineffective implementation rather than the need for new thinking, leading to a 'one more heave' turn of mind. Case 3 occurs where there is neither any strategy nor any will to manage change. Case 5 is a dangerous one as a potentially good strategy is poorly executed. As a result, the organization may pass a strategic advantage to a rival with better implementation skills.

It is also necessary to recognize that new strategic initiatives may sometimes fail for causes other than poor implementation. This may be because they were never intended to succeed, such as a political ploy on the part of a director. Sometimes a strategy fails because of inertia at all levels in the organization often caused by a lack of buy-in by those who had to make it happen—the middle level executives and the staff. These employees may lack enthusiasm because they are suddenly called upon to work with people who were once their competitors or because the strategy may cost them and their friends their jobs. A less cynical view would suggest that these strategic initiatives fail because many staff at all levels in the organization are unwilling to live with the dynamics of change. Overall, the table suggests that success is likely

Table 16.1 Impact of effectiveness of implementation on overall result

Case	Quality of Strategic Concepts	Effectiveness of Implementation of Strategies	Likely Overall Result
1	Good—creative and designed to achieve leadership through innovation	Good—implemented within targets set	Good—Strategy achieved as intended
2	Poor—unimaginative and bland	Good—implementation achieves competitive edge through speed, price, or quality	Probably indifferent result or lucky break
3	Poor—unimaginative and bland	Poor—stumbling through	Luck needed to avoid a disaster
4	None because circumstances make it impossible to plan ahead in any meaningful way	Fast response and adaptive tactics designed to exploit opportunities presented	May be best possible result in very uncertain conditions and can lead to high achievement by wrong-footing opposition
5	Good—creative and applied to achieve leadership through innovation	Poor—stumbling through	Transfer of strategic advantage to competition if they are able to implement your good strategy better
6	Good imitation of competitor strategy	Good—implementation achieves competitive edge by exploiting opportunities presented	Good—achieving fast follower capability and creaming the potential aroused by the innovator
7	Good imitation of competitor strategy	Fast response and adaptive tactics designed to achieve competitive edge through speed, price, or quality	Good—achieving 'me better' capability and both creaming opportunity created by innovator and also creating new markets.

to require both good crafting and good implementation of strategy. In practice, it is often difficult to determine whether a strategy failed because it was theoretically flawed or practically bungled. Either way someone will pay the price.

16.5 Strategic change management

THE successful repositioning of an enterprise to meet new strategic aims often requires the building of new **organizational capability**. Organizational capability is the collective skill of the organization developed to enable it to fulfil its objectives.

It is much greater than structure and usually combines structure, culture, and process. Wholesale organizational transformation impacts on the performance of the organization during the period of rethinking and uncertainty that precedes radical organizational transformation. It forces change on a variety of operational and strategic aspects of the business. Therefore, even if the will to change existed in the organization and all those involved were behind the proposed changes and wanted to see them implemented, the initiative would fail unless the organization had perfected the art of managing strategic change. The ability to achieve strategic change must rank as a strategic competence as it contributes to a key organizational capability and enhances effectiveness in this area.

Strategic change management resides at the heart of the strategy implementation process. It is about managing the changes for reshaping and refining the engines of strategy delivery expeditiously and while sustaining employee morale and motivation. Most often this means blending leadership, management, process, culture, and structure to create a new or revise an existing organizational capability so that it fits the new strategic intent of the business.

To make change happen smoothly requires both leadership and management. Leadership and management both drive the changes in systems, culture, and organization. But leadership and management are not the same thing. Leadership is about gaining and holding the hearts and minds of the people involved. Management is about co-ordinating the many detailed tasks involved in the change that requires good programme and project management.

Figure 16.2 may be helpful in illustrating how leadership and management have to guide the change of culture, process, and structure to achieve the new organizational capability required.

The model has five critical strands. Two of these—change leadership and programme and project management—run through the other three, culture, process, and structure change.

Change leadership is about communicating a vision that gains acceptance for the new direction. This is not a management task. Its objective is to win hearts and minds

Figure 16.2 The strategy implementation process

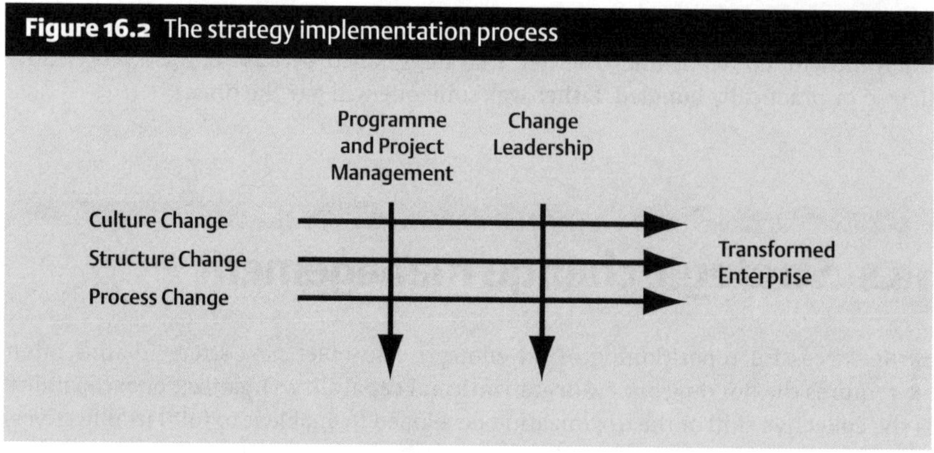

not to supervise the activities that need to be carried out to make the changes effective. It is emotional in content and motivational in purpose. Change management consists of a series of activities to supervise and control the vast array of tasks that need to be carried out if change is to be accomplished and the emotional and motivational energy of those involved is to be harnessed. Change leadership and change management act as the forces for change on process, culture, and structure—the three instruments of change. Process change typically requires a high level of programme and project management; successful culture and structural changes depend much more on effective leadership.

The five activities shown in Figure 16.2 come together to create a transformed organization with new organizational capability to match the needs of its strategic intent.

16.6 Change leadership: taking the hearts and minds with you

MANY leaders of organizations are better politicians than they are leaders. Progression up the corporate ladder is a function not only of ability but also of political talent. Those who are excellent at administrating an established business may not necessarily be good leaders of change, although they may be. The first requirement for an effective change leader is to convince followers that the change is for the good of the organization and not carried out for the personal benefit or aggrandizement of the leader. This can be quite a tall order. How do you persuade the employees of Air Touch and Vodafone that the acquisition of one by the other to create the largest cellular phone company in the world is good for the employees of either organization? Or how indeed do you persuade the employees and dealer network of Chrysler that the 'merger' between it and Mercedes Benz is good for them, the customers or the shareholders, or the American economy? And if you cannot, how much motivation and commitment would the leader get to drive through the changes that need to be made to realize the benefits put forward as the reason for the merger? If this cannot be achieved and the changes take too long to come through (as in the case of BMW and Rover), the benefits originally claimed will not materialize and the initiators of change may have to pay the ultimate price. In our experience, effective change leaders are those who genuinely believe that the proposed strategic change is needed to sustain the business. People often ask us how one can judge the genuineness of a leader's purpose. Our answer is that the staff can intuitively sense the authenticity of a proposed change. Very often they know the individual proposing the change and understand the underlying drivers of that person. Jack Welsh at General Electric was able to demonstrate the qualities of a good change leader and Tony Blair was also able to carry his party with him while he made the changes necessary to make the British Labour Party electable after eighteen years in opposition.

It would appear that good leaders emerge during times of adversity, probably because that is the time when most people are susceptible to being led and support the person who is willing to lead them out of a tricky situation (Tampoe 1989, 1998).

The issues of the management and leadership of change are intertwined and are addressed in Chapter 17.

16.7 Change management: programme and project management

To achieve strategic change, an organization needs to manage many different change initiatives in parallel. This often means setting up many small teams, each focused and resourced to achieve a specific outcome. The cumulative effect of these successful outcomes determines the success of the change initiative. To achieve cogency and synchronicity of the outcome of these different teams it is necessary to use two management techniques—programme management and project management. A programme is the embodiment of many projects, all of which, when completed successfully, realize an overriding objective. A project, on the other hand, is a discrete activity with a much narrower focus.

The issues associated with programme and project management are discussed in greater detail in Chapter 18.

16.8 Changing processes

Typically, the business processes within an enterprise will have been designed to support a previous strategy. A new strategy is almost certain to require radical change to some or all of these processes. This is not an easy thing to do and it is too rarely considered in practice. A good example is that of computer systems that support the operational activities of an organization. These systems often support specific functions or activities. Often the network is hardwired into buildings and other locations and individuals trained to operate them, allowing for the various idiosyncrasies of the system in use. An organizational restructuring or a commercial decision on pricing can completely change the way transactions need to be processed but very rarely has the knock-on impact of the decision on the computer system been considered or allowed for in the implementation dates. The resultant chaos is only felt by the operational (often very junior staff) who have to cope with angry customers and failing systems. BMW found that upgrading its UK factories to deliver cars of the same build quality as those of their German factories took much longer than they expected. This meant that the launch of the Rover 75 series had to be delayed with a serious impact on the company's bottom line.

Transporting procedures, practices, and standards across cultural (national and organizational) boundaries is an unenviable task; yet managers blithely go on acquiring and merging, ignoring this harsh reality. Good strategies are those that take these issues into account and allow for them. Perhaps Volkswagen is an example of a company that has thought through this issue before acquiring SEAT and SKODA. By deciding to use common platforms and components, the company very largely solved the process issue across Western and Eastern Europe, the USA, and South America.

Processes can be embodied in both information systems and organizational procedures and rules of operation. In these instances, it is important that the change team take the trouble to identify all the processes in use and to assess their scope and integrity. This may reveal that the processes depend on a structural form, reporting lines, and procedures that will not support the new strategic intent. In certain types of organization, for example, professional companies, the process is the individual. For example, a lawyer handling the sale of a house is the process driver. He or she will use both in-company procedures and the practices laid down by his or her profession to deliver a proficient and cost-effective service. Within organizations too there are groups of people who are process drivers and it is important to check that their role is not changed or modified by a change in strategic intent.

Chapter 19 outlines how processes may be effectively changed.

16.9 Changing culture

A CHANGE of strategy may require the culture of the enterprise to change. This is even more difficult than changing processes as culture is less tangible. An example of the need for cultural change has often occurred in recent years when companies have had to bring together multi-disciplinary teams to speed up the development of new products to reduce the time to market. These teams generally have people with mixed professional and technical disciplines (designers, engineers, production specialists, marketers, accountants, personnel, stylists, and so on) and can sometimes include people from different countries. Managing such groups, who have up to then not needed to recognize or acknowledge the existence of the others, and getting them to work collaboratively with one another is a mammoth and tricky task. Strategies that do not allow for cultural mismatches are unlikely to work.

What all this means is that if an organization which has run on bureaucratic lines wishes to become more entrepreneurial, it has a lot of work on its hands to change the mindset of its people to behave entrepreneurially. For example, their risk tolerance will have to be adjusted to accommodate a less certain decision environment and an organization where authority and power are more evenly distributed.

Chapter 20 examines cultural change in more depth.

16.10 Changing organizational structures

STRATEGIC change often requires that organizational structures and power bases change as well. It is unlikely that an organization can introduce a just-in-time procurement system without making significant changes to the way it operates its supply chain. The consequences of such a decision are far-reaching and touch on not only how the organization is structured but also how the supporting infrastructure—processes and culture—work to facilitate the changes. But shuffling people about within an organization has significant repercussions.

Organisations work well, not because the design is perfect but because the people in it work around the difficulties and imperfections of the organization. This means that individuals, in order to facilitate their work, build networks of people across their own organization and in other organizations. Restructuring the organization often breaks these support networks and introduces inefficiencies and ineffectiveness to a dynamic situation. The result may be chaos and a failed strategy.

Organisational structure embodies the power base of the management hierarchy and if the organization judges that decisions are better taken at the 'coal-face', then a structure and procedures that enable this to happen may mean a structure where power difference between management and workers is diminished. In recent years this has been achieved by removing layers of managers to create 'flatter' organizations. In these flatter structures, managers are forced to delegate power or get swamped by trivia.

In some organizations, the need for collaborative working between operational and functional units has to be achieved by strong networking rather than structural forms. Many people find it difficult to work in matrix structures where they have to be accountable to more than one manager and yearn for a clear chain of command.

Process infrastructures and cultures also affect organizational structure. An organization that is heavily dependent on information technology whether for direct selling or E-commerce may find that it needs a structure that is very different from one which still depends on person-to-person contact. Switching from one form to another is difficult and requires taking both staff and customers with you.

Chapter 21 examines the issues of designing and implementing changes in organizational structure.

16.11 Adaptability: a strategic capability

ADAPTABILITY is more a desirable characteristic than a specific activity. Adaptability is desirable in each of the five activities of the change model. In addition to designing processes, cultures, and structures that are capable of adapting to changing needs, change leaders and managers must also be tolerant of adaptive behaviour. Adaptability is not the same as flexibility. Adaptability is the ability to change nature in response to observed need. Flexibility is the capability to yield to external influences without changing nature. For example, car tyres are flexible in that they yield to the bumps and furrows in the road surface, but they cannot change their shape or their thread patterns to accommodate different surfaces. In that sense, the tyre is flexible but not adaptable. In periods of turbulence, when established revenue and profit streams can disappear overnight and where new opportunities appear equally quickly, the competence to take the organization by the scruff of its neck and refocus it on new objectives using new capabilities is of paramount survival significance. In Chapter 22 we discuss what we mean by adaptability and how such adaptive capability can be built into the fabric of the organization at both its emotional and transactional aspects.

16.12 Summary

THIS chapter has emphasized that however well thought out a strategy may be, it has little value unless it can be implemented effectively and within an appropriate time—a window of opportunity. The chapter introduces the reader to the five key activities needed to achieve this timely transformation—change leadership and management, process re-engineering, culture change or fit, and structural modifications or realignments.

The issues covered as part of the leadership activity are the need for both transactional management through techniques such as programme and project management and also transformational leadership which cannot be provided by a neatly described technique.

Process re-engineering stresses the need not only to introduce new processes but also to review and if necessary disband old and now defunct ones. Cultural and structural changes are the glue that brings the new transformed organization into pulsating life.

Finally, the importance of adaptability is stressed as a desirable strategic capability.

References

Ansoff, H, I., Declerk, R. P., and Hayes, R. L. (eds.) (1976) *From Strategic Planning to Strategic Management* (London: Wiley).

Charan, R. and Colvin, G. (1999) 'Why CEOs Fail', *Fortune*, 21 June.

Holman, Peter (1999) 'Turning Great Strategy into Effective Action', *Strategy* (Strategic Planning Society UK), Sept.

Pinto, J. K., and Slevin, D. P. (1988) 'Critical Success Factors in Effective Project Implementation', Ch. 20 in *Project Management Handbook* ed. D. I. Cleland. and W. R. King (New York: Van Nostrand Reinhold).

Tampoe, M. (1989) 'Leaders Do Not Deliver Projects, Teams Do', *International Journal of Project Management*, 7/1.

—— (1998) 'Liberating Leadership', The Industrial Society.

Chapter 17
Implementing Strategy: Leading Strategic Change

17.1 Introduction

LEADING change is not for the faint-hearted. Those in favour of the changes will, at best, give guarded support to those espousing the changes. Those wishing to retain the 'old' ways will fight long, hard, and noisily for things to remain as before. To quote Machiavelli:

> There is nothing more difficult to arrange, more doubtful of success, and more dangerous to carry through than initiating changes in a state's constitution. The innovator makes enemies of all who prospered under the old order, and only lukewarm support is forthcoming from those who would prosper under the new.

Strategic change initiatives usually involve a large number of people changing the roles they play. The transformations of roles, cultures, and structures have to be willed into being. Because of this, change requires strong leadership at all levels by both individuals and groups to maintain the collective motivation and drive of all those involved in the changes.

Leadership has many facets that can be summarized into two main types. The first is charismatic leadership which is mainly concerned with carrying the hearts and minds of the people involved in the change. The second is transactional leadership which is more task orientated and is concerned with making sure that a complex series of actions is planned, co-ordinated, and accomplished on time, within budget and to specification. These two separate elements of leadership are often confused. Both elements are essential to success. Few individuals are naturally good at both elements of leadership so that in practice the roles become shared across a leadership group. A further complication is that although the roles are separable, most real jobs will involve at least an element of both ingredients in differing proportions.

This chapter addresses the issues of leading change and the roles that are necessary to lead change. Chapter 18 looks at the mechanisms that are needed to manage projects and programmes.

Change leadership draws heavily on general leadership. It is a critical requirement and it can be carried out with varying degrees of success. In the ICL case, for example, there was no doubt in anyone's mind that radical change was needed to breathe new life into the company. Wilmot realized that he had two different leadership roles to perform. One was as change leader, in which role he spent many hours in one-to-many meetings to win support for his revised strategy. The other was as leader of a major corporation that still had to meet its commitments to its customers, shareholders, and creditors. As change leader, he recognized that speed of turnaround was important and he could only achieve this by winning the support, motivation, and commitment of the staff and management. As leader of an organization, he had to enthuse the same staff to deliver high quality outputs to achieve revenue and profit targets, without which the recovery would have faltered and the company would have ceased to exist. On the other hand, in the case of BMW, the change leadership was entrusted to others while Pischetrieder continued to lead the now much bigger BMW Group. His decision to delegate the role of leading the changes necessary in Rover to others may have cost him his job. As the initiator of the Rover deal, he had much more to lose if the promised turnaround failed to materialize than Wilmot who had been invited to help revive ICL's fortunes by the government and ICL's creditors.

This example highlights the vulnerability of chief executives who cannot deliver their promises, which are very often to deliver specified changes. Charan and Colvin (1999) in their article in *Fortune* magazine of 21 June 1999 list thirty-eight high profile chief executive officers who lost their jobs due to their inability to deliver their promises. Generally speaking, CEOs do not make decisions on their own, but when their vision is seen to fail, most of those associated with the vision and its execution tend to duck for cover. The leader is left on the high ground facing a firing squad of friends and enemies alike. Fortunately for most, these days, the guns are loaded with money rather than bullets so 'heads they win; tails they win'.

17.2 Leading and managing: a quick overview

THE leadership of change requires both leadership and management skills. It is therefore useful to review the fundamental differences between management and leadership. While management is mostly about maintaining the status quo, leadership is about creating the future. As Zaleznik (1977) points out:

> Managers and leaders are very different kinds of people. They differ in motivation, personal history, and in how they think and act . . . Managers tend to adopt impersonal, if not passive, attitudes towards goals . . . Leaders adopt a personal and active attitude towards goals. The net

result of this influence is to change the way people think about what is desirable, possible and necessary.

Benis and Nanus (1985) also draw this distinction. They say:

> To manage means to bring about, to accomplish, to have charge of, responsibility for, to conduct. Leading is influencing, guiding in direction, course, action, and opinion. The difference may be summarised as activities of vision and judgement—effectiveness—versus activities of mastering routines—efficiency.

It seems then that management is about efficiency and routine; leadership is about effectiveness and change.

Good leaders tend to create their opportunities by 'selling' new ideas and winning support for them from those they seek to lead. They display strong transformational skills. Transformational leaders engage emotionally with those whose help and support they need. Their emphasis will be on communicating the vision and over-riding objectives of the proposed activity. By doing this the leader(s) will remind people (who are deeply enmeshed in the detail of their day-to-day obligations) why they are going through the pain and added burden of these new actions and re-ignite their energy and drive. Zaleznik summarizes this well: 'Altering moods, evoking images and expectations, and in establishing specific desires and objectives'.

It is likely that by doing this a leader will be able to bring warring factions to the table and resolve their differences. Transformational leaders will display political and influencing skills, as they are good at sensing when to launch an offensive on any one of the many people on whom the project depends. They are able to couch requests and instructions in 'winning ways' and can live with ambiguity. This is because there will always be fuzzy areas around new initiatives and being tolerant of others' worries and fears yet allaying them by skilful manœuvring, requires the ability to 'hang loose' until a clear route forward can be sensed and firmed. Motivational and team-building skills are obviously a part of the transformational leader's armoury. This ability extends to both change makers and change receivers. Facilitation is another important capability. This means helping others achieve by pushing, prodding, and steering rather than doing it for them. The role encompasses that of a mentor and in that sense is a transformational one.

Good managers, on the other hand, are more likely to exploit the opportunities they are given. They usually work within a prescribed environment that often includes a territorial boundary, a set of objectives, and the resources to achieve those objectives. They depend on the quasi-contractual links with colleagues in other parts of the company to help them harness the corporate support they need to achieve their aims. Primarily, managers need to display transactional skills to do with planning, organizing, monitoring, and supervising. In this sense, they display the attributes of a transactional leader. A transactional leader is one who can plan and execute an implementation strategy with precision. Some of the key characteristics of such a person are precision of thought and execution. A transactional leader should be able to develop precise plans and to issue them, monitor, and re-plan as often as the changing nature of the project demands. Matching activities to individuals is also a trait that is prized in leaders. The ability to specify needs precisely and get them agreed by all those whose input is deemed essential is another transactional trait which is much valued in a leader. Searching for the truth and probing beyond the superficial are also traits that a transactional leader must have. In transactional mode, the leader will review progress with the various managers and staff involved with the changes and call to account those who are not pulling their weight. This can be interpreted as the management role of the leader, but that would be too simplistic shorthand for what the leader is doing in this instance. When leaders review progress, they seek to use the review, not only to assess progress but also to re-energize and motivate those being reviewed to continue to work at their assigned tasks. It is not an attempt to find fault but to help through mentoring and providing guidance and advice.

Great leaders combine transformational and transactional skills. They can enthuse and gather a group of willing followers; but they can also channel the goodwill and support they get to deliver a desired outcome. However, these can be conflicting characteristics. It is not easy to paint a visionary future and also to chart the map that gets you there. Often the visionary has to work hand in glove with a pragmatist to get results. Rarely can these dual traits be found in one person and so it is not uncommon to see leadership teams being formed that comprise people with these skills so that one can complement the other. These are very demanding qualities and this is why leadership is hard. Many people have some leadership qualities but only very few have the wide range of skills to rise above the shoal of able leaders.

17.3 The role of the change leader: why it is different from organizational leadership

LEADERSHIP has some general characteristics, but there are differences in leading change from leading an organization operating in a stable state. The leaders of organizations are often relatively free to set their own agendas. Change leaders are more likely to be involved in implementing strategic initiatives which they have not initiated and whose benefits they may not be totally convinced of. Change leaders are unlikely to have ready-made networks and processes and will have to create alliances and build networks in order to gain the support and resources for their change project. In other words, they have to use transformational skills to charm and win support and transactional skills to ensure that they deliver their promises. Change leaders have to depend more on influence, as they often do not have direct control of all the resources and people needed to achieve the changes they want. This makes change leadership very difficult, as some of the vital ingredients of leadership such as inner conviction may be lacking. For example, in the ICL case, there were many change leaders involved in implementing the changes proposed by Robb Wilmot and which the board had endorsed. Not all those leading the changes believed in them.

However, they all had one common objective that over-rode their doubts—survival of their careers and lifestyles that in the short term could only be achieved by ensuring the survival of the company. The beliefs and moral conviction that the leaders needed came from this underlying objective rather than the overt objectives to which they were working.

The leadership of change usually requires multiple leadership roles (as discussed in Sect. 17.5). The leadership task is not carried out by a single individual but is divided among several or many people. This is often because there are many simultaneous tasks to be accomplished and also because the nominated leaders are not necessarily the best leaders. It is not uncommon to find change leaders among 'doing' teams, providing colleagues with the emotional drive needed for success. It is the duty of programme managers, project managers and leaders, the change sponsors and change initiators to identify and harness the efforts of the change leaders. In late 1987, long after the recovery described in the case, the ICL board decided that the organization was still working at cross-purposes, with different divisions failing to support each other in the interests of the company. To correct this, the board, in its wisdom, chose to introduce a total quality programme into the company. Among the first things ICL did, at the instigation of the quality consultants, was to identify members of staff at all levels who were sympathetic to the quality programme, and send them for 'indoctrination' to a quality college run by the consultants. On their return they played the role of change leaders. They were able to allay fears about the programme by answering questions about it and were used to bolster morale throughout the long period of training that all ICL staff endured.

Change leadership is a political task and has to be done at all levels in the organization. At one end of the scale, it is necessary to keep the courage and enthusiasm of the board and other senior managers who, as the change programme hits obstacles, can falter in their belief in the benefits of the anticipated change. Within this group, there will also be those who wish the changes to fail but will be unwilling to make their feelings known. These 'sit on the fence till I know which side to support' types also need to feel that the board and the original sponsors still have the support of those that matter. The political task at this level is usually taken by or wished upon a senior director who is often the change leader at the highest level in the organization. He or she should be able to win and sustain the motivation and commitment of the board and other opportunistic junior directors and senior managers.

Against this role, we must contrast that of the programme and project manager. In the ICL case, the sponsors were the board and the government and creditors the initiators of the change. Even with this formidable backing, many change leaders found their efforts frustrated by managers and staff who felt threatened by the changes being introduced. The task of getting the logistics of change implemented usually falls on the change programme manager and project leaders. Programme and project managers do not have to be leaders and are not required to play leadership roles during a change process although the better ones usually demonstrate leadership behaviour. Project managers are drivers and are authorized and resourced to drive through change initiatives. They are not required to be political; but they have to be right. They are required to display inter-personal skills consistent with gaining support for their actions, but they are not expected to be diplomats. Programme managers have the task of synchronizing multiple projects so that they collectively deliver the programme objectives. The work of both programme and project managers is measurable and failure is often obvious and publicly visible.

The change programme manager is usually responsible for the complete change programme. He or she keeps the sponsor and other senior managers informed of progress and acts as the main conduit between the organization and the change programme. In addition, the programme manager needs to keep all the projects within the programme under review and ensure that they are progressing to plan and that they dovetail one with another. The other key task of the programme manager is to act as a mentor to the project managers or leaders reporting to him or her, providing them with the guidance needed to achieve their assigned objectives. The project managers have the dual role of keeping the teams reporting to them happy and motivated and ensuring that the organization continues to support the project with resources and essential support. This internal (to the team)/external (to the rest of the organization) role demands both political dexterity and transactional skills.

The design and implementation teams these project managers lead are the 'doers'. They are likely to be drawn from different parts of the organization. They will also be well versed in the way different parts of the organization function and the impact the changes will have on their particular part of the organization. Once they are knitted together as a team, they take on the unenviable task of making the changes necessary to realize the new strategy. This can often make them the butt of the organization's frustrations—as the initiators and sponsors are too distant from the rank and file and too powerful to be challenged. The team must therefore be made up of 'rugged' individuals who ride the punches and give as well as they get. Most importantly they must be achievers. The final group is made of those members of staff—at all levels—who have to live and work with the results of the change initiative. They are generally members of the different operational units whose task it is to keep the day-to-day activities of the business functioning.

The change leaders therefore need to be (adapted from Tampoe 1998):

- Confidence builders who can make leaders of their followers. During periods of change many people feel uncertain of their futures and worry about their ability to adapt their skills and capabilities to match that expected of them in their new roles. This saps their self-esteem and reduces their motivation. An effective change leader will work with different people to help them to release the leader within themselves and by so doing diminish their anxiety. By so doing, they are able to release the performance, loyalty, and commitment of those involved.
- Multi-faceted in that they can wear many faces and play many different roles. This is an important capability for leaders in change situations. They need to be able to display different leader behaviours to match the needs of their followers and the circumstances. This may mean tutoring and supporting some people and nagging others.
- Motivational by connecting with the emotions of their followers. Unless the leader is able to enthuse their followers with their vision and daring, it is unlikely that

they will carry the majority of those involved with them. Trotting out the arcane and well-worn metaphor of achieving shareholder value is more likely to demotivate and emphasize the wrong objectives. However, it is important that they spot the low points of the programme and the individual projects and step in to revitalize the motivation of the respective teams. Above all, the leader must be able to enthuse others and encourage them to renewed energy and determination to win.

- Trustworthy. It is unlikely that nominated leaders who are seen to be self-serving will capture the attention and the positive emotions of those being led. There must be sincerity in the actions of the leader and people must believe that the leader's motives are honourable.
- Outer-focused. To lead others it is necessary to understand them and their motives and aspirations. This means that while having his or her own convictions and beliefs, the leader must be able to tune into the mood of others to energize their motivational drivers.
- Performance not conformance orientated. The leadership actions must be focused on outcomes and not inputs. That is to say, to benefit from the potential of those they lead, leaders must get people to focus on tangible and desirable outcomes. By doing this, they enable people to understand why the future state is worth putting in all that hard work and enduring all that disruption for.
- Politically astute. While the project manager may take a more single-minded approach to the task, the change leader must react to the political climate and tune the play to match the mood of the organization as the changes work through. This means being political but not giving in to political expediency.
- Persistent and determined and not let project or programme constraints and considerations veer them off course. This can often mean fighting for scarce resources, particularly when the demands on these resources come from the 'normal' operational demands of the business.
- Quick-witted and able to comprehend the issues that may arise from a variety of disciplines even if they are not masters of any of the disciplines being used during the life of the change programme. This is mostly to be able to ask intelligent questions and evaluate the answers received.
- Convincing, so that they can get commitment to common objectives even if some of those involved may not fully support these and try to subvert them to meet their own specific objectives. This is a very common occurrence in project-based activity—one or more of the team members diverting the project towards modified goals—and unless stopped can lead to failed project and programme objectives. This does not mean that a rigid approach has to be taken. In fact, it suggests the establishment of an open forum for debate of contentious issues and a mechanism for dispute resolution which will get all the people involved behind the change programme again.
- Creative and be able to come up with solutions to obstacles and new challenges or be able to orchestrate such activity so that the projects and programme do not falter. Leaders generally tend to stay above the fray so that they can see the field of

play, the players, and the action objectively and intervene as appropriate. This means learning the tricky skill of being apart but yet being part of the action.
- Self-motivating especially when things are going badly, as there is unlikely to be anyone else to motivate them.

17.4 On whom should change leaders focus their transformational skills?

It is almost certain that events and the programme and project managers will force the change leader to spend more time on the transactional aspects of the change programmes. This makes it vital that change leaders deliberately set aside time for people-related activities. In the words of an ex-colleague, 'it is important to give people positive strokes', but who qualifies for such attention?

- Members of staff always suffer during periods of change. Their security is challenged. Their value and self-esteem are undermined. They may not have been told the whole picture and were not aware that anything needed changing. They may not have believed what they were told. They may have trusted the rumour mill which caused them more uncertainty and unhappiness. They may not like the 'sound' of the finished product/service/organization. During the changes they may have found their support network eroded and they may have had to create new ones, not knowing if those they are building networks with will be there at the end of the change implementation. This can be a very fraught and demotivating time for all those directly or indirectly involved in the changes.
- Customers and suppliers are often another group who find themselves at the receiving end of change programmes. All the familiar faces seem to have moved and the new ones are not familiar as yet. Sometimes well-established procedures and ways of working are erased as the new initiatives take over and these outsiders feel aggrieved that they were not consulted and that they were not given adequate notice to make the changes to their systems to enable a smooth transition. This becomes more important in those initiatives that depend on linked value chains and where electronic data exchange and just-in-time procedures are involved.
- The public and other organizations that are peripherally involved may also find cause for complaint and intervene to cause delay or to stop the change programme. Local authority planning officers and health and safety executives may find that what was proposed and what had come into being were different and made light of their authority and discretion.
- Distributors of the organization's products and those that stock spares and other ancillary accessories may also find that the changes have adversely affected their trading position. This is much more likely where new products hit the market at a

rate that makes obsolescence a serious threat to the 'small' business. Computer retailers suffer in this way because of the rapid obsolescence of processors and the erosion of the price of software and peripherals.

- The change receivers who have to live and work with the changes. Ignoring them during the change process development phase or even during the change initiation phase (see Chapter 18) can have significant repercussions as Shell discovered when it tried to dispose of a defunct oil rig in the North Sea. Having to pull back at the last minute was costly in both money and reputation. It was no comfort to the company that their accusers were wrong all along. Another example of a poorly executed strategy was the introduction of the Poll Tax by the Conservative Government. Whatever the merits or demerits of the Poll Tax, the country was not prepared in advance for its introduction and the result was an embarrassing retreat.

17.5 The multiple roles required for successful change

MANY roles are needed for successful change. Table 17.1 lists all those likely to be involved in a change programme and outlines their roles, their purpose, and the results they are expected to deliver.

Very often people have to take on these change roles in addition to their normal work-related role. For example, the change sponsor may be the board or it could be a line manager who needs to achieve change in order to meet targets. During a period of change, many people will wear two hats. However, the day-to-day operational hat will always take precedence unless there is someone around to remind them of the change programme obligations. This is a role that the change leader must play.

Table 17.2 shows how these roles were fulfilled in the ICL recovery actions. In the case of ICL there was very little time to establish formal structures and procedures to achieve the changes needed. Everyone in the company just had to run the business and also manage the changes simultaneously. There was, for example, no formal programmes office overseeing the changes; instead the executive directors and the divisional directors met weekly to review progress and iron out snags as they arose.

Table 17.1 The roles, purposes, and results of the change makers

Role	Purpose	Results
Change initiators	To propose the changes and get formal approval for them	Continued support for the change initiative
Change sponsor	To provide high level organizational support for the change programme. Some change is initiated from the top but other strategic changes can be initiated at divisional or business unit level but have corporate wide repercussions requiring director level support	Ensure the support of the board and other senior managers. Help the programme and project managers when asked
Change leaders	Individuals at all levels in the organization who believe in the changes and provide the motivation and drive needed to take their colleagues with them	Energize their colleagues and keep the changes coming
Change managers (programme and project managers)	To keep all the players on track, rooting for the change initiative and preventing the saboteurs from coming into play	Successful task achievement
Change designers	Work closely with the change initiators and the implementation team to design a process which can help the implementation team and which is still true to the ideas pushed by the change initiators	Design a change process that will steer the implementors to achieve the desired outcomes
Change implementors	Work to deliver the change initiative before its value and purpose are eroded by time or loss of interest due to lapsed time and implementation problems	Meeting all milestones
Review and consolidation team	A small team made up of the implementation team and probably the change initiators to review the outcome of the changes and to report back to the change sponsors	Smoothly operating end result
Change receivers	Those who have to operate in a new environment and cope with new structures, processes, and culture	Make a success of the changed environment
Change supporters	Those who believe in the changes and do their best to help it happen but are unable or unwilling to take a leadership or proselytizing role	Fuel the flames and keep the changes coming

Table 17.2 The roles and those who played them in the ICL case

Role	Purpose	Role Players
Change initiators	To propose the changes and get formal approval for them	Government and creditors initially. Robb Wilmot primarily on the tactics
Change sponsor	To provide high level organizational support for the change programme	The ICL board
Change leaders	Individuals at all levels in the organization who believe in the changes and provide the motivation and drive needed to take their colleagues with them	Newly appointed managers to various posts with clear 'guidance' on what was to be achieved and believers among the troops
Change managers (programme and project managers)	To keep all the players on track, rooting for the change initiative and preventing the saboteurs from coming into play	Executive directors and divisional directors of the company
Change designers	Work closely with the change initiators and the implementation team to design a process which can help the implementation team and which is still true to the ideas pushed by the change initiators	Mostly Wilmot with help from selected specialists advising on personnel, technical issues, and so on
Change implementors	Work hard to deliver the change initiative before its value and its purpose are eroded by time or diminishing interest due to lapsed time and implementation problems	Divisional Directors, their direct reports, and divisional staff
Review and consolidation team	A small team made up of the implementation team and probably the change initiators to review the outcome of the changes and to report back to the change sponsors that the changes have indeed occurred and been (it is hoped) successful	Weekly meeting of the executive directors and the divisional directors
Change receivers	Those who have to operate in the new environment and cope with the new structures, procedures, systems, and cultures	All staff and customers
Change supporters	Those who believe in the changes and do their best to help it happen but are unable or unwilling to take a leadership or proselytizing role	Whole group of frustrated managers in the 'old regime' who were grateful to have new leadership

17.6 Summary

IN this chapter we have discussed the role of leadership to achieve the changes necessary to implement a new strategy. We make the point that change leadership requires a clearly defined vision with concrete objectives and achievable stretch goals. It requires carefully mapped out change processes and an enthusiastic following of willing helpers and sponsors with adequate corporate power to provide support during the hard times and periods of doubt. During periods of change, the change leader sits in the middle of the action directing the traffic and the players until the desired outcome is achieved. It requires that the institutions and people being changed are emotionally engaged in the change process and will the new organization or culture into being.

We have taken special pains to separate out the leadership role from that of project and programme management that usually accompanies any change initiative. The role of the change leader is sometimes different from that of a leader in other situations, in that the change leader may be implementing the designs and aspirations of another person or group. None the less, we feel that the task of leadership, with its emphasis on engaging the emotions of those involved, and the task of management, with the job of systematically ploughing through the raft of actions needed to achieve change, must not be confused or subsumed into one role.

References

Benis, W., and Nanus, B. (1985) *Leaders: The Strategies for Taking Charge* (New York: Harper and Row).

Charan, R., and Colvin, G. (1999) 'Why CEOs Fail', *Fortune*, 21 June.

Macchiavelli, N. (1961) *The Prince*, tr. G. Bull (London: Penguin Classics).

Tampoe, M. (1990) 'Driving Organisational Change through the Effective Use of Multi-Disciplinary Project Teams', *European Management Journal*, 8/3, Sept.

—— (1998) 'Liberating Leadership, A Research Report', The Industrial Society.

Zalesnik, Abraham (1977) 'Managers and Leaders: Are they different?' *Harvard Business Review*, May–June.

Chapter 18

Implementing Strategy: Managing the Change Programme

18.1 Introduction

CHAPTER 17 examined the leadership of the change programme. This chapter looks at the supervisory aspects of managing strategic change. It is about the mechanics of taking the change concept from intent to reality. It is about dividing the whole task into manageable chunks, assigning these chunks to individuals or teams, allocating resources, and then monitoring achievement. This whole series of management activities falls under the categorization of programme and project management.

18.2 Programme management

PROGRAMME management refers to the umbrella activity that manages many projects simultaneously, so that they all meet their individual objectives and also satisfy the needs of the overall programme. Paramount among the issues that programme management supervises is that of inter-project dependency. Inter-project dependency occurs when one project within the programme produces output that is critical to another project within that programme. The delay of the lead project will harm the completion of the whole programme and will be costly in both resources and time. Figure 18.1 illustrates the inter-relationship between the projects that make up a programme and the achievement of the whole programme. It looks

Figure 18.1 Projects within a programme

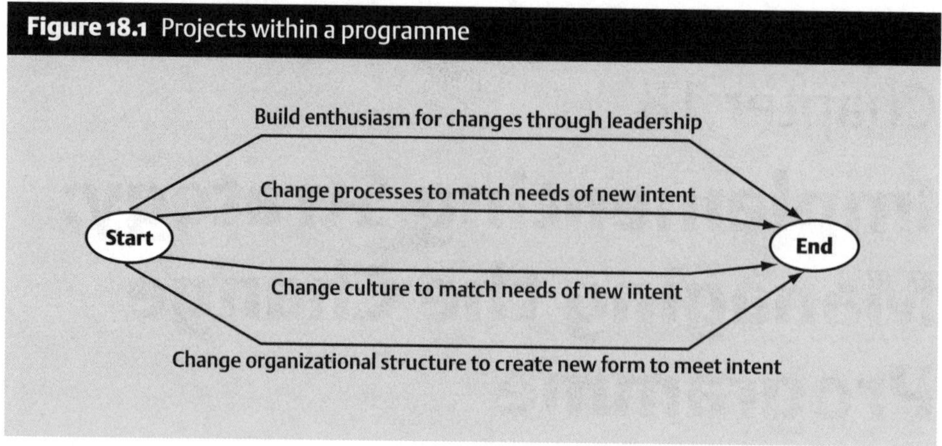

like and is a simple critical path network, where each project has its own more detailed network.

The role of the programme manager is often misunderstood. It is not the role of the programme manager to be a super-project manager. That is, the programme manager is not expected to act as the project manager of all the projects within a programme, using the project leaders as mere automatons carrying out the programme manager's instructions. The programme manager should be an enabler, acting as mentor, key and scarce skills provider, and administrative support to the projects within the programme. If the programme manager takes this more advisory role, the scope of the job is more likely to contain the activities in the list below:

- Create a programmes office. This office will provide the sub-project leaders and their team members with specialist skills, an administrative service including tracking the sub-project finances, resources, and time utilization.
- Liaise with the change sponsors and others who have an impact on the programme's success and ensure that they are 'on- side' throughout the programme's life. This could mean representing the programme to the board and other senior review bodies within the organization and taking a lead role in negotiating large contracts and other inputs that can derail the programme.
- Choose the sub-project leaders and then train them to manage their projects in accordance with the rules and objectives of the overall programme. This might mean persuading the sub-project leaders to use one rather than many project management tools such as software, using a common dependencies register, and a common means of tracking time and expended resources.
- Act as super-trouble-shooter by anticipating issues and problems, devising solutions, and then offering them to the sub-project leaders. More importantly, to get the sub-project leaders to take their eyes off the ball at their feet and scan the horizon for looming storm clouds.
- Review the progress of each project within the programme and encourage, cajole, and nag so that each project meets its deadlines.

- Negotiate for and obtain appropriate scarce skills from other parts of the company and facilitate wider co-operation from the organization as a whole.

Programme management may sometimes be achieved by informal means as shown in the EuroPharm case example.

18.3 Project management

THE change project has a minimum of four major phases, namely: initiation, change process design, implementation, review and consolidation.

The initiation phase

The initiation phase is mostly concerned with analysing the changes needed and building a case for them. The *change initiators* (as described in Chapter 17) will be actively involved during this phase. They usually tend to be senior decision makers and their advisers and direct operational managers. They tend to propose changes of a variety of types based on strategic or operational needs. Sometimes both needs can dominate simultaneously. Examples of such change initiatives are new products, new markets, new organizations, and strategic alliances. Because these changes can have significant current and future consequences, change initiators are usually required to justify their proposals by offering a carefully studied and documented case. Such a justification would not only cover the proposed changes, but also identify the risk to the business and the knock-on effects of the changes on other parts of the business. Because of the wider organizational implications of strategic change, it is customary for the change initiators to discuss their proposals with all those who may be affected by their proposals and to get their agreement to the changes. Where agreement is not received, they need to say so, so that the ultimate approvers know what support and dissension the proposal has within the organization. If this is not done, it is likely that the proposal will be rejected. Among the reasons given for the departure of Martin Taylor as chief executive of Barclays Bank was that he had proposed a demerger of the bank without a formal study of such a move and without winning support from fellow directors for it. That is certainly not the way to initiate a major strategic change for a company.

Typical outcomes of the initiation phase are a clear and emotionally engaging vision, strong conviction among the prime movers and their supporters that change is inevitable, and commitment from those in positions to resource and sponsor the change as it moves from initiation to completion.

The design phase

The design phase is all to do with defining the changes needed, designing the new order, designing the change vehicle, and preparing the groundwork for successful change implementation. Those involved in this phase are the *change designers*. In addition, it is necessary that the change management approaches and procedures be agreed so that the change process can be monitored and carefully steered into being. It is important to take time during this process. Rushing the thinking and planning at this stage will only create problems at the implementation phase and review and consolidation phases that follow. Far more people get involved at this phase—the *change designers*. It is likely that there will be nominees from different parts of the organization involved at this phase. The team that forms will be held responsible for designing a change process that will cause the minimum disruption and obtain the maximum support for the planned changes. It is likely that at this stage an individual is appointed to lead the change process. It is also likely that an embryonic implementation team will be created. This group of people will influence the change processes being designed and then take over the design for implementation. Not all of those assigned to the embryo implementation team will be supporters of or be released full-time to the change initiative. However, their early involvement will help get their buy-in and will also ensure that a core implementation team has formed so that the implementation can proceed with vigour from the very beginning.

The implementation phase

The implementation phase is about creating the new structures, products, cultures, and processes that need to be put in place for the organization to face its new future. Although the implementation teams (*change implementors*), with help from sponsors, will be driving forward the changes, it is likely that line managers and their staff will also be involved and affected by the planned changes. For example, a new product design, manufacture, and launch will involve people from marketing, sales, manufacturing, distribution, personnel, and finance. An organizational restructuring may involve the whole organization, with people at all levels affected by the transition to the new structure. Putting in place a strategic alliance could involve legal and contracts people, manufacturing, marketing, sales, personnel, finance, distribution, production scheduling, and perhaps others. As these examples show, every initiative, however simple it looks, usually has far-reaching ramifications. If managers fail to see the inter-linked nature of the changes they propose, strategic initiatives can fail. Unfortunately, our experience is that managers tend to underestimate the ramifications of strategic change.

Once the changes have been implemented, the organization must assess how well the implementation reflects the expected outcomes of the strategy. This final, *review and consolidation phase* requires the strategic implementation team, the line managers, and staff to ensure that the changes work and to highlight any modification that needs to be done to ensure complete compliance with the original intent. This phase is often forgotten. Most teams and organizations in general stop at the previous phase through sheer exhaustion. Summoning up the enthusiasm to review the implemented changes and to make sure that nothing has been overlooked is tedious work. Also by this stage, some of the more proactive people will have left the project, leaving a small group who are more likely to be administrators rather than project drivers. A downsized and deskilled team is unlikely to go in search of implementation

Box 18.1 Illustration of programme and project management

This example is taken from an organization seeking to develop effective human resource strategies to meet the challenges of a changing workforce and a more volatile market. The company recognized that it needed to implement a cogent human resources strategy that integrated the financial and career aspirations of its entire workforce. The problem was that some were highly skilled individuals and others were not. Some expected to work for the organization for a long time, and expected to progress to higher management. Others saw their stay as limited to a year or perhaps two before they moved on to do other things. The company determined that it needed to implement a series of actions to meet the needs of its workforce. Among these were:

- a career structure that matches the different needs of its employees;
- a communications policy and system to keep staff well informed about a range of organizational issues;
- pay scales that not only attracted good people but also held them for longer with a pay-for-performance methodology for future implementation;
- a training programme to develop all staff (juniors up to senior management and beyond);
- a recruitment/divestment policy and system that made the task of adding new staff and also removing poor workers easier and yet fair on all those involved.

To encourage the whole programme to be successfully implemented, the personnel director assigned the responsibility for each of these projects to the divisional personnel manager within the company that most needed the initiative. However, to avoid a plethora of systems and to ensure that the completed projects interfaced one to another, the personnel director appointed a programme manager with the responsibility of providing common project management services and of overseeing the progress of each project. In this way, matching needs, people, and initiatives, the personnel director achieved a company-wide programme within the costs and time-scales of the sub-groups within the organization.

failures and the operational staff may suffer the indignities of a poorly implemented change initiative. This is also the phase when the company learns about its ability to implement strategic changes and being able to refine this ability may prove to be life saving in the long term. It pays to set up a separate team to do the review. They are best selected from the implementation team, as this ensures continuity and ownership of what has been delivered.

18.4 The people in the change process and their relationships

All those involved in the four phases outlined above can be loosely described as change makers. Although they do not all get involved all of the time, they have played the important part of changing the direction of the organization and putting in place the organizational and cultural characteristics needed for the changes to succeed. The way these phases and the principal influencers relate to one another is shown in Table 18.1 on p. 216. Within each phase there may be many projects, all of them managed by a project manager or leader who is accountable to the programme manager and probably a line manager.

18.5 Measuring the success of strategic change programmes

Deriving meaningful measures of success for a change programme is always tricky. Traditionalists take the view that the programme must deliver what it promised and that there should be no compromises and no mealy-mouthed post-hoc rationalizations. Others take a more pragmatic view. They understand that designing and implementing a change programme is not like designing and building a house or many houses in a new housing development. Almost all change programmes are unique. If they were not, there would be little benefit from the vast investment in time and resources. Also they are organic, as people are involved and their views may change. Compromises have to be made and people's wishes accommodated if the final product is to be acceptable to the end users, so it is important to derive a set of measures which are not so loose as to be meaningless or so tight as to be constraining on the programme manager and the project teams. The measures must allow for justified and approved variations and they must be about things that can be measured.

It is likely that a set of success criteria along the lines listed below will be established as part of the strategic change programme.

- Declared targets for key deliverables for each phase and project within the overall programme. Depending on the type of project these key deliverables may encompass a set of soft and hard measures such as:
- Meeting stated purpose:
  (a) market share achieved at the end of the change programme;

(b) process efficiency improvement measured as reduced costs, increased attractiveness, and so on;

(c) visible changes in employee behaviour measured as improved communications, better co-operation, higher levels of innovation, and so on;

(d) return on investment, revenue, and profit as hard targets; and

(e) soft targets such as customer satisfaction, service quality, social and environmental factors, and employee satisfaction.

- They must have achievable but tight achievement dates for each activity within each project within the overall programme. These activities must also have resources and quality standards set at appropriate levels so that the programme is run effectively and efficiently.

EuroPharm used a cultural survey to measure the effectiveness of change (see EuroPharm case example)

18.6 Managing programme and project risks

CHANGE programmes are not without their risks. Sponsors can move on. Companies can get into financial trouble during the changes and the programme may have to be scaled down, slowed, or stopped. Key personnel with unique skills may move on leaving the project short-handed or short skilled during a critical phase. Original design objectives may have to be changed to meet changing circumstances. The change leadership may falter and diminish the motivation and drive of the organization for change. The programme and project management itself may be poorly carried out, resulting in the whole programme suffering from mismanagement or no management at all. The projects within the programme could have been poorly planned and their inter-dependence may not have been planned for at all. Dependencies between projects within the programme and on resources outside the programme may not materialize. For these and many more reasons, the projects and the programme may fail. The role of the programme manager is to identify these risks and, together with the project managers and others, to manage them.

Table 18.1 Relationship of change influencers and phases

Change phases/ influencers	Initiation phase	Development phase	Implementation phase	Review and consolidate phase
Change initiators	Likely to be quite involved at this phase. Also the advocates of the changes and responsible for getting senior management support and finance	Likely to be less involved but would wish to review and assess the design and then publicize it to help gain acceptance	Likely to be involved in bringing along the stragglers and encouraging the converted	Less likely to be interested in this phase
Change sponsors	Very actively working with the initiators to arrive at a fully justified idea for onward sponsorship	Involvement only when initiators and designers seek help	Involvement only when initiators, programme, and project managers seek help	Ensure that the organization is aware of the success of the programme and the lessons for the future
Change managers (programme and project managers)	Less active mostly during this phase but could be involved with the initiators helping them scope the task	Establishing the development team. Also keeping a sharp eye on the plans and actions to ensure consistency with original intent	Watching for distortions of the implementation and making course corrections to retain consistency with the original plan or its revision	Carry out the review to ensure that the original intent was achieved or learn from the failures of changes
Change designers	May be involved at this stage but most often chosen later	Very active during this phase. Checking back with the initiators to check that they are true to the original intent. And checking forward with the implementors for feasibility of their designs	Providing help to the implementors throughout this phase and modifying the design without losing integrity of the original intention and design philosophy	Co-operating with initiators and implementors to judge success and learn from shortfalls

Change implementors	Not involved at this phase	Some involvement when referred to by the designers	Fully active at this stage making changes happen	Contribute to the review and to explain changes and modifications made during implementation
Change reviewers	Not involved at this phase	Not involved at this phase	Not involved at this phase	Active at this phase to learn and feedback to the organization views on how all of the processes and decisions taken could have been better done
Change receivers	Almost certainly unaware of any activity to make changes	Might have inkling that something of significance is happening but uncertain of what and whether it would affect them	Feeling the full force of the change activity as their work and their equanimity is disturbed by the changes being made	Relieved it is all over and hoping that things will stay 'normal' for some time
Change supporters	No involvement	Little or no involvement but may point out matters of detail that can derail the programme during the implementation phase	Considerable involvement helping to overcome objections and circumvent obstacles	Give them comfort that supporting the changes was right and ammunition to publicize successes

18.7 Summary

THIS chapter has dealt with the issues surrounding the successful transformation of an organization to meet strategic aims. It has shown that many people, activities, and resources are involved and that unless the whole programme is well led and properly managed, the strategy may fail at the last hurdle. Finally, we wish to point out that however well the change programme achieves its objectives, the success of the strategy is finally tested in the furnace of 'real life' by the operational arm of the organization. Similarly, the eventual success or failure of the strategy must be measured against the ultimate impact the changes have on the business.

References

Macchiavelli, N. (1961) *The Prince*, tr. G. Bull (London: Penguin Classics).

Tampoe, Mahen (1990) 'Driving Organisational Change through the Effective Use of Multi-Disciplinary Project Teams', *European Management Journal*, 8/3, Sept.

Zalesnik, Abraham (1977) 'Managers and Leaders: Are they different?', *Harvard Business Review*, May–June.

Chapter 19
Changing Business Processes

19.1 Introduction

PROCESSES are the habits of organizations. They help organizations to operate on autopilot. This is achieved by codifying all those routine activities of the organization and then training people to use these processes to carry out their assigned tasks. Processes are put in place for many reasons but mainly to facilitate the efficient operation of the business, resulting in the prudent use of company resources by its staff and the norms of financial and physical resource usage. Processes are also a means of control and quality assurance as the process assists and monitors the way a transaction is carried out. Processes therefore have many uses. They can be used:

To support staff

- These processes are designed to help staff carry out their work with optimum efficiency and the minimum of stress. These can vary from the systems that help staff serve customers to those systems that help functional staff help their front-line colleagues.

To help customers

- These processes are designed to help customers access the organization and buy goods and services with minimum inconvenience. They also provide customer access to after-sales service and in general increase the customer's feel-good factor.

To control quality and service

- These processes are aimed at monitoring how well the organization is doing *vis-à-vis* its customers and suppliers. They enable customers to voice their satisfaction (or dissatisfaction) with the service they receive. In addition, these processes help monitor staff performance against standards and the organization's performance against its business targets.

To achieve financial control

- These processes are generally aimed at ensuring that the finances of the organization are used according to accepted norms of accounting practice and within the rules of the business and in accordance with any legal and statutory obligations.

To achieve management control

- These processes are put in place to ensure that management, at all levels, knows what is going on in the business. These systems are usually fed by the systems listed above but are not operations support systems, in that they do not directly facilitate day-to-day operations but do highlight the failure of the operational systems.

The challenge to the strategy implementor is that all these systems need to be checked and validated during a period of organizational transformation following the implementation of a revised strategy. Failure to modify these systems to match the new strategic capability of the business will result in the organization still functioning in the 'old' ways even though its people want to move it along its new chosen route. Process re-engineering therefore is an essential requirement of strategy implementation. Otherwise, as Deming (1986) quite rightly points out, 'The workers are handicapped by the system, and the system belongs to management'.

At the same time, it is necessary to take his warning that

> It is not sufficient to improve processes. There must also be constant improvement of design of product and service . . . All this is management's responsibility.

The point that Deming is making is that a management group who have decided on a series of strategic changes to renew and enhance the business cannot afford to stop at the promulgation of these changes. They must also put in place the underlying infrastructure that enables their staff to convert the ideas for change into the reality of change. Japanese companies entering the UK and US markets understood this very well. While building their factories and planning their sourcing, they made sure that their suppliers fully understood the quality and delivery implications of becoming part of their value and supply chain. They entered into long-term partnerships and invested in the education and improvement of their suppliers' capability before taking supply of the components necessary to make their cars, television sets, and other products (Oliver and Wilkinson 1988; Hammer and Champy 1993; also Nelson *et al.* 1998).

Both the IBAP and EuroPharm case examples show how systems changes were necessary as part of the process of implementing strategic change.

19.2 The eight steps to change business processes

THE steps to achieving effective changes to the process infrastructure are listed below.

1. Review all existing processes against the new strategic direction, especially to ensure that the inter-relationship between existing processes are understood in terms of knock-on effects.
2. Gain management agreement to the necessary process changes and then sell the need to all those who will eventually have to implement and use them.
3. Find best practice. Look for examples of good processes within or outside the organization rather than just update the present ones. It is not often that companies re-engineer their processes and it therefore makes sense to choose future processes carefully and well.
4. Develop the criteria and measures by which the effectiveness of the processes will be judged to prevent the new re-engineered processes falling foul of poor specification.
5. Revise existing processes by developing, refining, or redefining the processes needed for the new strategic direction being taken by the company.
6. Install revised/new processes, and
7. Publicize their presence to all staff and especially those using them in their work.
8. Remove outdated processes.

19.3 Step 1: Review all existing processes against the new strategy

THIS is the most practical way to begin. Carry out a quick review to determine whether current processes can satisfy the needs of the new organizational capability. Hammer and Champy (1993) suggest that the following areas be looked at:

- Broken processes—those already in trouble due to extensive information exchange, data redundancy and operational redundancy such as re-keying the same data. Other systems identified by them are inventory buffers, unutilised or poorly used assets, high levels of checking and cross checking and reworking.
- Important processes—those that impact on customers for example.
- Feasible processes—those that will yield to re-engineering and deliver quick returns.
- Complex processes—where the processes have many interconnections and dependencies and require above average training and maintenance.

Studying the organization to discover processes that fit these criteria does not have to be a large and cumbersome activity. Generally, it can be fulfilled in a few days for a medium-sized organization as its main purpose is to spot mismatches between current processes and future process needs. Out of this study the organization will be able to pinpoint the processes that need the most urgent changes and also what new processes are needed to help the organization meet its new objectives. In carrying out the review, it is essential that the reviewers are objective in their assessments. At every stage in their review, they must gain agreement from those who run the process that the reviewers' understanding of the process is correct and, more importantly, that they have understood the inter-relatedness of one process with another. The review process must also be used to gain agreement on perceived or real shortfalls and through this means gain the commitment of those who will use the new processes. The review must be a learning rather than a judgemental activity.

A manufacturing company carried out such an audit before it committed to a new strategic direction that attempted to introduce just-in-time supplier management. It found that the size and complexity of changes it would have had to make to the manufacturing and administrative processes would have been so extensive that the strategy it proposed to follow would have failed if attempted as a one-off activity. The directors had anticipated that these systems would have to be changed but it took an audit to highlight the cost and logistical complexity of the changes needed. Based on these findings, the organization chose a different strategic route that involved a phased implementation leading eventually to their 'ideal'.

These reviews often point up the fact that the flow of information is often at the heart of many organization design decisions and process efficiencies or malfunction. As Wind and Main (1998) point out:

> Computerized information does change the life of a business. It changes the way companies are organized, the way they are managed, the relationships among their people and with customers, suppliers and partners. It changes the scope and understanding of a business, the organization and flow of work, the way work is performed. It changes marketing and distribution; it lowers the barriers confronting entrepreneurs and reduces the differences between big and little companies.

19.4 Step 2: Gain management agreement to process changes

PROCESSES constitute a vital part of the power structure within an organization. As such, changing processes can often lead to a redistribution of power and with it a redefinition of the careers of many senior and junior staff. As Davenport (1993) points out, 'Process innovation involves massive change, not only in process flows and the culture surrounding them, but also in organizational power and controls, skill requirements, reporting relationships, and management practices'. Secondly, process changes can cause significant capital and revenue costs and dislocation to the smooth flow of the operation of the organization. Therefore, it is imperative that senior management agreement and sponsorship is obtained when changing processes. The costs and likely dislocation is often associated with new equipment, sometimes relocation of staff, early retirement or severance of staff, extensive training, and the potential impact on customer satisfaction and organizational reputation. Thirdly, even if the detail of how the processes work is not understood by top management it is only at the higher reaches of the organization that the interconnectedness of processes is fully understood. This means that top management backing is vital. To quote Davenport (1993)

> Process innovation is typically much more top down, requiring strong direction from senior management. Because large firms' structures do not reflect their cross-functional processes, only those in positions overlooking multiple functions may be able to see opportunities for innovation.

This backing from the 'top' of a company becomes even more important when the change project takes a long time. A typical time-scale to install a major new process is two to three years. Unless the commitment to the process changes are underwritten at the highest level, new management at the operational level, with different ideas, may derail the changes being carried out and with it the strategic initiative.

Many changes to processes involve the application of information and communications technologies. This invariably requires the involvement of the IT specialists. The marriage of IT specialists with other operational specialists and front-line workers is often a difficult one. Because the IT components often drive these processes, the IT staff take or attempt to take the lead role. But because they do not understand the processes this 'prima donna' attitude can spell disaster as costs, time-scales, and functionality can suffer. Top management must get involved to ensure that they do not allow the 'cart to get before the horse'.

The effect of time erosion on a strategic change project is illustrated by the example of an organization re-engineering its manufacturing control system. The company set up a project team to design the new system and bring it into being. The project took four years to complete. The project team had staff seconded from all the relevant units in the company. This established good early working relationships and achieved goodwill and co-operation of the whole organization. However, time, restructuring, and the promotion of key members eroded the relationships that existed between the project team and the operating units and the project team found that their original design and implementation plans were being questioned by new managers and staff in the operating units. Unmanaged, there was every likelihood that an expensive new facility would go unused. To correct this, the project team launched a major campaign to get the now much changed board to endorse the original strategy and to then inform and buy the co-operation of the new line managers and staff. As Davenport points out: 'The multidimensional scope of transformational change is an obvious driver of the time requirement. It is simply not possible to plan and implement major changes in multiple organizational systems and structures overnight'.

19.5 Step 3: find best practice

If the strategy is to become reality, then it is imperative that the processes that underpin the strategy are the 'best' the organization can afford. An effective approach is to learn from others and to ensure that the processes being installed are at least competitive facility for facility with those in competitor organizations. Watson (1993) points out, 'The objective of benchmarking is to change an organization in a way that increases its performance'.

Processes are deeply intertwined with the capability of people to deliver their obligations under a strategy. Individual capability must be blended in with the capability of the organization as a whole to marshal its diverse resources in a way that delivers competitive advantage. In this context, the term organizational capability takes on a wider and more integrative meaning as defined by Ulrich and Lake (1990), that is 'The ability of a firm to manage people to gain competitive advantage'.

In many instances, the ability of people to perform is tied in closely with the systems and processes that exist within the organization. They go on to suggest that people's performance is related to the processes that support them. 'Building organizational capability focuses on internal organizational processes and systems on meeting customer needs and ensures that the skills and efforts of employees are directed towards achieving the goals of the organization as a whole'.

Therefore, to attempt to imitate the processes of organizations with cultures or core competencies that are vastly different from one's own would be futile and counter-productive. It has become quite common during the period of benchmarking frenzy in the late 1980s and early 1990s for companies to stream to Marks & Spencer to learn how they managed their relationships with their suppliers. Partnerships have been a part of Marks & Spencer's way of doing business from its very inception almost 100 years ago. The company's founders saw it as a transformational relationship in which both parties derived mutual benefit. This did not mean that it was or is cosy or undemanding, but it is supportive and it does drive continuous improvement and cost reductions in the supplier organization much faster than would be the case if the supplier was left to its own devices. Those who sought to imitate them had often had adversarial or strongly transactional relationships with their suppliers. According to Latham (1994), the construction and building industry thrives on conflict-based relationships at every level in its dealings with both suppliers and customers. For such an industry or company within such an industry to attempt to emulate the Marks & Spencer approach, without significant changes to its values and behaviours, would be both naïve and futile.

This means that the processes being imitated must be drawn from organizations with similar cultural values and organizational capability.

19.6 Step 4: develop criteria and measures of process effectiveness

It is vital that as part of the strategy development activity clear measures of performance are defined for the organization. In particular, it is necessary to define target levels of efficiency and effectiveness for each process. This would be a vital requirement if organizations were depending on breakthrough strategies to achieve significant competitive advantage because breakthrough strategies require dramatic process and culture modification. As Strebel (1992) says:

> A discontinuous restructuring has to be implemented with speed in one jump. The speed of change means that deeply ingrained beliefs and behaviour will lag behind during the discontinuity. If the transition is to succeed, allowance must be made for the much slower change in beliefs and behaviour after the strategy, structure, business systems, and resources have been reorganized.

On the face of it, Strebel seems to be contradicting Davenport, quoted just above. However, both are making the important point that culture (beliefs and behaviours) can lag behind process changes at the working level. If the change makers (see Chapter 17) think that process change and culture change must march hand in hand then they may have to be satisfied with a slower rate of change.

For example, those who first introduced banking and insurance services over the phone had to make large investments in operational and capital costs to introduce a method of working which was radically different from any previous method of transacting confidential business with clients. The impact was phenomenal and created a discontinuity within the industry and large and significant benefits to the organization and the entrepreneur who first thought up the idea. In this instance, the prime source of competitive advantage and customer satisfaction was the speed and fluency with which customers could transact business with the bank. Defining the processes that enabled orders to be collected and processed instantly and also gave customers adequate safeguards against fraud and abuse was critical to this whole venture. Similarly, if an organization, such as Amazon, sets out to capture a large percentage of the reading public by encouraging them to browse and order via the Email it is imperative that the electronic messaging systems which support this sales thrust have clearly defined measures of success as regards response times and speed of order fulfilment. To quote Davenport,

> It is important that statements of objectives be specific and measures operational. Stating that a division will reduce the cycle time for introducing new products by 50% by 1993 is much more meaningful and helpful than stating that the division will increase revenue by 15%.

Re-engineering the process against clearly defined measures also achieves another objective—it heralds and underwrites in a comprehensive way the degree of change needed and sharpens the nature of the preferred new behaviour and operational attitudes. As Davenport says:

> A vision can also be communicated through a shift in the focus of existing, or through newly created, measures. New operating visions have turned some traditional measures on their ear. Leading companies have switched from producer time to customer time [when] measuring themselves on their ability to meet a delivery date.

The point being made here is that, where once an organization set out to get the longest delivery time a customer would tolerate, it now sets out to offer a delivery date which would surprise and please the customer by its proximity to the customer's preferred delivery date. To achieve this radical transformation in process efficiency and effectiveness, measures that challenge and redefine mindsets are needed. To quote Deming again, 'A vice-president in charge of manufacturing told me that half his problems arise from materials that met the specifications'.

The vice-president was pointing out that very often the errors found in the final product or output are the result of faulty specification at the beginning of the manufacturing process (at the time of design). In these cases, the final product will fail to please however good the workmanship or the manufacturing process during the fabrication of the product.

19.7 Step 5: revise and update existing processes to meet new operational needs

HAVING determined which processes need change, set in place a group of people to oversee the changes. At this stage it is probably important to take heed of the distinction made by Davenport (1993) between process innovation and process improvement as the nature, scope, and composition of the teams will vary. He says: 'Process innovation means performing a work activity in a radically new way, process improvement involves performing the same business process with slightly increased efficiency or effectiveness'.

It may be possible to implement process innovation as a stand-alone project distanced from the day-to-day activities of the organization. This is often possible if a new capability is being created. For example, when one of the authors set up a new research facility for ICL in Ireland, he was able to take a radical approach because he was not hampered or inhibited by carry over traditions from the research laboratories in the UK. The facility was set in a green field site. Its purpose was to carry out an entirely new research activity to do with UNIX-based systems. It was staffed by a completely new cadre of programmers and IT specialists drawn from the host country and the processes and cultures designed to optimize the investment of all those involved in the project were crafted to meet the needs of the facility. Again, in the experience of one of the authors, a practical way forward is to establish a single supervisory body (Programme Management Group) which plans and monitors the project while the changes are carried out in parallel under the supervision of line management in parallel with their line activities. The role of the supervising team is to facilitate the line activity *not* to command and control it. If, on the other hand, the new processes have to be brought into being within the framework of an existing organization with all the baggage that that entails, the problem is harder.

It is vital that incremental changes to processes are also carried out under the supervision of a single body. The reason for this is clear but often ignored. Most organizational processes interact with other organizational processes and therefore modification to one process can often have a knock-on effect on more than one other process. Unless these changes are co-ordinated and supervised to dovetail one into another, the organization could end up with systems which have suddenly gone out of synchronization one with another. It is also essential that different departments do not bring their revised systems on-line prior to checking that other systems that interface with their own are able to seamlessly link into each other.

This cautionary tale was missed by one company which ended up with different departments modifying their systems without reference to other departments who were also modifying their own systems. Within a short time, staff in all departments were working overtime carrying out manual tasks to overcome the confusion that was caused so that the business of the company could continue. It was a shambles.

As we have pointed out in Chapters 17 and 18, there are many players involved in change implementation. Hammer and Champy (1993) suggest five critical players:

- leaders—who authorize and motivate the overall re-engineering effort;
- process owner—a manager with responsibility for a specific process and the re-engineering effort focused on it;
- re-engineering team—who oversee its design and implementation;
- steering committee—a policy-making body of senior managers who develop the organization's overall re-engineering strategy and monitor progress;
- re-engineering czar—an individual responsible for developing re-engineering techniques and tools to achieve synergy across the company's separate re-engineering projects.

We have broken the leadership role into those of sponsor, initiator, and change leader of the individual sub-projects. The process owner is the change receiver in our categorization. We have broken up the re-engineering team and identified the key players within it such as change designers, change implementors, and review and consolidation team members. The steering committee plays a vital role as overseer of the change manager who is responsible for the programme. The role of the re-engineering czar we believe would be undertaken as part of the programme and would involve a team of designers, implementors, and reviewers. We have identified a group called change supporters who we feel have a vital role to play as they, as positive change receivers, oil the wheels for the implementation team.

19.8 Step 6: install new/revised processes

NEW processes essential for achieving the new strategic direction must be carefully integrated into the existing processes. New processes can take the form of management approaches, management systems, operational systems, or production systems. The critical issue with new processes is that of ownership once they are completed. To achieve this, it is important during the creation of these new processes to involve those units who will have to operate and maintain them once installed. They would need to know what is going on, agree the specifications, train their staff in their operation, and carefully take them over and embed them into their normal routine. Failure to do this will result in the operating units resisting the new processes and organization suffering the consequences of trying to force new systems and processes down the throats of unwilling recipients.

ICL, when it entered the mini-computer market, set up special sales outlets and support units and reaped the benefits of so doing. However, in contrast, when it set out to enter the personal computer market, it out-sourced the product and attempted to sell it through its existing sales outlets. Needless to say, the attempt failed. Part of the failure can be attributed to the fact that the initiative was taken at the very highest level of the company with little consultation with the 'troops'. The other part could be that the mainframe professionals who had to implement the decision thought that PCs were toys and not worthy of their attention or effort. Among the less political reasons were that there were few applications to support the hardware and the channels of distribution were new to the company and the industry. A strategic initiative, taken at the highest level to broaden the company's product offering, was broken at the wheel of ignorance.

A more recent instance of poor implementation of a changed process illustrates how carefully change tasks should be assigned. Here the problem was allowing one of the very few 'doubting Thomases' to manage a vital resource in the change process—those who would operate the new infrastructure. Although well-meaning, the manager was unable to comprehend the 'new' approach that the changes would deliver and was to some extent afraid of the changes taking place to the process under his care. In Hammer and Champy (1993) terminology, he was the process owner but did not believe in the revised process he was being offered and was taking considerable pains to make the transition harder and more cumbersome than it need have been.

19.9 Step 7: publicize their presence to all staff

PEOPLE experience trauma during a period of change. As Hammer and Champy (1993) point out: 'Jobs certainly change, as do the people needed to fill them, the relationships those people have with their managers, their career paths, the ways people are measured and compensated, the roles of managers and executives, and even what goes on in workers' heads'. As a consequence, those who depend on their knowledge of the existing processes and their idiosyncrasies will fight hard to retain existing processes because this helps them secure their own jobs. On the other hand, others will seek to make changes to processes to strengthen their power base and their stranglehold on the politics of the organization. Both groups need to be carefully managed if the appropriate processes are to be re-engineered. Publicizing why the changes are needed and then keeping all staff fully informed of progress can go a long way to allay their fears and retain their motivation. Effective communication can help staff to:

- buy into the new strategic direction;
- be persuaded that unless the processes within the organization change to match the needs of the new strategic direction of the organization it will remain bogged down in its history;
- understand that implementing process change causes major upheaval in organizations;
- realize that any horror stories they may hear have no foundation in fact or that the facts may be different from what the grapevine says and may have benign causes;
- recognize that changes are progressing well and that the end is in sight;
- publicise their own good news, thus diminishing the potential agony of others waiting for changes relevant to them to happen.

19.10 Step 8: remove outdated processes

MANY organizations fail to disband outdated or outmoded processes. Managers are too afraid to discontinue existing processes lest they have a function which no one understands but which could be vital to the smooth operation of the organization. The underlying cause of this unwillingness is ignorance. Most managers and staff inherit the processes they operate to get their job done and do not have a detailed enough understanding of their extent or ramifications. More often than not, they leave processes that serve their purpose well alone rather than tamper with them. However, failure to remove surplus or redundant processes undermines the strategic gains anticipated by the changes. It may often impose unnecessary stresses on the staff who have to operate them. This is a very common phenomenon in organizations that downsize as part of a rationalization programme but do not have the courage to redefine the work to match the lower level of resources. The result is that staff may become stressed and be too frightened or insecure to challenge the right of managers to impose harsh workloads on them.

19.11 Summary

IN this chapter we have reviewed the actions that need to be taken to ensure that outdated or inappropriate processes do not undermine the achievement of good strategic initiatives. The chapter outlines an eight-step process that organizations can follow when implementing changes to processes as part of a programme of strategic change. The chapter has also attempted to draw the distinction between modifying or introducing processes and amending or introducing new cultures to match the strategic aims and the process objectives.

References

Davenport, T. H. (1993) *Process Innovation, Re-engineering work through information technology* (Boston: Harvard Business School Press).

Deming, E. W. (1986) *Out of the Crisis* (Cambridge: Cambridge University Press).

Hammer, M., and Champy, J. (1993) *Re-engineering the Corporation: A Manifesto for Business Revolution* (London: Nicholas Brealey).

Latham, M. (1994) *Constructing the Team*. Final report of the Government/Industry Review of Procurement and Contractual Arrangements in the UK Construction Industry (London: HMSO, July).

Nelson, D., Mayo, R., and Moody, P. E. (1988) *Powered by Honda* (New York: Wiley).

Oliver, N., and Wilkinson, B. (1988) *The Japanization of Britain's Industry* (Oxford: Blackwell).

Strebel, P. (1992) *Breakpoints—How Managers Exploit Radical Business Change* (Cambridge, Mass.: Harvard Business School Press).

Tampoe, M. (1990) 'Driving Organisational Change Through the Effective Use of Multi-Disciplinary Project Teams', *European Management Journal*, 8/3 Sept.

Ulrich, D., and Lake, D. (1990) *Organizational Capability* (New York: Wiley).

Watson, G. H. (1993) *Strategic Benchmarking* (New York: Wiley).

Wind, J. Y., and Main, J. (1998) *Driving Change* (London: Kogan Page).

Chapter 20
Building the Culture for Successful Strategy Implementation

20.1 Introduction

THE success of any strategy depends on the vigour with which those entrusted with its implementation carry it out. It is often a group effort. One person may dream dreams but many are needed to give life to those dreams. As Deal and Kennedy (1988) point out: ' We need to remember that people make businesses work. And we need to relearn old lessons about how culture ties people together and gives meaning and purpose to their day-to-day lives'.

Schein (1992) goes further and attempts to offer an explanation of how culture comes into being. He says that culture is:

> ... a pattern of shared basic assumptions that the group learned as it solved its problems of external adaptation and internal integration, that has worked well enough to be considered valid and, therefore, to be taught to new members as the correct way to perceive, and feel in relation to those problems.

According to this definition culture is made up of 'shared basic assumptions' that are learned as the organization or society solves the problems it encounters in exploiting or reacting to internal or external threats and opportunities. This collective learning results in creating the values and beliefs that sustain and govern the political, contractual, and social relationships between an organization and its employees, customers, and suppliers. These values and beliefs help to combine their collective skills and capabilities towards the achievement of stated strategic goals through effective co-operation and collaboration. This suggests that if these strategic goals change, then there may be a need to develop new political, social, and contractual codes of conduct to meet the challenges of this new strategic thrust.

Newman and Chaharbaghi (1998) develop Schein's view of culture formation by suggesting that culture is: 'the by-product of a technology that has been developed in exploiting an opportunity'. The word 'technology' here suggests the capability of an organization as expressed by its core competence. Whether the culture of an organization is an outcome of the 'technology' it uses or whether the technology being used by the organization is a result of its culture is a hard question to answer. The reality is probably that it is a mixture of both influences. For example, the culture of those in an R&D laboratory can be significantly different from that of workers in the manufacturing plants. The R&D laboratory is usually staffed by scientists and engineers with much greater independence of action and with different personality traits from those of their manufacturing colleagues who may be more process bound. Their values, however, may be the same. Both groups may place high value on meeting their promises and deadlines to each other. We therefore encounter the possibility that culture may not be uniform throughout a large organization.

Culture comes in many guises. Culture is often embodied in mindset, tradition and professional conduct. Hofstede (1991) identified four main cultural characteristics:

- power distance, which he defines as the emotional distance that separates subordinates from their bosses;
- individualism which is the degree of independence that people show and their dependence more on their own abilities than on the community of which they are a part;
- masculinity/femininity which is interpreted as a tough/tender continuum;
- uncertainty avoidance seen as an individual's or organization's tolerance of risk.

Trompenaars (1993) identifies seven ways in which culture reflects itself in societies or organizations. Five of these refer to the way people relate to each other and cover such attitudes as:

- universalism versus particularism, where a distinction is made between the proposition that universal laws apply to everyone and the other that individuals are unique and universal laws must be adapted to individual needs;
- individualism versus collectivism where people take an individual or group persona;
- neutral or emotional where an objective or subjective view is taken of the relationship. The neutral view tends to be rational and unemotional. Those described as 'emotional' reflect feelings that people have when interacting;
- specific versus diffuse recognizes that in some instances going from the general to the particular is much better than getting straight to the point;
- achievement versus ascription where achievement is the basis of recognition and reward rather than age, social status, or other ascribed values.

In addition, Trompenaars sees people's attitude to time and the environment as being two further differentiators.

This means that those involved in culture change (all those discussed in Chapter 17) cannot devise a 'one size fits all' solution. They may need to develop subsets of a common new culture to meet the needs of the different organizational groupings. In the light of these observations, setting out to change the strategic direction of the organization without also making clear assumptions about the organizational culture necessary to achieve the new direction is a recipe for failure. If the new direction is dramatically different, then attempting to achieve it with the culture built and honed for a different strategy is both impractical and foolhardy. So how should those driving change approach the cultural changes they need to make?

Both the EuroPharm and IBAP case examples illustrate the need to change culture as part of strategy implementation and show some possible methods in use.

20.2 Nine activities to change the culture to support the strategy

THE following list, drawn from the consulting experiences of the authors, summarizes the main activities that will have to be undertaken to deliver the new organizational capability necessary to achieve the new intent. Although they read as a list, there is often overlap between the different activities and much retracing of activities before it all comes right. The organization will have to:

1. Sell the new strategic intent.
2. Interpret the existing organizational culture.
3. Develop group decision-making skills.
4. Introduce innovative mindsets that welcome change.
5. Develop skills and knowledge base.
6. Encourage staff to feel secure.
7. Develop means of helping staff deliver consistent performance.
8. Enable accessibility to management during periods of change.
9. Encourage thinking that focuses on the outside world.

In this chapter we explore each activity and seek to justify its inclusion.

20.3 Activity 1: sell the new strategic intent

IT is vital that the strategic intent, so finely honed and developed as the driver for the proposed changes, is convincingly sold to all those involved in effecting the changes.

Box 20.1 Example: Selling the new strategic intent in ICL

In 1980 ICL had arrived at a crossroads. It had large quantities of unsold mainframes and, consequently, significant cash shortfalls. The City and bankers lost confidence in the top management of the company and refused further finance until a new top team was appointed. Consequently, Robb Wilmot took over from Chris Wilson and there followed a significant reshuffling of a revised pack. Once he had understoood the reasons for ICL's state, Wilmot spent weeks touring the UK and overseas offices explaining to as many staff as he could what the issues were and what he planned to do about them. The speed with which he grasped the issues facing the company and the conviction with which he sold the solutions to managers and staff resulted in a mobilization of the energy of those in the company. His message was clear. Survive, become profitable, and then grow profitably. That was a message all ICL employees could understand and work for. It enabled easy decision making at all levels and explained many actions which otherwise would have seemed arbitrary.

In addition to selling the idea of the need for change, it is also important to show that the new direction is the 'right' one. This is much harder as the proposals predicate a future state and therefore allow room for considerable debate on whether the intended actions and directions will lead to the future performance that the organization thinks it needs to survive and grow. For example, there was much debate about the benefits of privatizing government-owned businesses during the mid-1980s and later. This debate intensified as the once public utilities started shedding fat and their new shareholders and directors spread their bread thickly with the profits this action generated. The debate still goes on about whether the balance is right between the interests of shareholders, employees, and consumers as represented by their interest groups, the industry regulators, and the politicians. The latter are quick to make scapegoats of the directors of the privatized utilities whenever their poorly informed constituents complain about services and/or prices.

The effective selling of the strategic intent and the rosier future that that will bring to all levels of management and staff is a prerequisite to the successful implementation of change and the achievement of new behaviours among those working for the business. To do this, the leaders must ensure that all those involved in the process of change understand how the practical changes required relate to the new strategic intent. This may require new senior management talent.

20.4 Activity 2: interpret the organizational culture

BEFORE changing the culture of an organization it is necessary to determine what its present culture is. This means identifying what values, beliefs, and behaviours predominate. There are many different ways to dissect the culture of an organization and indeed there are many definitions of organization culture; for example, Deal and Kennedy (1988) identify four generic cultures. These are:

- Tough-guy macho culture—a world of individualists who regularly take high risks and get quick feedback on whether their actions were right. Among the organizations or professions in which, they claim, this culture prevails are: police and other emergency services, surgeons, construction, cosmetics, management consulting, venture capitalists, advertising, television, movies, publishing, sport—the entire entertainment industry.
- Work hard/play hard culture—fun and action are the rule here but employees take few risks. According to Deal and Kennedy, sales organizations, real-estate, computer companies, automotive distributors, door-to-door sales, mass consumer sales companies, office equipment manufacturers, and retail stores are likely to have this culture.
- Bet your company culture—a high-risk slow feedback organization. Typically, it refers to companies that invest large sums now to recover them over time. Examples given by Deal and Kennedy include oil companies, aeroplane manufacturers, capital goods companies, mining and smelting, investment banks, architectural firms, computer design companies, actuarial function within insurance, and the armed forces.
- Process culture—in the view of Deal and Kennedy low-risk, slow feedback organizations such as banks, insurance companies, financial services, government, utilities, and heavily regulated industries such as pharmaceuticals display this culture.

To Deal and Kennedy's classification one can add those of Reddin (1970) or Bennis and Nanus (1985), whose segmentation of management and leadership style predicated the resultant organizational culture, and Goffee and Jones (1998) who suggest that organizational cultures could be classified as networked, fragmented, communal, and mercenary. Reddin's managerial styles would result in cultures that could be classified as bureaucratic, developmental, executive, and benevolent autocratic. The application of Bennis and Nanus's leadership style would create organizational cultures that are formalistic, collegial, and personalistic. Tampoe, from an analysis of culture maps derived from employee opinion surveys carried out for many companies, has found that the cultures could be classified as the combination of the following four key behavioural traits—independence, inter-dependence, inner-focused, and outer-focused.

The usual process of analysis begins by carrying out some form of culture survey and then interpreting the results against some chosen segmentation. While this approach is useful, it suffers from the disadvantage of being prescriptive and so does not allow for the identification of variants and new categorizations.

A more sophisticated way is to draw cultural maps of organizations. These maps do not try to categorize the culture by predetermined titles; instead they extract the cultural norms in a more eclectic way. The maps show, for example, that businesses that are project based are very team focused rather than organization focused. In these companies, the project teams work to the objectives of the project rather than the business and show little interest in the business or its strategic purpose. This is compounded by the fact that members of the team can, often, easily find new employers. Similarly, organizations that have staff involved in managing a process 365 days of the year and 24 hours a day relate more to the process than the business. Shift workers who are often working when the rest of the organization is absent from the workplace may feel that the organization runs on their shoulders alone. They may tend to isolate themselves from the business and in turn to feel isolated. Staff working for an applications software development business feel 'independent' of the company, probably because they can find employment elsewhere while associates of the company relate more closely to the business because they see the business as their prime and most favoured customer. When two or more culture maps of organizations representing different time periods are compared one with another, the impact of strategic initiatives on the culture of the enterprise are clearly visible. For example, strategic initiatives such as the introduction of share option schemes, out-sourcing of services, divestments, and acquisitions materially alter the culture of the organization and the attitudes and behaviours of the staff.

What all of these and many other empirically tested cultures show is that 'there are horses for courses' and that the organization in seeking to exploit new strategic aims must ensure that the culture of the organization fits these aims. Failing this, the

Box 20.2 Example: Recognizing cultural difference at National Grid

The National Grid Company had over 7,000 kilometres of wires stretched across the length and breadth of England and Wales. When seeking to optimize its asset base, the company decided to break into the communications industry by stringing fibre-optic cables along the earth wires. Realizing that the communications industry was very different from their main power transmission business, the directors chose to set up an entirely different company staffed with telecommunications specialists and ran it entirely separately. Today Energis has been floated on the UK stock market. It has a market capitalization of £2.5 bn. and boasts of customers such as Vodafone Airtouch, BBC, Mirror Group, Lunn Poly, Boots, the Post Office, and other companies who wish to transfer data around the country.

Energis was successful and it is probably likely that Energis would have been less so if it had been set up as a sub-department of National Grid's main transmission business as the culture of the transmission business is very different from that of Energis.

organization must develop this new initiative away from its current culture in a separate organization.

The National Grid example (Box 20.2) shows that culture and strategy are related more closely than is often considered. A culture that is appropriate for one type of business or technology may be totally inappropriate for another type of technology. Understanding what type of culture currently exists is a necessary first step in honing culture to strategy. It may be more realistic to try to avoid sharp cultural mismatches than to expect to design the perfect culture for a new strategy.

20.5 Activity 3: develop group decision-making skills

BEING able to make decisions quickly and effectively during a period of organizational change lies at the heart of effective change management. This is often because there are fewer precedents on which to draw when making decisions in a new organizational context. Therefore, staff need access to other individuals or groups with whom to discuss and develop new decision paradigms. If this is not achieved and a company-wide decision framework evolved, each operating unit will seek to optimize its position within the corporate whole and use its knowledge and political power to win decisions that favour its own survival. In the long run, this may not be too good for them or the company. Committees and working groups tend to further this unit-centred approach to decision making and decision taking. Their members tend to protect the interests of the group they represent. This tends to compound the fact that during periods of change, particularly when old hierarchies are tumbling, the urge to protect each mini-empire within the organizational whole is even greater. Decision making becomes a survival tool and people play the system to gain their own security. Unless this is changed and people are made to see that survival of the whole is more likely to ensure survival of the few, strategy implementation will fail. How this is achieved depends on the current culture of the organization. Very often, change implementation fails because the implementors disagree with the new direction. It is therefore vital that decisions that have a significant impact on people's lives and futures should, wherever possible, be made collectively rather than by a small 'elitist' group (see Box 20.3, for example).

Another approach to achieving similar ends is to appoint an individual as a catalyst. This catalyst has the freedom to roam among managers and staff exploring ideas and testing the reaction to new approaches. This can work very effectively in organizations where there are 'management fiefdoms' and the habit of collective decision making and responsibility for those decisions is not a common occurrence. An example from a consultancy assignment serves to illustrate this approach (see Box 20.4).

Box 20.3 Example: Group decision making in Xerox

In the early 1980s Xerox Corporation found itself in serious trouble from aggressive marketing and product development by Canon. The company fought back by adopting two key strategies designed to focus the behaviour of its people. The first was competitive benchmarking which focused on improving performance against its competitors and the other was the quality of management initiative. Part of this approach was to encourage the concept of family groups where staff from different operating units were brought together to tackle critical issues. The task of the team was to develop a solution and then sell it to their colleagues so that the ideas were adopted and implemented. The directors found that by taking this approach, decision making was slower but decision implementation was faster and the overall time between recognizing the need for change and achieving the change was faster.

Group decision making, however, has its pitfalls. The tribal effect can cause a whole group of intelligent people to be misled by one ill-informed but opinionated individual into willingly falling over the cliff. There have to be safety railings that prevent this from happening. Deal and Kennedy (1988), talking about corporate tribes, emphasize the risks associated with a culture with a 'quick-fix' mentality, especially when reality proves them wrong. They say: 'The worst of the culture comes out in lack of thoughtfulness or attention; the tendency is toward the kind of back-of-the-envelope calculations that can backfire'.

They contrast this decision-making approach with that of decision-making processes in capital-intensive organizations such as oil companies evaluating investments in oil exploration or aircraft manufacturers considering the development of a new aeroplane. In their view, these are 'bet-your-company' decisions (organizational change decisions are very similar) where, in their view: 'The agenda will include ten pages for review, but the meeting will spend two hours on each page'. And contrasted with the faster feedback culture where: 'Managers typically have one hundred pages to review in a two-hour meeting'. They also point out that many managerial decisions are based on few 'real' facts and have open-ended outcomes. In these situations, although managers may go through the rituals and procedures of investment appraisal, uncertainty, and risk assessment, when push comes to shove, they, in Deal and Kennedy's words: 'gather people in a room, review *available* information and data, and if pressed "decide" as best they can'.

However, if this means that those in the room agree with the decision and make every effort to make it reality, the chances are that it will be a 'good' decision—because everyone is committed to making it work. That is what is needed when making decisions which require the whole organization to change their habits, forgo their hard-fought positions, and enter uncharted waters in the hope of reaching nirvana.

Box 20.4 Example: A consultant as an aid to improving group decision making

A divisional manager in a newly privatized utility chose to provide resident consultancy support to all his managers to help them manage the transition from a public utility into a profit-focused privatized utility. The consultant worked with the divisional director and his management team to design and implement the new organization and then remained to help each manager to train and influence change within their individual patches. To ensure the consultant was used, he covered the consultant's costs on his divisional budget. The result was a very focused and close-knit organization and rapid change.

20.6 Activity 4: introduce innovative thinking that welcomes change

It would seem that in this hurried world in which we live, people have little time to take their eye off the ball and see the distant horizon. Discussing this in his book, an immensely powerful commentary on the loss of the 'soul' in the workplace, Whyte (1994) says that those managers: 'cultivate a work-force unable to respond with personal artistry to the confusion of global market change'.

Innovation in the context of change is having the mental agility and willingness to discard old habits and accept new ones. This means that an organization is willing to move with the times and to grasp the challenges as they arise. A significant inhibitor to thinking the unthinkable is the complacency of many staff in relatively 'secure' employment. Many members of staff have narrow views of the challenges faced by the organization and refuse to comprehend the 'unthinkable'—that the organization may have exhausted its current capabilities and now finds itself vulnerable to new challengers. For example, many staff who, in the very early 1980s, worked for the mainframe computer manufacturers such as Burroughs, ICL, UNIVAC, Digital, Honeywell, and IBM were reluctant to accept the threat posed to their jobs and their companies by mini and micro-computers. These attitudes, born partly of ignorance and partly from complacency and arrogance, meant that drastic action eventually had to be taken in many of these companies.

Strategy implementation is very hard to achieve in an organization where those involved in the implementation process cannot think 'outside the box'. As Kantrow (1988) points out: 'We must somehow find a way to loosen the bonds of tradition—but loosen them selectively—and then reattach them to new and different objects'. The task of 'loosening the bonds of tradition' is relatively easy if the need for change is visible and incontestable, for instance, if the company is losing money and it is self-evident that it is heading straight for the rocks. On the other hand, if the company is doing well, the task is much harder. Kantrow does also point out that cosmetic changes will not deliver the sense of purpose necessary to get the new show on the road. He says: 'A generation and more of bad decisions at US Steel cannot be remedied by changing the corporate name to USX, but there is obviously some hope that the new name appellation will lead recollection away from those decisions and the thinking that led to them'.

Unless they are able to face new ideas and new challenges with new ways of doing things, they are likely to fall back on the 'old' ways and this often results in failure. It is often necessary to encourage people to think outside the 'box' by establishing channels of communication and decision making that not only encourage them to act innovatively but also provide on-site support to staff to help them take the newer routes.

Ideally, of course, an organization would evolve along with its customers and its markets. Such an organization would adjust its cost base, its processes, its people policies, and product offerings to exploit current trends in technology and society and match the needs of those it serves. By so doing it will avoid the sudden course corrections that many more myopic organizations are forced to take to survive. In practice, most enterprises depend on period changes, of course, with injections of new blood at director level to stay afloat and prosper. De Geus (1997) has examined the reasons for this. His conclusions may perhaps be summarized as that these companies have learnt to learn continuously.

20.7 Activity 5: develop skills and knowledge base

If the strategic changes require the staff to learn and display new skills and competencies, it pays to structure the new learning formally. Staff, faced with the challenge of their day-to-day job and the need to learn new skills, will tend to spend time on the activity that demands their attention and effort most—their day-to-day obligations. Similarly, if staff need to build new sources of information and new networks of colleagues in order to achieve in the new structure, leaving them to do this 'in their own time' is likely to be slow and inefficient. Managers need to develop learning tools and initiate projects to ensure that the new tool kit is in place so that staff will begin to use them and discard their old ways.

Learning tools take many different forms. The most popular of these are the change workshop that organizations run to introduce their staff to the new concepts and values and to help them begin to behave in the new way. Others could be an electronic directory of 'Who's Who' and 'Where and What'. This often takes the form of a company Yellow Pages and is very effective in speeding up the formation of communication channels and decision communities. A bulletin board of 'tough' issues can also be helpful. Employees with issues or problems that do not have a ready answer may pose the problem to a wider audience by using electronic or physical bulletin boards calling for help from anyone who has had to deal with the same or similar problems. This often reveals that their difficulties are not unique to them.

20.8 Activity 6: encourage staff to feel secure

STRATEGIC transformations usually result in some form of people displacement. In recent years, downsizing has become so common a means of achieving corporate results that it has broken the psychological contract that exists between staff and the company. This has meant that during periods of change staff feel deeply insecure. This sense of insecurity demotivates people, makes them reluctant to try new things and new ways. Providing confidence in management's good intentions is therefore a vital prerequisite to achieving successful strategy implementation.

There are many actions that companies can take to give staff a sense of security without making them complacent. First, staff must see that their departing colleagues are being well cared for and the company is doing all it can to help them secure a new career or happy retirement. This can be achieved by setting up an internal placement register, providing external out-placement support and good redundancy terms. Unfortunately this was not done in the early years of rationalization and downsizing and the whole process was seen as management 'dumping' their once loyal and useful members of staff. Today a whole industry has developed to support staff who are affected by downsizing.

Getting the balance right between a sense of security and complacency is always important. Secondly, formal training programmes can be put in place to help staff with coming up to speed with their new tasks quickly. Training supported by a mentoring programme and a help desk can help staff feel more secure. Thirdly, regular information about those who have left and why would also help. Very often staff feel that their colleagues have been silently and invisibly spirited out of the company in a surreptitious and clandestine manner. If this feeling grows, it can do considerable harm to their own sense of security and to their opinion of the honesty and integrity

Box 20.5 Example: Results of effective staff support during change

A major UK company handled this issue by providing a lot of external and internal support. At first staff were sceptical of the company's intentions, but later on, when their colleagues found 'better' jobs or better quality of life through the company programme, the company found that more people wanted to leave than to stay.

of their managers. Making all changes in staff positions as open as possible will cure this problem. Finally, it is important that people are able to assess their own worth to the company and to the wider market place. In many cases, staff who have worked for the same company all their life or for many decades lose a sense of value of their own skills and capabilities. This is because they have not tested their worth in the market place. Showing that their colleagues who left were able to find new well-paid jobs will help those who are staying behind to feel assured of their employability. There may be the risk that staff will begin to apply for jobs elsewhere. This risk is probably exaggerated and is worth taking as it will help calm staff down and get them refocused on their new roles.

20.9 Activity 7: develop means of helping staff deliver consistent performance

DURING periods of transformation and strategy implementation it is vital that the organization helps the staff understand and interpret changes in a positive way. Failure to do this could result in performance degradation either because of stress and uncertainty or because the staff really do not have clear goal and role definitions. This help can take the form of information systems or procedures and rules that make clear the new routines and processes of the company. By so doing the company removes fear and uncertainty and clarifies each individual's new position in the changed organization. Very often these aids to performance improvement can take the form of mentors, suggestion schemes, weekly group talk-ins where people can air their fears and point out shortcomings without fear of recrimination.

In many organizations, performance is enabled not only because of the underpinning processes that support staff but also because of an intricate web of associations and links which enable staff to 'work around the system' to get things done. When organizational or process change disrupts these networks it affects the performance of staff. Their contacts have moved on or left, people they trusted are not available to answer questions or solve problems, and others have taken vital information with them when they left. Management must recognize these disorienting situations and put in place a set of actions and mechanisms that will ameliorate this dislocation and subsequent performance degradation.

Box 20.6 gives a simple example of managing the dislocation caused by change and its consequent impact on performance.

Box 20.6 Example: Helping staff to deliver consistent performance

A multi-national company adopted a simple mechanism to overcome the problem of uncertainty after a major reorganization. It set up a help desk to which queries could be routed. If an individual tried to contact a colleague and failed, they telephoned the help desk which did two things:

- it logged the incident so that it could determine the number of times the individual was sought by colleagues, and
- re-routed the call to someone else with appropriate knowledge who was unknown to the caller.

20.10 Activity 8: enable access to management during periods of change

POWER balances shift most dramatically during periods of strategic change. As a consequence, the decision-making process within organizations is disabled and people feel the need for leadership and guidance. During the period of settling in most people find it difficult to pinpoint sources of new power and therefore decisions do not get made in the time-scales that make for efficient operations. In these circumstances, until new hierarchies, structures, and behaviours are established staff must understand how and who they can go to, to get answers to questions that affect their day-to-day work. Due to the volatility of the situation, managers tend to withdraw power from the working levels lest local autonomy causes dissonance. Unfortunately, this slows down the changes and harms the implementation of the new strategic intent. Until such time as the new organization is embedded and

Box 20.7 Example: Improving access to management using Email

One very effective approach was that adopted by a senior manager in a UK company. He invited all staff to Email him with their concerns, whatever they were. He would read each letter and answer the staff member within a day of receiving the Email. At first the workload was high, but as the answers filtered back and staff passed the answers to their colleagues and all the staff realized that he could be reached easily, the letters dwindled to a small number and then disappeared. Open access to the power base removed concerns and also helped dissipate power to other levels in the organization through the simple expedient of creating a channel by which people could quickly gain access to the source of power.

routine re-established, decision-makers will have to be prepared to work harder and be more accessible to their staff. This may not be an effective way of handling localized decision making and a more appropriate method would be to delegate limited decision-making authority to lieutenants at the working level even if these nominees are not formally appointed managers and to encourage staff to be both self-appraising and self-correcting.

20.11 Activity 9: encourage thinking that focuses on the outside world

TIMES of change tend to pull people's attention inwards and away from those the changes are meant to serve. This is a natural tendency and results from the fact that people are relearning their jobs and this activity absorbs more of their time than when they are functioning in routine mode. The dangers of this are that the organization goes in on itself and becomes desensitized to what is happening outside its immediate sphere. It is during this time that competitors are able to make inroads into established customer relationships as customers feel, often justly, that the organization is more concerned about itself than those it is changing to serve.

An example of inner-focus resulting in loss of revenues is taken from a major international company whose sales staff found themselves continuously battling against indifference at the centre of the company during a period of major strategic transformation. Their frustration was caused by staff in various operational units absolving themselves from making decisions by blaming the restructuring activity. Central apathy was not new to the sales staff but prior to the changes they knew how to mobilize the organization. During this period of change, they had lost their contacts and their unofficial support networks and found themselves battling against their organization and the competition. Sadly, some significant accounts were lost during this period due to poor site service and slow pricing decisions. The lost accounts remained lost for a good many years until the competition had a reorganization and the same thing happened to their salesmen.

20.12 Summary

ALL organizations have a set of shared values and beliefs that they call their culture. Some of these values and beliefs evolve over time as the company grows and the work that is carried out in it and the behaviours that help it prosper become better understood. Others may reflect the beliefs and values of its founder(s). Either way, change makers cannot afford to ignore the culture of the organization when they attempt to make the business jump new hurdles or switch from flat racing to steeple chasing. You have to use horses that are most suited to the course.

References

Bennis, W. and Nanus, B. (1985) *Leaders: The Strategies for Taking Charge* (New York: Harper & Row).

Deal, T. and Kennedy, A. (1988) *Corporate Cultures* (London: Penguin Business, 1st pub. Addison-Wesley, 1982).

de Geus, A. (1997) *The Living Company: Growth, Learning and Longevity in Business* (London: Nicholas Brealey).

Goffee, R., and Jones, G. (1998) *The Character of a Corporation* (London: Harper Collins Business).

Hofstede, G. (1991) *Cultures and Organizations* (New York: McGraw-Hill).

Kantrow, A. M. (1988) *The Constraints of Corporate Tradition* (New York: Harper and Row).

Nelson, D., Mayo, R., and Moody, P. E. (1998) *Powered by Honda* (New York: John Wiley & Son).

Newman, V., and Chaharbaghi, K. (1998) 'The Corporate Culture Myth', *Long Range Planning*, 31/4.

Reddin, W. J. (1970) *Managerial Effectiveness* (New York: McGraw-Hill).

Schein, E. H. (1992) *Organizational Culture and Leadership* (San Francisco: Jossey-Bass).

Trompenaars, F. (1993) *Riding the Waves of Culture* (London: Nicholas Brealey).

Whyte, D. (1994) *The Heart Aroused* (London: The Industrial Society).

Other books of interest in this area

Francesco, A. M. and Gould, B. A.(1988) *International Organizational Behaviour* (Upper Saddle River, NJ: Prentice Hall).

Lawler III, E. E.(1992) *The Ultimate Advantage: Creating the High-Involvement Organization* (San Francisco: Jossey-Bass).

Sathe, V. (1998) *Culture and Related Corporate Realities* (Homewood, Ill.: Richard D. Irwin).

Chapter 21
Implementing Strategy: Managing Structural Change

21.1 Introduction

Faced with changing the organization, most managers reach for a pen and blank paper and redraw the organization chart. This may show decisiveness but it reveals a very superficial understanding of the nature of organization. **Organizational structure**, which is what can be drawn on an organization chart, only shows how the management intends to manage the enterprise and in particular the lines of management reporting and control. Organization structure has very little to do with what the organization needs to be nor with what it really is. What the organization needs to be depends on the **Organizational forces**. These are the strategic drivers that dictate how an organization has to behave to achieve its strategic intent. The real current shape of the organization, which depends on how it really operates day to day and is probably the result of how it has grown over time in reaction to organizational forces, is the **Organizational form**. The design of organizational structure depends on understanding both organizational forces and organizational form. All three aspects of organization have to fit into the broader context of **Organizational capability**. It is organizational capability which is required to implement strategy successfully. Effective organizational capability is a result of a good balance between culture, business processes, and organization.

An analogy may help to understand these distinctions. A Formula One racing car is designed to handle the forces at play when it is driven at high speeds. These forces (wind resistance, adhesion, manœuvrability, strength, speed among others) determine its form or shape. Underneath the shape is a rigid structure that supports the form and enables the driver to attempt to control the car against the external forces.

On the day of the race, the capability of a competitor is determined by how well the structure and form of the car, the skill of the driver, and the expertise and morale of the support team all come together to respond to the forces.

In this chapter we will describe how organizational forces, organizational form, and organizational structure relate to each other and how organizational capability can be enhanced by wise choices of organizational structure in relationship to changes in processes and culture, as discussed in Chapters 19 and 20.

21.2 Organizational forces

FORCES are the predominant drivers that are essential to the achievement of the strategic intent. If the strategic intent has changed, there is likely to be a change in the forces. The aim of organizational change is to react to this change in forces.

Mintzberg (1991) identified seven forces that impact on an organization. These are:

- *direction*—the strategic vision or intent of the organization;
- *proficiency*—the ability to achieve results using knowledge and skill;
- *innovation*—the need to be creative and to learn in order to exploit 'new' things or ideas;
- *concentration*—to focus energy on a specific market or to gain specific results;
- *efficiency*—to get the best benefits from the resources and capabilities used;
- *co-operation*—working together towards common aims;
- *competition*—constructive conflict that leads to ascendancy of one of the contestants over the other.

Other possible forces include speed of response and acquisition of knowledge.

These forces may apply at either a strategic or operational level. For example, direction might be a very important strategic force for an organization in crisis seeking a way out of its troubled past, while to another, innovation could be the strategic force that drives it to develop its strategic innovative capability. Innovation might be an operational driving force in an organization in which fast development of the next model is critical rather than a strategic innovative capability.

These seven forces apply in some degree to all enterprises but their relative importance varies significantly. Similarly, a change in strategic intent may alter the relative importance of the forces. To adjust organization in response to a change in strategy, it is necessary to begin by understanding the forces and attempting to bring them into play. This is what organizational form does.

21.3 Organizational forms

ORGANIZATIONAL form is the organization as it currently exists and operates. Form tends to grow and change gradually and therefore to be determined by the organizational forces of the past. Redrawing the organization chart does not change the form of the organization, but this and other management actions may influence form indirectly.

The organizational forms proposed by Mintzberg (1991) are:

- The *entrepreneurial form* where power resides with an individual and decisions of any importance are taken by that individual. This is very often the case with start-ups and in organizations that are owned by an individual—usually a founder. However, it is also found in turnaround situations where the 'rescuer' takes back power until the ship is righted.
- The *professional form* where the 'professionals' and their direct helpers operate autonomously. The structure and formal disciplines come from their professional training and precedents and tried and tested methods. Legal practices are a good example where those in Chambers may practise under a common corporate title but actually work independently of each other in accordance with their specialist knowledge and expertise. This is also possibly true of hospitals, accountancy firms, and similar professional organizations. This can be considered to be a special use of an entrepreneurial structure.
- The *adhocractic form* best described as a project form. It is free of organizational boundaries and given a specific task with specific budgets and resources. It is often used for innovation and other out-of-the-ordinary activities with short life spans.
- The *machine form* usually understood to be bureaucracies and process-driven organizations where efficiency and consistency are the driving forces. Manufacturing companies and many administrative establishments tend towards using this form.
- The *ideological form* where the organization is bounded by a strong belief or ideology. Mintzberg suggests that a kibbutz is a good example. Some start-ups can fit this form when the driving force is a group of individuals with complementary skills attempting to influence others to their viewpoint; for instance, Greenpeace and similar lobby groups can fall into this category too.
- The *political form* where the organization is required to carry out conflicting objectives. Mintzberg sites regulatory agencies as an example. In the UK, the Ministry of Agriculture, Fisheries, and Food has been likened to an organization which is structured to satisfy the 'farming interests' and the 'consumer interests' and is judged to have failed as it leant towards the stronger farming lobby.

Mintzberg makes the point that the ideological and political forms are not often found in practice.

To these we would like to add two others:

- The *lateral form* where people and departments work across organizational boundaries to achieve common aims. The lateral form differs from the adhocractic or project form in that the individuals collaborating remain within the formal structure but reach out to others to create a network that contributes to their achievement. Galbraith (1994) says that a lateral organization, 'no matter what its form, is a mechanism for decentralising general management decisions. It accomplishes the decentralisation by recreating the organization in microcosm for the issue at hand'.
- The *networked form* which is not dissimilar to the lateral form except that there is much greater 'hardwiring' between the different nodes in the network. Those involved in the network can be at any level within the organization. Usually, many of those involved act as formal links or gateways to their departments or work units. Committees and special interest groups tend to form into networks.

In complex organizations, different forms may exist in different parts of the organization.

Form tends to grow in response to organizational forces. Table 21.1. illustrates the dominant relationships between forces and forms.

Table 21.1 Forces and organizational forms

Forces – underlying drivers of the business	Forms – How the organisation behaves
Direction	Entrepreneurial
Proficiency	Professional
Innovation	Adhocracy
Concentration	Diversified
Efficiency	Machine
Co-operation	Ideological
Competition	Political
Speed of response	Lateral
Knowledge acquisition	Networked

Source: Adapted from Mintzberg, 'The Effective Organization: Forces and Forms', *Sloan Management Review*, winter 1991.

21.4 Organizational structures

ORGANIZATIONAL structure differs from organizational form in that managers can change the structure by direct action. However, the changes are not likely to be effective unless they are made after consideration of forces and form.

Mullins (1999) summarizes the key objectives of organization structure as follows:

Structure is the pattern of relationships among positions in the organisation and among members of the organisation. Structure makes possible the application of the process of management and creates a framework of order and command through which the activities of the organisation can be planned, organised and directed and controlled. The structure defines tasks and responsibilities, work roles and relationships, and channels of communication.

Mullins sees structure as essential to order and good management. Structure facilitates the ordered inter-relationship of different organizational components such as roles, tasks, responsibilities, accountabilities, and authority among the people in the organization. It also helps put people, process, and resources into context so that they can realize meaningful outcomes.

Organizational structures formalize relationships and indicate where the formal sources of power reside in the organization. Structures also facilitate decision making because they formalize hierarchies and define the degrees of authority across the organizational divide. Structuring can, in the words of Lawrence and Lorsch (1986), strengthen: 'The quality of the state of collaboration that exists among departments that are required to achieve unity of effort by the demands of the environment'. On the other hand, the structuring, while segmenting the organization into meaningful groups with their own lines of command, responsibilities, and accountabilities can, in the words of the same authors, tend towards creating a: 'Difference in cognitive and emotional orientation among managers in different functional departments causing isolation and self-sufficiency of purpose, resources and deep desires for independence thus breaking the "system" '. This suggests that structuring will eventually result in a tendency for different units to isolate themselves from each other and operate across unit boundaries in a transactional manner.

Adopting different management styles may modify the effects of structure. For example, a structure designed to provide high degrees of conformity and compliance can be benevolently applied, giving people within it a framework of acceptable behaviour but leaving them to operate within that framework to optimize their personal contribution to the company.

Various forms of organizational structure exist and are recalled here to help the reader. More detail about them and their impact on organizational performance and order can be found in organization textbooks such as in Mullins (1999), Porter, Lawler III, and Hackman (1975), Feldman and Arnold (1985), Mitchell and Larson (1987), and Schein (1992). The more commonly described and recognized forms of organizational structure are:

- The *entrepreneurial structure* where, usually, a single individual determines the direction and future of the organization and manages it towards that objective using other people to supplement his or her specialist skills and know-how.
- The *functional structure* divides the organization into key activities such as sales, accounts, R&D, personnel, and manufacturing. There is much greater formality within such a structure but it is still centrally controlled and the chief executive very often determines strategy and requires the heads of the functional units to deliver their part of the puzzle.
- The *divisionalized structure* divides the organization into major themes (by products,

by geography) and each theme is functionally organized. The structure is still formal but power is decentralized within certain strategic and operational guidelines. This form of decentralized structure is effective as long as the different units do not need to work closely with other units within the organization.

- The *matrix structure* where the organization is simultaneously structured both functionally and divisionally. In such structures, the divisional personnel manager, for instance, is subject to the jurisdiction of both the corporate personnel function and the divisional head.

Organizations rarely function as prescribed in their structure charts or 'organograms'. It is more likely that the structure is distorted or moulded to take on the shape or form which best fits its purpose and which enables its people to do what their tasks demand. So, while the structure describes how all the different pieces of the organization come together, it is the form that determines its efficacy.

21.5 Optimizing the design of organizational structure

WE have seen how organizational structure has to take organizational forces and form into account. Mintzberg (1991) describes how forces and form interact. In his view:

> the effective organization plays LEGO as well as jigsaw puzzle. The pieces of the game are the forces that organizations experience; the integrating images are the forms that organizations take. Together they constitute a powerful framework by which to diagnose and deal with the problems organizations face.

He suggests that the internal and external forces impact on the organizational structure so that it reshapes the structure into an organizational form most appropriate for the circumstances of the time.

To take another motoring analogy, a well-designed and implemented organization structure is very much like a multi-purpose vehicle (MPV). Within the same physical frame it can take many different forms to meet the needs of the different tasks it is required to fulfil. The seats are the work units that can be added to, or removed or reconfigured to meet the needs of the owner. With all its seats in place it becomes a school bus. With its seats removed it becomes a van. With its seats stretched flat it becomes a caravan and with just four seats in place it becomes an executive carriage. An organization also has to have this flexibility. Some tasks that it has to carry out demand consistent, unremitting, repetitive action. Others require it to act spontaneously. Between these two extremes it may have to take mixed forms to achieve different levels of flexibility and agility.

Figure 21.1. illustrates how different forms can exist within a functional structure.

Figure 21.1 Varying forms within a single structure

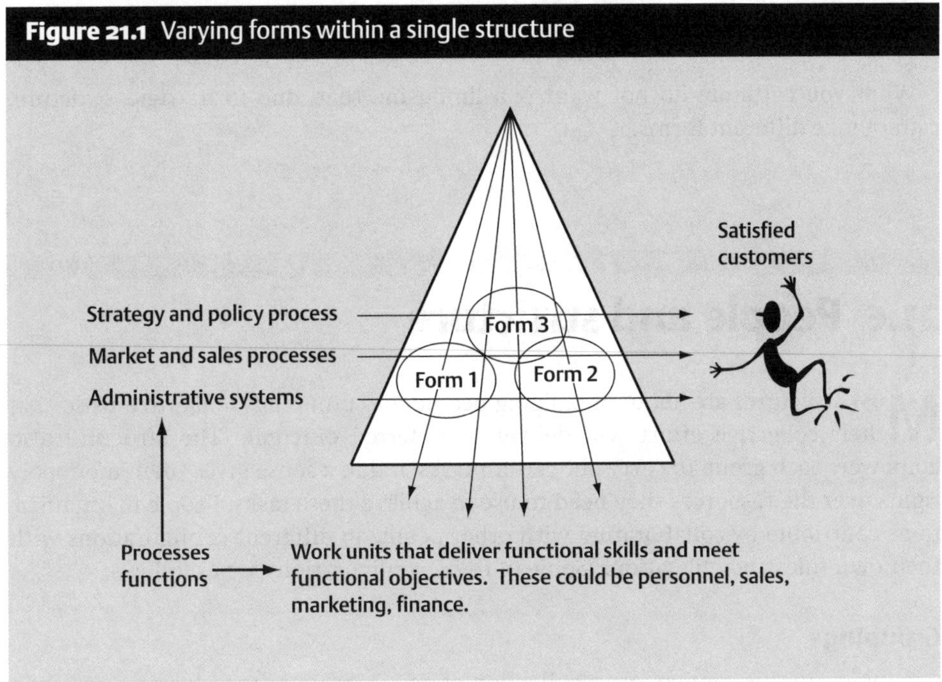

The pyramid represents the structure. Within it are a variety of work units (departments, teams, and so on) operating vertically through the structure. Across this structure are processes and systems that group different work unit skills and capabilities into products or services that are delivered to customers. The way these different work units have to combine to meet customer needs dictates the form that the organization takes to meet that need. For example, the figure displays three different forms made up of a combination of different processes and work units.

Form and structure tend to relate to some extent. For example, one would expect an entrepreneurial structure to mirror an entrepreneurial form. However, it is also possible to have an entrepreneurial form in a divisionalized structure where the divisional head behaves as an entrepreneur. Even matrix structures can have entrepreneurial forms. For example, in the early 1980s it became common practice to encourage the establishment of 'skunk works' and 'intrapreneuring' within organizations to bring about dramatic change or to encourage innovation within the environs of more bureaucratic structures.

If we return to our MPV analogy, what we see is that, depending on the need, the seats can be reconfigured. For example,

- the force is 'we need to transport four children to school';
- the structure is the vehicle;
- the form is a seven-seater.

If, on the other hand, the MPV were needed as a load carrier we would have:

- the force is 'I need a load carrier to transport granny's wardrobe to our house';

- the structure is the same vehicle;
- the form is 'remove all seats except the driver's seat to create a flat load space'.

What you certainly do not want is a limousine that, due to its rigid structure, cannot take different forms.

21.6 People and structure

MOST structures are about organizing people into groupings and/or teams so that their collective effort will deliver a preferred outcome. The structure also empowers each group to carry out certain tasks and in a sense gives them monopoly rights over the resources they need to use to achieve these tasks. People in organizations contribute by collaborating with other people in different configurations with their own rules and obligations. Some of these configurations are as follows.

Groupings

Groupings, in this context, are a collection of people brought together to carry out a specific function of a routine kind, in conjunction with a set of processes. For example, a collection of sales clerks whose activities are helped and monitored by a sales order process would be a group even though they may not be a team. Groups who are supported by processes find that what little cohesion, common purpose, collaboration, and communication they may need are usually provided for them by the process that supports them.

Teams

Teams, in this context, are a collection of people brought together to fulfil a specific purpose, of a routine or non-routine kind, and against a set of criteria, usually targets covering money, outcomes, and resources. Teams, generally, have cohesion and common purpose. This directs their actions and encourages them to cohere, collaborate, communicate, and co-ordinate their activities. These acts of collaboration and communication tend to build a sense of community among team members and have transformational consequences.

Project teams

Project teams are a special case. They usually sit outside the normal organizational structure. They are entrusted with the task of bringing about change to the environment in which they operate. They usually have clearly defined objectives, their own budgets, finance, and resources and tend to be self-sufficient. The sense of common purpose and collective responsibility for achievement tend to create a common ethos leading to strong bonding during the life of the project.

Distributed teams

Distributed teams are loose-knit groupings of people that form and re-form to match the needs of the tasks and objectives they contribute to. Distributed teams are not physically co-located as their physical presence is not as vital as having access to the thoughts, ideas, and outputs of its members. Communication between them is often transactional rather than transformational. Team members are, often, connected to each other using computers and communications networks resulting in a collection of people supported by computer-supported work group systems. Members enter and leave as they see fit or are invited to do so.

In determining structure, it is important to know how the people within the organization need to be grouped and ranked to achieve the strategic intent in the most economical and effective way.

21.7 Structure and leadership

IN Chapter 17 we discussed leadership as it applied to a change leader. Leadership in that context was contrasted with management and the point made that during periods of change and uncertainty people need both emotional reassurance and formal guidance over the actions they take. Our point was that in change situations operational controls must be tempered with emotional support in the form of transformational leadership. That was a special case. In this chapter, we look at leadership as a concomitant of structure and seek to point out that in any normally functioning organization it is inevitable that the people in it need leadership and that it is important to marry leadership style and structure. Failure to do this can result in a dysfunctional organization where the structure stifles the adoption of the leadership style most relevant to the organization's strategic intent.

It is important not to confuse structure with style. Styles can be applied within any structure or form. However, some styles go better with certain types of structures than with others. For example, a machine form organization can be run paternalistically, scientifically, or participatively (Vroom and Deci 1989). Similarly, a professional form can be run dictatorially by the leader. Whichever style is adopted, the main objective of the machine structure is to deliver consistent behaviours from those in it. However, it is important that the style is consistent with the strategic intent and the organizational culture and that the structure facilitates both, as the following example from Hewlett-Packard shows (Box 21.1).

The Hewlett-Packard example makes the point that structure and culture, although related, are different organizational elements and have to be treated differently yet coherently to achieve radical changes. You can change the structure to meet new strategic aims without harming the culture. More importantly, in making the

Box 21.1 Example: Hewlett-Packard

From all accounts Hewlett-Packard has been a success story. It has maintained its record of revenue and profit growth over many years, even when its competitors faltered. Some of this success has been credited to a culture that is able to spot and quickly exploit new opportunites. In late 1998 the company's performance faltered and its board decided to split the company into a computer business and a medical and measurements products business. This change in structure was undertaken, according to its chief executive Lew Platt, to overcome the '*complexity, breadth and loss of accountability*' that the company suffered. This was a radical move for H-P and aimed at making the company '*become more agile, accountable, focused*' and also '*easier to understand*'.

All very good reasons for making radical structural changes. The actions of the H-P board reinforce the significant role that organizational structure plays in achieving strategic intent. However, when asked whether the cultural values embodied in the H-P way need to be changed, Lew Platt pointed out that the two new companies (H-P's new computer business and its medical and measurements business) 'Need to be built around those five (cultural) values, which are more or less timeless'.

The article does not spell out what exactly these five values are but from generally available sources they seem to be relate to business practices, people practices, and management style. Among those often quoted are:

- market expansion and leadership based on new product contribution;
- customer satisfaction second to none:
- honesty and integrity in all matters;
- belief in our people;
- open door policy.

Source: Adapted from *Fortune*, 29 Mar. 1999.

structural changes within the expectations of the culture, much of the disorientation and demotivation that usually follows can be avoided.

21.8 Organizational capability

WHILE organizational structures are essential to the successful management of enterprises, **organizational capability** is necessary to achieving its aims. Organizational capability requires more than a well-considered organizational structure. Organizational capability is greatest when organizational structure, business processes, and culture are all aligned with each other and with the strategic intent of the corporation. Organizational capability does not happen overnight. It is an evolutionary, trial and error process that eventually results in a capability that suits the organization best. Galbraith (1994) says that: 'The organization acquires a capability when it can consistently and effectively execute the task. By that time the company has figured out what kinds of people perform the task best, what information they need, how to measure performance, and how to structure effort.'

Mohrman *et al.* (1998) make an even more startling assertion that:

> In highly competitive environments, the organizations that win are the ones that succeed in combining difficult-to-combine organizational capabilities. In the auto industry, for example, Japanese manufacturers gained significant competitive advantage in the 1970s and 1980s by being able to combine low cost, high quality, and brief time to market.

Thus they emphasize the fact that well-structured organizations enable the creation of organizational forms that are able to exploit the forces that influence an organization and give it competitive strength. Pascale and Athos (1983) identify seven critical elements for effective organizational capability. They encapsulated these elements into a '7S' model as illustrated in Figure 21.2 and listed below.

- *Strategy* is a 'plan or course of action leading to the allocation of a firm's scarce resources, over time, to reach identified goals'.
- *Style* is 'how key managers behave in the company'.
- *Systems* are the rules and guiding principles that staff use in carrying out their jobs. They can also encompass the processes that support people at various levels in the organization.
- *Shared Values* (super-ordinate goals) are over-arching beliefs and norms of behaviour used by those in the organization.

Figure 21.2 Extended 7S model

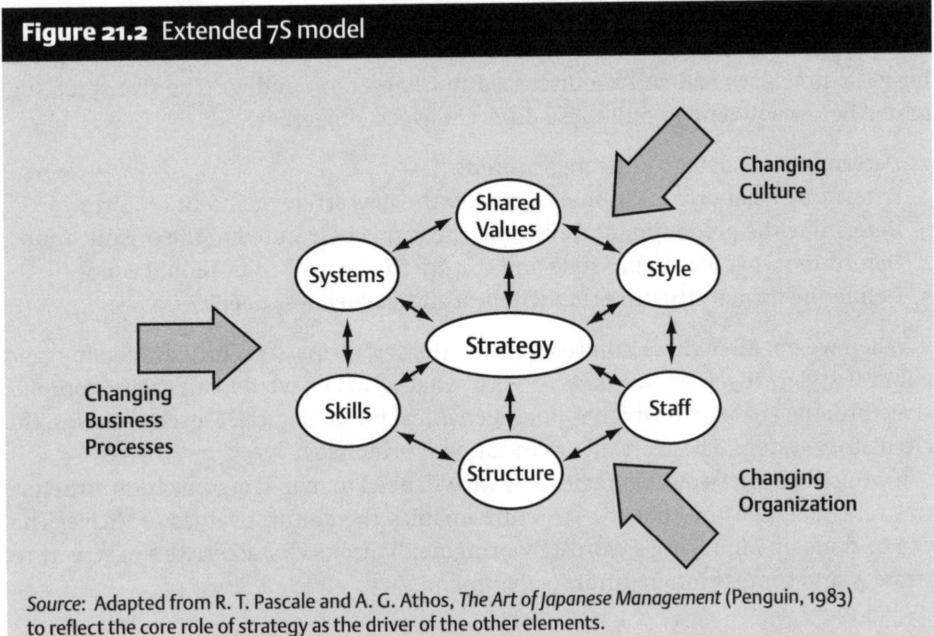

Source: Adapted from R. T. Pascale and A. G. Athos, *The Art of Japanese Management* (Penguin, 1983) to reflect the core role of strategy as the driver of the other elements.

- *Staff* represents the different types of people that the organization needs and who bring with them specialized knowledge and capability, that is, engineers, IT specialists, and so on.
- *Skill* refers to the distinctive capabilities of individuals and encompasses both knowledge and the ability to apply that knowledge to beneficial effect. The increasing trend to out-source certain skills that are needed by an organization makes this distinction more important than it was at the time the model was created.
- *Structure* is the formal distribution of power and accountability within the organization, usually represented by an organization chart.

Generally speaking, all organizations, at whatever level, will comprise these seven elements, even though the importance of each will differ. For example, a small group or team within a larger enterprise will need some strategy, even if the strategy is only a clear statement of what is expected of it. The team will certainly need staff and skills and where there is staff there will be shared values and style. They will have systems and structures to help them do their jobs and to position them within the organization. Organizational capability is underpinned by its structure.

21.9 Determining organization structures to fit strategic aims

It is difficult to prescribe a rule of thumb for selecting the ideal structure. It is also important that changes in structure are considered in parallel with the changes in business processes and culture discussed in Chapters 19 and 20. The five steps suggested below will tend to pull these different aspects together.

1. Determine the change in strategic intent.
2. Determine what organizational capability the new strategic intent requires.
3. Determine the predominant forces and the forms best suited to the organization.
4. Determine what leadership style and culture the organization should adopt.
5. Define the formal structure that will best suit its business needs.

When we put all of these different strands (forces, forms, structure, leadership, and cultural styles) together, we end up with what Drucker would call: 'Very complex structure, the analogy to which is not mechanical but biological. Muscles, nerves, the circulatory system. These are all organisational principles'.

If we are to achieve our strategic aims we will need to match organization structure to strategy and ensure that the structure enables the cultural values to thrive. This can be done (in Mintzberg's words) by bringing: 'Various characteristics of structure, strategy and context into natural co-alignment'.

Step 1—Determine the change in strategic Intent

It is important to revisit the strategic intent and make sure that its purpose and objectives are clearly understood. This is vital. An organizational form that is at odds with the strategic intent will harm the business even if it does not prevent it from trading. For example, if the strategic intent requires that the organization is innovative but the structure is 'machine', the responsiveness of the organization will suffer but it could get by, by using project teams for the innovation. However, the predominance of the 'machine' structure and culture will stifle the 'adhocery' needed to achieve the innovation needed by the business.

Step 2—Determine what organizational capability the strategic intent requires

Use the '7S' model or something similar to configure the organizational capability treating teams, groups, project teams, and distributed teams as the building blocks. For example, for an organization seeking to be innovative, the '7S' model may look like that in Table 21.2.

Table 21.2 Matching organizational design criteria to the 7S model

'7S' elements	Likely choice for organization needing to be innovative
Style	Participative
Systems	Standards that prescribe the quality of outcomes and specify resources, acceptable behaviours, and limits to authority. Mostly facilitative rather than controlling
Shared values	Collaborative and co-operative, forgiving, learning
Staff	Specialists of various disciplines with strong self-drive
Skills	Inter-personal skills to influence and drive through change such as persuasiveness, determination, listening and learning, etc.
Strategy	Getting results, quickly
Structure	Informal with ease of inter-organizational transactions within a loose-knit hierarchy where power resides with the innovators

Step 3—Determine the forces and forms best suited to the needs of the organization

The strategic intent and the strategic context will impose certain constraints and offer opportunities. It is important that the organization is structured to optimize these. Ideally, the organizational designer needs to understand which of the seven forces listed by Mintzberg need to predominate. For example, an organization that needs strong direction is more likely to benefit from an entrepreneurial configuration. This is most likely to be the case when an organization is faltering and is in need of strong leadership. In these situations it is often right to appoint a 'trouble-shooter' who takes the organization by the scruff of its neck, suspends democracy for a short time, and takes whatever action is necessary to get the business back on even keel. This is also an effective form for start-ups where the founder(s) drive the organization towards a future of their imagining. If, on the other hand, the driving force were innovation, it would be most likely that the organization would benefit from the careful use of adhocratic structures where teams form and disband as the circumstances dictate. It is unlikely that innovation would thrive in an organization using the machine form that is likely to encourage ordered behaviour and stifling convention. Organizations can have different forms embedded in them. For example, it is possible to conceive of the organization defined above as having an R&D laboratory using an adhocracy form. Its manufacturing plant is likely to have a machine form, a sales and marketing organization that is diversified, corporate functions that are professionally structured, and new business ventures that are entrepreneurial.

Step 4—Determine what leadership style and culture the organization should adopt

It is important to decide how the different forms co-exist. As was pointed out before, most organizations will comprise all the forms identified (entrepreneurial, professional, adhocracy, diversified, and machine). It is also likely that diversified forms will incorporate the other four. The linkages between the different forms often cause problems. Those in the adhocracies and entrepreneurial forms have difficulty interrelating to people in the machine forms who are required to be more conformant and can frustrate their adhocractic and entrepreneurial colleagues.

Step 5—Define the formal structure that will best suit its business needs

An organization should be structured to achieve its strategic intent. It is important that the structure enables the organization to respond to the internal and external forces that affect it and take the form that most suits its business needs at that time. This form is then managed using a culture that is most suitable for that form. For example, if the strategic intent is to be the lowest cost producer in the organization's chosen segment, it is likely that the driving force is efficiency and the organization would take on a machine form. This would allow it to have a more rigid hierarchy, more formal lines of command and decision making, much higher levels of process-dominant working and training that fit the staff to be consistent and tolerant of repetitive work. If, on the other hand, the strategic intent dictates that the organization needs to be highly innovative, it is likely that it would take an adhocratic form, where there is control by the provision of specific goals, where decision making is less formal, and where power is more evenly distributed. Training would be geared towards deductive and inductive reasoning and efficacy.

21.10 Summary

IN this chapter we have discussed how organizations should be structured to achieve their strategic intent. We have shown how the different elements of organizational design such as style, leadership, systems, skills, and so on fit together to deliver organizational capability. We have urged that organizational designers structure organizations so that they match the strategic intent and by so doing exploit organizational capability to the fullest. The caution is that poor structures will make all those involved perform cartwheels and contort themselves and the systems and structure to achieve their assigned goals. In this situation, people are apt to spend more time fighting the system than achieving the strategic intent of the organization.

References

Drucker, P. F. (1970) *Technology Management and Society* (London: Pan).

Feldman, D. C., and Arnold, H. J. (1985) *Managing Individual and Group Behaviour in Organizations* (New York: McGraw-Hill).

Galbraith, Jay R. (1994) *Competing with Flexible Lateral Organizations* (Reading, Mass.: Addison Wesley, Organizational Development series).

Kay, J. (1993) *Foundations of Corporate Success* (Oxford: Oxford University Press).

Lawrence, P. R., and Lorsch, J. W. (1986) *Organization and Environment* (Cambridge, Mass.: Harvard Business School).

Mintzberg, Henry (1991) 'The Effective Organization: Forces and Forms', *Sloan Management Review*, winter.

Mitchell, T. R., and Larson, J. R. (1987) *People in Organizations: An Introduction to Organizational Behaviour* (New York: McGraw-Hill International edn.).

Mohrman, S. A., Galbraith, J. R., Lawler III, E. E., and associates (1998) *Tomorrow's Organization (Crafting Winning Capabilities in a Dynamic World)* (San Francisco: Jossey-Bass).

Mullins, Laurie J. (1999) *Management and Organizational Behaviour*, 5th edn. (London: *Financial Times*, Pitman Publishing).

Porter, L. W., Lawler III, E. E., and Hackman, J. R. (1975) *Behaviour in Organizations* (New York: McGraw-Hill).

Pascale, R. T., and Athos, A. G. (1983) *The Art of Japanese Management* (London: Penguin).

Schein, E. H. (1992) *Organizational Culture and Leadership* (San Francisco: Jossey-Bass).

Vroom, V. H., and Deci, E. L. (1989) *Management and Motivation* (London: Penguin).

Chapter 22
Adaptability: A Strategic Capability

22.1 Introduction

THE purpose of this chapter is to examine how enterprises can build the strategic capability essential to their future survival in turbulent times. Strategy is mainly about the future, which at best is only partially predictable. It follows that planned change alone is inadequate as a mechanism for managing the future. While some uncertainty can be handled by planned change, some can only be handled by being responsive to new challenges and opportunities as they occur. This means that even if an enterprise has understood its capabilities, analysed its opportunities, and set in place strategies to optimize its success in the future, it is still necessary for it to be able to handle unexpected events. To do this, it needs to be adaptable.

Ansoff, Declerk, and Hayes (1976) point out that sensitivity to future uncertainty makes organizations approach their strategic processes with different objectives. They suggest that there is a choice between three possible ways forward. These are:

- *Planned change*—to prepare organizational structures, processes, and culture in anticipation of an identified need;
- *Adaptive learning*—a natural organic process, that provides for learning and mutual adjustment in complex organizations;
- *Planned learning*—a mixture of adaptive learning and planned change that injects some planning into organic change, some dynamism into rigid planning, and some adaptability into the final result.

Managers, when deciding how to implement agreed strategies, will be largely concerned with planned change. They will be helped in this by applying the strategic analysis and implementation guidance described in the earlier parts of this book. These measures are necessary but not sufficient. Managers need also to concern themselves with the ability of their organization to exploit new opportunities and threats. This requires them to consider how the organization should develop the capability of adaptive learning so that it can track dissonant elements and adapt to them and then incorporate these adaptive skills into planned learning. This does not mean that there is no planning of change but that there is an additional ability to adapt to the unforeseen and be capable of planned learning.

22.2 Planned change

PLANNED change as a mode of strategy formulation and implementation implies that the organization is operating in an environment in which the future may either be predicted or created. Where such predictability exists, prescriptive models and approaches can be used to position the organization to exploit them. This often means applying a set of rules to project the organization from the present into the future. Much of the approach described in this book tends to assume that at least some degree of planned change is both possible and necessary. This prescriptive model of implementing a preconceived strategy has natural attractions to managers who like to feel that they have taken appropriate and necessary steps to succeed in the future. It fits naturally within the traditional view that managers are responsible for the command and control of the enterprise. It does, however, imply that the enterprise can determine the future state by its own actions and that it can control or neutralize competitor responses. This is only true under very particular circumstances such as a near-monopoly or cartel. It may be appropriate, for instance, for utility companies to take this view. The local gas or electricity company may be able to dominate a geographical area despite the efforts of regulators and competitors. Managers in these organizations can devise structures and systems that seek to create order and routine as a means of achieving control. Such organizations tend to manage external disruption by the application of predetermined rules and procedures. In this sense, such organizations tend to be procedural and formalistic in their culture, organization, and processes and find that this approach serves them well. Safety and security of supply demand that they operate to stringent standards and create a mindset that is preconditioned towards conformity and pre-planned behaviour. Command and control concepts tend to influence their management practices and tend to preclude adaptability as an organizational competence. As Waelchli (1989) points out when discussing forms of viable organizational systems: 'the practice of management has been the practice of controlling or limiting variety in natural systems, of suppressing entropy so that the remaining natural forces within a system could move it towards man's chosen goals'.

Those whose enterprises operate in more volatile environments need to take a more adaptive view on the grounds that they cannot depend on their predictions being correct or that their planned actions are appropriate for the future. However, at this point, the bold part company with the others. The bold set out to create their own futures by thinking themselves outside their current 'box'. The timid and not so bold, accept the limitations of their current 'box' and plan to optimize the opportunity and resources they currently enjoy. This latter approach may often lead along the road to downsizing and contraction.

The planned change approach depends on a good knowledge of the industry and market place. Beyond these it is likely to draw from a rich seam of material on the expected trends for the future. These range from Nostradamus to present day prophets. Many of these are such good reading that they have become best sellers. See, for instance, Handy (1989), Naisbitt (1982), Toffler (1980). Many of these futurologists expound the view that the world is experiencing unprecedented turmoil and a devastating rate of change—a new age as fundamentally different from the industrial age as the industrial age was from the agrarian. Some of the most important changes these and others predict include:

- blurring of industry boundaries as physical assets become less important than sources of information;
- blurring of organizational boundaries as networks replace hierarchies and nation states;
- switch of the centre of power to Asia that may dominate the twenty-first century as the USA has dominated the twentieth;
- globalization of markets as integrated teams and systems allow activities of all kinds to become independent of time or location;
- the inexorable growth of knowledge-based businesses;
- changing demographics with 'grey power' replacing 'youth culture' as the dominant force in the market.

Futurologists are often able to detect future trends correctly but their views need to be applied with caution. The problem with many predictions is not so much that they are wrong; but that the time-frame of take-up and the size of the market created is difficult to determine with any accuracy. For example, there were predictions made in the early to mid-1980s that the new capabilities of computers and telecommunications would have dramatic effects on work patterns with a significant number of people working from home. While many people do now have computers at home and use them to enhance their working practices, relatively few have abandoned traditional working patterns so that there has not, as yet, been a major reduction in demand for office space or commuter transport. The change has resulted in addition rather than substitution; the predicted revolution in working patterns has not occurred—at least not yet.

However, we must accept that futurologists can contribute to strategic thinking by introducing new patterns of thought and indicating the shape and nature of the new 'waves of change'. They spend time contemplating these changes and provide a far wider and richer picture than those who are wedded to the coal-face. They do help others think the unthinkable and give validity to the 'unthinkable' thoughts of the 'average' strategist and manager. They can therefore be engines of innovative thinking and catalysts for change. Their ideas, appropriately sifted and modified, can be used in planned change.

Futurists can never predict everything that matters to an enterprise. This can best be demonstrated by examining what has occurred in the recent past but was not predicted. During the years 1998 and 1999, the following events took place:

- the Tiger economies of the Far East collapsed;
- the US Congress attempted to impeach President Clinton;
- the European Commission was dismissed;
- Microsoft became the largest company in the world by market valuation;
- the highly regarded chief executive of BMW was dismissed;
- the Japanese economy failed to recover from the recession of the early 1990s.

None of these events was widely predicted and these are just examples. For any particular enterprise, unexpected events may invalidate the best-laid plans. It is this that makes adaptability so important.

22.3 Adaptability as a strategic capability

ORGANIZATIONS that operate in strongly competitive markets cannot take an approach based solely on plans that anticipate a predictable future. Instead, strategists have to allow for future uncertainty and find ways of dealing with it. They have to be able to sense change quickly and respond to it. They have to be more adaptive and find evolutionary routes to survival. This means that, like an army preparing for battle, they need to hone their techniques, define different possible scenarios, and define different approaches to handle each scenario and practise their moves until it becomes second nature to them. Armed in this way, they enter battle prepared to respond to the enemy. This contrasts strongly with the approach taken by many who plan a campaign based on a single most likely scenario and hope that they have chosen the right option from the many on offer.

Companies that have taken adaptive routes have realized that to be adaptive they need to spread accountability and responsibility more widely across the organization and have built cultures that are tolerant of change and risk. Examples of companies that seem to have achieved adaptability include Hewlett-Packard, Sony, and Asea Brown Boveri (ABB).

In 1966 Hewlett-Packard built digital controllers, in 1968 its first hand-held calculators, in 1980 its first personal computer (PC). Today it is recognized as a major supplier of laser and inkjet printers, PCs and palmtops. It is acknowledged to have a culture of innovation and a workforce who welcome and react favourably to change and challenge. The adaptability of Hewlett-Packard appears to originate in the values of its founders and in the attitudes of its employees who seem well attuned to continuing change.

Sony started by making transistor radios in the 1950s, television sets using Trinitron technology in the 1960s, and produced the walkman in the 1970s. In the 1980s it offered the world the CD player and is today deeply engrossed in the entertainment software business. Sony's adaptability appears to be derived from its identification of a clear competence in miniaturization and how it should be exploited for maximum competitive advantage. Sony also had for many years in Akio Morita a chief executive with rare visionary gifts.

Asea Brown Boveri (ABB) seems to have achieved adaptability through its organizational architecture. Two previously somewhat centralized enterprises (Asea and Brown Boveri) were divided into many quasi-independent businesses. Percy Barnevik, the chief executive of ABB after the merger, said that he hoped that the new organization would prevent any employee from hiding where they were unaware of the needs of customers.

All three companies have been successful in rapidly changing market places so that these examples suggest that adaptability is an advantage for survival in the harshly competitive global economy. The examples also suggest that adaptability may have different forms. There is adaptability of mind, so that new ideas are embraced and used and also adaptability of organization, so that the capability of the organization can be quickly transformed to match the needs of new situations and opportunities presented to it.

Adaptability is not the same as flexibility. The car tyre is flexible in that it bends and distorts to absorb shocks and unevenness on road surfaces but it returns to its original shape when it comes to rest. A rubber tyre would be adaptable if it were able to change thread patterns, size, and strength of the tyre walls to meet different terrains.

Adaptability is not necessarily a function of size. Some small to medium-sized organizations are rigid in structure and mindset. Often these are companies that are family owned or where control rests in the hands of a founder or founders. They tend to perpetuate the strategies that made them successful in the first instance and reject any views that question the validity of continuing the original strategy into the future. Fearful of learning new 'tricks', they tend to take a 'let them eat cake' approach to their employees, customers, suppliers, and other stakeholders.

Conversely, large organizations with established bureaucracies can modify their strategic drivers and their organizational focus to be adaptable in the markets they seek to exploit. Abegglen and Stalk (1985), writing at the height of the accepted wisdom that Japanese management had cracked the issues of dealing with the uncertain future, point out that: 'the primary source of competitive advantage exploited by Japan's leading international Kaisha has changed four times. First, the primary source of advantage was low wage rates, then high-volume large-scale facilities, then focused production. Today, the emerging source of competitive advantage is high flexibility.'

Some attempts have been made to identify the general characteristics of organizations that will improve their chances of responding successfully to rapid change. Benton (1990) advocated increasing individual freedom within the organization as the key to managing in turbulent times but leaves open the question of how an enterprise can be managed strategically in this new more liberal culture. Pettigrew and

Whipp (1991) examined how some companies managed to survive change successfully in four different industry sectors. They concluded from their research that the five keys to success were:

- the ability to be sensitive to changes in the external environment;
- the quality of their leadership of change;
- effectiveness at linking strategy to operational change;
- the tendency to treat human beings as assets rather than liabilities;
- the ability to maintain coherence as change occurred.

These would seem to be the principal characteristics needed in an adaptable enterprise.

Most generally, advocates of adaptive organizations make a strong case for creating a sense of continuing change within the organization so that employees are not afraid of change.

22.4 Adaptive learning systems as sources of strategic advantage

ADAPTABILITY is the ability of an organism to modify itself to meet the demands of the environment within which the organism lives at a rate consistent with the survival and growth of the organism. Survival and growth require the ability to exploit current strengths and grow new ones with which to benefit from future opportunities. This means attacking the environment in two ways—exploit and change to exploit in the future. Ansoff, Declerk, and Hayes (1976) point out that:

> A firm relates to its environment in two distinctive ways, (1) through competitive (or operating) behaviour in which it seeks to make profitable the goods/rewards exchange with the environment. (2) through entrepreneurial (or strategic) behaviour in which it replaces obsolete products/markets with new ones which offer higher potential for future profit.

An adaptive organizational system that is strategically focused will need to take both perspectives into account and mould the organization to ride both currents. In Gell-Mann (1994) terms, those organizations that wish to survive over the long term without intermittent periods of turbulence and disorientation must: 'learn or evolve in the way that living systems do' so that they anticipate and/or influence the future and therefore are not surprised by it. Organizations that operate in complex or turbulent environments must become adaptive to survive and thrive. They need to understand their different parts and also understand how these different parts relate and interact to make the whole much greater than the sum of the parts. This leads us to require the organization to understand its core competence which, according to Hamel and Pralahad (1985), 'represents the sum of learning across individual skill sets and individual organizational units'. Seen in this light, all organizations, however complex, can be adaptive, renewing, and concurrent with the environment within which they have their being. Lacking the understanding of their 'real' strength makes it hard for organizations to carry out meaningful strategic analysis and strategy formulation and implementation. This is because it makes it harder for the organization to find those specific strategic options that 'fit' both the system being affected and the wider system within which the corrected system resides. Gell-Mann (1994) suggests that concentrating on the information flows, particularly, 'What are the regularities and where do accidents and the arbitrary enter in?' can be of immense benefit in formulating and anticipating future trends. In essence, he suggests that previous data, behaviour, and experiences are studied for patterns of commonality and predictability and a schema or mindset formed which enables an individual to interpret current data and to predict its impact on the individual in a real world context. A comparison of the interpretation with the real world experience enables the individual to confirm or modify the schema so that it can better interpret new occurrences in the future. What seems to be emerging as a critical faculty in these turbulent times is the ability of the organization to learn from its history. By studying past successes and failures, an organization can determine which of its organizational capabilities have the adaptability to enable it to face and overcome future challenges or exploit future opportunities. However, such a study must have a reference point. It seems that the most meaningful reference point is the core competence of the organization. Others such as strategic assets (Kay 1993) or end products or brand images are but 'outcomes' of the effective deployment of the organization's core competence.

22.5 Planned learning organizations

PLANNED learning organizations combine the characteristics of planned change and unplanned adaptability. The planned elements can be those activities associated with exploiting cash cows in known markets. The unplanned aspects can be focused on the innovative and entrepreneurial activities of the business. Inherent in planned learning systems is the need for effective information flows. Without these, no system can adapt to its environment or realize that its plans are invalid or inappropriate. It is information that makes planned adaptability viable. As pointed out by Gell-Mann and reiterated by Waelchli (1989), 'A prime characteristic of viability in a system is the presence of massive flows of information within the system and between the system and its environment'. This is true of both planned and adaptive learning organizations. The difference is in how the information is interpreted, decisions made and acted on. In planned systems, information is processed by rule of thumb for all those routine cases that have been anticipated and encoded into the systems and processes of the business by its management. When exceptions occur, the system highlights them as out-of-the-ordinary occurrences and attracts management attention. Adaptive learning systems, on the other hand, process information at the local level and take decisions at the local level using guidelines, cultural values, and expressed goals of management. The lack of control in any situation can often be traced to information overload leading to confusion in the controller.

In our view, the approach that is appropriate for turbulent times is a planned adaptive organization.

22.6 Building a planned adaptive organization

A PLANNED adaptive organization can be likened to an aircraft. An aircraft can be designed as a fighter plane or a jumbo jet. A jumbo jet is built to be stable in the air. Disabled, it is designed to glide down rather than plummet. It is capable of free movement in the air but it is much less agile than a fighter plane. A fighter aircraft, on the other hand, is designed to be unstable in the air. This instability makes it immensely manœuvrable and enables it to duck and weave and if necessary fall out of the sky in an instant. A hierarchically structured and planned organization is much more like a jumbo jet than a fighter plane. Organizations that need to be adaptive must be designed like fighter aircraft with an inherent tendency to go off the straight and true unless deliberately held to its course by their human and automated processes.

The principal characteristics of a planned adaptive organization are:

- flexibility built into their information systems to enable organizational entities to be grouped and regrouped to meet the needs of the business without losing financial or operational control;
- leadership, not in the sense of charismatic behaviour but in the sense of mentoring and influencing appropriate behaviours from colleagues while at the same time keeping adequate control of the functions they are responsible for so that everything works to expectation;
- effective followers—people who can adapt to the changing needs. Generally they would be proactive and be willing to learn new skills and equally willing to shed old, outdated, and irrelevant skills;
- flexible groupings of people within loose-knit boundaries so that they can group and regroup as the need dictates. In this sense they should be like participants in a water-ballet where their stability comes from their ability to float and their form from the choreography;
- highly tuned sensors to catch the mood swings and change precursors and alert the organization to impending icebergs;
- directors who have flexibility of mind and can re-orchestrate the organization to match the changing needs;

- strategic processes which *continuously* scan the horizon and alert the organization to any change that will materially affect the fortunes of the business. The word continuous is the key;
- fast implementation capability to put new strategies quickly into play;
- a critical understanding of its intellectual capital and its ability to apply its implicit and explicit knowledge to new situations.

22.7 Summary

MANAGERS would ideally like to operate in a predictable world. While this may be possible in some localized businesses, the majority of managers operate in a globally competitive environment where turbulence is a constant. It is therefore unlikely that managers can take a command-and-control view of their role or in their planning and strategies. In the field of strategic management, the command-and-control view leads to a step-by-step approach from analysis, choice, and implementation. Such an approach is useful but not enough. The extra ingredient required is adaptability to handle unforeseen events, which occur and are significant however well future trends have been understood.

Adaptability is therefore a critical organizational capability for success. Adaptability is not only a function of size but rather of mindset, leadership style, culture, processes, and organizational structure. There are analogies with living systems that react to their environment. Some parts of an enterprise need to be more adaptable than other parts.

It is necessary to combine the elements of the prescriptive view of strategic management with the characteristics of an adaptive organization. This ideal may be called a planned adaptive organization. The principal characteristics of a planned adaptive organization may demand radical re-engineering of the social fabric of the organization to produce the characteristic described in this chapter.

References

Abegglen, J. C., and Stalk, G. (1985) *Kaisha: The Japanese Corporation* (New York: Basic Books Inc.).

Ansoff, H. I., Declerk, R. P., and Hayes, R. L. (1976) *From Strategic Planning to Strategic Management* (London: John Wiley & Sons).

Benton, P. (1990) *Riding the Whirlwind* (Oxford: Blackwell).

Gell-Mann, M. (1994) *The Quark and the Jaguar: Adventures in the Simple and the Complex* (London: Abacus).

Hamel, G., and Pralahad, C. K. (1994) *Competing for the Future* (Harvard, Mass.: Harvard Business School Press).

Handy, C. (1989) *The Age of Unreason* (London: Business Books).

Kay, J. (1993) *Foundations of Corporate Success* (Oxford: Oxford University Press).

Naisbitt, J. (1982) *Megatrends* (Warner Books).

Pettigrew, A., and Whipp, R. (1991) *Managing Change for Competitive Success* (Oxford: Blackwell).

Toffler, A. (1980) *The Third Wave* (London: Pan).

Waelchli, F. (1989) 'The VSM and Ashby's Law as illuminants of historical management thought', in *The Viable System Model*, ed. R. Espejo and R. Harnden (Chichester: John Wiley & Sons Ltd).

Epilogue

STRATEGIC management is about taking action now, based on uncertain information to improve the chances of surviving in the future. Success cannot be guaranteed as witnessed by the many companies that hit stormy times after long periods when they have appeared to be models of excellence. It may be that excellence is a myth and that it is more constructive to think of enterprises as living beings that suffer ups and downs in lifetimes of differing but always finite length. Under this analogy, no enterprise can be immortal. An enterprise that enjoys a brief and glorious life may be as relevant as an example of management good practice as an enterprise with a long but uneventful history. There is a parallel with human achievement. Schubert died before his thirtieth birthday but ranks among the greatest of composers.

Strategic management must address context, process, choice, and implementation and is most likely to be successful when these four areas relate effectively to each other and are given equal importance. Conversely, strategic failure is very often the result either of poor understanding of the peculiarities of the context or of a failure to implement strategies successfully.

The strategic management process may be summarized as distinct steps.

1. Understand the issues by studying the specific **Context** in which the business operates and which gives rise to the opportunities for exploitation using the capabilities of the organization.
2. Evaluate all of the issues by relating them to the **Strategic Intent** of the organization.
3. Undertake a **Strategic Assessment** of the current status and the opportunities available.
4. Derive a set of **Strategic Options** that can be meaningfully and profitably exploited.
5. Make a **Strategic Choice** of a preferred option that is feasible for implementation within the constraints of the context and has the commitment of those most involved in making it happen.
6. Put in place an appropriate **Strategy Implementation Process** to create the new **Organizational Capability** to achieve the chosen strategy. This invariably requires the alignment or realignment of the culture, processes, and structure of the organization to the new strategy.
7. Examine the **Structure, Processes** and **Culture** of the enterprise to see what can be done to make it more **Adaptable**.

These steps allow for enormous variation in style and in the nature of the strategic circumstances in which the strategic process is being applied. The steps do not have to be carried out in sequence. Sometimes, the choice may have to be made first and the model used to determine the most effective approach to implementation. At other times, an organization that cannot be changed within the time-frame of the opportunity may go back through the model to offer a strategy or strategic intent that matches the organizational capability of the business. The particular situation may require that the steps be carried out concurrently rather than in sequential mode. However, each of the steps will have to be taken by formal or informal means whether strategy is being formulated for a high technology start-up or a large insurance company established for 200 years. The uniqueness of the final answer is the result of careful thought as to what will work best within the style of the enterprise and with the time, resources, and effort available to each.

Adaptability of strategy, organizational mindset, and organization structures and processes is a necessary capability for sustaining an enterprise in turbulent times. The strategy makes sure that adaptability does not deflect the business away from its main objectives or the exploitation of its core competencies. The adaptability ensures that unplanned events can be accommodated without disrupting the smooth and even progression to greater growth and prosperity.

We would not claim that the advice in this book is revolutionary, rather, that it is a compendium of the better thinking that has occurred in the field of strategic management over the last fifty years. We have been influenced in our judgement of what constitutes 'better' thinking by our experience of what seems to improve the chances of success in practice.

Part VI

Case Examples

Introduction to Case Examples

PART VI is made up of six case examples. Each briefly describes events that occurred and that have some significance for strategic management. There is a short commentary on each case example and several questions for discussion. The commentaries are not complete analyses but rather attempt to highlight those aspects of the case which relate to concepts described in the rest of the book.

Table 1 lists the case examples, their industries and sources.

The case examples are from six different industries that represent a range in terms of strategic management. Three are manufacturing companies and three service companies. At the times to which the case examples refer, three of the case examples were quoted companies, two were privately owned or privately controlled, and one was a government agency.

The sources of the case examples are indicated in Table 1. The cases examples on BMW and Marks & Spencer are compiled from newspaper reports. The advantage of this source is that the stories are intrinsically interesting which is why they were reported in the press in the first place. BMW and Marks & Spencer are both well known and visible so that readers are likely to have some background knowledge to enrich the details in the case. On the other hand, public sources do not report all the inner workings of these enterprises and may be influenced either by the companies

Table 1 Case examples, industries, and sources

Case	Industry	Principal source
ICL	Mainframe computers	Detailed account by company secretary and personal experience
Nolan, Norton	Management consulting	Personal experience
BMW	Car manufacturing	Newspaper reports
Marks & Spencer	Retailing	Newspaper reports and company annual reports
Intervention Board for Agriculture	Government agency	Personal experience
EuroPharm	Pharmaceutical company	Personal experience

themselves or by the interests of the reporting journalists. The danger with this kind of case example is that a good story may be only rather loosely related to what actually went on and that some important details are hidden.

The other case examples depend to a great degree on personal experience. This source has the advantage that details are available which would be unlikely to become public, occasionally for reasons of commercial confidence, but more often because they would not make a very interesting story. The danger with personal experience is that it is seldom impartial. Two observers of the same events may tell a different story because their interests or responsibilities were different.

The case examples also vary importantly in their focus. Some are more oriented towards strategy formulation and some towards implementation, but it is hoped that all the cases give a glimpse of each or at least raise questions for discussion on each aspect.

The case examples differ also as to the time when the events described occurred and the length of time described. In two cases, the events happened over ten years ago. This has the advantage that events can be described objectively and with the greater clarity of hindsight. Two were unfolding as the book was written, which leaves uncertainty about the final outcomes but has the advantage of greater immediacy. The period of time described ranges from a few months to several years. Strategic management does normally take several years from conception to implementation so we hope that some of the case examples illustrate this. On the other hand, a shorter time span allows important events to be described in more depth.

The case examples are based on fact but clearly not all the facts can be included in a short account. We have tried to give a fair account of the facts as we understand them, but no doubt there may be those who think that we are biased. Needless to say, none of the case examples is meant to be an example of either good or bad management practice.

Case Example 1
ICL: The 1981 Crisis

History of ICL

ICL (International Computers Ltd.) was created in 1968 as a result of a merger between ICT and English Electric Computers. The British government supported and indeed brokered the deal. This merger was the latest in a series of mergers which had gradually consolidated most of the UK-owned suppliers of punched card and computing equipment to create the UK's flagship in the world computer industry. The government wanted Britain to take a strategic role in what it considered was the technology of the future and saw ICL as the obvious choice to counter-balance American dominance in this area. In 1968 ICL was one of five significant mainframe computer suppliers in the world. The others were IBM, Burroughs, Univac, and Honeywell. Siemens had a significant share of the German market but did not have a presence in any other country. CDC, NCR, and GE were also known suppliers with a small market presence as indicated in Table C1.1.

IBM's dominance was partly fuelled by the growing presence of American subsidiaries in Europe who were required to buy and install IBM equipment to achieve compatibility with their parent's computing systems in the USA. As American industrialists bought up large chunks of European business, so the hegemony of IBM grew. In many countries, a domestic supplier was a significant competitor to IBM but only in that single market. In the UK, ICL had a larger share of the market than IBM and was particularly strong in the public sector, where it benefited from a 'buy British' policy. ICL was weak in all the other European countries. Outside Europe, ICL had the lion's share of the South African market and of some Middle Eastern and Far Eastern markets. ICL's strength, where it existed, was built on its long-standing business in punched card equipment and on its presence in ex-British colonial territories. Both these advantages were declining in their importance over time.

Throughout the 1970s, ICL retained its independence as a designer, maker, and supplier of mainframe computers and related services. ICL inherited two incompatible ranges of computers from its constituent parts. ICT, the dominant partner in the

Sources: Marwood, D. C. L. (1992) 'ICL: Crisis and Swift Recovery' in *The Manager's Case Book of Strategy*, ed. B. Taylor and J. Harrison (London: Heinemann).

Both authors worked for ICL and observed the events in this case example first hand.

Table C1.1 Market shares of European mainframe computer market 1969

Computer company	Germany	UK	Italy	France	Benelux
IBM	57.1	30.4	68.8	65.7	51.8
ICL	2.3	43.0	—	5.6	5.5
Univac	8.3	2.1	13.0	1.7	4.3
Siemens	20.7	—	—	—	1.9
NCR	2.0	2.7	—	—	3.8
Honeywell	1.6	5.6	—	—	2.6
CDC	1.5	—	—	—	1.9
GE	1.6	3.2	7.8	8.5	10.0
Burroughs	—	2.2	—	—	2.3
Other	4.9	10.8	10.4	18.5	15.9
	100%	100%	100%	100%	100%

Source: Adapted from *Fortune*, 15 Aug. 1969.

merger, had developed and successfully launched the 1900 series in the early 1960s. The 1900 series had been introduced a few years before the IBM 360 series and was incompatible with it. Compatibility was an important issue in the computer industry at the time, as it was expensive for customers to switch from one range to another. Once customers had made a choice of computer range, they tended to be committed to this range for a long time. ICL's installed base of 1900 computers was thus an important business asset in gaining future sales.

ICL's other component, English Electric Computers, on the other hand, had developed and marketed the System 4 range. The hardware was compatible with IBM's 360 range and the System 4 range was introduced at almost exactly the same time as the 360. English Electric had had limited success in selling the System 4 range in direct competition with IBM. In general, like ICT, it had been more successful in the public sector where there was a degree of national preference than in the private sector where it was selling a compatible product in direct competition with IBM.

After the merger, ICL concentrated on selling the 1900 but continued to offer System 4 if this seemed more likely to win the business. This burdened ICL with two different and incompatible ranges of computers and the costs of supporting the customers of these different ranges. In early 1970 the company decided to develop and launch a new computer range called the 2900 series to replace both the 1900 and System 4 ranges. The development of the 2900 series demanded heavy investment over a number of years to design the computers themselves and to write their operating system software. In addition, ICL's existing users were faced with the daunting task of re-programming all their existing applications software to run on this new range with its new and quite advanced operating system. As well as the cost of buying a new computer, ICL's customers therefore had to pay for a sizeable support team to make the transition from 1900 (or System 4) to the 2900.

In the early 1970s, Digital Equipment Corporation and a few other companies launched mini-computers. These machines met most of the needs of the majority of customers and cost much less to buy and maintain. At about the same time, packaged software began to appear which offered customers significant savings compared with writing their own bespoke software. Naturally, more of this software was written for the IBM 360 series as IBM had a larger installed base. The introduction of these cheaper and easier to use computers and software widened the choice available to customers and reduced the cost of computing to the customer. It also meant that mainframe vendors had new competitors for the expenditure which companies were making on computing. ICL was pinched by both these trends. Its mainframe sales suffered, but ICL did respond by hastily developing a new small 2903 computer. Although the model number suggested that the 2903 was a member of the 2900 series, it was in fact hastily and cheaply developed as a stopgap to respond to the new mini-computers. The 2903 was successful in the market and achieved a far greater return on development investment than the larger ranges. ICL's strength in mini-computers was further strengthened in 1976, with the acquisition of Singer Business Machines, whose 1500 range was a mini-computer specifically designed to support network operations. Both the 2903 and 1500 ranges had a price and functionality which made them attractive to the market, but they were incompatible with each other and required separate development teams to keep up with market changes. This extension in its product range came too late to save ICL from the fall in mainframe sales revenue and profit.

By the later 1970s, ICL was supporting four separate ranges of computers while spending massively on developing a fifth. The first 2900 series machines were just entering service at this time, but this did not mean that development expenditures, particularly for software, had yet ended. Not surprisingly, by this time, the cost of keeping up with emergent new technologies was proving too expensive for the company. Tugendhat (1973) records that IBM spent $5,000m. to develop its 360 series in the early to mid-1960s. During the later years of the 1970s, ICL was struggling in the market place with IBM as a much larger and extremely capable competitor, while its development resources were being stretched to breaking point.

In May 1979 the Labour government (whose policies had been in favour of intervention in industry when it was in the national interest to do so) lost the general election. The new Conservative government led by Mrs Thatcher believed in market forces and was reluctant to support failing businesses. The new policies, combined with high interest rates, the high value of the pound, and a recession, placed enormous pressures on British manufacturers; many did not survive through the next few years. About this time the 'buy British' policy adopted by government departments, public utilities, and local authorities also ceased. This compounded the problems for a now relatively smaller and more vulnerable ICL.

The storm gathers

By late 1979, ICL's major problem was the widening gap between the funds needed to continue developing new computers and software and the funds likely to be available from operations. The board accepted slightly lower growth targets and management strove to increase revenue while reducing product costs. Particular measures included the closure of a plant in Manchester in May 1980 with the loss of 900 jobs. Some of ICL's world-wide rental base of computers was sold. This raised immediate cash but removed a guaranteed future cash stream, thus increasing financial risk.

ICL's financial situation continued to deteriorate rapidly during the summer of 1980. Profitability for the year to September 1980 was sharply reduced by aggressive pricing in the market place by IBM. Even after reducing its prices to match IBM, ICL's volume of orders fell below targeted levels. Forward projections indicated an ever-growing development fund gap. ICL's responses included a ban on recruitment that even included new graduates who formed the lifeblood of ICL's technical staff. A much larger and newer factory at Winsford in Cheshire was closed with a further loss of 2,500 jobs. The results for the year to September 1980 published in December 1980 showed an increase of 15% in turnover but a decrease of 46% in profit. The share price plunged to about one-third of its value a few months before.

By January 1981, ICL was unable to tell whether it would over-run its existing cash facilities and exceed its legal borrowing powers after the end of March 1981. At the AGM on 3 February, the chairman disclosed a pre-tax loss of over £20m. for the first quarter (Oct.–Dec. 1980) of the 1980/1 year and a forecast loss for the full year of £50m. There were doubts whether ICL's bankers would continue support. ICL's customers also began to feel uneasy. Mainframe computers represented a capital investment and needed continuing support from the manufacturer, so customers were reluctant to buy if there were doubts about the long-term future of their chosen supplier.

There were discussions with potential partners aided by ICL's merchant bankers. The board pressed the government for an immediate decision on financial support and took legal advice on whether and when ICL might have to cease trading. On 18 March, the government and ICL's four UK bankers met with ICL and its advisers and offered a support package of UK bank overdraft facilities to the end of March 1983. The guarantees were limited to two years because this was felt to be enough time to conclude a merger or some other arrangement with a strong partner.

Throughout March and April 1981, efforts continued to find a suitable longer-term partner. At the same time, management strove to cut back costs and planned a third manpower reduction.

The crisis breaks

On the 8 May 1981, the government notified ICL that, under powers in its guarantee agreement, it proposed to nominate three new directors. At an historic board meeting on Sunday 10 May, which lasted for seven and a half hours, the chairman and managing director resigned and a new chairman (Mr Christopher Laidlaw, a deputy chairman of BP) and a new managing director (Mr Robb Wilmot, a senior executive of Texas Instruments) were elected. The government had four aims:

- to ensure that its guarantee was not called;
- to maintain its own computing capability which was very largely on ICL equipment;
- to enable that capability to be enhanced and developed;
- to maintain a substantial computer capability in the UK.

The new management team therefore had clear objectives dictated to them by the government and also, perhaps even more importantly, by circumstances. Within eighteen days, Robb Wilmot put forward to the board cost reduction proposals which involved a further cut of 5,200 jobs, temporary short-time working at certain plants, and a voluntary early retirement scheme. The board decided that the adverse effects on the company's reserves required an issue of redeemable preference shares. The new chairman spent June and July battling to get agreement for ICL to issue £50m. of preference shares. These could only be placed with the banks (no one else would accept them) if they were covered by the government's guarantee. By the end of July this had been achieved.

In the new management team, the key players were the new chairman (Christopher Laidlaw) and the managing director (Robb Wilmot). The former focused on the financial aspects of the strategy and with relationships with institutions and the City. The latter focused on the technology, product, market, and people issues. Success depended not only on their separate skills in their areas of expertise but also on their ability to work together. They were of very different ages and completely different backgrounds but were able to achieve leadership as a team of two.

Meanwhile, the manpower reduction programme went ahead although no financial benefits would result until the second half of the year. Customer confidence began to improve and there was an increase in orders in June. Senior management devoted great time and effort to encouraging customers to believe in ICL's future. The board was aware that the restoration of confidence depended on awareness that the government's financial support would not end abruptly and on producing a sensible new product strategy and a viable financial structure.

Meanwhile, Robb Wilmot spent much time formulating a new strategy. The new product strategy was for ICL to supply a fully networked product line and not just the mainframe element. Since ICL did not have the necessary resources to do this on its own, this new product strategy required that ICL should form new collaborative agreements with suitable partners. There was a need to keep the staff of ICL at all levels informed on the need for change, the new strategy, and the actions needed to make it work. This formed an important part of Robb Wilmot's work during his first few months at ICL.

The most important collaboration was with Fujitsu, a world leader in sophisticated computer technology, who were at least nine months ahead of any competitor in developing CMOS gate array chips. These had a significantly better speed/price capability than other technologies available at the time. The advantage to ICL was to be able to use the latest Fujitsu technology as the basis for its future mainframe designs. This would reduce the cost of future mainframe development and allow additional investment in small systems development. The potential advantages to Fujitsu included increased volume of sales, access to the European market, and ICL's know-how in computer applications. In September, Robb Wilmot signed heads of agreement with Fujitsu. While the main area of collaboration was to be technological, the arrangement would also cover ICL marketing Fujitsu's latest IBM-compatible M380 mainframe in selected markets.

In parallel with the Fujitsu relationship, the board approved a proposal by Robb Wilmot to collaborate with the MITEL Corporation of Canada over electronic PABX (telephone exchange) systems so that ICL could offer PABXs as part of its co-ordinated data voice and text networked product line.

At the same time as these external arrangements were being made, management took action internally to cut costs. The company was reorganized, office space reduced, tighter controls were applied to overseas subsidiaries, inventory handling and debt collection were improved, and better business forecasting was put in place. In the early autumn, management and the board sought an operating budget for 1981/2 aimed at bringing the company back to break-even. The cost base, particularly in manufacturing, was still too high. The board was also aware of the need to 'clear out the stable' in the year-end accounts for the current year (1980/1), to be published in December. There would have to be a delicate balance between a heavy trading loss plus large write-offs and maintaining customer confidence. There was also the effect on ICL's net worth; too heavy an impact here could trigger a statutory obligation to consult shareholders.

By this time it was clear that further finance would be necessary. One particular need was to finance further manpower reductions so as to make 1981/2 profitable. The government was prepared to help by paying up-front for new equipment. On the other hand, it took the view that after helping with the original guarantee and with the issue of preference shares, it was now the turn of the ICL shareholders to come up with money; this would require a rights issue. The board therefore decided to sound out, on an insider basis, the three major ICL shareholders to seek their support for a rights issue.

The five weeks from mid-November to mid-December 1981 were the real 'high risks, high stakes' period for ICL. During these few weeks, ICL was exposed to a crisis of confidence in four different but inter-locking areas. If the government refused to extend its guarantee beyond 1983, Fujitsu would not consent to long-term collaboration. If Fujitsu did not commit, the three major shareholders would withdraw their support for the rights issue. If the rights issue could not be underwritten, ICL could not afford to carry out the 2,500 redundancies. If these redundancies did not take place, ICL could not offer the prospect of a return to profit and the confidence of the banks and customers would finally evaporate.

On the night before the Fujitsu chairman returned to Japan, the government confirmed its extension of the guarantee. The formal agreement was signed with Fujitsu. On 15 December, ICL's results were released showing a trading loss of £55m. plus extraordinary expenses for redundancies of £78m., a total loss of £133m. This cleaned the stable but reduced shareholders' funds to only £72m. A one-for-one rights issue was announced at the same time to raise £32m. The success of the issue was announced on 25 January with 95% acceptances.

ICL had turned the corner financially but the work to implement a new and viable strategy had only just begun. Over the next several years, ICL's management worked to implement the new strategic direction. This did not prevent ICL losing its independence. Standard Telephones and Cables (STC) took over ICL. Robb Wilmot left at this time, leaving Peter Bonfield, his second in command, with the task of continuing the process of implementing the new strategies for ICL. Shortly after STC took over ICL, STC's other businesses ran into trouble so that STC (including ICL) was in turn taken over by Northern Telecommunications of Canada (Nortel). Fujitsu then bought an 80% share in ICL from Nortel in 1990.

Interestingly, ICL's strategies, which had been put in place so hurriedly, tended to survive these successive changes of ownership. For most of the 1980s, both revenues and profits showed steady increases. When IBM hit its own crisis in the early 1990s, ICL seemed to be enjoying comparative prosperity. The relationship with Fujitsu has generally been a happy one—perhaps because the logic of the original alliance with Fujitsu realized enough synergy to sustain a permanent relationship.

References

Jebb, F. (1996) 'ICL looks back in Languor', *Management Today*, July.

Tugendhat, C. (1973) *The Multinationals* (London: Pelican, Business and Management).

Commentary on ICL case example

This case example describes a crisis that occurred some years ago. The passage of time allows the facts to be viewed more objectively than would have been possible at the time.

Context

The crisis dominates the context. The central issue for ICL was survival. The case demonstrates how important a crisis can be to trigger a radical change in strategy. The case demonstrates the importance of finance as a driver of strategy, but also that strategy itself has to address business fundamentals. In this case, these fundamentals involved product, market, technological change, political change and external relationships, as well as finance. The strategic response to the crisis had to co-ordinate all these different aspects.

The strategy formulation process

The strategy formulation process bore little resemblance to the carefully orchestrated staff-supported process of textbooks. The crisis required decisions to be made by a very small group of people (predominantly just two). For most other staff, discussion was not encouraged; they had to do what they were told or leave. This demonstrates that effective leadership style varies with circumstances and that more authoritarian styles may be required in emergencies.

The process was driven by the financial crisis which meant that not only was a new strategy needed but that this new strategy had to be recognized and understood by existing and potential financial supporters. These included the government, major banks, and existing shareholders. The relative importance of these different groups of stakeholders varied rapidly and significantly over the period between May 1981 and 25 January 1982. The strategy formulation process had to deliver the right message to the right group at the right time over this period.

Strategic intent

ICL's strategic intent changed very sharply and suddenly as a result of the 1981 crisis. Before the crisis, ICL saw itself as a manufacturer of a complete range of mainframe computers, peripherals, software, and services. Computing was seen as a 'strategic' national industry. IBM was the dominant supplier but there was room for other manufacturers. The desire to remain a full range producer was deeply embedded in ICL's culture. This was what the government had created ICL to be. This 'intent' had remained unchanged and largely unquestioned since ICL's creation. ICL was heavily dependent on public sector orders and hence inclined to align itself with government thinking. Also, all its existing customers required continuing support across the full range.

The main threads of the new strategic intent were to move from providing mainframe computers to providing computer networks, to change from a manufacturer into more of a service company, and to operate by alliances as well as owned resources. Above all, perhaps, it was clear that ICL had to survive as a commercial company; it could no longer rely on government support.

Strategic assessment

An objective assessment of ICL, even before the rapid descent into crisis, should have revealed that ICL's aspiration to be a supplier of a complete mainframe range on a world-wide basis was extremely high risk given its available resources. ICL was in essence committing itself to achieving as great results from its research and development as a direct competitor over ten times its size. It was not difficult to make this assessment; the problem was that the consequences of such a negative assessment were unacceptable both within ICL and to the government. It took a crisis to change this.

ICL had other weaknesses that a strategic assessment should have revealed. In spite of its long-standing overseas interests, ICL was UK centred in an industry which was global in technology and product offerings. South Africa was ICL's most important overseas market, but was becoming isolated from the world economy due to its apartheid policies. There were strong reasons apart from money to think that ICL could not survive for long in its present form.

A cultural assessment would also have produced interesting findings. Salesmen and accountants, both disciplines that tend to emphasize the short term over the long term, were dominant in ICL's management. ICL also had a strong technical streak, originating from ICL's pioneering contributions to computer technology, which tended to equate strategy with technological advance and expected research to attract government funding by right. By the late 1970s, ICL had obvious strategic problems but they were rarely discussed.

An assessment of the external environment might have identified the changes in the technology and the impact these changes were having on the mainframe computer industry. It is apparent that ICL did not understand or did not act vigorously enough on its understanding of these changes before the crisis broke. The recession and new government policy meant that gradual changes in technology and the industry triggered a crisis over a period of only a few months.

Strategic choice

While there were risks attached to staying with the 'full product range in all markets strategy', it was not easy, before the crisis, to define viable alternative strategies.

A change to selling IBM-compatible computers might have provided access to the growing packaged software market but would have required major new development expenditure. It would also have meant that much of the development expenditure on the 2900 series would have been wasted. It would also have caused ICL to let down its existing customers who required compatible computers of increasing power for the future. A change to IBM-compatibility might also imply competing on equal terms with IBM for the future business of ICL's own client base. Even loyal customers, forced to convert to an IBM standard, were clearly going to find IBM rather than ICL mimicking IBM an attractive choice.

Another possible choice might have been for ICL to limit its market scope either geographically or by industry. This had the disadvantage that it would have reduced the size of market open to ICL without reducing the level of funding needed for research and development. It would merely have accentuated ICL's existing problems.

ICL would evidently have benefited from a partnership or merger with another player. The difficulty was in finding a partner. European governments tended to support their local company while the US vendors such as Univac, Burroughs, or Honeywell all had their own problems and incompatible computer architectures.

At no stage, as the crisis approached, was a major change of strategic direction seriously considered because there seemed to be no attractive choices available. The change in strategy may be attributed to Robb Wilmot personally but the radical change in direction could perhaps only have been made in an atmosphere of crisis.

Strategy implementation

There is little material on strategy implementation in this case example. It is, however, clear that the strategies that were put in place in a few months took several years to implement. The new strategic intent served ICL well for a decade.

Questions for discussion on the ICL case example

1. ICL survived the 1981 crisis. The changes implemented in the 1980s were not only effective at the time but also created a durable organization which has survived through difficult trading conditions. What factors contributed to this outcome?
2. Could the management talent that undoubtedly already existed within ICL have achieved the changes introduced by the new management team in 1980? If so, how? If not, why not?
3. In a time of crisis, one man was able, with the help of others, to drive through a new strategy. What are the advantages and disadvantages of formulating strategy in this way? Under what conditions might this approach be most effective? When least effective?

4. Would the recovery of ICL have been any more successful if the strategy work had been commissioned from a firm of consultants? Would it have been useful to call on consultants at the time of the crisis? If so, what terms of reference would you have given the consultants?
5. Did the changes in 1980/1 increase ICL's adaptability?

Case Example 2

Nolan, Norton & Company Inc. 1985–1987

The origins of Nolan, Norton & Company

Richard (Dick) Nolan and David (Dave) Norton founded Nolan, Norton & Company, Inc. in 1975. Nolan, Norton was a firm of management consultants specializing in advising large companies on how to get the best business value from their investments in information technology.

Dick Nolan had been a professor at the Harvard Business School for several years. His research had led to several articles in the Harvard Business Review. These articles had generated interest among general managers because, unusually at the time, they considered the use of computers as a business rather than a technical issue. Dave Norton had recently completed his doctorate at Harvard Business School after an earlier career as a management consultant. Harvard Business School encouraged its staff to maintain active contact with business by undertaking consulting assignments. The foundation of Nolan, Norton & Company marked an expansion and formalization of such activities.

Nolan, Norton & Company was incorporated as a 'Subchapter S Corporation'—a specialized corporate form under US company law. This form combines the protection of limited liability with some of the tax advantages of a partnership for a small number of owners. The two founders and their families owned all the equity in Nolan, Norton.

Nolan, Norton & Company's business

Nolan, Norton & Company specialized in assisting large companies (most of its customers were on *Fortune*'s list of the 100 largest US corporations) to derive the

Source: Compiled from unpublished sources.

maximum benefits from their investment in information technology. In the later 1970s, most large companies were increasing their expenditures on computing equipment very fast. Nolan, Norton was notably successful in providing practical methods by which boards could feel comfortable that they were making sound investment decisions in the unfamiliar area of computing. Normally, the firm's principal client was the board member responsible for information technology. At that time, it was unusual for board members to have much technical knowledge of computing. Conversely, it was typical for the head of the computing services department to be technically knowledgeable but not a member of the board. Nolan, Norton's special skill was to be able to communicate both with the computer technical staff and with the board and thereby assist them to understand and resolve the management issues arising from the rapid spread of information technology. Nolan, Norton consultants usually presented the results of their assignments to the assembled board. These presentations often generated lively interest and discussion.

The firm was successful and grew rapidly between 1975 and 1980. This growth resulted partly from word of mouth referrals from one client to others. Other marketing mechanisms included a publication, *Stage-by-Stage*, circulated free to some hundreds of senior information technology executives in large companies. Nolan, Norton also ran seminars, which were free and by invitation only, targeted at this same group. Both the seminars and *Stage-by-Stage* were serious attempts to build and to make known to a selected audience a body of knowledge on how best to manage information technology. The knowledge was based on both leading-edge theory and emerging best practice.

By 1980, Nolan, Norton was doing an increasing amount of work in Europe, mostly for the subsidiaries of US multinationals. This justified the opening of an office in London to serve clients throughout Europe. The London office continued to serve the European operations of US multinationals and soon began to win work from large British and Scandinavian companies. In practice, its operations were concentrated in northern Europe where English was acceptable as a working language.

Nolan, Norton suffered a sharp downturn in its US business during the recession of 1982. About one-quarter of the staff was let go at this time. Apart from this one setback, the firm continued to grow profitably and earned a reputation as a leader in its field.

Nolan, Norton's business purpose

Nolan, Norton & Co. had a very clear business purpose. This was to maintain intellectual leadership in the management of information technology and to develop practical ways in which managers could apply these ideas in practice. It saw itself as having to 'write the book' on the new art of information technology management. This purpose implied that, as the scope of information technology moved from a supporting role (such as payroll), through an operational role (such as banking terminals or airline check-ins), through to enabling completely new ways of doing business, so the scope of Nolan, Norton's activities would have to follow. Nolan, Norton's purpose did not change over the years, but the growth in the scale and importance of information technology inevitably required that Nolan, Norton would have to broaden its activities to continue to meet this purpose. Gradually, the nature of Nolan, Norton's work changed from the effective business management of information technology resources to assisting clients to understand the effects of information technology on their business strategies.

Internal structure of Nolan, Norton

To achieve this purpose, Nolan, Norton had a clear strategy of being 'one firm', operating with a coherent but extendible framework of ideas. To support this idea, the organizational structure had three dimensions—geography, client, and practice.

The geographical structure consisted of a headquarters in Lexington, Massachusetts. Over time, branch offices were opened in London, Chicago, Milan, New York, and San Francisco. Each consultant was assigned to one branch but moves between branches were common. For instance, the London office always had Americans working in it on postings lasting from a few months to several years. The basic management tasks of generating revenues, controlling costs, and assigning staff to projects were carried out in the branches.

A single client manager oversaw the relationship with each client. The client relationship might involve several separate projects run out of several different offices. A project manager was responsible for the success of each project. Project managers reported to client managers on the quality of the project and its contribution to the client relationship. Project managers were responsible to branch managers for meeting the project budget and for developing the skills of staff assigned to the project.

The third dimension of the organizational structure related to developing the ideas and practices of the firm. Practice leaders were responsible for extending the best of current practice within Nolan, Norton, for developing external relationships with external experts, and for running internal seminars to develop the knowledge of staff in each practice area.

Each consultant, at any time, might have roles in each of these three dimensions. For instance, a consultant might be working on two projects, be project manager for one of them, and at the same time be spending some time assisting in a particular practice area. In addition, while these dimensions determined role, roles were to some extent independent of level of seniority.

There were three broad levels of staff—consultants, managers, and Principals. Most staff joined as consultants and would be promoted to manager when they had enough experience of client work to manage projects. Managers might in turn be promoted to Principal when they were seen to have made a general contribution to the firm either as business managers, client managers, or practice leaders. There was intense competition for promotion to Principal, announced once a year.

The two founders retained ownership of the firm but distributed a high proportion of earnings to staff by way of profit-sharing schemes. The twenty or so Principals benefited particularly from this.

Management processes

The ideas of the firm were spread through a structure of intellectual frameworks and methods that could be shared internationally and with clients. The management process that supported the transmission of professional ideas between consultants was therefore critical to Nolan, Norton's success. Many of the ideas were presented using diagrams and pictures. Nolan, Norton maintained a database of such pictures shared by all the offices. This graphical database existed before computer graphics software was capable of supporting it. The database was automated using Apple Mac computers as soon as the necessary technical capability became available.

Nolan, Norton's marketing depended on engaging potential clients intellectually in these frameworks. This could lead to a discussion of specific issues and hence to consulting assignments to help resolve the issues. Nolan, Norton's relationships with its clients were nearly always good and were often maintained over several years. Managing mailing lists of the names of the key individuals who already were, or might become, clients was an important management process.

Typically, the longer relationships with clients would start with an assessment of the status of information technology across the customer's business, then the necessary changes would be planned and finally implemented. Nolan, Norton consultants nearly always worked in joint teams with staff from the client. Another important management process recorded the time spent on each project by each consultant and so provided information on which consultants were available to work on new projects. The assignment of consultants to projects was a critical management process as it could affect the profitability of the office, the quality of work done, and the rate of personal development.

People and culture

The internal culture of Nolan, Norton was derived from and encouraged by the values of the two founders who had different but complementary capabilities. Dick was an inspirational leader with a natural ability to make work seem fun. Dave was both an extremely capable management consultant and a dedicated manager with enormous enthusiasm for measurement and control. The two made a powerful combination.

Nolan, Norton staff all came from the computer industry. They had therefore lived through the excitement of working in a fast-growing industry and all could have found other jobs very easily. Their choice to work for Nolan, Norton required a willingness to take a risk with their careers, as the firm was small and initially not well known. It is likely that Nolan, Norton staff were in general more creative and less risk-averse than the average 'computer professional'. Working for Nolan, Norton was generally more exciting than working for a larger and more bureaucratic enterprise.

Early in its life, Nolan, Norton developed a clear set of values and a distinctive culture. Staff were almost invariably dedicated to working hard and were highly committed to helping their clients to manage their computing better by introducing the innovative management practices pioneered by Nolan, Norton. Nolan, Norton had a clear objective of staying ahead of the field by pursuing new ideas and making these ideas work in practice. This strategy was supported by the sponsorship of industry research work, the fostering of relationships with relevant universities, and by heavy investment in staff development.

In order to pass this culture and body of knowledge to new members of staff, all new recruits to Nolan, Norton spent two weeks at the headquarters in Massachusetts. This time was spent partly in formal learning sessions, but also gave the opportunity for new recruits to meet and get to know the senior members of the firm personally. In addition, it was usual for the entire firm to meet once a year, often at a ski resort, for sessions lasting two or three days. The time was spent in exchanging ideas and 'show-casing' best practice. The emphasis was on the content of professional work and the ideas of the firm rather than on business results. These meetings cemented personal relationships and maintained Nolan, Norton's distinctive culture. They also provided opportunities to discuss, clarify, or refine Nolan, Norton's business purpose and long-term business direction.

Strategic issues in 1985

External

In 1985, the business climate was still generally favourable for Nolan, Norton. The recession of the early 1980s had passed. Changes were, however, occurring in the external business environment. Many large companies, and hence Nolan, Norton's clients, had now installed mini-computers in addition to their large central mainframes. These were often owned and operated by a single department with its own information technology budget and staff. Central computer departments began to lose their overall control of computing. Relationships between the central and divisional computer departments were often strained. There was often therefore no longer a single person who could be the focus of Nolan, Norton's relationship with a large corporation. If Nolan, Norton was seen as too close an ally of the central computing department, it might be difficult to have good relationships with divisional computing departments. The arrival of personal computers in large numbers by the middle of the 1980s compounded even further this problem of the decentralization of the control of computing within the client.

While the internal control of computing was tending to fragment, the overall effect of information technology on business was becoming wider and more fundamental. Computing was beginning to affect the business strategies which clients were pursuing. Management consulting firms such as McKinsey and Boston Consulting Group, who had traditionally built their practices on corporate and business strategy, began to see that information technology was becoming a driver of change that they could not ignore. Such firms often had the advantage over Nolan, Norton of existing high level relationships with clients. Nolan, Norton had typically enjoyed higher level relationships than purely technical consultants had, but its base of high level contacts in a large client was usually narrower than the strategy consultants had.

To address the new customer needs, Nolan, Norton began to seek to help clients to identify and implement new ways of doing business that used computers to transform their operations. Such transformational assignments were much larger than Nolan, Norton's previous work which had been limited to assessing, advising, and assisting in the specialized function of information technology. Transformational assignments also required a broader range of skills in the consultant team. Nolan, Norton was a relatively small firm (perhaps 200 professional staff world-wide) and could only take on a handful of such projects at a time.

Internal

There were limits to growth within the existing organizational structure. A number of attempts had been made to pass day-to-day general management of the firm away from the two founders. These had all been unsuccessful. The reasons for this were diverse but the common factor was probably that many of the Principals had close personal association with the founders and so would bypass or undermine management decisions with which they did not agree.

The aspirations of the two founders, Dick Nolan and Dave Norton, were also important. They had founded an enterprise that had grown from a back-bedroom operation into a growing and profitable business that was perceived as a leader in its field. But they had not yet derived significant financial benefits from this success. They had distributed the profits widely and generously and there was no market for their equity. Obviously either selling out or a public offering could be attractive.

It is also possible that the recession of the early 1980s had left its mark on their aspirations. During this time, they had to make painful decisions and had seen bankers interfering in day-to-day management decisions. Dick and Dave had no desire to repeat the experience of having to lay off staff whom they knew well in the next recession, whenever that might be.

Nolan, Norton had very significant strengths in terms of focus, unique and well-tested methods, the quality of its relationships with its clients, and the dedication and skills of its staff.

On the other hand, there was a distinct mismatch between the scale of the opportunity now presented and the resources available. Resources were stretched to open new offices and to staff very large projects. At the same time, many large companies were seeking assistance to resolve similar difficulties. Consulting assignments cannot wait, so competitors would fill the gap if Nolan, Norton could not. If it were going to respond to the opportunities, then Nolan, Norton would have to grow faster than could be achieved by internal development alone.

The need for choice

The awareness that Nolan, Norton was facing a 'strategic inflection point' did not occur at any defined moment. There was certainly a realization that the market place was changing and that the niche which Nolan, Norton had exploited so successfully was unlikely to continue to exist in the same form. The need for larger resources was also apparent, both to meet new competition and to achieve rapid international growth.

Various ideas for future direction were considered and some were taken as far as exploratory discussions. One possibility was to build joint ventures of strategic alliances with major partners in the major countries. The Milan office opened in 1983 was a prototype, as the operation in Italy was a joint venture with a leading Italian systems house. This strategy would leave Nolan, Norton relatively small, highly international, and very specialized. Nolan, Norton would generate ideas internationally and work with local partners to deliver these ideas in their local market. Overall scale would come from having a number of such partnerships in the major markets. The staff of the larger and locally resident partner firms would be strong in local connections, and have enough staff to do the bulk of the work.

There was also considerable effort devoted to the development of new services, particularly related to achieving business transformation through the extensive exploitation of information technology. These efforts achieved some success but were perhaps limited by the relatively narrow base of skills within the firm. There was also a tendency to try to devise standard methods for tasks that were intrinsically more complex and subtle than those that Nolan, Norton had previously worked on. Nolan, Norton was rich in computer technical skills but much less so in fields such as the management of people and change. There would clearly be advantages in a merger with a partner with counter-balancing skills.

A third option was to remain specialized in the management of information technology itself. Nolan, Norton had specialist skills in areas such as measuring the scale and risk of computer projects. Nolan, Norton could have survived in a role similar to that of a consulting engineer in civil engineering projects. Though viable, this option did not fit well with Nolan, Norton's business purpose and did not appeal to staff who had scented the appeal of more general work.

Finally, Nolan, Norton could have continued as it was with a small share of a very big market, growing by internal development as best it could. Although apparently easy to implement, this option also involved risks.

In summary, Nolan, Norton was doing well but there were signs that it might have to make a strategic choice about its future. There were four broad strategic options—continue with no change, find a single partner, find multiple national partners, or focus on technological issues.

Internal discussions on strategy

The options were discussed openly between the two owners and the twenty Principals. The Principals met regularly every month and these meetings were extended two or three times a year into off-site events lasting several days. Although the Principals had no 'equity' in a financial sense, it was apparent that their collective commitment to the future direction of the firm would be crucial to success in a people-oriented business like consulting.

While there was naturally a range of opinion among those concerned, the technical focus option was perhaps the first to be dropped. Although it had its advocates, it was generally unattractive emotionally to most staff. Fee levels for technical work were generally lower, so it was also unattractive for future earnings levels. There was also a feeling that the time had come for some kind of fundamental change which eliminated the 'continue as is' option.

A consensus emerged that selling the firm as whole would be preferable to trying to maintain its integrity with separate relationships with partners in different countries. It may be that the experience of the Italian joint venture influenced this. The joint venture had been quite successful but had involved a great deal of time and effort to make it so. Clearly, a suitable acquirer had to be large and international. Two potential acquirers—Peat Marwick and Saatchi & Saatchi—emerged, presenting different prospects for the future.

Saatchi and Saatchi had started as an advertising agency but were growing rapidly at this time. Their concept was to become a supermarket of professional services combining advertising, management consulting, and financial services. This approach offered autonomy to Nolan, Norton as a business unit within a family of autonomous professional service firms.

Peat Marwick was keen to absorb Nolan, Norton into its existing management consulting operations. Peat Marwick had identified its information technology consulting capabilities as being weak in comparison with some of the other large accounting firms, particularly Arthur Andersen. Peat Marwick therefore saw Nolan, Norton as being able to strengthen its existing consulting practice more quickly than would be possible by internal development. Peat Marwick saw Nolan, Norton as having a catalytic role in leading and enlivening its much larger information technology consulting practice.

Both potential acquirers saw Nolan, Norton as offering apparent synergy with their existing businesses, but synergy of different kinds. Peat Marwick was eventually chosen and terms agreed. There were few dissenters within the Nolan, Norton Principals, who were offered the prospects of personal gain from earn-out payments spread over five years. The rest of the staff of Nolan, Norton was perhaps less happy. Some felt that they had joined Nolan, Norton because it was an exciting place to work and that large accounting firms were not known for their fun cultures.

Strategy implementation and results

Nolan, Norton began working jointly with Peat Marwick in the autumn of 1986 and formally merged into (or was acquired by) Peat Marwick in March 1987. At almost exactly the same time, Peat Marwick merged world-wide with Thomson McLintock to form KPMG.

The synergy between Peat Marwick and Nolan, Norton turned out to be less than had been expected for several reasons. Peat Marwick, and later KPMG, operated in a very decentralized way. In the USA, for instance, there was a KPMG office in every major city, dealing mostly with middle-sized enterprises in that city and region. This middle market was the core of KPMG's business and the source of its main strengths. However, it offered few opportunities for introductions to the large multinational companies for whom Nolan, Norton's services had been specifically designed.

KPMG did, of course, have its fair share of large multinationals as clients. However, in these, the audit partner tended to be seen by the client as a specialist adviser on matters related to accounting and tax. It was not easy to extend this technical relationship to provide more general management advice nor into a different specialist area.

There were also significant differences in culture between KPMG and Nolan, Norton. Both were dedicated to excellence but they defined excellence differently. Nolan, Norton believed that innovation was a necessary ingredient of excellence, so that every client assignment had to include something entirely new. Peat Marwick saw excellence as consisting of the careful implementation of well-tested ideas. Nolan, Norton saw itself as an agent of change; Peat Marwick saw itself as guaranteeing and attesting quality to established standards.

Finally, a merger between the two large accounting firms happened at the same time as Nolan, Norton, a small specialist firm, was being absorbed into the management consulting practice of KPMG. The amount of management attention available within KPMG to address the specific issues of Nolan, Norton was limited.

Commentary on Nolan, Norton case example

Context

The case describes a smaller business than the other case examples. It is also a good example of a knowledge-based business. This case example illustrates how strategic change can become necessary even when there is no change in strategic intent. It also illustrates how, particularly in smaller companies, there can be a significant overlap between the aspirations of individuals and the strategic needs for the business as an entity.

Strategic intent

The strategic intent was very clear in Nolan, Norton. Its central elements were the desire for intellectual leadership in the emerging field of the management of information technology and a commitment to translate ideas into working practice. This strategic intent did not change, but as information technology spread its influence wider and wider, this strategic intent required a change in other aspects of the business in response to the changing needs of clients and new competition.

Strategic choice

Nolan, Norton certainly had a range of choices available. The case example illustrates how a strategic choice is made by a combination of logic and emotion. It also demonstrates how different groups of stakeholders can influence strategic choice.

Strategic assessment and strategy implementation

Nolan, Norton had very distinctive culture, organizational structure, and management processes. Each of these had been designed or evolved to suit the needs of its business. A strategic assessment of Nolan, Norton before the merger with KPMG should have highlighted the importance of these in maintaining the business. After the merger with KPMG, there were changes in the culture, systems, and organization of Nolan, Norton. These changes were made for a variety of reasons but were not aligned to any clear strategy for Nolan, Norton within KPMG.

The differences in culture between Nolan, Norton and KPMG were extremely significant in the years after the merger. The differing views of excellence meant that Nolan, Norton people sometimes found KPMG people dull, while KPMG people sometimes found Nolan, Norton people a bit wild and 'unprofessional'.

Organizational structure was changed as Nolan, Norton was absorbed into a KPMG structure. This was particularly difficult in the USA where a centralized Nolan, Norton had to work within a very decentralized KPMG.

There was also a tendency to impose KPMG's management processes on Nolan, Norton. These processes did not match Nolan, Norton's needs as well as the processes which had been specifically designed for its own use. For example, Nolan, Norton's basic reporting system had worked on a weekly cycle; KPMG's was monthly. While attempts were made to maintain Nolan, Norton's professional idea transmission systems and meetings, these tended to be reduced because of changes in reporting lines and to save cost.

Stakeholder structure

Three stakeholder groups emerged in determining the future of Nolan, Norton—the two founders, the Principals, and the other staff. As a small entrepreneurial firm with the two founders still active in day-to-day management, it was impossible to separate the strategy of the firm from the personal ambitions and desires of these two individuals. Professional service firms have few physical assets, so the value of the businesses largely derive from the skills and knowledge of the people. This therefore necessitated a strategy process in which the Principals were actively involved and strategic choices were generally acceptable to this group. It may be that the interests of the rest of the staff were given less weight than they deserved.

Exit strategies

The aim of strategy is usually to ensure the long-term success of the enterprise. Entrepreneurial firms may be an exception to this. An effective exit strategy may be as important as the long-term survival as an entity.

Synergy

There is a tendency to over-estimate synergy in mergers. Research results support this view and it was certainly the case here.

Questions for discussion on Nolan, Norton case example

1. Nolan, Norton was a successful company that faced a changing market. Selling out was one strategic option. Was this the only option? What might have been the advantages and disadvantages of other options?
2. How would you expect the views of the main stakeholder groups within Nolan, Norton (the two owners, the twenty Principals, and the staff) to differ on the question of the future of the company?

3. Saatchi and Saatchi was a possible alternative purchaser of Nolan, Norton with different intentions from KPMG Peat Marwick. How might their different intentions have affected the outcome?
4. What additional measures might KPMG have taken to make their acquisition more valuable to them?

Case Example 3

BMW in 1999: Victim of Poor Strategy or Poor Implementation?

On Friday 5 February 1999, Mr Pischetsrieder resigned as chief executive of BMW. His departure was attributed to his decision to buy Rover in 1994 and then to fail to make it profitable. It seems clear that either BMW's strategy had been wrong or it had failed in implementation. BMW's products were highly successful in the very competitive executive car sector and its take-over of Rover appeared to be a calculated move. What had gone wrong?

The world motor industry

Motor cars are among the more desirable possessions of an individual. An MIT study carried out in the mid-1980s called the car the 'Machine that changed the world'. Yet in the closing years of the twentieth century, after years of steady growth, this industry was experiencing a slowing down in growth in sales and over-capacity. As Bob Eaton, joint chairman of DaimlerChrysler, said in *Director* magazine of March 1999, 'World-wide automotive capacity today stands at 66 million units. Demand on the other hand, is only 51 million units. But in the year 2002 world wide capacity is expected to be 79 million units chasing demand of only 61 million units'. The car industry is mature and almost global. Table C3.1 summarizes the position.

It is evident that by 1999 the industry had become quite concentrated, with the five largest companies sharing 54% of the world market. Of the other seven groups with over 2% of the world market, BMW and Honda perhaps stand out for the perceived brand image of their products. BMW, in particular, could claim to have become an 'aspirational' brand in that to many it was the car which they hoped they might own

Source: Compiled from newspaper coverage.

Table C3.1 World market shares of top twelve motor manufacturers

Company	Additional interests	World market share (%)
General Motors (USA)	Opel (Germany), Vauxhall (UK), 50% of Saab (Sweden), Partnerships with Suzuki and Isuzu (Japan). Produces Prism with Toyota	16.4
Ford (USA)	Jaguar (UK), Aston Martin (UK), Volvo Cars (Sweden), Minority shares in Mazda (Japan) and Kia (Korea)	13.5
Toyota (Japan)	Lexus(Japan), Produces Prism with GM	9.1
Volkswagen (Germany)	Audi (Germany), Bentley (UK), Skoda (Czechoslovakia), SEAT (Spain)	8.0
DaimlerChrysler (Germany)	Mercedes Benz (Germany), Chrysler (USA)	7.5
Fiat (Italy)	Ferrari (Italy), Maserati (Italy)	5.4
Nissan (Japan)		5.3
Honda (Japan)		3.8
Hyundai (Korea)		2.3
PSA (France)	Peugeot (France), Citroen (France)	3.9
Renault (France)		3.6
BMW (Germany)	Rover (UK)	2.2
Other		19.0

Source: Adapted from *Time*, 8 Feb. 1999.

as a symbol of having arrived in their careers. For instance, job advertisements sometimes specifically mentioned a BMW as among the perks.

Many of the 'additional interests' shown in the central column of Table C3.1 had been put in place by mergers and other moves made during the 1990s.

'Other' includes the smaller Japanese manufacturers, newcomers such as Daewoo in Korea, Proton in Malaysia, as well as many specialist manufacturers such as TVR, Westfield, Morgan, Venturi, and Porsche.

Market conditions in 1999: a mature industry

Bob Eaton's figures suggested that both demand and capacity would grow by about 20% between 1999 and 2002. A compound growth rate of about 6% a year is healthy in comparison with many other industries, but is modest compared with the rates of growth of the car industry since the Second World War. The continuing excess capacity meant that competition would remain intense.

Brand has traditionally been very important in this industry, but cars are losing their individuality. Most mass market products and some luxury brands look very much like each other and offer much the same mix of driving experience, safety, comfort, and after-sales care. Most of the parts beneath the skin come from the same component manufacturers, thereby reducing the uniqueness of the motor car.

It has been claimed that survival in the market is now a function of volume and strong marketing. Cost reductions come from volume, automation, interchangeable and out-sourced systems, and strong procurement capability. Eaton saw the solution to differentiation as one of building 'desirable cars'. By this he meant making cars that people wanted to buy, mainly those with social cachet such as Mercedes-Benz, BMW, Porsche, Audi, Jaguar, and a few other 'brand' names. These cars have waiting lists and hold their value well. The other makers will have to fight it out in the market place. One way to do this is to own the means of production of the more price-sensitive cars. Here the Japanese manufacturers have an edge and so does Ford, whose models have always sold well to the price conscious.

By 1999, many large and mature markets, such as the USA and Europe, were reaching saturation. In the USA, the American manufacturers had lost ground. They had already ceded 30% of the market to foreign competitors and were in danger of losing more as European manufacturers feeling the pinch at home invaded the US market for the second time in twenty years. Volkswagen's new Beetle was selling well in the USA although it had yet to take off in Europe. *Fortune* (15 Mar. 1999) reported that 'For the 1999 model year, which began on October 1 [1998], four of the five top sellers (Camry, Accord, Civic and Corolla) are made by Toyota and Honda. The only domestic car is the Ford Taurus, whose biggest customer is Hertz.' It seemed from this quote that the American giants were in trouble again. But they were not the only ones. Clearly, there were strategic issues for the players to resolve.

New entrants: the supplier's challenge

More and more of the finished motor car and truck incorporates complete sub-assemblies from systems suppliers such as Magna of Canada, Bosch in Germany, and TRW in the USA. The industry now has car assemblers and car systems developers whereas once it just had car makers. As Zwick (1999) points out: 'The car industry, like the computer and consumer electronics industries before it, is going modular, and the percentage of a car that is actually manufactured by traditional car companies is getting smaller and smaller as a result'.

The modularity comes from the fact that manufacturers are buying in complete sub-assemblies rather than parts that they then assemble into cars. This means that the car you buy is made up of a plethora of parts and sub-assemblies supplied by a wide range of component manufacturers rather than by the car manufacturer. Zwick points out that the systems suppliers named above: 'are taking on their own global role alongside the global car assemblers. The advantage to the car makers includes faster delivery times, more flexibility and more manageable inventories, as well as redefined labor arrangements.'

One of the key advantages of the Systems Suppliers is that they enable smaller car makers to operate viably and give the lie to the oft-quoted statement that you have to be big to benefit from economies of scale. It would appear that, in the car industry, size and profitability are not necessarily synonymous.

Government influence on the industry

There has been a build-up of legislation to make cars 'cleaner' and to discourage people from using their cars. Measures, which have already occurred in some markets and are likely to increase, have included increases in fuel taxes and charges for the use of cars in cities. Financial support from governments has become harder to obtain. In the UK and USA, except for a few exceptions, companies have to finance their own growth. This contrasts with a desire at one time for governments to sustain prestigious industries such as cars and airlines as indicators of national virility. The reason is that a diminishing public purse has made such subsidies almost impossible to make. As Womack, Jones, and Roos (1990) pointed out: 'The investment finance systems behind the other Western producers in Europe (as opposed to British Leyland) have been more effective, at least in providing companies the funds necessary to weather crises'.

In this regard, Womack, Jones, and Roos were referring to the fact that the French government still supported its industry and that family interests supported companies such as Fiat, BMW, and Porsche. Close ties with major European banks helped companies such as Daimler Benz.

Growth by acquisition or merger

There seems to be a natural limit to growth by evolution, that is, the increase in market share, revenue, and profit through the sale of a particular brand. Once evolutionary growth hits its limits, companies are faced with more aggressive options such as mergers and acquisitions. Mercedes Benz is a good example of a company that had eventually to merge with an American manufacturer to grow its business. The company went from being a purveyor of large, expensive luxury vehicles to producing cars for a much wider spectrum of buyers. Widening its product offering did change its fortunes and increase its market share, but it needed to merge with Chrysler to make a significant difference to its size, financial strength, and market reach.

Table C3.1 shows clearly how the giants in the car industry have sought to reposition themselves by widening their product portfolio by acquiring smaller manufacturers and by acquiring weaker competitors. This is not a new phenomenon. Mergers and acquisitions were often justified on grounds of size: 'financial firepower, technological depth and brand presence' (Martin 1999).

Mergers such as DaimlerChrysler were carried out to help expand market share, enter new markets, and plug product gaps. Above all, this trend seems to be fuelled by a feeling in the industry that (*Time*, 8 Feb. 1999) 'The economies of scale increasingly favour the multinational giants. And more of the smaller firms are deciding they'll fare best by joining with a strong partner.' Earlier acquisitions such as that of Vauxhall in the UK and Opel in Germany by GM were to facilitate market entry. Other mergers such as those that created the British Leyland Motor Corporation were engineered by government intervention to strengthen the national industry.

Survival by staying small and specialist

However, there are detractors from the view that mergers will solve the capacity problem in the auto industry. Takahiro Fujimoto (an economics professor at Tokyo University and a member of MIT's International Motor Vehicle Programme) is quoted in *Fortune* (15 Feb. 1999) as saying: 'I do not think there is any logical, economic, or strategic reason why only five to ten giant automakers need to survive in the world'.

John Kay (1999*b*) points out that despite the many mergers over the years a study of comparative figures for the industry between 1969 and 1996 shows that:

> The world motor industry has become steadily less concentrated. Larger participants have been losing market share, and the number of makers at all scales of production has been increasing. Frequent alliances, consolidations and mergers, in which failing companies have been picked up by their competitors, have not been enough to offset these basic facts of market evolution.

Fortune (15 Mar. 1999), examining this trend, suggests that 'overcapacity has been a fact of life in the auto industry for decades remaining steady at about 25% of total production capability'. The article also points out that: 'Mergers don't always reduce it [over-capacity]; they often only put it under one roof instead of two'.

The article argues that mergers enable the joint entity to spread research and engineering costs over a larger volume. But it points out that it reduces the ability of the mega-giant to respond to the market—something the smaller companies such as Honda and BMW can do. The article says: 'Honda and BMW are only a fraction of General Motors' size, but that hasn't prevented them from handily outperforming the General for the past 20 years. Put two lumbering companies together and you get one that runs worse, not better.'

Peter Martin, writing in the *Financial Times* of 9 February 1999, soon after the board-room bust-up at BMW, supports this view. He makes the case that small can be beautiful in the auto industry, provided that by small is meant companies such as Honda and BMW. Specifically, he says: 'The minimum size of an efficient plant is coming down, thanks to automation and pre-assembly of components. So if BMW is in some sense too small, it cannot be for the traditional reason of production efficiencies.'

If these sceptical views on the value of mergers are right, why does the rush to merge or acquire continue?

The BMW story

BMW is a long-established company. It has been around for nearly eighty years. At first, it manufactured aero-engines and motorcycles but its reputation is now based on its cars. The Quandt family owns 46% of BMW and has remained a friend of BMW even when times were tough. For example, in 1959, when the company suffered reverses and was almost sold to Daimler Benz, it was Herbert Quandt who bought 30% of the shares in the company and prevented the take-over. Since then, the family has stood by the company and supported it. The family is unlikely to support any moves to sell it to a predator, so growth had to come from exploiting its current product range and developing new products to enter new markets or to acquire or merge with another company.

Engineering excellence

High quality engineering is in BMW's blood. In 1936 the company unveiled the type 328 motor car at the Motor Show. It was a great car, as Jenkinson (1984) points out in his history of AFN Ltd, who started selling BMWs in the late 1930s. In his view: 'It was quite obvious that even the supercharged Shelsley model Frazer Nash could not cope with this newcomer from Germany, which AFN Ltd. was marketing as the Frazer Nash-BMW TT model'.

He also says that even then: 'The smooth and lively little 6 cylinder engine (Type 315) and the independent front suspension and rigid chassis was a complete break-through by English standards of the time'.

BMW is also excellent in its production process. As Kay (1993) points out, BMW had: 'A system of production which gives the company a particular advantage in its chosen market segment, a world-wide reputation for product quality, and a brand which immediately identifies the aims and aspirations of its customers'.

It was in the late 1950s and early 1960s that the general car-buying public began to recognize BMW as a manufacturer of excellent cars with driver appeal. With the 1500 and then the 1602 and 2002ti, it chose a segment of the industry which was, until then, not tapped with any real earnestness—a production saloon with high build quality which was fun to drive. From this beginning, the company built up its reputation but its customer base was primarily among aficionados. It was only in the 1980s that the car became a fashion icon and began to sell in volume.

Financial strength

The support of the Quandt family, a healthy order book, and good sustained profitability has provided BMW with the money to innovate and refresh its product line. In addition, the company has good financial backing from its bankers in Germany and elsewhere. Its excellent market presence also contributes to its financial strength; BMWs are rarely discounted.

BMW in 1994

BMW was a small player in a global village of giants (or perhaps dinosaurs) who were about to embark on the acquisition spree of Table C3.1. BMW had a good image. Its cars were bought by the 'upwardly mobile', but BMW was lucky not to be narrowly typecast like Porsche as a 'yuppy' toy—an image that could at times conflict with social values. On the face of it, BMW had successfully differentiated itself in a way that its competitors might envy and had a strategy which seemed capable of delivering continuing success.

There were, however, several reasons why BMW needed to consider a new strategy. First of all, a merger boom was taking place in the industry. Managers always find it difficult to stand back at such times; deliberate inactivity may appear like a lack of drive. In spite of the Quandt family holding, BMW management may have felt that it was a question of either acquire or be acquired. Also, of course, mergers can provide both excitement and reward to the managers involved. Another factor was that BMW's direct rival Mercedes Benz began to move like a spring chicken. Mercedes Benz accelerated its new product development programme. Over the next few years it changed from a company with three products to one which spanned the whole spectrum from the A class to the S class with C, E, and M class saloons and variants filling critical gaps in its range.

BMW had some catching up to do but it was well placed to meet the challenges posed by Mercedes Benz and Audi. In the luxury sporty car segment, it had a much healthier percentage of the market. It had some impressive new models such as the revamped 3 and 7 series coming on stream. The 5 series continued to be the class leader as the best-rated executive car in the industry. In addition, its recently launched Z3 was proving successful.

In 1994 BMW acquired Rover from British Aerospace.

Rover

Rover was the result of many mergers over many years. In the great merger boom of the late 1960s, British Motor Holdings and Leyland Motors merged to become British Leyland Motor Corporation. British Motor Holdings was itself a merger between Austin, Morris, Coventry Climax, Guy Motors, Daimler, and Jaguar cars. Leyland was the result of various marriages between Leyland, Standard-Triumph, Associated Commercial Vehicles, Rover, and Aveling-Barford. These mergers were hardly ever rationalized. In most cases, the resulting companies were an unholy combination of work practices, car designs, and ad hoc cannibalization. The factories were rarely streamlined to accommodate the products of the merged organizations and the workforce continued as if nothing had changed. Michael Edwardes made a valiant effort to clean up and went part way towards achieving structural and product changes. He tamed the unions and got working practices under control. He validated the management staff and introduced designs and products from Honda to remedy the appalling product line-up which the company offered. This had gradually brought the company back to life but had in the process cost the British taxpayer a large fortune. Eventually the British government sold Rover to British Aerospace.

By 1994, British Aerospace no longer saw Rover as a core business and by this stage it was politically feasible to sell Rover to a foreign owner. The sale to BMW gave Rover, for the first time in a very long time, an owner with a history of sticking by its subsidiaries during hard times and one that was willing to invest money and technological capability in it to pull it out of the mire. At the time, the popular view was that BMW had pulled a fast one on Honda whose existing technical relationship with Rover made them a more obvious acquirer.

The purchase of Rover by BMW

It is certain that BMW executives knew about the whole sorry saga of Rover. Mr. Pischetsrieder did not buy Rover on a whim. His decision to buy Rover Cars from British Aerospace (BAe) in January 1994, was: 'Based on sound analysis by Pischetsrieder and his strategy director Hagen Luderitz.' The paper goes on to say that

> they (Pischetsrieder and Luderitz) saw that, in the long term, BMW could not retain its position as an independent premium car maker with an output of only 600,000 cars a year. The rising costs of developing models and pricing pressure from volume-car makers, led by Ford, General Motors, Volkswagen and Toyota, would mean BMW's wide margins would be squeezed.

This quote suggests that BMW saw Rover as important in increasing its scale of operation.

One motivation may have been that it was becoming harder and harder to keep up with development. The Rover acquisition clearly offered some economies of research and development. As Gavin Gaskell, UK managing director of BMW, has pointed out: 'The market we are competing in gets more and more aggressive every year. The new products that come to the market are very, very good. And just take a look at our customers. Their expectations are increasing dramatically every year.'

On the other hand, there was no plan to integrate manufacturing. Rover cars continued to be made at Longbridge and BMW cars in Bavaria. The effect of the merger was therefore to make the BMW group into two 600,000 a year producers not one 1,200,000 unit.

BMW's brand strategy seemed to be that Rover would produce the lower end models for its range. These models had to compete directly with mass producers such as Toyota, Ford, and VW in a market in which BMW had no particular competence. The BMW brand would retain its strong position in the higher priced segments.

Land Rover was a further complication. It was reported at the time of the take-over that BMW had been particularly attracted by Land Rover as giving it a strong position in the growing 'off-road' or 'sports utility vehicle' segment in which Land Rover's position was strong. BMW's strategy seems also to have been a little unclear in this area, as in 1998 BMW announced that it was developing its own SUV model, the MX5.

The proof of the benefits of the acquisition should have been in the results and it is clear that the strategy failed. In the five years between 1994 and 1998 BMW's investments in Rover have been variously estimated at between £3 bn. and £5 bn. (including Rover's losses in the period). It also cost BMW management time—time that might have been better spent within the BMW stable. This money and management time were spent on a company that Wolf (1999) describes as: 'A long-running disaster, the residue of a company that once had half the British market'.

Mr Pischetsrieder resigned on 5 February 1999. The *Sunday Times* of 7 February 1999 reported: 'His position had been weakened by Rover's slump and his own admission that BMW should have moved quicker to address the problems'.

References

Carter, M. (1999) 'Car Trouble', *Director*, Mar.

Jenkinson, D. (1984) *From Chain Drive to Turbocharger—The AFN Story* (London: Patrick Stephenson Limited).

Kay, J. (1993) *Foundations of Corporate Success* (Oxford: Oxford University Press).

—— (1999*a*) 'The Car that Lost its Way', *Financial Times*, 17 Feb.

—— (1999*b*) 'Sometimes Size is Not Everything', *Financial Times*, 3 Mar.

Martin, P. (1999) 'Cut to the Core', *Financial Times*, 9 Feb.

Taylor III, A. (1999) 'The Automakers: More Mergers. Dumb Idea', *Fortune*, 15 Feb.

Wolf, M. (1999) 'Carmaker's Auction', *Financial Times*, 22 Mar.

Womack, J. P., Jones, D.T., and Roos, D. (1990) *The Machine that Changed the World* (New York: Rawson Associates).

Zwick, S. (1999) 'World Cars', *Time Magazine*, 1 Mar.

Commentary on BMW case example

Context

The motor industry is one of the major world industries and by the 1990s was mature. It seems that evolutionary growth was limited and the industry saw mergers and acquisitions as the answer. By 1999, the industry had consolidated into a few giants and many minnows. The giants may not have been as profitable as the specialist makers but their size gave them buying power and the ability to exploit markets better, to improve production techniques, and to meet customer demands of more for less. It seems that BMW felt that it had to react.

Strategic assessment

We have no hard evidence about how BMW assessed either BMW itself or Rover in 1994. It would have been very desirable to take a very hard look at what synergy the merger might realistically achieve. Scale economies in production could only be made in production by more rationalization of production than was attempted and probably more than was politically feasible. Similarly, it is difficult to see a clear brand and model strategy for the combined company. Other points relevant to a strategic assessment would have been on engineering compatibility and cultural differences.

Strategic choice

BMW had the same kinds of options as the rest of the industry. It could remain a small or medium-sized provider of luxury sporty cars selling to a small but loyal, informed, and well-heeled customer base and grow by evolution and internal strength. It could grow by acquisition, buying into other European or Japanese companies. It could invite acquisition by a large manufacturer and like Jaguar, Ferrari, and others find itself a good and appreciative home. The Quandt family would probably have rejected this third option out of hand.

Likely candidates for acquisition or merger in Europe were few—perhaps Renault, Peugeot/Citroen (both much larger), or Volvo. The only possible Japanese company would have been Honda, which had at least some strategic similarities to BMW. Relations between Honda and BMW became strained over the Rover deal but were not necessarily poor before that.

In the end, the strategic choice for BMW seems to have been between buying Rover or remaining an independent specialist manufacturer.

Quality of strategy implementation

It would appear that BMW were too slow to make the savings and efficiencies needed to make Rover a viable car plant. The deal made with the unions came too late to save the company. The politicians dithered and the work and the opportunity envisaged by Pischetsrieder and Luderitz were lost. Poorly executed strategy is enormously costly for those involved and for the bystanders. However, it is worth recording that it cost Ford almost as much to get Jaguar right. So perhaps in another five years Rover will be contributing significantly to the bottom line and will have helped the company to enter a new market segment to compete successfully with the mainstream products of Ford, GM, and Toyota.

Kevin Gaskell, the UK managing director of BMW, remains optimistic (*BMW Magazine* 1/1999): 'the acquisition of the Rover Group by BMW means that we can enjoy economies of scale—manufacture, research and distribution—and at the same time offer products to very different market sectors'.

On the other hand, maybe Pischetsrieder can be blamed for dragging BMW into a disastrous alliance or for mismanaging a great new opportunity for the company. Perhaps the strategy was right but the execution failed BMW, Rover, and Britain. Either way, Pischetsrieder ran out of time and paid the price.

Questions for discussion on BMW case example

1. BMW is a successful company with an excellent brand image and loyal customers. Could it have survived on its own in an industry where giants were teaming up to create mega-giants?
2. How should BMW have assessed the suitability of potential acquisitions or partners? How good a fit was Rover with BMW's strategic need for a suitable acquisition? Would any other company have been a better fit if BMW had moved in time?
3. If you had been an adviser to Mr Pischetsrieder in 1994, what advice would you have offered him to make the Rover acquisition a success?
4. How would you rate the Rover acquisition strategically in the light of subsequent events?

Case Example 4
Hard Times for Marks & Spencer

Introduction

For many years, the name Marks & Spencer (M&S) has been synonymous with excellence in British retailing. Its March 1998 results showed that M&S stood out as the most profitable of the major retailers in the UK (see Table C4.1).

In May 1998 M&S reported its results up to the end of March 1998. Turnover at £8,243m. had increased by 5% and profit before tax at £1,168m. by 6%. It was noticeable that over 94% of the profit had been earned in the UK, reflecting the advantages to a retailer of a strong market share. Marks & Spencer was well regarded in other ways than for its financials. In 1997 *Management Today* rated it third among Britain's

Table C4.1 Comparison of turnover and profit of leading UK retailers 1998

	Sales (£M)	Pre-Tax Prof. (£M)	Margin %	Year end date
Tesco	16,452	728	4.4%	28 Feb 1998
J.Sainsbury	14,500	719	4.9%	7 March 1998
Marks & Spencer	8,243	1,168	14.2%	31 March 1998
ASDA	7,620	405	5.3%	3 May 1997
Safeway	6,979	340	4.9%	28 March 1998
Kingfisher	6,409	521	8.1%	31 January 1998
Boots	5,022	432	8.6%	31 March 1998
John Lewis	3,117	153	4.9%	31 January 1998
W.H.Smith	2,850	143	5.0%	31 May 1997
Dixons Group	2,774	219	7.9%	2 May 1998

Source: Company Annual Reports.

Source: Compiled from newspaper coverage and annual reports.

most admired companies, moving up one place from the previous year (Merriden 1997).

The 1998 Annual Report exuded confidence and announced a major investment programme to provide more selling space. In the UK the space was to increase from 10.6 to 12.5m. sq.ft. (an 18% increase) and overseas from 2.7 to 3.8m. sq. ft. (a 41% increase). The increase in space in the UK was on top of the recent acquisition of the Littlewoods chain. The principal thrust of this phase of overseas expansion was to be Europe and the Far East.

Yet, during the winter of 1998 and early 1999, it became clear that all was not well with this once great business. Matters came to a head at the Annual General Meeting on 18 May 1999 when Peter Salsbury, the new chief executive, had to report that profits had fallen by about 50%. Sir Richard Greenbury, the chairman and Salsbury's predecessor as chief executive, was absent from the AGM. What had gone wrong and what did Salsbury plan to do about it?

History of Marks & Spencer

Although founded much earlier, Marks & Spencer first came to national prominence after the Second World War as a leading clothes retailer. In a postwar world of scarcity and dubious quality, the St Michael brand offered customers a guarantee of value and quality. Marks & Spencer stores appeared on most leading High Streets throughout the UK.

The promise of value for money was backed by well-implemented strategies. Marks & Spencer built long-term relationships with its suppliers, who were mostly small, British, and little known in their own right. Marks & Spencer and the St Michael brand created value by providing a critical link between manufacturer and customer. The Marks & Spencer brand was of value to manufacturers in reaching an expanding market for clothes. Customers needed Marks & Spencer to monitor the quality of the product to high standards and to provide a full range of clothes from a fragmented textile industry. Marks & Spencer also offered its customers other advantages. Every branch offered the same range of goods so that customers could return goods to any branch for cash provided the labels and receipts were intact. M&S became known for its internal efficiency and simplicity of administration. M&S was also noted for the way it treated its staff and for its training schemes. As a result, it built up a high quality staff who made their careers with the company. In almost every way M&S became the model which set the standards among leading UK retailers. The traditional strengths of Marks & Spencer have been summarized by John Kay (1999):

> The external architecture of Marks & Spencer's organisation was built around an almost Japanese relationship with suppliers; detailed influence on product specification and design as part of relationships sustained over many years. Its internal architecture was centred on permanent employment relationships, strong organisational routines, and a shared sense that there was a Marks & Spencer way of doing things.

In the 1970s, M&S embarked on a major change in its product strategy by moving into food. M&S focused on high quality food at relatively high prices. It offered prepared meals and food of high quality that required little effort in preparation to a customer base that sought convenient good food. With more families with two full-time job holders, there were more and more households in which time was scarcer than money; M&S had picked a growing segment of the food market. M&S was early into the use of chilling food rather than freezing it. It also used its strengths in distribution and date stamping to emphasize food freshness. By choosing this segment of the food market, M&S avoided competing too directly with the major food retailers. For them, this segment was a relatively small part of their total sales and they had no incentive to try to undercut M&S on price. Over the next twenty years, M&S gradually expanded its food retailing space so that by 1998 food sales reached £3.1 bn. compared with £4.8 bn. for clothing and footwear.

During the 1980s, M&S also extended its range of activities within the UK into financial services. These have achieved a reputation for solid rather than brilliant performance. M&S again seemed to target a specific market segment and offer value. M&S's financial business has grown steadily and has been consistently profitable. By 1999 financial services provided 18% of group profits.

The UK has always been Marks & Spencer's base but it has made a number of separate attempts to expand internationally. In Europe, Marks & Spencer opened stores, similar in appearance to the larger UK stores, in major cities in France, Germany, Spain, and Belgium. It entered the US market by acquiring Brooks Brothers, an up-market clothing chain, and Kings Super Markets. It entered the Canadian market in 1973 by acquiring D'Allaird's and Peoples. By 1996 it was trading in Canada under the three names—Marks & Spencer, D'Allaird's, and Peoples and had a total of 47 stores. M&S also had stores in the Far East. By the mid-1990s, there was talk of global retailing and global retail brands and it was clear that M&S aspired to global status for itself and its St Michael brand (*Economist* 1995).

Overseas operations tended to be less successful than the UK business. For instance, the Canadian operation lost money in 24 of the 25 years between 1973 and 1998. While the reasons for this relative lack of success varied in detail between different markets, two recurring factors were the lack of the strong UK supply and distribution support and the lack of the M&S culture among staff, many of whom had joined the group by acquisition.

Sir Richard Greenbury

No account of the recent history of Marks & Spencer could fail to mention Sir Richard Greenbury as a major force. Richard Greenbury joined Marks & Spencer in 1952 and rose through its ranks to become joint managing director in 1978, chief operating officer in 1986, and chief executive in 1988. In 1991 he took over from Sir Derek Rayner as chairman while remaining chief executive.

Sir Richard became chairman of M&S at a difficult time for the UK clothing industry. In addition, M&S had admitted that its acquisitions in the USA had been ill judged and badly timed. Under his leadership over the next eight years, M&S relentlessly increased its market share in both the food and clothing markets and branched out into new areas such as jewellery, furniture, luggage, and sandwiches.

Sir Richard was a very visible chief executive as Hollinger (1998) puts it: 'His control over every aspect of the business was legendary. Visitors to his cavernous office in Baker Street pass chairs piled with next season's jumpers, waiting for the chairman's seal of approval on colours, price and quality.' During his period as chairman, the profits before tax of M&S grew from £615m. to £1,168m.

As well as his dominating position at M&S, Sir Richard became more widely known as a senior figure in British business. One particular public role was to chair a commission that produced the Greenbury report into directors' remuneration.

Signs of trouble

The first sign that all was not well in the house of Marks & Spencer appeared with the announcement on 3 November 1998 of the results for the six months to 30 September. In the first decline in thirty years, operating profit for the half year fell to £327m. from £428m. the previous year. The profit figure was further reduced by a £64m. write-off for 'reduced carrying value of overseas assets'—an admission that M&S had overpaid for some of its overseas acquisitions. Public attention was distracted from the results by a very visible row about who should succeed Sir Richard Greenbury. Sir Richard Greenbury had flown to India the day after the results were announced but then returned to London on 8 November in the midst of an acrimonious and embarrassingly public dispute over his succession.

Sir Richard was already 63 and therefore already past the normal retirement age of 60. The intention was that Sir Richard should hand over his role as chief executive but remain chairman for a time. The board had not agreed a successor as chief executive and there were two internal candidates. One candidate, Keith Oates, was deputy chairman. He had joined M&S in 1984 as finance director and was now 56. He had considerable international experience, was a gifted communicator, and was well known to the London financial community. The second candidate, Peter Salsbury, had, like Sir Richard himself, spent his entire working life in M&S. At 49 he had been with M&S for 28 years and had great depth of knowledge of the retail business and also of most aspects of M&S's management. He was little known outside M&S and was seen by some outsiders as a slightly grey figure. It was no secret that Sir Richard Greenbury preferred Salsbury to Oates, the retailer over the 'bean counter'.

After a few days of tense meetings of the board and smaller groups of non-executive directors, it was announced that Peter Salsbury would take over as chief executive and that Keith Oates would take early retirement. Sir Richard would remain as non-executive chairman. The non-executive directors also presented detailed job descriptions that clearly separated the roles of chairman and chief executive. It was made clear that it was intended that in future different people would hold these two posts.

More bad news

Early in 1999, M&S issued another profits warning. As Hollinger (1999*a*) reported at the time:

> In his first official act as chief executive designate of Marks and Spencer, Peter Salsbury announced a surprise profits warning and gave details of Christmas trading so dire that some pundits were left wondering whether the flagship of British retailing had finally been sunk.
>
> Questions have been raised over M&S's products, pricing, management and strategy. In effect, over everything. The company once so beloved of the British establishment now can do nothing right, it seems. Outsiders accuse M&S, for example, of having been too complacent, of ignoring changes in the domestic market which have finally caught up with it. Competitors had improved their performance, but M&S carried on as if it 'could still control the marketplace', according to one retailer. At the same time, the autocratic style of Mr Salsbury's predecessor made the company more risk-averse, leaving it without the ability to innovate, says another. 'They have to bring that ability back to management and to their supply team. It is a deep rooted problem'.

In April 1999, M&S announced that it was to close all its stores in Canada. This raised obvious questions about the future of its Brooks Brothers and Kings Super Markets businesses in the USA. Both were making modest profits but neither had ever made a satisfactory return. M&S denied any immediate plan for closure but admitted that 'the business is undertaking a strategic review, and all areas are being looked at' (Tomkins 1999).

In the early months of 1999, M&S announced other changes to its operations, leading to job losses. Three board directors, 230 head office, and 250 store management jobs disappeared, leading to savings estimated at £20m. a year.

Further details of results and the changes made in response became public at the Annual General Meeting on 18 May 1999. M&S announced pre-tax profits before exceptional items of £655m. for the year to 31 March down from £1,114m. in the previous year. Almost £400m. of the decline in profits was in the core UK retail business. It seems that a number of fashion misjudgements had been made. As a spokesman for the company said:

> Grey was the fashion colour so we bought into it, but the mistake was that we bought it for everybody. Older customers wanted colour and we were missing it. By the time we realised, it was too late to buy more colour. We'd had a successful year previously, so we were confident and bullish about buying. On reflection we bought too much fashion and too much grey

Apparently customers felt much the same way. Steiner (1999) recorded the comments of two mature ladies: 'They have gone for street cred. but I'm in my forties and there is nothing for my age group'; 'For my age group [65] there has been absolutely nothing we can buy this year. Now it's all teenage'.

It seemed that the expansion scheme announced the previous year was also partly to blame for the troubles. Some stores had building work reducing sales space, investment in new tills, and refurbishment of the Littlewoods branches acquired in

1998 together knocked £90m. off profits. The expansion had also led managers to focus on property and processes instead of the customer. Powerful entrants to the clothing market—mail order and supermarkets—had generated increased competition in the market place with aggressive marketing and discounting. The home furnishings business was down due to cyclical factors and the food business was flat.

The overseas retail business reported an overall loss of £15m. after a profit of £67m. in 1998. The strength of the pound sterling and economic turmoil in the Far East were cited as the principal reasons for this reverse. The Middle East stood out as an exception with sales far exceeding estimates.

Only the financial services business reported an increase in profit from £89 to £110m. M&S seemed to be succeeding in positioning itself as a low-cost alternative to traditional providers in sales of unit trusts, pensions, and life assurance.

The new chief executive, Peter Salsbury, announced a four point recovery programme to address the problems and to restore the value of the shares:

> 1. We must create clear profit centres with simpler management structures, faster decision-making and distinct targets for shareholder value.
> 2. We must change the way we buy goods, both in the UK and overseas, by giving our selling and marketing functions more say in what we offer.
> 3. We must restore profitability overseas by reorganising our local businesses to serve their local customers.
> 4. We must build on the success of our financial services business.
>
> In short, we must aim every part of our organisation towards the customers it serves.

The reaction to Peter Salsbury's statement at the AGM were reported by Peggy Hollinger (1999*c*):

> Cutting out bureaucracy to allow more rapid decision making, and taking a life-style approach to buying and displaying products in the stores are two of the most welcome changes. 'In the past, M&S has behaved more like a wholesale buyer of products such as shirts and trousers, rather than thinking about the sort of person who was buying the item and what else they could sell to that customer' said one analyst.
>
> The most interesting evidence of the new broom sweeping through M&S came from the finance director who set out a number of accounting changes that for the first time gave outsiders an indication of how changes are being forced through this conservative and centralised retail business. Now store managers will not only be responsible for the goods they sell, and for feeding information back up the supply chain but they will also be held responsible for the results.

There was some cynicism from the audience as to whether these new strategies would be implemented successfully. One analyst said: 'It is everything they should be doing, but will they actually drive these disciplines through the business? You cannot take it as read, particularly as it is the same group of people who have been there for years'.

On 22 June, Sir Richard Greenbury announced that he would retire immediately from the chairmanship leaving Peter Salsbury to implement the new strategies. Peter Salsbury commented on Sir Richard's departure (Willman 1999): 'The executive directors needed active impetus from the top that Rick was unable to provide'.

Sir Richard himself was reported to have found his three-day a week non-executive role unsatisfying and commented: 'The board will be spending the next three days on discussing a few hundred pages of its new strategy. I don't feel comfortable about presiding over that.'

Marks & Spencer appointed headhunters to look for a new chairman.

Sources

Bartram, P. (1999) 'Saving St Michael: An Interview with Sir Richard Greenbury', *Director*, Feb.

Economist (1995) 'Retailing Survey', 4 Mar.

Hollinger, P. (1998) 'Company Profile: Marks & Spencer', *Financial Times*, 27 Nov.

—— (1999*a*) 'Man in the News: Peter Salsbury', *Financial Times*, 16 Jan.

—— (1999*b*) 'M&S shake up to claim 250 store management jobs', *Financial Times*, 10 May.

—— (1999*c*) 'On your Marks for a Counter-Offensive in the High Street', *Financial Times*, 19 May.

Kay, J. (1999) 'Perennial Hits Hard Times', *Financial Times*, 20 Jan.

Marks & Spencer Plc, *Annual Reports*.

Merriden, T. (1997) 'Britain's Most Admired Companies', *Management Today*, Dec.

Steiner, S. (1999) 'How Grey Cast a Shadow over Profits at M&S', *The Times*, 19 May.

Tomkins, R. (1999) 'M&S to Close all 38 Stores in Canada', *Financial Times*, 29 Apr.

Willman, J. (1999) 'Greenbury Steps Down a Year Early at M&S', *Financial Times*, 23 June.

Commentary on Marks & Spencer case example

Context

The retail business has specific characteristics. Retailers always have to get the locations and scale of their outlets right and to fill them with the right offerings to match their customers' tastes. The supply chain is also critical. All these issues were as important to M&S as for any other retailer.

The immediate context is dominated by the sharp fall in profits. This was particularly dramatic in a company that had been known for slow and deliberate growth over a long period of time. The central dilemma was how to understand the causes of this fall and what new strategies to introduce to correct it.

It is apparent that personalities were a significant factor in the context. Sir Richard Greenbury was a very dominant personality. Not only does it seem that he had set a distinctive management style but, more immediately, the succession battle may have distracted managers from issues more directly related to the business.

Other issues posed by the context included international expansion and finding profitable uses for M&S's great strengths in its people and reputation.

Strategy formulation process

M&S has traditionally been a slightly secretive and centralized organization so that it is difficult for an outsider to understand how its strategy formulation process works. There was a decision in 1998 to go for major expansion in space, particularly in the Far East. It would seem that this decision, which with the benefit of hindsight now looks unwise, was made with the strong support of Sir Richard Greenbury. It may be that querying decisions supported by Sir Richard was not seen as career enhancing. The strategic review undertaken in the early months of 1999 appears to have marked a new style of strategy formulation under Peter Salsbury's more democratic leadership.

Strategic assessment

Any strategic assessment of M&S must explain M&S's very long period of outstanding success as well as its short-term problems. Clearly M&S had such a large share of the UK market in quality convenience food and clothing that these areas offered limited growth potential. The obvious growth opportunities were financial services and overseas.

The St Michael brand had an excellent reputation and universal recognition in the UK. Overseas the brand itself was of variable value. While still carrying weight in some markets, it was clearly not yet a global brand. The brand might also become stretched if applied to too many different product areas.

M&S had always targeted a particular segment of the market—the relatively affluent middle-classes who had money to spare and wished to buy goods on value for money rather than price alone. Many of these customers had been captured in the late 1960s and early 1970s—when the post-war baby boomers were beginning to have money of their own to spend. They remained loyal to the brand and had brought up their children to value it too. However, the boom years of the early and late 1980s resulted in these second-generation M&S customers looking to more prestigious brand names. This left M&S with their traditional, but ageing, customers who were now a diminishing market. M&S seems also to have misread the needs of these customers by seeking to follow fashion which had never been a competence. The company seems to have misread the demographic changes and continued to function more as a guarantor of quality and value rather than having any deep understanding of its customers' needs.

There may also be an arrogance about M&S. M&S managed to avoid having sales until very recently. It was slow to allow customers to use any credit cards other than its own to pay for goods. It did not sell other prestigious brands. It did not seem to want to make it easy to shop at M&S. These distinctions from the practices of other retailers were a strength as long as M&S had a dominant position but became weaknesses as other retailers caught up and surpassed them in many ways. Time seemed to have passed M&S by.

Historically, M&S had great strengths in its UK supply chain and in its staff. This supply chain is of little help overseas and may be a hindrance by being too UK centred.

M&S has historically been highly profitable and there must be a question of whether this level of profitability can be sustained. M&S's way of working has been exceptional, but what have they done recently to keep so far ahead of competitors that they can earn much higher profit levels than their industry? Maybe M&S is not doing badly now with its profits halved; maybe it was just doing unsustainably well before.

Strategic choice

M&S has to make choices about the scope of its product line and the scale of its retail operations in the UK. It seems that in 1998 M&S may have made unfortunate choices in both these areas—the space was too much and the buying decision process too insensitive to the needs of real customers as opposed to style and fashion.

M&S also has to make choices about its overseas development. Clearly it has been trying to become more international or even global in its brand and outlets but not all the attempts have been successful.

Finally M&S has to make choices about internal processes, about how it runs its business.

Strategy content

The case example gives a fairly complete idea of the new strategies chosen by the new management. The four-point recovery plan is very clear. It is a little disturbing that the back-up documentation took 'a few hundred pages' to record.

Strategy implementation

The case gives some insight into how changing financial processes can be used to make other changes happen. It is, of course, too soon to judge whether the strategies put in place by the new chief executive will succeed, but M&S has many strengths to build on. The recovery plan may be just what is needed to return M&S to its previous glory. The quality of the implementation may be the critical factor.

Questions for discussion on the Marks & Spencer case example

1. To what would you attribute Marks & Spencer's difficulties in 1999?
2. What is the core competence of Marks & Spencer? What relevance does this core competence have in assessing M&S's moves into (*a*) food, (*b*) financial services, (*c*) overseas markets?
3. What lessons can be drawn about strategic leadership from the case example? What are the advantages and disadvantages of a dominant leader like Sir Richard Greenbury? Could the leadership succession have been better handled?
4. How would you assess Peter Salsbury's four-point recovery plan. What practical measures would you suggest to implement it successfully?
5. How would you assess the strategic management of Marks & Spencer in the light of events of 1999 and since.

Case Example 5
Strategy Implementation in the Intervention Board for Agricultural Produce 1990–1993

Background to strategic change in UK central government departments

For many years before the oil crisis of 1973, UK public expenditure rose at about the same rate as gross domestic product. The financial crisis of September 1976, combined with pressure from the IMF and other financial institutions, finally forced the Labour government to recognize that real cuts in levels of public expenditure were inevitable. Pressure for cuts grew even more intense after 1979 with the election of a Conservative government who added political will to financial necessity in its search for savings in public expenditure. The demand for public services continued to increase, however, due to higher levels of unemployment, increasing pensions costs as a result of increasing longevity, and increases in both the demand for and cost of health treatments in the NHS. It became very clear that, if supply were in any way to match demand, it would be necessary to achieve 'more for less' from the public sector.

Since the Northcote/Trevelyan report of 1855, changes in the civil service had been achieved more or less in an evolutionary way. The increases in productivity now seen as necessary, however, could only be achieved by transforming the complete concept of public service provision—in other words, by radical change in the way that public sector organizations saw their role in the world. This required a considerable change in both the way things were done and the thinking behind the changes.

Source: This case example was contributed by Roger Lovell who was Director of Establishments at IBAP between 1989 and 1993.

From a strategic viewpoint, the principal need was to understand precisely what each public sector organization was endeavouring to achieve. For too long many departments had seen themselves as in business to 'administer', without ever considering what they were supposed to be administering and in consequence knowing whether or not they had achieved their objective. A successful outcome to many was therefore that they had survived. When self-preservation becomes the *raison d'être* of an organization, it is proof that the means have taken over from the ends.

Over the next several years, the UK government launched a series of separate initiatives, each with its own specific focus. The overall objective was 'more for less'. The means were based primarily on perceptions of private sector practice as there was a widespread belief that the private sector was more efficient.

The *Financial Management Initiative* of 1982 aimed to discover what the objectives of each department were, how much they cost, and the means to measure them. The exercise quickly exposed that in many cases objectives within different parts of the same organization were in conflict. For example, part of the Department of Health and Social Security was intent on spending as little as possible of potential benefits, while other parts aimed to assist the claimant to obtain as much benefit as possible. Such contradictions were reinforced in terms of whom the staff saw as their customer. For example, the agricultural adviser saw the farmer in the field as his or her 'customer', while staff in headquarters looked to the Secretary of State as their 'master'. This lack of clarity in aims was further reinforced by the emphasis placed upon the importance of 'policy' work as opposed to 'management' at the top of the service. Not only did policy work have kudos, but the management of resources to obtain better value for money was seen as inferior and unnecessary. As so often occurs, attitudes influenced internal systems and processes. Promotion and reward systems were so geared towards policy, as opposed to execution, that the latter was frequently downgraded and often ignored.

By 1988 it was recognized that a structural reorganization might be one way to redress this imbalance. *The Next Steps Initiative* therefore aimed at separating policy from execution. Those parts of the existing departments whose work related directly to execution were hived off into Executive Agencies whose chief executives were responsible to Parliament for delivering agreed objectives. For instance, the Driver and Vehicle Licensing Authority (DVLA) was set up as an agency with objectives related to efficiency in issuing licences. To this end, each Agency was required to produce a Framework Document which established the boundaries of its responsibilities and clearly identified objectives.

The aim of the separation was also to place the Agencies in greater contact with and awareness of their customers or clients. This led in 1991 to the *Citizen's Charter Initiative* which aimed to improve customer service and *Competing for Quality* which, among other things, considered the notion of out-sourcing of peripheral tasks while retaining core activity in house.

The Intervention Board for Agricultural Produce (IBAP)

It is against this background that the Intervention Board became an Executive Agency in 1990. Unlike all other Agencies, however, IBAP was already a separate government department in its own right, having been established in 1972 in preparation for the UK joining the then Common Market. Its function was to administer the Common Agricultural Policy, while policy responsibility was held with its sister department, the Ministry of Agriculture, Fisheries, and Food (MAFF) and the EC Commission in Brussels. The role of chief executive was therefore fraught with contradictions and a duality of responsibilities.

IBAP's objectives were complicated, as several different outside organizations had influence over them. The European Commission handled the Common Agricultural Policy for the whole of the European Union and allocated European Funds. IBAP's expenditure and running costs were determined by the UK Treasury. For political direction within the UK, IBAP was answerable to four separate arms of the British government. IBAP's responsibilities covered the whole of the UK, so ministerial responsibility was pooled between the Secretary of State for Agriculture in England, and the Scottish, Welsh, and Northern Irish Secretaries for their respective countries. This representation was also reflected in membership of IBAP's Policy Board which also lent itself to occasional regional bias.

That said, the chief executive of IBAP was a career appointment from MAFF, staffed by a person two grades below the head of MAFF. Hence, while reporting to the Minister for policy directives, the chief executive reported to the head of MAFF in terms of his or her 'pay and rations' and, in particular, future promotions. Crossing the Ministry had the potential for unpopularity for the chief executive and possible damage to his or her future career.

IBAP was responsible for spending about £3 bn. of taxpayers' money. This required proper control which was enforced by having five sets of auditors from Europe and the UK examining accounts and systems annually. Hardly surprisingly, the culture of IBAP was one of compliance with little being challenged or reviewed. Against this background, IBAP became an Executive Agency in 1990 and began trying to improve its functioning by the introduction of more modern methods of management.

Implementing strategic change in IBAP

IBAP faced four primary challenges:

- to restructure and become a Next Steps Agency;
- to relocate 350 of its 1,150 posts from Reading to Newcastle as a result of the government's desire to move jobs away from the south east;

- to change its *modus operandi* to become more customer oriented as a result of the Citizen's Charter;
- to carry out competitive studies under the Competing for Quality initiative to consider outsourcing its peripheral services as opposed to keeping them in house.

Central initiatives

All four initiatives were imposed from outside IBAP by central departments such as the Treasury and Cabinet Office. The management board of IBAP had no choice but to implement them whether or not they would make IBAP more economic, effective, or efficient. As such, the initiatives ran the risk of imposing a solution to a problem which had yet to be diagnosed.

In practice, what tends to happen under such circumstances is that the organizations themselves tend to adapt the initiative as best as possible to suit their circumstances. Sadly this often results in the initiative itself becoming the end in itself rather than the means to it. Examples are numerous, but perhaps the most recent is the directive to restructure in order to delayer organizations. Any restructuring exercise should in the first place consider what needs to be done; this should be followed by an assessment of the skills needed to do it and consideration of the number of staff required and the most sensible way of organizing the work. This might be termed the pro-active approach.

Instead, virtually all departments considered what they had at the time; in some cases, they reduced particular layers indiscriminately and claimed to have complied with the initiative. The most ridiculous case was a department which reduced to seven grades but kept twelve pay bands. They were then surprised when their personnel department had almost twice the difficulty in posting people that they had had before and created an organization almost twice as rigid, when one of the prime aims of the initiative had been to create more flexible organizations.

An example of such behaviour at IBAP was the achievement of BS 5750 status for application development in its computer services. Apart from installing a bureaucracy of 10 people in the Project Support Office out of a total computer staff of 70, it failed to produce a single system to time, quality, and budget. This was because compliance to the BS 5750 system became the objective as opposed to producing high quality, timely, and economic computer systems. Thus such 'kitemarks' became the master rather than the slaves that they were intended to be. Examples of the same behaviour have also occurred for later initiatives such as investors in people, benchmarking, activity based costing, and individual performance pay, all of which are sensible if used in the correct context. The problem was that the Treasury and Cabinet Office, well meaning though they might have been, gave such systems a seal of approval which was often interpreted as 'tablets of stone' within agencies.

Restructuring

Many newly formed Executive Agencies rejoiced in a degree of liberation from their parent departments, for instance, in greater freedom in recruitment. IBAP, on the other hand, was already a government department and therefore already possessed such freedoms. While on the surface it produced a Framework Document along with the other Agencies, it was in practice receiving little if any of the benefits. The changes outlined in the Framework Document proved particularly difficult to sell to the staff, despite launching parties and so on, particularly since any attempt to renegotiate staffing terms and conditions with the Treasury fell on deaf ears. Using the terms coined by Argyris, it seemed that the 'espoused values' of the Treasury to allow greater freedom and flexibility were not matched by their 'theories in use' (Argyris and Schon 1978). To put it more colloquially, the Treasury were unable to 'walk the talk'.

Nevertheless, working within its own parameters, IBAP decentralized budgetary control with the aim of placing the responsibility for allocating money as close to the point of contact with the customer as possible. Initially, however, any move towards decentralization of financial resources was fiercely resisted by the finance department who saw the initiative in win-lose terms. In other words, instead of seeing the organization as a whole become more effective and efficient in a win-win situation, they saw merely a loss of financial control to the new budget holders. Rather than appreciate that power is a dynamic which expands and contracts, they saw it purely as a fixed supply, the surrender of any part of which would lose them influence and control.

It was also less than ideal, therefore, that initiation of decentralisation of budgeting was driven by the Director of Establishments and linked to a series of personnel delegations in order to provide an umbrella for the initiative. And, while a strong degree of control was necessary in terms of the payment side of the organization's work, there was considerable room for movement as far as other systems were concerned. For example, applications for special leave had to be approved by a personnel officer rather than the line manager who was obviously in a much better position to judge the legitimacy of the application.

Other initiatives included bringing part-time staffing conditions into line with full time staff, along with a system to allow people to apply for vacancies that interested them, instead of being moved on a compulsory basis every three years.

The top-down approach to change, while successful in many cases, often fails to reach the 'hearts and minds' necessary to bring about transformational change—in other words, trying to move from a traditionally bureaucratic approach where people do not do things because nobody said they should, to having them use their own initiative to solve the problem. To this end, all personnel and office services staff were asked to define their own objectives and then state the best and most consistent service they would provide day after day. The results were highly commendable and probably far in excess of any targets which might have been set from above. Not only did the staff match the published targets but they steadily improved upon them quarter after quarter.

IBAP also reduced the number of layers of management. The aim of this was to make lower levels take decisions rather than wait for specific instructions. In some cases, lines of command became so large that managers had to find different ways of control. Managers were forced to manage by outcome as opposed to process. Previously, managers had told someone what to do, how to do it, and watched over them to ensure they did it their way. Now managers had to identify jointly with the staff what the required outcome was and, through coaching and support, allow the staff to decide the most effective way of achieving the outcome. The ability to cope with this way of working tended to depend upon the personality of the managers and staff. Those tending to be more creative found it both refreshing and liberating. Those imbued with a command and control mentality naturally found it harder. Their inability to control by using the old methods due to the increased span of command, however, eventually forced them to operate in the new more empowered manner.

Overall, therefore, while the central initiative of Next Steps itself provided little if any benefit for the organization, the mere existence of an externally generated initiative allowed internal change agents to harness the mood for change to endeavour to make the organization more effective using other means.

Relocation

The central government aim of relocating 37,000 staff from the south east of England to areas of lower employment was in itself noble. In the late 1980s, turnover among IBAP's clerical staff in Reading had climbed to over 40% a year so there did appear to be some advantage to IBAP in relocating 350 of its 1,150 posts to Newcastle. Unfortunately, by the time much of the relocation to Newcastle had taken place, the 1991/2 recession had started. The effects of the recession were heavier in Reading than in Newcastle so that IBAP found itself spending money to create jobs in an area which two years afterwards had a higher attrition rate of staff leaving than Reading. As a result, the relocation of IBAP jobs was a failure from an economic perspective. The central relocation policy, however, had its roots in socio-political aspirations and no benefits were ever felt by IBAP itself. In fact, apart from the discrepancies in retention and the cost of relocation, IBAP had ultimately to cope with the difficulties of managing people in two sites 300 miles apart.

Customer service

As with the Next Steps' initiative, the good intentions of the Citizen's Charter to improve customer care across the public service provided opportunity for IBAP to use such support to its advantage. This resulted in a variety of initiatives including the formation of quality circles and focus groups, both in house and with customers, together with customer satisfaction surveys. It also provided the opportunity of emphasizing the role of the internal customer for service areas within the organization.

Operational conflicts soon started to arise, however, when defining who the customer was. Some saw Ministers in London, others Commissioners in Brussels and others the local trader receiving or paying money, as their customer. Of greatest note, however, was the identification of the conflict between the desire to create an organizational culture that created greater freedom for individuals in responding to the needs of the customer or client (an empowerment culture) with the strict command and control systems operating within IBAP. While it is fully recognised that taxpayers' money must be spent prudently and correctly, it does not follow that every single activity within the organization should be controlled in the same manner. Sadly, the culture of the organization was so ingrained with the command and control type mentality, particularly at Management Board level, that it pervaded the whole organization. This was highlighted in remarks made by many members of the Management Board when complaining about the 'dead hand of the Treasury' always stopping them from taking the initiatives they wished, being replicated throughout by junior managers who saw the Management Board in the same way. This 'victim mentality' is sadly all too prevalent in the public sector where everyone is blaming others; waiting for things to get better (by which they mean returning to some distant serendipity), and denying problems. This they do by having a flexible assumption of truth. In other words, they genuinely believe that they are powerless and yet have no hard evidence to prove it because they never test it.

This rather myopic view of the world was particularly prevalent at management board level and was highlighted in a piece of research carried out by Bath University and published in the British Institute of Management Journal of May 1994 (Brooks and Bate 1994). This ethnographic study looked particularly at the behaviour and language of members of the Management Board just after Agency status, only to find that they saw change as a culturally deviant activity since they saw nothing wrong with previous systems and culture. In other words, they were in business to 'maintain' rather than to 'change'. Such an attitude also reflected a view that the public sector was in business to provide a service to, rather than for, the customer which was particularly reflected in things such as a reluctance to extend office opening times to suit customers' needs.

In practice, in a small way, the more empowered methods described above started to take hold at the lower levels of the organization and had the potential of forcing change from below.

Outsourcing

The systematic and structural changes of the late 1980s tended to operate in a top-down manner. So much so that many people lower down the organization felt little impact (Lovell 1992). All this was to change with the introduction of the Competing for Quality initiative. IBAP was required to compare in-house activities with services bought in from outside contractors. Ironically in this instance, the Agency had anticipated the initiative and had already contracted out much of its IT work. As regards other services market tested, for example, messenger services, word processing, internal audit, and so on, all in-house teams won. The primary reason for this was the involvement given to those involved at the start, thereby giving them ownership of the exercise and an opportunity as the service provider to understand customer requirements. In this they were successful in being able to 'stand in the shoes' not only of the customer but also of the contractor in being able to see the situation from a different perspective. Most importantly on the IT side, the Agency was able to retain sufficiently qualified staff to act as intelligent customers for future requirements and control of the contract.

The overall results of the changes in IBAP

By 1993 therefore, IBAP had embraced the four initiatives. During the period 1990–3, IBAP management endeavoured to establish a new way of operating through system and process improvements and to change the culture. Sadly, as the more dynamic managers who set up the changes moved on and were replaced in many cases by more traditional command and control managers, the organization settled once more into its familiar culture, as the Bath study referred to above had predicted. Instead of achieving second order or transformational change as intended by the initiatives, the general antipathy to change resulted in little more than a marginal transition to a new status quo. Such a state of affairs suited most members of the management board; those it did not left. In other words, 'exit' replaced 'voice' due to frustration.

The initiatives themselves provided above all else an opportunity for internal change agents to endeavour to change the monolith as much as possible while the political wind of the initiative was still prevalent. Once this passed, the traditionalists steadied the ship and sailed onwards after the slightest change of course.

One is tempted to say that the organization might have done things differently without the imposition of the external change initiatives. The most sensible way to manage such organizations is to set them highly challenging outcomes, not outputs, and ensure that they are capable of being measured accurately from outside, and then allow the chief executive and his team to deliver—in other words, treating them in an adult manner. Sadly, the central departments seemed unable to do this since they acted as parents distrusting the child. Despite protestations to the contrary, it must also be questioned just how committed the central departments were to transformational change themselves since they, like the finance department above, saw power in win–lose terms.

The Management Board was not unhappy therefore since their power base remained largely untouched. It is questionable just how much of an empowered culture one should have with so much public money to control and this provided numerous excuses for inaction. It is fair to say that the Treasury have endeavoured to provide agencies with greater and more meaningful freedoms in recent years. The reality is however that such organizations will never succeed in transforming themselves unless a new way of viewing work is implemented and everyone in the organization takes full responsibility for their actions, as opposed to blaming others.

Commentary on IBAP case example

Context

The context has two distinct elements—the general changes in the UK public sector and the specific context of IBAP as an entity. Much of the interest in this case example is a result of the interaction between these two contexts. The case example raises issues of whether strategies and the resulting changes can succeed when the strategies are formulated outside the entity in which the change is to occur. This issue is as common in the private sector as in the public.

Strategy formulation process

The strategies were formulated in the centre and then imposed on IBAP. Separation of formulation from implementation seems to reduce the chances of success.

Strategic intent

The strategic intent to achieve 'more for less' was translated into central policy directives. IBAP was required to implement these directives without any specific consideration of the strategic needs of IBAP which were extremely complex because of its multiple reporting lines. It is apparent that the chief executive of IBAP was confronted with an extraordinarily difficult leadership task as he or she had to implement a strategy derived from objectives which were not related to any assessment of IBAP's strategic needs.

Strategic assessment

IBAP before 1990 was a traditional bureaucratic organization. There seems little doubt that there were opportunities to increase its efficiency and effectiveness by clarifying its objectives and applying the right management techniques. These were broadly the aims of the central government initiatives.

Strategy implementation

Change in IBAP was driven from the outside often in a top-down manner. There were both advantages and disadvantages in this. One advantage of this within IBAP was that it allowed those who already wanted change (potential change leaders) to 'hitch their colours to the mast'. They could use the opportunity to bring about their own personal change agendas that they have long harboured themselves but have had little chance to implement due to the general inertia.

Secondly, the initiatives forced IBAP to start to re-examine its operations in the light of more current management thinking. This was demonstrated for example in forcing the organization to draw up a 'Corporate Plan', within the responsibilities laid down in the Framework Document, to identify and measure objectives and to monitor its progress.

Thirdly, the introduction of more empowered methods of working within IBAP allowed greater creativity and satisfaction for the staff while still operating within a structured framework. The decentralization and delegation of budgets started to create a more realistic association between activity and cost.

On the negative side, while the enthusiasts for change used the opportunity to force their often private agendas for change, the vast bulk of IBAP carried on as before, albeit with an impression of activity. In other words, they complied but were not committed. Many waited for a return to command and control. This occurred to some extent in IBAP after 1993 when a new management team became less committed to instilling a culture of empowerment.

In IBAP, initiatives were created and driven centrally without due regard to the particular needs of the organization, or copied blindly from the private sector despite the failure of its impact in many cases. If objectives are correctly identified, strategy implementation will be executed best if the individual organization is given the freedom to carry on and achieve the objectives as they know best. Nothing short of a significant change of 'mind set' will do in creating lasting change.

IBAP did attempt to change its culture, systems (business processes), and organization, but the systems and culture changes in IBAP did not reinforce each other as well as they might have done. The aim was to generate a Theory *Y* culture in which managers try to create an environment where staff potential can be brought to the fore in a creative and flexible climate. Sadly, too many of the IBAP systems still operated under a Theory *X* culture which attempts to control staff tightly.

Mintzberg (1983) describes public sector organizations as 'the Instrument' with a dominant external coalition in the shape of Ministers and so on enforcing their influence on the organization. In the case of IBAP with its multiplicity of policy stakeholders, this is undoubtedly true. The power of the chief executive to dominate the internal coalition and meld the strategy of the organization to his or her will, however, should never be underestimated, particularly when considering the functional knowledge and expertise resting within the business.

References

Argyris, C., and Schon, D. (1978) *Organizational Learning* (Reading, Mass.: Addison Wesley).

Brooks, I., and Bate, P. (1994) 'The Problems of Effecting Change within the British Civil Service: A Cultural Perspective', *British Journal of Management*, 5: 177–90.

Lovell, R. (1992) 'Citizen's Charter: The Cultural Challenge', *Public Administration*, 70/3: 395–404.

Mintzberg, H. (1983) *Power in and around Organizations* (Englewood Cliffs, NJ: Prentice Hall).

Questions for discussion on IBAP case example

1. This case is an example of the new managerialism in action. What general advice would you offer a government trying to improve the efficiency of departments and agencies with public sector values and culture?
2. In 1990 IBAP faced four primary challenges. What suggestions can you offer the management team at IBAP as to what more they might have done to manage their change programme to meet these challenges?
3. How can the public good and commercial reality be successfully reconciled in general? How can managers develop commercial and public sector values among their staff to ensure that one is not sacrificed on the altar of the other?
4. How can managers measure their success in environments in which objectives are ultimately political rather than meeting the expectations of shareholders?

Case Example 6

Implementing Strategy in EuroPharm UK 1993–1998

Introduction

The UK and Europe remain an attractive place for the pharmaceutical industry to operate and many of the biggest companies are based here. The UK and Europe offer these companies a rich market funded by taxpayers in the form of their National Health Services and able and well-qualified staff. However, in recent years, the industry has been going through major changes. Like other industries, the pressures of global trading have challenged their established ways of working. Some have responded to the challenges of the past decade by acquiring or merging with other equally powerful players in the industry. These marriages such as Glaxo-Wellcome transformed the merged group into mega-corporations overnight. Others have extended their product range and all have tried to accelerate new product development.

In the UK the industry has suffered some adverse publicity. Pharmaceutical companies were cast as the fat cats of the health care sector when governments were looking to contain costs in the National Health Service (NHS). Indeed, very recently, one of the very largest has hinted that it might pull its R&D out of the UK altogether if the government's licensing arrangements continue to restrict their opportunities to sell new products into the market here.

The industry has remained an attractive field of employment. Historically, terms and conditions have been well above average and there has been relatively generous provision for training and development. Many of the organizations had a relatively informal culture, highly educated employees, and an atmosphere where merit was rewarded. Mobility within the industry, nevertheless, was relatively high and

Source: This case example was contributed by Gary Saunders who worked as a consultant to EuroPharm UK during the period described.

increased as consolidation proceeded. This was especially evident in the sales and marketing functions, but also included R&D workers. Consolidation, therefore, had less impact on employee numbers than might have been expected.

The pharmaceutical industry operates in a highly regulated market. There are stringent guidelines on the release of drugs to the market. These can include the length of time drugs are tested before release, on whom or what they can be tested, and on detailed and carefully monitored field trials. Finally, permission to release the drug has to be obtained from a government agency in each country separately. Another aspect of the industry is that in most cases the health services of various countries are their largest customers. These monopsonists not only have the choice of supplier (except in rare cases), they can also influence the price of the drugs being sold. This does not mean that the industry is powerless to influence the way it is regulated and paid for its expertise and know-how, it just means that it has some very powerful organizations lined up against it; organizations with considerable influence. In addition, the public can be drawn into any debate about drugs, their testing, and pricing as they are emotive subjects and politicians feel that the large and rich companies in the industry are fair game. The growth and success of a company is often based on a single drug or a few drugs and it is this that is not understood by the public. The industry can be likened to a horse race. Every company tends to research into sure-fire money spinners such as cures for AIDS or cancer and often the first past the post makes the most money from the vast investment in R&D associated with each product. Few other industries bet the whole company on one or two discoveries. Patent laws further compound this pattern of revenue and profit achievement. The patent laws cover a period of thirty years. Within this time-frame, the company has monopoly rights to exploit the product under patent. At the end of the patent period other manufacturers can make the drug which becomes a 'generic'. Naturally, the longer the time available within patent, the higher the potential profit. In the current context of drug development and exploitation, the time to win approval keeps increasing and this means that the commercial life of the product decreases, adversely changing the revenue and profit profile of the product.

Companies that survive and grow in this industry need to create organizations that can manage this diverse range of challenges. They need highly able and dedicated staff in their R&D laboratories, effective distribution channels, and marketing strengths to exploit the 'winning' products.

Short history of EuroPharm UK

EuroPharm UK is the UK subsidiary of a pharmaceutical company with its headquarters in mainland Europe (EuroPharm). EuroPharm has been in business for over a century. By the early 1990s, it operated across a wide range of markets, not just in health care. It had a strong position in a relatively small number of therapeutic areas and its product range included a few blockbusters. However, the portfolio was ageing and the pipeline of replacements was still a few years away. Believing that the prices being paid for acquisitions were unrealistic, it decided to correct this imbalance by internal development rather than getting involved in the consolidation spree within the industry. It was felt that while mergers and acquisitions may deliver economies of scale, this may often lead to the new larger organization losing its way, as managers focus too much on making the new integrated organization work effectively. EuroPharm, therefore, focused on its strategy, organization, and culture to become more competitive rather than seeking possible partners or acquisition targets. Getting better performance out of existing resources was, in its view, its most critical challenge. It also felt that effectiveness was more important than cost reductions.

By the early 1990s, EuroPharm UK was well established and successful and was among the top ten companies in the UK market. Its reputation within the parent company was high and it was considered to be one of the most skilled and most profitable of the national subsidiaries of EuroPharm. However, the market in the UK was becoming ever more complex and the company was beginning to tackle the implications of changes in the National Health Service (NHS).

EuroPharm UK was organized very much along traditional lines and comprised:

- *Sales* regions with Profit and Loss responsibility.
- *Marketing* organized by therapeutic area as was normal for the industry.
- *R&D* in two chunks—research centre which formed part of a global research activity and country-specific regulatory/registration functions. This too was normal for the industry, although the regulatory and registration functions were gradually evolving into a more pan-European function.
- *Commercial* included financial planning and control, accounting, customer orders, purchasing, and IT. They also established a direct selling team which was considered unusual.
- *Human Resources* had personnel and training (including Sales Training) but as the changes progressed, Sales Training became the responsibility of the Sales Department. During the changes a people development function was added to the HR portfolio.
- *Business Development* was a project-based department who undertook studies on new markets, integrating offerings across business groups, for example, in Diabetes where they used meters from Diagnostics and drugs from another division within the company. Business Development was the nearest thing to a strategy group in EuroPharm UK.

Despite its success, EuroPharm UK recognized that it had to face up to the following future challenges:

- falling income from a key product due to the aggressive entry of generics;
- the switching of other key products from prescription to over-the-counter medications;
- uncertainty about the new product pipeline;
- negative impact on profitability caused by allocation of more central costs from the parent;

- poor exchange rate compared with past;
- the prospect of closure of the UK research centre and the effect this was having on motivation;
- pressure on headcount;
- loss of key people as the company, in light of its opposition to merger, was seen to be likely to fall down the industry league table.

Culturally, there were tensions within EuroPharm UK. There was tension between the regional sales business units that were put in place to mirror the way the NHS was structured and the Europeanization of the business group. In practice this meant that the regionalized sales units were attempting to drive the organization towards fragmentation, while the whole organization was seeking to gain economies of scale and leverage through a more integrated organization, particularly in the areas of R&D, patenting, registration, and so on.

It would seem to an outsider that the energy spent on internal politics, if redirected, would have made it a far more effective company and that there was much to be gained by initiating changes to its culture and ways of working.

Changing EuroPharm UK

The management of EuroPharm UK decided to re-engineer the business rather than seek short-term gains by downsizing. They therefore set out in 1993 on a journey of exploration that eventually meant defining a vision, changing culture, structure, and process and finding a means of assessing how well the change process had worked. At the beginning of the change programme, EuroPharm UK had 350 employees. When the programme was declared closed in 1998, it had 500 employees. It was felt that there was no need for a formally structured change management activity as the size of the task and the interdependencies could be managed using workshops and cascade briefings. The workshops and briefings, in addition to being a change management mechanism, also helped maintain morale and motivation during the period of change. The chief executive was supportive of the programme throughout which assisted the continuity and integrity of the programme.

The strategy process began by attempting to define what business the company wished to be in, in the future, and what changes were needed to arrive at their new destination. They began by taking a wider view of their business. They considered nursing homes, insurance, and pathology laboratories and they experimented with home care for diabetics. They sought internal measures of effectiveness and efficiency by developing a kind of scorecard of organizational health that led to such actions as culture surveys to test and validate views about the climate and the creation of a strategic planning process based on identifying critical success factors. Out of this process of strategic exploration and assessment they decided that they had to:

- develop into an integrated health care company providing products and services for education, prevention, diagnosis, and treatment;

- improve the efficiency and effectiveness of their distribution channels to exploit new products coming through the development pipeline.

This, in turn, meant that they had to develop corporate capabilities that would help them to:

- make short-term tactical decisions but with very long-term horizons;
- maximize current year profits but maintain long-term viability based on the perception of customers;
- retain and grow existing talent in an environment of increased competition for quality staff and aggressive recruitment from other companies;
- expand their field forces, mirroring US trends;
- ensure fit between corporate values and individual values.

This early work was driven by the management team with support from the business development department. This more 'wholesome' approach to improving EuroPharm UK's performance became the yardstick for the changes and led to the creation of a vision.

Building and promulgating a vision for the future

The managing director launched the visioning process by running a workshop involving the top 40 or so managers. They developed the skeleton of a long-term Vision for the company. After this, cascade events run by these top managers were used to challenge and refine this skeleton. More than 90% of people in the company attended one of these events. This offered them the opportunity to understand, test, and refine the Vision to ensure that it was valid and applicable in the real world. The outputs from these were then considered at a second management workshop. This workshop produced a statement of the Vision and Values of the organization that has guided action ever since and is still in use today. The Vision was to position the organization as an 'Integrated Health Care provider within an innovative and progressive culture'.

The Vision meant that the company had to achieve two things:

1. to focus the business on the objective of becoming an integrated health care company;
2. to articulate a vision of the employment experience needed to attract, retain and motivate the best people and to develop the values of the business into those of:
   - flexibility;
   - increased individual responsibility;
   - working more effectively;
   - adding value
   - alignment rather than management.

Managing the change efforts

Shortly after the Vision was drafted, a network of volunteer change agents was set up to help implement Vision initiatives in local areas and to provide a direct communication mechanism to and from the MD. Regular meetings of the network focused on improvement projects and cross-functional initiatives. Membership was rotated regularly so that about 25% of all employees had been involved over three years. This structure has helped maintain continuity in spite of changes in the senior team.

Measuring the success of changes made

One of the core activities that was initiated and driven by the change agents was an employee survey. This employee opinion survey covered a wide range of issues but focused primarily on such issues as motivation, management style, communications, team and individual needs, among other organizational climate factors. The survey was used to measure progress and to prioritize corrective action where needed. By using the volunteer network to promote the survey, response rates of over 90% were achieved. During the period of this change initiative, which lasted five years, the employee opinion survey was conducted twice and the improvements achieved measured. In particular, neural network models were used to identify a value for motivation of the employees. This value increased by a factor that was higher than pure chance during these five years, thus validating the approach taken at least as far as developing and retaining its staff are concerned.

Impact of the changes on the company

The impact on each of the functional areas is discussed below.

Sales force

The sales force lacked commercial focus with the result that they were not working within limits that reflected the company's overall business environment. This had to change. In addition there was internal conflict between parts of the sales force resulting in reduced efficiency. Customer bases, workload, and sales targets needed to be shared and business planning had to become a team activity that involved every representative. The sales force structure had to be flexible and adaptable to match the changes taking place in the NHS—its major customer. The sales force went through major change in 1992 when regional business managers were appointed with budgetary responsibility for their territory. As a result, activity rose and investments were made more wisely.

As workload increased, new processes had to be developed and implemented to support the field staff.

- A comprehensive performance management process was created to assist in the management of poor performance and the identification and development of potential.
- Development centres were set up and followed through with planned career moves and other development activities—in some cases, clearly breaking the mould of traditional career paths. This process was increasingly important to staff motivation in an organization with a flatter structure and contributed to cross-functional working and the maintenance of the knowledge base of the company.
- New technology in the form of a new electronic territory management system (ETMS) was deployed to improve communication and record sharing within the Sales Force.
- A team of NHS liaison specialists was set up to influence the influencers and innovators in UK health care and was the first of its kind in the UK pharmaceutical industry.

By 1998 the company had a flexible field force that was used to change. Representatives achieved increased days on the road through a vacancy management programme, changes in training, and a reduction in time spent on non-selling tasks. Moving administrative staff to frontline positions had increased the numbers of people in direct selling positions. Effort was more evenly distributed over the customer population, so that coverage and frequency of calls increased, giving rise to more competitive 'noise' levels in the market place.

Research and Development

The R&D group had to be more commercial and business orientated to help the company meet the challenges posed by the market. It, therefore, set about creating a bold and challenging mission for itself based on the EuroPharm UK Vision. In support of its mission, it identified critical success factors and core processes that needed improvement. In 1996, the R&D management team embarked upon a quality management programme as part of a series of initiatives designed to help it become more effective and efficient.

Multi-functional teams undertook process improvements. They:

- defined and described the processes for R&D;
- aligned the processes with the department's standard operating procedures and published them on the company Intranet—these are being used for training purposes;
- identified measures that could be applied throughout the process;
- agreed and collected benchmarking data;

- introduced a Business Planning Calendar into which the department's critical success factors, core processes, and objectives were integrated as a comprehensive system for running the department's business.

R&D's considerable investment in business excellence has resulted in:

- improved ability to meet demanding time lines for clinical trials;
- an ever-increasing flow of work into the department;
- less work contracted out (now time and cost-competitive with contract research organizations);
- major contributions to pivotal development studies;
- management of the European submission of key new products;
- improvement in inter-departmental working;
- early licensing of key products.

The R&D department is now better prepared than ever to meet the challenges that lie ahead. It is more commercially aware than in the past and, as a result, its staff understand and are more able to contribute to the achievement of the company's strategic objectives.

Commercial

The commercial department had previously focused on customer care. It had to widen its brief to embrace purchasing and information technology as well. In essence, it took on the role of the department which specialized in contractual relationships and process infrastructure.

The new structure included:

- a commercial accounts team to support the defence of medicines coming off patent. The team manages the entire process of dealing with wholesale and retail pharmacy customers for these products, with around 60% coverage of the retail pharmacy market in this way;
- a customer service team which has evolved to reflect the need for higher levels of customer care;
- account management principles to build ongoing working relationships with major customers;
- a telesales function with both office and part-time external home workers. The team has been highly successful in generating sales in support of the generic defence campaigns;
- an IT group which has established a number of key accounting systems for a new business venture and managed financial support for its first year in business;
- support activities for the new over-the-counter business, establishing new processes and procedures for dealing with grocery accounts and for controlling activity;
- managing the financial impact of the divestiture of a small business and then provided financial/management accounting support to the new owner.

At the same time, headcount has decreased and costs have increased only in line with inflation. This was achieved through a clear focus on improving efficiency and effectiveness in meeting the changing needs of the business, supported by continuing investment in technology.

People management and development

The HR team had to adopt a more strategic role in support of the Vision. This would mean partnering internal customers to identify priorities for the achievement of their objectives and developing a better understanding of the contribution of HR initiatives to business success. This has meant changes to processes used by the department, its approach to carrying out its role, and the use of technology to improve its efficiency and cost-effectiveness. HR people began their reinvention by spending time developing an understanding of the business issues the company was facing and, derived from this exploration, the people management and development needs of the company. This resulted in:

- increased use of IT which has improved the capacity of the department to track people development by supporting the continuing professional development of all staff and the implementation of personal development plans;
- reduction of training time of sales representatives by five weeks and reducing hotel costs and time away from the field;
- a project management approach to managing priorities and workloads;
- alignment of people management and development initiatives to better fit with business objectives by seeking sponsorship from leaders outside the department. This helped define priorities, manage customer expectations, and deliver to deadlines;
- implementation of the performance management process which has enabled the creation of cross-functional development centres. These development centres have helped to support a culture of self-development and have played a key role in retaining people with potential.

Marketing

The marketing function needed to make high performance repeatable, to develop ways of sharing knowledge, and to establish sound processes. It also had to develop enough talent to withstand the erosion of good staff to other parts of EuroPharm. It had to supplement its current ways of working by introducing a strategic planning process and processes to improve its own internal efficiency.

To manage the changes within its own department it:

- set up cross-functional teams to map processes and identify efficiency improvements;
- set up a cross-functional steering team to manage each product and a portfolio (mix of products of differing ages, growth trajectories, and market appeal) management approach was developed. This portfolio management system is now regarded as the best example of its kind in the whole of the company;

- identified efficiencies in promotional operations, standardized processes, and identified departmental training needs using a team made up of product managers and marketing assistants.

The department's achievements include:

- growth of market share in core products and product line extensions;
- vigorous defence against 'genericization' and competition from alternative molecules;
- successful launches of new products;
- entry into a new therapeutic area;
- targeted maintenance of mature products;
- successful out-licensing deals;
- significant improvement in pre-marketing of new products.

All this has been achieved with significantly reduced promotion and investment expenditure. This has been made possible through a shift in the balance of administrative and operational staff facilitated by ongoing people development.

A benchmarking exercise with nine other major pharmaceutical companies showed staffing levels, departmental structures, and compensation levels and confirmed the efficiency and effectiveness of the department.

Business development

The purpose of the business development team was to 'Build Business through Partnerships'—internal partnerships as well as external. The business development team played an important role in promoting the Vision and being a catalyst for change.

Notable successes were:

- entry into a joint venture in generics;
- the re-launching of the over-the-counter business;
- evaluation of a large number of new market opportunities;
- forecasting the future health care environment through the Healthcare Environment Audit;
- cross-divisional synergy projects;
- partnerships with other healthcare organizations.

The business development team played an integral part in establishing the link from strategic objectives down to individual objectives throughout the company. As well as its core role, the department developed an internal consulting capability that enabled it to cascade objectives into appraisals so that the critical success factors reach everybody.

Commentary on EuroPharm UK case example

Context

The ethical pharmaceutical industry has been characterized by high R&D expenditure, long-term planning, and has operated in a highly regulated market. In the past ten years it has been going through major change on a national and global scale. These changes have, to some degree, been triggered by changes in the regulatory regime.

Change in regulations in Europe has had a significant impact in respect of patent protection and generic prescribing. This in turn has put pressure on time to market for new products. At the same time, new technologies demanding new skills have emerged and the financial risks of leading edge research have escalated.

The market for generic pharmaceuticals has grown dramatically while entry costs have reduced and the speed of generic substitution has accelerated. In response, pharmaceutical companies that had traditionally covered a relatively limited range of therapeutic areas have expanded their research capability to move into new areas.

But the most obvious changes in the industry have been a trend to consolidation, the decline of family-owned companies, and the globalization of R&D. Of the top ten global pharmaceutical company list of ten years ago, only half are still there. The rest have combined or fallen out of the list as others who were combining went past them.

Strategy formulation process

The UK company had a clear understanding of what it had to do. The pressures for change came from the wider industry and the parent company reluctance to buy itself out of trouble. The whole organization had to get fitter fast and also grow new muscles. The UK management team saw the need to do this and succeeded in getting approval for the changes from the parent company. The issues seemed fairly obvious. The solutions, however, were not. The visioning process used by the UK management resulted in a clear statement of intent and, following that, an understanding of the strategic options open to the business.

Strategic choice

The choice to attack the cultural values and streamline the operational processes was among the options it had. It could, again, have taken the easier and more short-term route of 'bribing' sales teams and R&D groups to deliver increased productivity. However, it chose a route that more accurately mirrored the values of its staff, for whom ethical behaviour and environmental concerns featured highly. The recognition of the needs of staff also featured in the process of change adopted by the company.

Strategy implementation

Changing the culture and with it the structure and retaining the ability to continue to adapt the structure to meet new challenges were essential ingredients of the 'new' organization. In this sense, EuroPharm UK set out to become an adaptive organization and seems to have achieved this aim.

During the period of change, the MD, his management team, and the 'change champions' provided strong leadership. The leadership focused first on winning hearts and minds through the development of the corporate vision and the progress of change was managed using formal project methods and measured using such tools as the opinion surveys. All of this helped to keep the momentum going at the working levels and also to give ownership of change to the staff. It was, unquestioningly, a winning formula.

The cultural changes achieved during this period were profound and made it easier to achieve an organization structure which, while focusing on specific areas of expertise, was still able to function as an integrated, collaborative, and co-operative unit. Accompanying the culture and structure changes were the changes and improvements to the processes, particularly the distribution channels, so that as a whole a new adaptive, integrated, and invigorated organization was born to compete with the now emerging giants of the industry.

Only time will tell if the philosophy adopted by EuroPharm, to grow by building internal capability, will prove more durable than those pharmaceutical companies that attempted to meet future challenges by just getting fatter through mergers and acquisitions.

Questions for discussion on EuroPharm UK case example

1. What are the strengths and weaknesses of the strategy implementation process in EuroPharm UK?
2. The process of strategy implementation described was designed for an organization of about 500 people. What would need to be different for an organization of 5,000 or 50,000 people?
3. Do you think that there may be both commercial needs for performance and ethical values in the sales force at EuroPharm? What would you do about this?
4. Could the change programme have been executed more quickly? What would have been the risks of haste?

Glossary

Adaptability The capability of an enterprise to react quickly to opportunities and risks and convert them into business advantage

Business Processes The systems, procedures, and habits of an enterprise which enable it to execute activities efficiently and consistently

Business Strategy The strategy for a single business or activity which describes how that business will succeed in its chosen market place against its competitors

Capability The ability of an individual, a group or organisation to exercise a set of skills pertinent to an activity

Competitive Advantage Any advantage that an organization may have which enables it to meet the needs of its customers better or more cheaply than its competitors

Competitive Strategy Synonymous with Business Strategy (q.v.) but with particular emphasis on competitive advantage.

Complementors Other businesses from whom our customers buy complementary products. Complementors are therefore very different from competitors

Content of Strategy See Strategy Content

Context The enterprise as a whole within its external environment viewed both objectively and subjectively. The background against which all strategic management takes place

Core Competence The combination of technologies, processes, resources, and know-how into a unique organizational capability which confers sustainable competitive advantage to its owner

Corporate Advantage The means by which a multi-business corporation adds value beyond the value of the sum of its individual businesses

Corporate Strategy The additional element of strategy required in a multi-business or multi-activity enterprise in addition to the separate business strategies for each business or activity. Describes how that corporation intends to achieve Corporate Advantage

Culture The pattern of shared basic assumptions and beliefs which a group of people has learned as it solved its problems

Function The major activity areas of an enterprise, for example, Marketing, Operations, Finance, Organizational Development, Knowledge Management, Information Systems

Functional Strategy Ideas and actions for how a particular function will support the realization of the Business and Corporate Strategies.

Leadership The achievement of desired results by winning active and willing co-operation of others by capturing their interest, motivation and energy

Management The achievement of desired results by organizing people and resources to fulfil their obligations within the terms of a contractual relationship

Mission Statement A written statement which describes the strategic intent of the enterprise with the aim of capturing the imagination and support of all groups of stakeholders

Organizational Capability The ability of an enterprise created by harnessing its resources, internal processes, systems, and skills

Organizational Forces The strategic drivers that dictate the way an organization has to behave to achieve its strategic intent

Organizational Form The shape that an organization has to take in order to release the forces needed for it to achieve its strategic intent

Organizational Structure The way an organization is arranged to enable it to be effectively and efficiently managed

Parenting Advantage Corporate advantage derived from the ability of a particular corporation to add value to its businesses more effectively than its competitors

Process See Business Process, Strategy Formulation Process, or Strategy Implementation Process

Programme Management The umbrella activities that manage many projects simultaneously

Project Management The activities to manage a project to achieve its objectives within budget and on time

Resources Typically divided into physical resources (fixed assets and equipment), human resources (people and their skills), and financial resources (cash and the ability to raise cash)

Strategic Assessment A judgement of the current position of the enterprise in relationship to its environment and in its ability to realize its strategic intent—one of the three logical elements of the Strategy Formulation Process

Strategic Choice A major choice made by an enterprise to secure its future success. One of the three logical elements of the Strategy Formulation Process

Strategic Intent The highest level purpose of an enterprise which drives the strategy formulation process. One of the three logical elements of the Strategy Formulation Process

Strategic Options The available set of possible future actions from which a strategic choice can be made

Strategy Ideas and actions to secure the future of the enterprise

Strategy Content The strategies, learning, intentions, and initiatives resulting from the Strategy Formulation Process and driving the Strategy Implementation Process

Strategy Formulation Process The process by which strategies are thought about, conceived, compared, and chosen within an enterprise. It has three logical elements: Strategic Intent, Strategic Assessment, and Strategic Choice

Strategy Implementation Process The aggregation of all activities aimed at putting strategies into practice. Essential elements include the leadership and management of efforts to change processes, culture and organizational form

Structure See Organizational Structure

Selected Bibliography

The books and articles listed below have been selected as suitable further reading on strategic management. Most should be readily available in management libraries. Most should be accessible to general readers. Some have been specifically referenced in the relevant chapters.

ANDREWS, K. R. (1971) *The Concept of Corporate Strategy* (Homewood, Ill., Irwin)

ANSOFF, H. I. (1987) *Corporate Strategy* (Revised Edition, London, Penguin)

ANSOFF, H. I. DECLERK, R. P., HAYES, R. L. (1985) *From Strategic Planning to Strategic Management* (London, John Wiley & Sons, 1976)

BADEN-FULLER, C. and STOPFORD, J. M. (1992) *Rejuvenating the Mature Business: The Competitive Challenge* (London, Routledge)

BARLETT, C. A. and GHOSHAL, S. (1994) 'Changing the Role of Top Management: Beyond Strategy to Purpose' *Harvard Business Review* Nov/Dec

BATE, P. (1994) *Strategies for Cultural Change* (Oxford, Butterworth Heinemann)

BENIS, W. and NANUS, B. (1985) *Leaders: The Strategies for Taking Charge* (New York, Harper and Row)

BOISOT, M. H. (1998) *Knowledge Assets* (Oxford University Press)

CAMPBELL, A. (1999) 'Tailored, not benchmarked: A Fresh Look at Corporate Planning' *Harvard Business Review* Mar/Apr

CAMPBELL, A. and ALEXANDER, M. (1997) 'What's wrong with Strategy?' *Harvard Business Review* Nov/Dec

CANNON, T. (1994) *Corporate Responsibility* (London, Pitman Publishing)

CHANDLER, A. D. (1962) *Strategy and Structure* (Cambridge, Mass., MIT Press)

CHARAN, R. and COLVIN, G. (1999) 'Why CEOs Fail' *Fortune* 21 June

COLLIS, D. J. and MONTGOMERY, C. A. (1995) 'Competing on Resources' *Harvard Business Review* Jul/Aug

—— (1998) 'Creating Corporate Advantage' *Harvard Business Review* May/June

COLLINS, J. C. and PORRAS, J. I. (1996) 'Building Your Company's Vision' *Harvard Business Review* Sept/Oct

CUMMINGS, S. (1993) 'The First Strategists' *Long Range Planning* Vol. 26 No. 3 133–135

CYERT, R. and MARCH, L. (1963) *A Behavioural Theory of the Firm* (New York, Prentice Hall)

D'AVENI, R. A. (1994) *Hyper-Competition: Managing the Dynamics of Strategic Manoeuvring* (New York, The Free Press)

DAVENPORT, T. H. (1993) *Process Innovation, Reengineering work through information technology* (Cambridge, Mass., Harvard Business School Press)

DE GEUS, A. (1988) 'Planning as Learning' *Harvard Business Review* Mar/Apr

—— (1997) *The Living Company: Growth, learning and longevity in business* (London, Nicholas Brealey)

DE KARE-SILVER, M. (1997) *Strategy in Crisis* (London, Macmillan)

DE WIT, B. and MEYER, R. (1999) *Strategy Synthesis: Resolving Strategy Paradoxes to Create Competitive Advantage* (London, International Thomson Business Press)

DEAL, T. and KENNEDY, A. (1982) *Corporate Cultures* (New York, McGraw Hill and Penguin 1988)

—— (1999) *The New Corporate Cultures* (London, Orion Business Books)

DEMING, E. W. (1986) *Out of the Crisis* (Cambridge University Press)

DRUCKER, P. (1955) *The Practice of Management* (paperback edition, Oxford, Butterworth Heinemann)

—— (1990) *Managing the Non-Profit Organization* (Oxford, Butterworth Heinemann)

—— (1994) 'The Theory of Business' *Harvard Business Review* Sept/Oct

EGAN, C. (1995) *Creating Organizational Advantage* (Oxford, Butterworth Heinemann)

FARNHAM, D. and HORTON, S. (1993) *Managing the New Public Services* (London, Macmillan)

FRUIN, W. M. (1997) *Knowledge Works, Managing Intellectual Capital at Toshiba* (Oxford University Press).

GADDIS, P. O. (1997) 'Strategy Under Attack' *Long Range Planning* Vol. 30 No. 1 Feb.

GARRATT, B. (ed.) (1995) *Developing Strategic Thought* (London, McGraw-Hill)

GOODWIN, P. and WRIGHT, G. (1998) *Decision Analysis for Management Judgment* (Chichester, Wiley)

GOOLD, M. and CAMPBELL, A. (1987) 'Many best ways to make strategy' *Harvard Business Review* Nov/Dec

—— (1987) *Strategies and Styles* (Oxford, Basil Blackwell)

GOOLD, M., CAMPBELL, A. and ALEXANDER, M. (1994) *Corporate-Level Strategy: Creating Value in the Multibusiness Company* (New York, Wiley)

GRANT, R. M. (1995) *Contemporary Strategy Analysis* (Oxford, Blackwell)

GRINYER, P. H., MAYES, D. and MCKIERNAN, P. (1988) *Sharpbenders: the Secrets of Unleashing Corporate Potential* (Oxford, Blackwell)

HAMEL, G. (1996) 'Strategy as Revolution' *Harvard Business Review* Jul/Aug

HAMEL, G. and PRAHALAD, C. K. (1989) 'Strategic Intent' *Harvard Business Review* May/June

—— (1993) 'Strategy as Stretch and Leverage' *Harvard Business Review* Mar/Apr

—— (1994) *Competing for the Future* (Cambridge, Mass., Harvard Business School Press)

HAMMER, M. and CHAMPY, J. (1993) *Reengineering the Corporation. A manifesto for business revolution* (London, Nicholas Brealey)

HANDY, C. (1989) *The Age of Unreason* (London, Business Books)

HARRIGAN, K. R. and PORTER, M. E. (1983) 'End-game strategies for declining industries' *Harvard Business Review* July/Aug

HENDERSON, B. (1984) *The Logic of Business Strategy* (New York, Ballinger)

—— (1989) 'The Origins of Strategy' *Harvard Business Review* Nov/Dec

HILL, T. and WESTBROOK, R. (1997) 'SWOT Analysis: It's Time for a Product Recall' *Long Range Planning* Vol. 30 No. 1 Feb.

HINTERHUBER, H. H. and POPP, W. (1992) 'Are you a Strategist or just a Manager?' *Harvard Business Review* Jan/Feb

HOFSTEDE, G. (1991) *Culture and Organizations: Software of the Mind* (Maidenhead, McGraw-Hill)

IDENBERG, P. J. (1993) 'Four Styles of Strategy Development' *Long Range Planning* Vol. 26 No. 6 Dec

KAPLAN, R. S. and NORTON, D. P. (1992) 'The Balanced Scorecard—measures that drive performance' *Harvard Business Review* Jan/Feb

KAY, J. (1993) *The Foundations of Corporate Success* (Oxford University Press)

KONO, T. (1984) *Strategy and Structure of Japanese Enterprises* (London, Macmillan)

KOTTER, J. P. (1995) 'Leading Change: Why Transformation Efforts Fail' *Harvard Business Review* Mar/Apr

LAWRENCE, P. R. and Lorsch, J. W. (1986) *Organization and Environment* (Cambridge, Mass., Harvard Business School)

LEONARD-BARTON, D. (1995) *Wellsprings of*

Knowledge (Cambridge, Mass., Harvard Business School Press)

LEVITT, T. (1960) 'Marketing Myopia' *Harvard Business Review* Jul/Aug

LISSACK, M. and ROOS, J. (1999) *The Next Common Sense: Mastering Corporate Complexity through Coherence* (London, Nicholas Brealey)

LOCKE, R. R. (1996) *The Collapse of the American Management Mystique* (Oxford University Press)

LORANGE, P. and ROOS, J. (1992) *Strategic Alliances : Formation, Implementation and Evolution* (Oxford, Blackwell)

LOVELL, R. (1994) *Managing Change in the New Public Sector*. (London, Longman).

LYNCH, D. and KORDIS, P. L. (1988) *Strategy of the Dolphin* (London, Hutchinson Business Books)

MAISTER, D. H. (1993) *Managing the Professional Service Firm* (New York, Free Press)

MATHUR, S. S. and KENYON, A. (1997) *Creating Value: Shaping Tomorrow's Business* (Oxford, Butterworth Heinemann)

MAYNE, J. and ZAPICO-GONI, E. (1997) *Monitoring Performance in the Public Sector* (London, Transaction Publishers)

MCINTOSH, M., LEIPZIGER, D., JONES, K. and COLMAN, G. (1998) *Corporate Citizenship* (London, Financial Times/Pitman Publishing)

MCKIERNAN, P. (1992) *Strategies of Growth: Maturity, recovery and internationalisation* (London, Routledge)

—— (1997) 'Strategy Past; Strategy Futures' *Long Range Planning* Vol. 30 No. 5 Oct.

MILLAR, D. (1992) 'The Icarus Paradox: How exceptional companies bring about their own downfall' *Business Horizons* Jan/Feb

MINTZBERG, H. (1987) 'Crafting Strategy' *Harvard Business Review* Jul/Aug

—— (1994) *The Rise and Fall of Strategic Planning* (London, Prentice Hall)

MINTZBERG, H., AHLSTRAND, B. and LAMPEL, J. (1998) *Strategy Safari* (London, Prentice Hall)

MOORE, G. A. (1991) *Crossing the Chasm* (New York, Harper Collins) paperback edn. 1995

MOORE, J. F. (1996) *The Death of Competition*. (Chichester, John Wiley & Sons)

MOSS KANTER, R. (1983) *The Changemasters*. (London, George Allan and Unwin)

NATHAN, J. (1999) *SONY—The Private Life*. (London, Harper Collins Business)

NEWMAN, V. and CHAHARBAGHI, K. (1998) 'The Corporate Culture Myth' *Long Range Planning* Vol. 31 No. 4 August

NORMANN, R. and RAMIREZ, R. (1993) 'Strategy and the Art of Reinventing Value' *Harvard Business Review* Sept/Oct

OHMAE, K. (1982) *The Mind of the Strategist* (New York, McGraw Hill) Penguin paperback edn. 1988

—— (1988) 'Getting Back to Strategy' *Harvard Business Review* Nov/Dec

OWEN, G. (1999) *From Empire to Europe*. (London, HarperCollins)

PASCALE, R. T. (1990) *Managing on the Edge: How successful companies use conflict to stay ahead*. (New York, Simon & Schuster)

PASCALE, R. T. and ATHOS, A. G. (1983) *The Art of Japanese Management* (London, Penguin).

PETERS, T. J. and WATERMAN, R. H. (1982) *In Search of Excellence* (New York, Harper and Row)

PETTIGREW, A. and WHIPP, R. (1991) *Managing Change for Competitive Success* (Oxford, Blackwell)

POLLITT, C. (1991) *Managerialism and the Public Services: The Anglo-American Experience* (Oxford, Blackwell)

PORTER, M. E. (1985) *Competitive Advantage: Creating and sustaining superior performance* (New York, Free Press)

—— (1987) 'From Competitive Strategy to Corporate Strategy' *Harvard Business Review* May/June

—— (1996) 'What is Strategy?' *Harvard Business Review* Nov/Dec

PRAHALAD, C. K. and HAMEL, G. (1990) 'The Core Competence of the Corporation' *Harvard Business Review* May/Jun

QUINN, J. B. (1978) 'Strategic Change: Logical Incrementalism' *Sloan Management Review* Fall

QUINN, J. B. (1992) *Intelligent Enterprise* (New York, Free Press).

RAPPAPORT, A. (1986) *Creating Shareholder Value: The New Standard of Business Performance* (New York, Free Press)

ROSENBLOOM, R. S. and SPENCER, W. J. (eds.) (1996) *Engines of Innovation.* (Cambridge, Mass., Harvard Business School Press)

RUMELT, R (1991) 'How much does industry matter?' *Strategic Management Journal* March 12:167–186

SCOTT, M. C. (1998) *Profiting and learning from Professional Service Firms* (Chichester, Wiley)

SCHEIN, E. H. (1992) *Organizational culture and leadership* (San Francisco, Jossey-Bass)

SCHWARTZ, P. (1991) *The Art of the Long View* (New York, Currency Doubleday) paperback edn. 1996

SENGE, P. M. (1990) *The Fifth Discipline: The Art & Practice of the Learning Organization* (New York, Doubleday)

SIMON, H. (1964) 'On the subject of the Organisational Goal' *American Science Quarterly* 9 June 1–22

SLATTER, S. (1984) *Corporate Recovery: A Guide to Turnaround Management* (London, Penguin)

SLATTER, S. and LOVETT, D. (1999) *Corporate Turnaround: Managing Companies in Distress* (London, Penguin)

STACEY, R. (1993) 'Strategy as Order Emerging from Chaos' *Long Range Planning* Vol. 26 No. 1 Feb.

STALK, G., EVANS, P. and SHULMAN, L. E. (1992) 'Competing on Capabilities: The new rules of corporate strategy' *Harvard Business Review* Mar/Apr

STEWART, T. A. (1998) *Intellectual Capital* (London, Nicholas Brealey)

STREBEL, P. (1992) *Breakpoints—how managers exploit radical business change* (Cambridge, Mass., Harvard Business School Press)

SWANN, G. M. P., PREVEZER, M. and STOUT, D. (1998) *The Dynamics of Industrial Clustering* (Oxford University Press)

TAMPOE, M. (1990) 'Driving Organisational Change Through the Effective Use of Multi-Disciplinary Project Teams' *European Management Journal* Vol. 8 No. 3 September

—— (1994) 'Exploiting the Core Competences of your Organisation' *Long Range Planning* Vol. 27 No. 4 (66–77)

—— (1998) 'Getting to know your organisation's core competences' in *Exploring Techniques of Analysis and Evaluation in Strategic Management* (eds.) Ambrosini, V. with Johnson, G. and Scholes, K. (London, Prentice Hall)

TROMPENAARS, F. (1993) *Riding the Waves of Culture* (London, Nicholas Brealey)

WACK, P. (1985a) 'Scenarios: uncharted waters ahead' *Harvard Business Review* Sept/Oct

—— (1985b) 'Scenarios: shooting the rapids' *Harvard Business Review* Nov/Dec

WALDROP, M. M. (1992) *Complexity: the emerging science at the edge of order and chaos* (New York, Simon & Schuster 1992, Penguin 1994)

WATSON, G. H. (1993) *Strategic Benchmarking—How to rate your Company's Performance against the World's Best* (New York, Wiley)

WERNEFELT, B. (1984) 'A Resource-based View of the Firm' *Strategic Management Journal* Vol. 5 171–80

WHITTINGTON, R. (1993) *What is Strategy—and does it matter?* (London, Routledge)

WILSON, I (1994) 'Strategic Planning Isn't Dead—It Changed' *Long Range Planning* Vol 27 No. 4 August

WIND, J. Y. and Main, J (1998) *Driving Change* (London, Kogan Page)

WOMACK, J. P., Jones, D. T. and Roos, D. (1990) *The Machine that Changed the World* (New York, Rawson Associates)

ZALESNIK, A. (1977) 'Managers and Leaders: Are they different?' *Harvard Business Review* May/June

ZEITHAML, V., PARASURAMAN, A. and BERRY, L. L. (1990) *Delivering Quality Service* (New York, The Free Press)

Index

D

E

P

Q

R

S

T

U

V

W

X

Z